INTERIOR DeSIGN

FAIRCHILD BOOKS, INC.
NEW YORK

INTERIOR DeSIGN

PRACTICAL STRATEGIES FOR TEACHING AND LEARNING

Katherine S. Ankerson
University of Nebraska-Lincoln

Jill Pable
Florida State University

Director of Sales and Acquisitions: Dana Meltzer-Berkowitz

Executive Editor: Olga T. Kontzias

Senior Development Editor: Jennifer Crane

Art Director: Adam B. Bohannon

Production Manager: Ginger Hillman

Senior Production Editor: Elizabeth Marotta

Copyeditor: Yonie Overton

Cover Design: Adam B. Bohannon

Book Design: Renato Stanisic

Library of Congress Catalog Card Number: 2007938129

ISBN-13: 978-1-56367-558-4

GST R 133004424

Printed in the United States of America
CH11, TP13

For all the members of the Interior Design Educators Council
who continue to advance and evolve the interior design profession.
Your passion for student achievement is the lifeforce of the future.

CONTENTS

PREFACE

Interior design as a human cultural activity has proven to be a necessary undertaking that enhances human existence, meaning, and function. In surprising contrast, interior design has been recognized as a full profession by this name relatively lately—since the early 20th century. Therefore, it may be more accurate to say that interior design as a profession has recently coalesced rather than been invented or discovered.

Interior design is now an accepted activity within human society and an acknowledged part of the pantheon of design fields. This fact is evidenced by the National Design Awards, which "celebrate the best in American design in a variety of disciplines, including architecture, communications, fashion, interior, landscape and product design."[1] These awards seek to broaden awareness of the role of design in daily life, and it is on this intimate scale of daily life that interior design excels.[2] Like some other areas of study, interior design is intertwined with many disciplines such as psychology, anthropology, ergonomics, history, and sociology. It is telling that other fields with similar diverse roots, such as furniture design, view interior design as a prelude to their own emergence.[3]

Interior design's expansion is accompanied by an increasingly sophisticated academy of researchers and writers who rightfully propose, consider, and debate the vast ground of the profession's growing realm of knowledge. It is thus through these and other activities the interior design profession will establish and maintain its claim to utility and delight with its public. In the midst of this dynamic growth and change, it is fitting that a reference be developed to help educators bring their students to a pedagogical understanding of this complex and diverse field. Numerous generic educational reference texts exist, and many colleges and universities feature Centers for Teaching and Learning toward this end, but it could well be argued that the nature of interior design education warrants a collection of content dedicated to its unique needs. The distinctive nature of the studio experience, the comprehensive nature of the design process, and the complexity of the knowledge that interior designers must know all point to the logic of a customized educational reference that interior design educators can call their own.

This book is designed to serve as a resource that brings a foundation of clarity to the complex task of interior design teaching and learning. The writing style expressly avoids the "academic-ese" approach, and care has been taken to select educational theory and content that is most relevant to interior design education and that will withstand the test of time. Whenever possible, examples punctuate the text, providing specific suggestions for applying concepts to the interior design learning experience. The text is designed for a diversity of educators from the first-time instructor to the seasoned educator seeking to reevaluate and refresh their techniques.

The realities of interior design instruction are that educators sometimes must adapt their teaching to new conditions quickly, with the classroom strategy used on Wednesday developed the preceding Tuesday night. This book was designed to serve educators in these harried times and, when more time allows, to assist in the development of an entire course, the consideration of learning theory, or the revamping of a studio experience. It is organized into ten chapters, as follows.

Chapter 1, *The Importance of Interior Design Teaching and Learning*, orients the reader to the book's approach and provides guidance regarding the location of specific information for typical educator needs.

Chapter 2, *The Nature of Interior Design Education*, discusses interior design higher education and the unique qualities of interior design as a field, and it identifies the challenges, responsibilities, and choices that a career in academia involves. This chapter also discusses the characteristics defining today's learners and learning theory that affect pedagogical choices.

Chapter 3, *Course Preparation*, provides guidance on constructing a course and the development of key documents, including the syllabus, schedule, and course materials.

Chapter 4, *Managing and Guiding Learning*, offers basic information on choosing from a growing multitude of learning techniques; how to ensure that testing is effective and fair; and how, in general, to facilitate successful classroom experiences.

Chapter 5, *Studio Learning*, offers information regarding one of the hallmarks of design education—the studio. Strategies and examples of activities, the studio as a classroom, the critique, and examples of both formative and summative evaluation techniques are presented.

Chapter 6, *Teaching and Learning at a Distance*, presents an overview of distance learning in interior design, including potentials, pitfalls, and successful strategies. Specific case studies offered by an array of faculty experienced in teaching at a distance give concrete examples in a variety of settings and courses.

Chapter 7, *Trends in Interior Design Teaching and Learning*, discusses paradigms that affect interior design educators' approaches to the teaching task, including sustainability, collaboration, diversity, and changes in how interior designers are redefining the scope of their activities and learning.

Chapter 8, *Improving Teaching and Learning*, offers examples and guidance that can enhance one's teaching. Evaluation techniques, strategies to understand and implement improvements, and methods to strengthen and maintain relationships with faculty and administration can assist new and seasoned educators alike.

Chapter 9, *Essays and Inspirations*, offers first-person insights into the very human experience of interior design teaching and learning. Essayists discuss the feeling of standing on the front lines of seeking tenure, teaching as an adjunct educator, and administering an interior design program. Notably, the interior design learner also offers insights here on what it's like on the receiving end of education.

Chapter 10, *The Teaching and Learning Physical Environment*, discusses the critical factor of physical facilities in interior design education. This chapter is particularly helpful to educators anticipating new construction or renovation to their teaching facilities.

Assisting learners to emerge as professional interior designers is a challenge worthy of lifelong examination. It embodies, among other things, nudging others to new heights of seeing, awareness, and rethinking how things are done. With this book we hope to start a needed conversation that engages educators and learners in helping interior design education evolve toward a future that better serves the public—the reason for the profession's very existence. It is perhaps not too grandiose a vision to believe that a world served by well-educated, confident, and energized interior designers ready to envision and create superior environments is a world closer to reaching its full actualization and potential. Education is where this journey starts.

ACKNOWLEDGMENTS

It is a daunting task to create a guide with the lofty goal of making an impact on teaching and learning in interior design. Such a broad undertaking necessarily engages the advice, writings, and thoughts of many educators, researchers, and other experts, which has made the creation of this reference a joint effort in the full sense of the phrase.

We are reminded of the individual talents, the passion for teaching, and the desire to influence the profession each time we gather with fellow interior design educators, and we stand in awe of the diversity of viewpoints, great teaching ideas, and passionate drive that so many of our colleagues continually exude. This work would be incomplete without the shared wisdom and insights of seasoned educators and the exuberance of instructors who have only recently begun their education careers.

Our association with the Interior Design Educators Council (IDEC) has allowed and encouraged a sharing and networking among our peers and has served as a critically important mirror of the diverse set of educational programs, academic settings, visions, and missions that characterize interior design education. In this multiplicity, however, there exists a singular goal among us for excellence in our students and for the furthering of this very necessary profession.

Many persons have contributed significant effort, writings, and/or images to this work. Specifically, we extend a heartfelt thank-you to:

Tom Allisma
AMA Alexi Marmot Associates
Jo Ann Asher Thompson
Abimbola Asojo
Rula Awwad-Rafferty
Sarah Block
David Brooks
Ann Camp
Lynn Chalmers
Stephanie Clemons
Holly Cline
Shauna Corry
Samuel Duncan
Lindsey Ellsworth Bahe
Jean Edwards
Paul Eshelman
Veronica Fannin
Betsy Gabb
Pat Hilderbrand
Lynn M. Jones
Lori Kinley
Jane Kucko

The Joint Information Systems Committee e-Learning and Innovation Team
Christine Lee
Jacqui McFarland
Rachelle McClure
Anna Marshall-Baker
Caren Martin
Carl Matthews
Hannah Mendoza
Trisha Otto
Nate Perkins
Ronald Phillips
Marlo Ransdell
T.L. Ritchie
Douglas Seidler
Ruth Tofle
Erin Trafholz
Lisa Tucker
Kerri Ann Uchida
Jennifer Webb
Eric Wiedegreen
John Weigand
Stephanie Watson Zollinger

Others, too, have left their mark on this book. Students past and present have inspired and encouraged this work, knowingly or not. Their insights included here represent a seldom-tapped but obviously important aspect of effective education. Also, writers and thinkers in other fields such as architecture, education, facilities management, and philosophy have flavored the ideas and the approach of this work.

We are grateful to the staff of Fairchild Books—especially Olga Kontzias, who deserves special mention for her unwavering support of interior design education and belief in the need for this project. Other Fairchild staff, including Jennifer Crane, Adam Bohannon, and Elizabeth Marotta, lent their expertise and talents to its pages. Andy Sieverman of Newgen-Austin/G&S facilitated a smooth production process. This project is also the beneficiary of review comments provided by Jim Postell of University of Cincinnati, Theodore J. Drab of Oklahoma State University, and Christiana Lafazani of Virginia Commonwealth University.

A special thank-you to our family and friends, who supported this work with prayer, emotional support, and understanding.

Lastly, we the authors would like to thank each other for a most happy collaboration. Such a paired effort requires a significant measure of patience and humanity, and the care, humor, and positive outlook that were dedicated to this work made the writing odyssey the exciting adventure that it was.

Kathy Ankerson
Jill Pable

ENDNOTES

1. National Design Awards (2007). What are the National Design Awards? Retrieved 10/20/07 from www.nationaldesignawards.org.
2. Honey, P., Anderson, B. & Dudek, M. (2007). Interior Design's Social Compact: The Missing Aspect of Our Quest for Professional Legitimacy. *Proceedings of the 2007 International Interior Design Educators Conference*, Austin, Texas, pp. 91–92.
3. Postell, J. (2007). *Furniture Design.* New York: Wiley.

SECTION ONE

Meeting the Challenge

CHAPTER 1

The Importance of Interior Design Teaching and Learning

Design education is unique amongst fields of study—it is an integrator and connector of knowledge, forming links between ideas, information, people, and objects.[1] The utility of design education is in its pursuit of understanding how humans interact with their world. Some go so far as to proclaim that design is on the frontier of remaking liberal education in the twenty-first century, drawing emphasis away from the idea of teaching "what is and what has been" and toward the concept of an education "grounded in possibility."[2] Whether these lofty predictions prove true or not, the relationship between user, experience, information, and product are vital insights to the human experience.

Fields under the collective design umbrella are perhaps primarily united in their collective use of the term *design*, yet beyond this commonality, they diverge in important ways. Interior design is not the same as architecture, nor is it interior decoration. In this growing realization of interior design's distinctive identity, significant steps are being accomplished to provide tools that help interior designers do what they do better. The Interior Design Educators Council has long offered vibrant regional and national conferences that help educators stay abreast of new developments in research, practice, and education. New website initiatives, including InformeDesign and DesignIntelligence, are expanding existing boundaries. Initiatives in distributing new research and educational knowledge by professional organizations such as the American Society of Interior Designers, the International Interior Design Association, Interior Designers of Canada, and the National Council for the Qualification of Interior Designers are similarly helping interior design to claim its rightful place of integrity amongst its sibling professions in the built environment.

For all its progress as a field, however, interior design may suffer from a lack of vision in its teaching potential, as well as a lack of resources to remedy the situation. In addition to their enthusiasm, creativity, and design prowess, design educators require enhanced comprehension of the nuts and bolts of how ideas are learned to successfully impart insight to their students in a lifelong, meaningful way. In the words of one design education administrator, "design educators need a more technical understanding of learning and will need to reexamine their priorities in order to make room for more projects that encourage good learning—even at the cost of bad design."[3] It is time to consider the unique nature of interior design teaching and learning, and its embrace of both theoretical and applied content in courses that span lecture, seminar, and the complexity of the studio experience.

It is both interesting and ironic that prerequisites for success as an interior design educator in today's post-secondary systems are often much more stringent about one's design capability than about possessing the teaching skills to successfully impart these skills to others. Yet, as many educators and students know, being a good interior designer does not automatically mean one can teach well. This text represents an initiative to breach an educational gap, helping interior design educators better understand and prepare for the significant challenges and changes that today's learners, the growing breadth of interior design curricular content, and higher education teaching environments all pose.

We acknowledge the substantial variety of backgrounds interior design educators possess, including those embarking on a teaching career after years of practice, graduate students moving directly from their own studies to an academic life, and those educators who already possess years or even decades of teaching experience. The intent of the text is to offer insights to all these groups, recognizing the valid contributions of full-time educators, researchers, and instructors, adjunct instructors, and graduate teaching assistants alike.

A second reason for this publication is more directly pragmatic. The choices one must make when establishing one's academic career in interior design education are many, including type of institution, nature of the department, and issues of responsibility in research, teaching, and service. Placing the academic career within the larger canvas of life is a tricky endeavor best approached with foresight. It is said that authors are often compelled to write the book they wish they had had themselves, and that is true here with regard to choosing an academic home.

USING THIS BOOK TO BEST ADVANTAGE

This book is designed to offer a logical exploration of interior design education when digested in the given order of chapter presentation. However, it is further useful when seeking focused information for tasks both new and seasoned educators invariably encounter. Table 1.1 offers suggestions for helpful content categorized by task.

The content of this book is also a continuing education experience approved by the Interior Design Continuing Education Council for three hours of credit. Materials for completion of the course credit are available through the Interior Design Educators Council at www.idec.org.

Coleman and Sosnowchik's 2006 report *Interior Design Trends and Implications* concludes that the three primary elements for evaluating the strength of an interior design academic program are pedagogy, faculty, and resources.[4] Given the importance that quality teaching and the overall caliber of the faculty imply for higher education institutions, and by extension the larger interior design profession, we hope this work might serve as a helpful reference that furthers successful learning and progress toward this end.

TABLE 1.1: CHAPTERS THAT CAN ASSIST WITH VARIOUS EDUCATIONAL TASKS

Task	Chapter	Topic
Preparing a new course	3(B)	Matching course goals to measurable outcomes
	3(C)	Basic course construction and syllabus preparation
	3(D)	Selecting and creating course resources
	4(A)	Techniques for learning
	7	Trends in teaching and learning
Reinvigorating classroom learning strategies	2(D)	Today's student
	2(E)	Learning theory
	4(A)	Techniques for learning
	4(C)	Classroom management
	7	Trends in teaching and learning
	8	Improving teaching and learning
	9(A)	Reflections of seasoned educators
	9(F)	The learner perspective
Teaching for the first time	2(A)	The nature of interior design education
	2(C)	Contributions of adjunct faculty
	2(D)	Today's student
	2(E)	Learning theory
	4(A)	Techniques for learning
	4(B)	Giving tests and assigning grades
	4(C)	Classroom management
	7	Trends in teaching and learning
	8	Improving teaching and learning
	9(C)	Observations from adjunct educators
	9(D)	The graduate teaching assistant experience
	9(F)	The learner perspective
	11	Definitions
Managing the academic life	2	The nature of interior design education
	3(A)	Managing time and the demands of teaching
	8	Improving teaching and learning
	9(B)	Achieving tenure and maintaining life balance
	9(D)	The graduate teaching assistant experience
Managing studio classes	5	Studio learning
	7	Trends in teaching and learning
Choosing an academic job opportunity	2(A)	The nature of interior design education
	2(B)	The roles of the full-time academic
	9(B)	Achieving tenure and maintaining life balance

(continued)

TABLE 1.1 *(continued)*

Task	Chapter	Topic
Assessing progress	4(B)	Giving tests and assigning grades
	5	Studio learning
	8	Improving teaching and learning
Working with technology	3(D)	Selecting and creating course resources
	6	Teaching and learning at a distance
	7	Trends in teaching and learning
Planning interior design educational facilities	10	The teaching and learning physical environment

ENDNOTES

1. Buchanan, R. (December 2000). Design and the Organization of Learning. Keynote address, *Re-Inventing Design Education in the University* Conference. Perth, Western Australia.
2. Dinot, C. (December 2000). Looking for Design in the Twenty-First Century University. Keynote address, *Re-Inventing Design Education in the University* Conference. Perth, Western Australia.
3. Jackson, B. (December 2000). Supra-Design: Transforming Design Education for the Age of Lifelong Learning. Paper presented at *Re-Inventing Design Education in the University* Conference. Perth, Western Australia.
4. Coleman, C. & Sosnowchik, K. (2006). *Interior Design Trends and Implications.* Grand Rapids, MI: Council for Interior Design Accreditation, p. 44.

CHAPTER 2

The Nature of Interior Design Education

In his keynote address to the conference *Reinventing Design Education in the University* in the year 2000, Notre Dame educator Dennis Doordan stated that "design is about the fact that things can be other than they are."[1] This description is deceptively simple, yet captures the profound task that design undertakes. The same might be said about education, which seeks to bring learners to higher understanding and capability. Both design and education are marked by the challenge a quality outcome represents—a functionally and aesthetically pleasing design for users in the case of the former, and a knowledgeable and confident student for the latter. It is the fearless person indeed who engages in the teaching of design, combining both of these challenges into one monumental endeavor.

This book is about just that—teaching design, or specifically interior design in a successful fashion that leaves the student changed for the better and maintains a sense of achievement and fulfillment in the educator. Were this task not already daunting enough, the current age is a potentially pivotal time in human history with regard to many things, including how societies educate their members.[2] In a 2003 paper, *Growing a Discipline: Evolving Learning Practices in Interior Design*, Dr. Jacqueline Vischer and Dr. Tiiu Poldma discuss the growing need for "educational tools for Interior Design that are unique to the needs and requirements of its disciplinary base and which go beyond borrowed knowledge. The unique knowledge base of Interior Design as a discipline refers to the knowledge and competencies needed to interact with users and clients, as well as to the specifics of interior space problem solving. In addition, a more dynamic philosophical debate is to be encouraged on how these knowledge areas, competencies, tools, and skills are transmitted in the context of a university education."[3]

A logical starting point is to acknowledge that interior design and its attendant education does in fact differ from other fields in that it is the only profession that addresses physical environments at an intimate, personal level.[4] In this way, interior design represents a unique manifestation of human culture's evolution such that it can recognize the value of the micro level of human experience.

This issue shapes programming, graphic representation, and verbal communication in a way that is different from architecture. Similarly, interior design is concerned with decisions of space and non-structural change significantly more comprehensive than is addressed in interior decoration. It is the integration of the social sciences, construction, psychology, technology, aesthetics, and many other areas that makes interior design both so challenging and also so full of opportunity for discovery.

To introduce the topic of education and design education specifically, this chapter will discuss interior design in a larger world context, including that of academia in general, and finally addressing the nature of institution types and the characteristics of different academic positions.

THE UNIQUE HIGHER EDUCATION ENVIRONMENT

A joke recently rippled through academic circles as to what Rip van Winkle would find were he to wake up now from his 100-year sleep. Amidst a bewildering scene filled with talking devices people hold to their ears, screens with moving images, and elderly people kept mobile with artificial joints, only one place looked familiar to Rip—the schoolroom, still outfitted with desks and a blackboard, albeit a whiteboard rather than a chalkboard.[5]

While this story takes the idea to the extreme, many have concluded that education, including higher education, has not kept pace with other societal advancements.[6] The public spotlight is beginning to acknowledge this, and new reports are calling for reforms and modernization.[7] There is new emphasis in higher education on instilling portable skills such as creativity, critical thinking, and connectivity across disciplines.[8] The explosion of information and the growing maturation of communication methods has compelled a switch from content memorization to knowing where and how to find answers, along with the ability to filter out irrelevant or discredited "noise."

In some ways, interior design and its academic institutions are ahead of this curve of change. Interior design has always engaged in the creative, the collaborative, and the personal.[9] By its nature, the design process integrates disparate information into a cohesive whole. It is no small surprise that business schools are now integrating the design process learning model into their own curricula.[10]

Current Pressures and Influences on Higher Education

Higher education with its model of research, teaching, and service has long enjoyed an elevated status and respect in society. During the past twenty years, however, economic pressures, population increases, technological advances, communication access, and globalization have projected pressures and influences on both the shape and delivery of higher education.

The Pervasiveness of the Business Model

Higher education's consistent heavy dependence on labor costs has compelled a rise in the cost of obtaining a degree. These increasing costs coupled with new conditions of global competition and Western culture's embrace of the market economy has lately infused the university experience with the market process.[11] This is manifested in various ways, including the embrace of a consumer attitude toward higher education by learners and a new emphasis on academic accountability. This push for accountability (evident in the emphasis on standardized testing in the K-12 arena) is also affecting arts programs in higher education, as a recent white paper on *Quality in Art Education* by the National Association of Schools of Art and Design (NASAD) attests.[12] Continual pressures on institutions to cut costs is a by-product of perceptions regarding business model competition. The growth in private arts and interior design educational institutions is also placing pressure on public institutions to remain competitive and relevant.[13]

Technology

New opportunities in learning fostered by computerization and mass communication are in effect dissolving the concept of the traditional classroom. The physical transaction of education is now being drawn away from brick and mortar home campuses to meet learners where they are, both literally and figuratively speaking.[14] Some futurists predict an age when the academic institution as it is currently known will fade away to reveal a cross-institution, à la carte system of courses where learners construct their own personalized curricula. Online course systems such as those of the Curriki.org Global Education and Learning Community offer examples of this idea in the K-12 environment.

New Learner Attitudes

New communication methods and other influences from such sources as the entertainment and gaming industries have resulted in an evolution of learner expectations about information content, pace of access, and delivery. Increasing learner age, cultural, and other diversities have challenged educators to manage their learning styles and temperament contrasts. These new learner characteristics have greatly influenced teaching styles (moving from top-down authoritative approaches to user-centered methods), the design of higher education physical learning facilities, and educators' tactics in working with learners' emotional and behavioral traits.

Changing Popular Perceptions of Interior Design

This time of great cultural and educational change is also accompanied by evolving attitudes toward design in general, and interior design specifically. Where once interior design was viewed as a feminine, elitist pursuit primarily concerned with color and surface finishes, the current age is experiencing a crossroads of technology, prosperity, and culture. This is raising the bar of popular expectation for comfort, convenience, and aesthetics, bringing the positive effects of design into the arena of public visibility and consumption. This turn of events has prompted Mark Dziersk, president of the Industrial Designers Society of America, to call the current decade the new "Golden Age of design."[15]

The new fascination with design has resulted in both positive and negative effects for interior design education. Heightened student enrollments in many interior design programs reflect design's new public image. However, the popularity of interior design "reality" television shows has resulted in inaccurate perceptions of the field by new interior design students that must be addressed by educators.[16]

The Particular Challenge of Practicing Design and Teaching Interior Design

The creative decision-making process makes interior design an alluring career. However, this also makes it difficult to teach well. Interior design engages people in comparatively high-level cognitive thinking that is divergent, rather than convergent, in its choices. In the words of Rittel and Webber, this makes interior design a "wicked" problem, not a "tame" one.[17] When compared to

Tame problems	Wicked problems
Can be stated clearly and definitively.	Have no definitive problem formulation.
Have a built-in rule for stopping the problem-solving effort.	Have no 'stopping rule' (nothing in the problem tells you when you are 'done'; you can always try for a better solution).
Have answers or solutions that are correct or wrong, true or false.	Have answers that are not true or false, but rather "more appropriate" or "less appropriate" or "good" or "bad".
Have answers that can be tested for correctness, usually immediately.	Have no immediate or ultimate test for the correctness of solutions.
Have a well-defined set of legitimate operations (rules) for solving the problem.	Have no rules or specified legitimate operations for solving the problem ('anything goes') and no defined range of acceptable solutions.
Have clear problem classes for which 'textbook' treatments exist.	Are unique (textbook knowledge and experience with other problems does not necessarily apply).
Have symptoms, causes, and consequences that can be clearly distinguished.	Can be considered mere 'symptoms' of other (wicked) problems.
Allow for a second try if the first effort does not succeed.	Offer only one chance to find a solution. The next time it's a different problem.
Can be solved through trial and error (learning from mistakes is a legitimate strategy).	Do not allow trial and error; failure has significant consequences.

Figure 2.1 Interior design often involves dealing with complex problems. A side-by-side comparison of "tame" and "wicked" problems shows the vivid contrast. Adapted from H. Rittel & M. Webber (1973), "Dilemmas in a General Theory of Planning." *Policy Sciences* 4(2): 155-169. Applied to architecture in T. Mann (2004), *Time Management for Architects and Designers*. New York: Norton.

mathematics, for example, the complexity of interior design becomes clear, as Figure 2.1 shows.

The Benefits of the Academic Career

Given the significant challenges of higher education, why would one commit to a full-time academic career or even part-time teaching? The answers to this vary greatly, of course. With challenges come the possibility of great achievement and satisfaction. One educational writer sums up the toil and the rewards thusly:

> Certainly we all have our own reasons for pursuing such a career in spite of the long years of master's- and doctoral-level studies, the arduous process of writing a dissertation, and the terrible uncertainties of the job market. But one common hope among those with whom I attended graduate school and whom I meet today at academic conferences was and remains the desire to live a professional life constituted on principles of energetic and forthright intellectual activity in which one's broad theoretical beliefs, passionate devotion to lively and creative thought, and eager tackling of the most difficult questions of interpretation and identity could be incorporated into one's daily work.[18]

Other sources similarly extol the virtues of the academic life. A 2006 *Money Magazine* ranking of the top 50 jobs in America places post-secondary teaching at number 2 in desirability, based on projected job growth, pay, stress level, flexibility in work environment and hours, creativity, and other considerations. However, the authors caution that salaries at the low end can indeed be low, a fact often encountered by adjunct instructors and graduate teaching assistants.[19]

Many factors ultimately influence the satisfaction or drudgery of a teaching job. Faculty camaraderie and personalities, salary, teaching facilities, curricular organization (or the lack of it), and opportunities for personal professional development can each figure heavily into an educator's opinion of their work. The relative importance of each of these and other factors is a matter of personal choice.

Interior Design Education Issues and Academic Preparation Expectations

As in any discipline, the current and future health of the interior design profession depends in part on the vitality of its educators. In 2007, a collection of professional organizations and practitioners in interior design came together to begin a dialogue that addresses the currently dwindling number of interior design educators.[20] Increasing student enrollments, baby boomer educator retirements, and the higher salaries professional practice offers may be contributing factors to this problem. Educators, practitioners, and members of industry are beginning to discuss an academic path for practitioners to become educators so that their expertise can be shared with interior design students. A 2006 white paper by the Interior Design Educators Council outlines a new degree type called the Master of Interior Design (MID) that would serve as a "terminal 'professional' teaching degree" that is "distinct from, but an equivalent alternative to, the Ph.D."[21] This new degree's specific nomenclature and accreditation are issues that remain to be resolved.

This lack of interior design educators represents both a cause for concern and a call to action for current educators to urge appropriate students to consider an academic career. For new graduates, the situation represents a unique opportunity to enter a career where significant demand triggers the happy circumstance of potential multiple job opportunities and the negotiation for an enhanced salary.

The MID offers another potential career path that may eventually complement the Master of Arts (M.A.), the Master of Science (M.S.), the Master of Fine Arts (MFA), the Doctor of Education (Ed.D.) and the Doctor of Philosophy (Ph.D.) degree options. The Master of Architecture (M.Arch) degree is also often acceptable. Teaching positions vary in their academic preparation requirements, and generalities are difficult to make. However, several perceptions usually hold true:

- An M.A. or M.S. degree can be an incremental step toward achievement of a doctoral degree. Some institutions also accept the M.A. or M.S. degrees as sufficient for an academic career in the design fields.
- The MFA degree is often seen as a "terminal" degree and is accepted by some institutions as sufficient for an academic career in the arts.
- A doctoral degree remains the preferred choice by research institutions.

Institutions sometimes reconsider their minimal qualifications for faculty academic preparation in response to evolving societal expectations, and the addition of extra requirements or degrees is sometimes required of instructors after hiring or as a prerequisite to promotion and tenure. Professional interior design licensure places additional expectations on interior design educators to take identified quantities of continuing education courses. Given the quickly changing nature of the profession, these extra learning experiences are a necessary endeavor regardless of institution or licensing mandates.

INTERIOR DESIGN ACADEMIC HOMES

Interior design programs of study across North America are diverse and housed in a variety of institution types and academic locations. The particular institution type sets the stage for the overall value system for all colleges, departments, and programs. The academic home is often an influential factor in the mission and goals of the individual program.

Implications of Institution Type

Higher education is composed of several common types of institutions. These may be categorized by their funding sources and allocation, type of degrees offered, and their primary mission.

The first level of categorization identifies an institution as a university or as a college. A **university** typically has a broad curriculum, and offers advanced academic degrees (graduate degrees) in addition to undergraduate degrees (bachelor's degrees) in quite varied subjects. For instance, the University of Wisconsin-Madison is a university, offering 136 undergraduate majors, 155 masters programs, and 110 doctoral programs.[22]

The term **college** may refer to an independent public or private institution or to an undergraduate division of a university. If an independent institution, the degree offered could range from an Associate's Degree (two or three years) to a Bachelor's Degree (four or five years). If within a larger university structure, the term **college** is used to distinguish a division housing programs or departments that are somehow similar.

Often institutions are categorized by their primary funding and oversight. The general categories include public; private, non-profit; and private, for-profit. Within the public sector, institutions may be further distinguished by whether the institution was established as a land-grant institution. Land-grant institutions were initiated by the Morrill Act of 1863 and established in the mid-nineteenth century across the United States with several purposes in mind. There was and remains a broad social responsibility aspect to land-grant universities, typically including tripartite requirements of research, teaching, and outreach or service.

Private institutions, whether non-profit or for-profit, maintain more autonomy in their structure and philosophy than a public institution. For students, tuition is typically higher at a private institution, as public funds are not used to supplement salaries, grounds, building upkeep, and the like.

There exists a further delineation of institution type based upon overall mission. Some institutions integrate a substantial research component in the requirements faculty must meet in addition to a proportional ratio of teaching and service. Others cite teaching as their primary mission and faculty are expected to maintain currency in their field through publication and service. As might be expected, the **teaching load** (the number of courses per term an instructor is expected to teach) varies substantially in the varied institutional types. In *The Academic Self: An Owner's Manual*, Hall cites examples of teaching loads in terms of courses taught per semester. Research schools range from teaching loads of one course each semester, two courses each semester, or perhaps three courses one semester and two the following. In these positions, faculty are expected to research, apply for, and successfully obtain research funding, such as grants, and disseminate resulting research through presentations and publications. Teaching schools typically contain an expectation to teach a minimum of three courses each semester, with emphasis on service in addition to teaching.[23]

Where do interior design programs fall in terms of institution type? Janetta McCoy, Denise Guerin, and Margaret Portillo conducted research describing the institution types of 120 responding interior design programs. Seventy-three indicated they were based in public institutions, 27 in private non-profit, and 17 in private for-profit institutions. Within the public institutions, 43 indicated the primary institution mission as teaching, one as service, and 29 as research. Of the private non-profit responses, all indicated teaching as their primary mission. Of the private for-profit institutions, teaching was indicated in 16 of the 17 responses, with service as the primary mission of one.[24]

Implications of Program Home

From largest to smallest in terms of power and size, the structure extends from university to college to school to department to program. Interior design may be a program or a department within an overall college or school in a university setting. Both the academic home and the length of program vary from institution to institution. Two-year programs are typically located at community colleges. Three-, four-, and five-year programs are typically associated with a bachelors (or higher) degree. Professional program accreditation is provided by the Council for Interior Design Accreditation (CIDA), formerly known as FIDER. A list of accredited programs may be found at www.accredit-id.org. Accreditations of programs through North American Schools of Art and Design (NASAD) or the National Kitchen and Bath Association (NKBA) are also possible; however, these accreditations are not recognized as the overarching professional program accreditation CIDA provides.

Examples of interior design academic homes include the College of Architecture, College of Visual and Performing Arts, College of Fine Arts, College of Business, College of Arts and Sciences, College of Agriculture and Human Ecology, and many others. Within these broad structures, there may be a program of interior design; architecture and design; clothing, textiles, and interior design, or some other combination. Challenges exist within each setting to define the parameters of interior design education and teaching requirements while simultaneously maintaining good relations with neighboring programs.

Likewise, the number of permanent faculty teaching in a program varies depending upon the overall program size and number of enrolled students, the mission of the institution, and the program's academic home. Typically, one or more adjunct professors are hired to supplement the permanent teaching faculty. The most common numbers of permanent interior design faculty for interior design programs are three to four. In McCoy's research, the responding programs indicated as few as two permanent full-time faculty members of interior design combined with an additional four adjunct (or otherwise supporting) faculty in a fine arts academic unit. This number contrasts with the largest program of nearly five full-time permanent faculty supported by over sixteen adjunct and part-time faculty within interior design academic units.[25]

Each of these widely varying settings has advantages and disadvantages for faculty members. Some instructors perceive a general academic bias against teaching institutions and a higher status ascribed to research institutions. For example, Hall observes that "certainly those hard-working academics employed at schools that emphasize teaching rather than research often feel misunderstood, undervalued, or ignored by the profession as a whole. Once employed at teaching schools, young academics may indeed break productive connections with the larger profession; fall out of the conversation in their fields of specialization; and sink into silence and resentment under the weight of papers, exams, and committee work."[26] Clearly, finding the right fit between an instructor's educational background, professional experiences, area of expertise and comfort, and personal and professional goals is paramount. In the authors' opinion, association with an institution maintaining teaching as its primary mission is no less legitimate than an institution engaging in significant research. Likewise, the pressure of research and grant-related activities in a primarily research-oriented institution can be cumbersome. No matter what the institution's orientation, maintaining currency in the profession is critical for all instructors, either through continuing education experiences, research, service, or all three paths. Faculty must carefully guard their time to ensure their personal renewal in order to offer their best to learners. Maintaining ties with colleagues through professional organizations is also important to an enduring sense of academic participation and contribution to the profession.

QUALITIES OF FULL-TIME, PART-TIME, AND GRADUATE ASSISTANT ROLES

While institutions vary greatly in their faculty policies and titles, generally instruction is carried out by full-time faculty, part-time (or adjunct) faculty, instructors, visiting lecturers, or graduate teaching assistants. Other categories sometimes exist as well, such as an outside practitioner whose presence in a class exceeds that of a guest speaker, yet who officially lacks the class-time involvement or credentials to be identified as an adjunct instructor.

The Tenure System

Like the titles given to faculty, the presence and application of the tenure system also varies by institution. Despite consistent criticism of the tenure system as antiquated, many still proclaim its protections for academic freedom, meaning the ability of an instructor to offer their own point of view on a subject without fear of recrimination or being fired.[27] Theoretically, the tenure system promotes intellectual autonomy and allows original thought to flourish without intervention. The downside of the tenure system can be seen in those tenured faculty who reduce their productivity or cooperation with others, using their tenure as a shield against firing for what may be justifiable causes.

The quantity of tenured positions has grown more slowly than non-tenured positions in recent decades, and institutions carefully consider tenure applicants because of the lifelong economic and professional relationship it establishes.[28] The proportion of non-tenured faculty has increased four times more rapidly than tenured positions since 1975, due in part to the growth of the American community college system and its heavy reliance on adjunct instructors. Currently only 35% of all who teach on all types of campuses in the United States are tenured or on the track to receive tenure.[29] Typically, tenure is only granted to full-time faculty.

Full-time Academic Positions

The full-time academic career varies in its responsibilities and is influenced by the mission and priorities of the hiring institution.

Typically, a full-time position in interior design requires that one engage in teaching, research or creative scholarship, and service in identified proportions. (These three activity categories are described further in Chapter 3.) Some institutions maintain an emphasis on teaching and may reduce or eliminate the requirement for original research or creative works. Other institutions emphasize research and subsequently reduce the teaching load to two or fewer courses per term. Full-time positions are not necessarily tenure-track, and some institutions use a contract system that is tied to performance evaluations in lieu of a lifelong tenure agreement. In some interior design departments, only the program chairperson is a full-time academic and all other instructors are part-time. Most commonly, there are three to four full-time interior design faculty within an interior design program.

In a full-time, tenure-track position, one begins an academic career as an assistant professor. After an identified probationary period (often six years in the tenure system), the educator petitions for tenure and promotion to associate professor simultaneously. After another six years, some but not all educators attain the final step of promotion from associate professor to full professor. It is possible to apply for tenure or promotion early, but these exceptions are carefully scrutinized by most institutions.

A full-time position usually carries with it expectations for contributions to the institution at various levels, such as student advising and service on committees. Some educators use a tenured position as a springboard to positions in higher academic leadership, such as department chairperson or dean.

Usually, full-time faculty are provided a private office, phone, and technology by the institution. An institution typically expects that a full-time faculty member will be a consistent "resident" within the department, attending faculty meetings and holding regular office hours commensurate with their teaching load to assist learners outside of class.

Full-time academic positions are not necessarily tenure-earning or permanent. At some institutions, **instructor** is a title given to faculty that are full time, are on two- to three-year renewable appointments, and have teaching and service but not research responsibilities. Similarly, **visiting lecturers** may engage in teaching or research full time with a one year appointment term.

Part-time (Adjunct) Academic Positions

Part-time faculty are present in many interior design academic programs. Usually, one or more adjunct faculty are hired to supplement the permanent teaching faculty and minimum qualifications vary by institution. The flexibility of hiring part-time faculty offers institutions obvious advantages to address the ebb and flow of student enrollment and gaps in faculty expertise or experience. Part-time faculty play a vital role in the learning experiences of students and often possess qualities that complement the skills and orientation of full-time faculty.

Part-time faculty often maintain a vital and direct connection with the profession, either through current or recent practice. Full-time faculty often must make contributions to research, service, or other pursuits that prevent them from full immersion in daily professional practice. Thus, adjunct professors fill an important teaching niche and provide current knowledge of products and procedures for learners. The qualities and contributions of part-time faculty are further discussed later in the chapter.

Part-time benefits vary by institution. Usually part-time faculty do not have access to healthcare and similar perks. They are often compensated on a per-credit-hour basis for the term. An office shared with other part-time or graduate teaching assistant faculty may be provided, along with a shared computer and phone. Part-time faculty are generally expected to maintain office hours commensurate with their teaching load but otherwise do not have to be present on campus.

Graduate Teaching and Research Assistant Positions

Graduate students are a diverse group, ranging from those students pursuing a graduate degree immediately following undergraduate or professional studies, to those with one to thirty or more years of professional practice experience. As the title suggests, departments with graduate programs often offer limited numbers of paid departmental assistantships to their graduate students. This opportunity can be a valuable way to build rapport with department faculty, opening doors to research projects and guided teaching opportunities. These assistantships may be awarded based on grade point average, suitability of skill to the position's responsibilities, stated need, or other criteria. This provides the graduate student with supervised teaching experience while simultaneously enhancing the department's course offerings. A graduate assistant may be assigned to assist a full-time faculty member with research or with class instruction. Some institutions permit graduate teaching assistants to teach undergraduate courses without daily full-time faculty guidance. Graduate teaching assistants are usually not permitted to teach other graduate students.

Other graduate assistantship benefits vary by institution. Usually graduate assistants do not have institutional access to healthcare and similar perks, although some institutions do address this situation. This issue is compelling some institutions' graduate students to form unions.[30] Some institutions offer private or shared office space with phone and technology to graduate assistants. Graduate assistants may be asked to hold office hours to assist undergraduate students but are usually not required to attend faculty meetings.

Meeting the Challenge of Interior Design Education

This chapter provides only a cursory outline of the multiple career issues and decisions facing the interior design educator. The academic life is many things both positive and negative, but most would agree it is seldom boring, and it can be exhilarating. An informed understanding of the nature of program homes, institution types, and position types can help educators define the best situation for their personal circumstances and preferences.

A. THE ROLES OF THE FULL-TIME ACADEMIC

Full-time interior design academics are present in a wide variety of institution types. Two-year colleges, five-plus-year research universities and private arts institutes are but three of these classifications. An academic's potential assigned responsibilities are nearly as diverse and relate closely to the mission of the institution. Typically, these activities will be in one or more of four categories of teaching, research/creative scholarship, service, and leadership (although some would group leadership under the service category). This section will address these four academic categories at length, defining their meaning and offering others' points of view on these components of the academic life. First, however, it is helpful to discuss the academic career in general and finding one's peace within its framework.

TAKING OWNERSHIP

When considering an academic job opportunity, it is important to seek the right fit, taking into account one's own proportional preferences for teaching, research, service, and leadership activities. Some interior designers will know the type of work they wish to engage in early on and can consciously engineer their personal academic and professional preparation to match these goals. Other interior designers enter the academic life during or after professional practice, which can sometimes lead them to enhance their qualifications or brush up on needed research knowledge.

Ultimately, it may matter less how one arrives at the conclusion to become an academic and more how one reacts to the opportunities it provides, taking ownership for one's career. In his book *The Academic Self*, Hall calls this self-reflection "moving between writing your own text and operating within the larger text of academia."[31] This mental negotiation implies the need to articulate one's values and priorities while simultaneously finding a home and role within the larger institution. When coming from professional practice to academia, this negotiation may involve several phases, including fact-finding, experimenting, and experiencing. Hall and others offer several observations that can help an academic maintain personal balance while simultaneously achieving success as expressed through tenure and promotion:

- Know the institution's and larger academic community's expectations of research, service, and teaching and be willing to accept those consequences.
- Do not succumb to a fear of failure. Academics must engage in documentable vita activities to succeed but should not think of failure to receive these honors and awards as a life shortcoming.
- Avoid a sense of ego or entitlement with victories. Sometimes successes are highly dependent on chance, such as being in the right place at the right time for a grant's acceptance.
- Avoid "self-willed ignorance." Be sure that the action plan of accomplishments for earning tenure melds with the institutional mission and expectations.
- Actively seek out answers from the institution if expectations are unclear.
- Understand that a career is subject to certain forces not under one's direct control. Budgets, changing institution priorities, and other unexpected issues are a common part of the academic experience.[32]
- Make teaching, research/creative scholarship, and service fit together, each complementing the other. This can simplify an academic's to-do list considerably. For example,
    - Bring the classroom experience to research, if appropriate. Teaching experiences can generate research questions or provide participants for research studies.
    - Let research findings influence teaching, improving technique and broadening point of view.
    - Influence teaching with service by engaging learners in local or national activities that give back and boost learner empathy (see Figure 2.2). Service projects can also easily serve as the foundation for research studies.

Academics choose their professional values, behaviors, and definitions of success in response to and in negotiation with the professional community. It is often an active choice either to engage in that community or to encourage the dichotomy by remaining isolated in intellectualism. While more difficult than the "academic diva" approach, the path of critical participatory dialogue with

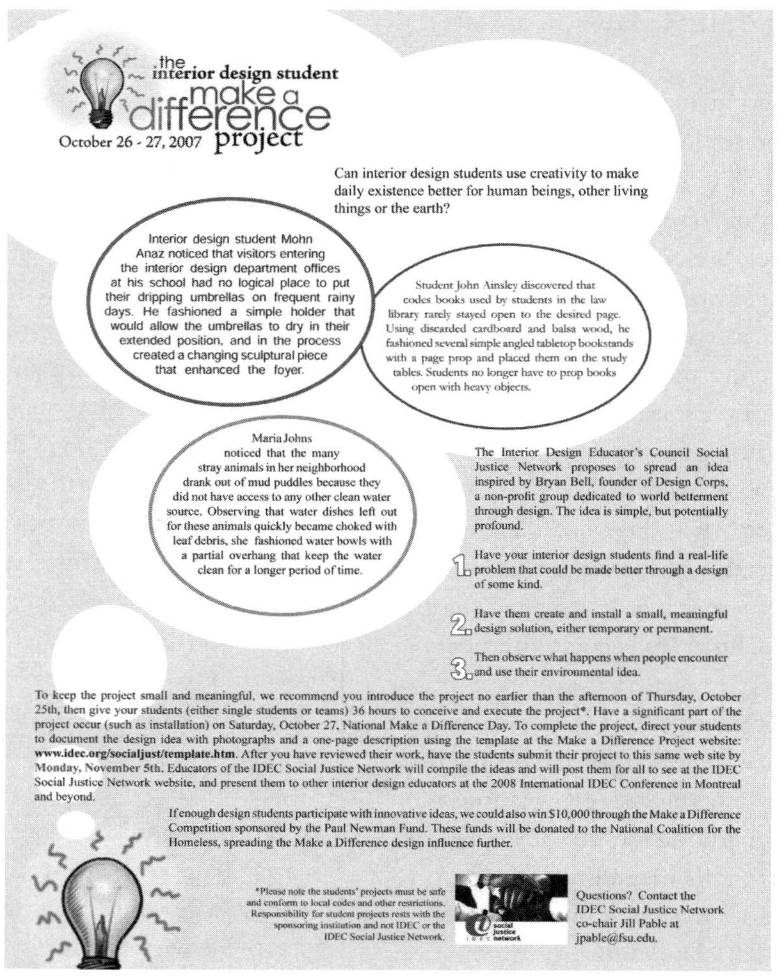

Figure 2.2 The Interior Design Educators Council's Social Justice Network has created a national service activity for interior design students called the "Make a Difference Project." The interior design instructor creators intend to propose a conference presentation of the results that will in turn provide vita items for their personal records.

others can lead to long-term happiness and positive growth.[33]

THE FOUR PRIMARY ACTIVITIES OF THE ACADEMIC CAREER

Academics are primarily engaged in teaching, research/creative scholarship, service, and leadership in their career activities. Some engage in all of these on a daily basis, while others segment their year with focused engagement in primarily one or two areas at a time. This section will discuss considerations of each and offer an interior design academic's personal perspective on what it is like to live the experience.

Teaching

The opportunity to engage learners in dialogue and prompt new understanding is among the most thrilling aspects of academia. There are few situations other than education where people spend money to be held accountable to the words and point of view of another. Teaching can indeed be a joyful task, and some academics feel that the youthful vigor of their learners rubs off on them as well.[34] It is little wonder that some educators who have advanced to leadership roles removed from teaching yearn for a return to a daily chance to work with learners.

Interior design educator and associate professor Carl Matthews of the University of Texas at Austin found that his teaching priorities influenced his choice of institution. He draws great satisfaction from engaging interior design learners and professional firms in educational partnerships:

> When I made the transition from full time professional interior design practice to full time teaching, I was terrified of losing my contact with practice and eventually my relevance as a studio teacher. This fear drove me to return to practice during holiday and summer breaks. For ten years I loved the routine: teach in the peaceful city of Lincoln, Nebraska during the semester and return to New York City, San Francisco or Seattle during school vacations.
>
> One of my primary reasons for moving to the University of Texas at Austin was the unique opportunity to combine my passion for studio teaching with my desire to maintain a strong connection with major design firms. At UT during the Spring of the third year of study and the Fall of the fourth year of study, Gensler, Dallas, Wilson Associates, Dallas, and Sussman Tisdale Gayle Architects, Austin, donate their time to co-teach my design studios. Each semester I meet with the firms to determine which of the projects in their office would be most academically meaningful and challenging to the students. Students meet with the professionals on a bi-monthly basis to review and present progress on their projects.
>
> This close relationship with the firms has benefited us all. Professionals are energized by the youth, creativity and enthusiasm of the students. Students are inspired and motivated by the professionalism and knowledge of the practitioners. And I have the great joy of watching both groups flourish while staying current with the daily workings of the industry.

Research and Creative Scholarship

Teaching is largely a local phenomenon. Research, however, takes one's voice out to the farther academic community and beyond. Institutions often desire that their academics' ideas be known and respected beyond the bounds of campus, and each researcher's work adds to the collective perception of the institution. National and international recognition of researchers is often a stated priority for research institutions and a condition for promotion and tenure.

Research can be quite enjoyable, and the opportunity to address a question or solve a puzzle can provide immense satisfaction in the thought of making a contribution. Research can also be a nerve-wracking experience because it implies putting one's investigation and synthesis out there for others to criticize and tear apart. Scrutiny from the academic community through rejection letters or edits to research articles resembling the carnage of Bull Run can ruin one's day. A positive attitude and the ability to look at comments as constructive criticism rather than personal rejection is necessary during these times. A community of peers can provide a valuable service in that all academics engaged in research/creative scholarship can share similar experiences.

Research and scholarship are typically valued highly, in fact sometimes more highly than teaching, in tenure and promotion.[35] Endeavors that institutions regard as research vary widely. Examples include scholarly books published at a university press, textbooks, scholarly monographs, journal articles, book reviews, and editing projects. Creative scholarship is another category many institutions equate equally with research for interior design academics. Winning or placing in design competitions is a common path toward recognized creative scholarship. A common thread in the value placed upon particular research and creative scholarship activities is both the review process and the perceived prestige of the publication or other venue.

Interior design academic Dr. Caren Martin of the University of Minnesota integrates a sizable research agenda into her career activities. Her experiences in professional practice served to spark questions that her later academic career provided the means to explore:

> Having been an interior design practitioner for over seventeen years enriches my current role as educator/researcher. That knowledge also gives me an advantage in the classroom as I bring first-hand practice to students. It is for that reason I have tremendous passion about improving practice and practitioners as a way to improve quality of life and protect the Earth.
>
> When I entered graduate school in the mid-90s, my passion was to find out why interior designers were held away, segregated, often, from the full scope of the project in a multidisciplinary firm and sequestered to being "color-picker-outers." Also, very few interior designers would freely admit this situation. I had always worked in larger, full-service firms as had many of my colleagues. I began my research to determine if interior design was a profession as a way to understand the lack of confidence of interior designers and to ask why interior designers were considered of less value to the design process than, say, architects. My research was based on a theory of professionalization, as without that theoretical foundation it would just be my opinion—and that is not research. Learning about the research process was challenging. I had to learn to sharpen my logic, become knowledgeable about research methods and statistical analysis, omit subjective thinking, and improve my writing skills.
>
> In the end, my research determined that based on an established theory of professionalization, interior design is a profession. Of course that pointed out other aspects of the profession that I wanted to explore: what did the public think? Subsequently, I conducted a national survey of the public's opinion to determine if they believed that interior design was a profession. It was a scary undertaking but exciting to determine which findings were "statistically significant." Study design that results in quantitative analysis can be harder to structure in social science types of investigations, but complementary to the richness of qualitative analysis and subsequent findings. It is important to try to address both over the course of one's research agenda.
>
> Research is the underpinning of any endeavor, especially a professional one. It is how a doctor knows how to treat the pain you have in your arm; likewise it is how an interior designer knows how the interior environment can help a dementia patient's quality of life. Personally, research also feeds all other aspects of my academic pursuits. Understanding the power of research enables me to impart a curiosity about and reliance on research among students who will be practitioners in a few short years. Research and its symbiotic relationship to practice also was the inspiration for InformeDesign®, a Web site launched in January 2003 that

transforms research into evidence-based design criteria for use by practitioners, created with Dr. Denise Guerin.

Overall, engaging in a vibrant research agenda has enriched my experience as an educator and as a person. As my skill as a researcher develops with each investigation, I am able to bring more into the classroom on a personal level with my students, bring my findings to the attention of colleagues for the purpose of discussion, and impart information to the public that can influence perception, policy, and even law.

Service

Many institutions also require their academic members to engage in activities that provide assistance to others. In promotion and tenure documents, service is often broken down by scope of influence into categories, and service can take many forms at these varying levels:

- *Department.* Service on committees, student advising, overseeing materials libraries, maintaining technology, developing local conferences and colloquia
- *College/University.* Service on committees, reviewing institution grant proposals, serving as an advisor to college teaching and learning institutes, serving as a faculty senator
- *Community/Local & regional.* Judging local design competitions, offering presentations to the public, serving as a leader in local-level professional and civic organizations, volunteering to help with local/regional causes
- *Community/National & international.* National service to professional organizations such as the Interior Design Educators Council (IDEC), the American Society of Interior Designers (ASID), the International Interior Design Association (IIDA), and Interior Designers of Canada (IDC); sponsoring and facilitating national conferences; creating an institute that addresses a broad-scope issue

Service for academics can invigorate a life that is often steeped in writing, grading, and thinking and can "keep the walls of the ivory tower from crowding out the sun."[36] That is, service projects can connect theory and stated beliefs to practical action, bringing a sense of reality to an academic's experience. Service can also further the outreach mission of the institution. Conversely, an academic's lack of service, some would say, is an abdication of responsibility. D. Hall describes the relationship between service and one's broader career thusly:

> In reading, interacting with, and responding to the very complex texts of our institutions—which is what most service is, after all—we are not being pulled away from our work, we are doing our work as cultural/textual critics. If we define service as somehow opposed to our work, then we have deliberately chosen a professional self-identity that is neither collegially responsible nor even intellectually nuanced.[37]

Rula Awwad-Rafferty is chairperson of the interior design program, coordinator and associate professor at the University of Idaho. Her engagement in service has provided benefits for both herself and her students:

> Hands-on learning, civic participation, and service learning make possible opportunities to explore timely, critical, and enduring issues of meaning, purpose, and moral integrity. The growth, sensitivity, and sense of personal responsibility and empowerment which comes from such encounters are immeasurable.

Senator Robert Kennedy perhaps said it best: "But history will judge you, and as the years pass, you will ultimately judge yourself, in the extent to which you have used your gifts and talents to lighten and enrich the lives of your fellow men. In your hands lies the future of your world and the fulfillment of the best qualities of your own spirit."

Service to others is the essence of being vibrant in the world, of adding value to the world, and being part of that large, complex tapestry we call life. The service paradigm is interdisciplinary, action-oriented, culturally reflective and integrated. I have embraced it as the foundation for who I am and what I do as a human being, as a scholar, as an educator, as a mentor, and as a designer and community member.

I believe that educators hold a most sacred trust in their hands—the future. The sense of wonder and fulfillment that the diversity of experiences, ideas, faces, backgrounds, and perspectives we encounter in and outside of class is energizing. My credo is to be an effective faculty and community member who honors and advances the tenets of human rights, honoring respect, dignity, self realization, and basic human needs through both action and thought. I strive to do this by recognizing the complexities and diversity in places, people, and cultures, and by structuring a strongly engaged, inclusive, and innovative learning experience for my students. The world around us is a canvas for all these possibilities, which can be engaged both intuitively and intentionally through service.

For example, students in my Universal Design class at the University of Idaho complete 20 hours of service, working with an organization that serves the needs of people with disabilities. The intimate connection that the students developed over the service period, the structured reflections after each encounter, and observed change in attitude and perspective may have not been as effective had it not been for this service component in the class. When students take initiative and become involved in service activities, great things can happen. The design of the College of Law Legal Aid Clinic, work with the Fair Housing Commission, and the design of the Student Multicultural Center have all been examples of student-driven initiatives on my campus. I am very proud of these students, and know that through their continued commitment the world will be a better place.

I have also grown personally from my experiences with service. Living in a migrant farm workers' community while conducting my Ph.D. field research provided me with great insights into the intricacies of itinerant life, the built environment, and issues of law and inclusion. Learning firsthand from the workers placed a visible face on my research questions. I have witnessed the crystallization of this experience with a new generation when the students in senior Interior Design studio worked with Shoshone Bannock tribes to design a veterans' center. In the process they learned about design leadership, sense of place, sustainability, cultural values, and the participatory process.

I have become more aware of holistic thinking and have gained broader and deeper understanding of the complexity and interrelatedness of issues. "Real life scenarios," problem based learning, and community building have become easier for me to grapple with through my engagement in service. Through a continual process of evaluation, introspection, and learning, my own knowledge and philosophy have developed along with my students. I now utilize a more grounded application to theories, methods, and experiences that previously lacked context. Further, I am more comfortable with relinquishing authority in favor of becoming a learner in the team. With these skills I am able to communicate a vision, facilitate a dialogue, and help achieve results on university committees as well as in other service arenas.

As designers and design educators, we sometimes tend to gloss over or superficially appreciate the contextual relationship between design and the rest of the world, forgetting the ecosystems character of the designed environment. When we focus completely on our own disciplines, we forget to notice its connection and reciprocal relationship to other facets of human endeavor, such as economy, politics, health, and industry. Grounded service allows us to delve deeper and bridge these chasms. Combining service, education, training, and commitment enables me to build an engaged career that I love.

I urge interior design educators to break open the box of what is standard operating learning procedure to embrace new ideas grounded in service and look at the world with passion and renewed perspective. Strive to incite critical and creative thinking in students, and let service learning elevate and make real an endeavor's context so it builds intellectual commitment and deep engagement. Let students leave not only with knowledge of necessary concepts, but with the tools that allow them to make critical, creative, and responsible decisions in their future lives as designers and professionals.

Mahatma Gandhi has said, "The difference between what we do and what we are capable of doing would suffice to solve most of the world's problems." This sentiment embodies what I believe to be the role of an effective and engaged educator. We are stewards of the future, and we can choose to play a part in making it better and making a difference.

Leadership

Higher education institutions are often operated in a hierarchical leadership structure. In public institutions, program chairs report to department chairs, who are in turn guided by deans that report to provosts. Private institutions similarly have a clear chain of authority that takes cues from the business management model. Some academics elect to advance their careers by moving from traditional teaching, research, and service activities into leadership roles that engage them in distinctly different concerns such as budgets, personnel decisions, and campus initiatives. These positions offer the advantage of exerting a greater influence on institution activities and overall guidance than otherwise would be possible.

Interior design academic Dr. Jo Ann Asher Thompson serves as Vice Chancellor at Washington State University Spokane and is also the editor in chief of the *Journal of Interior Design.* She attributes her success in leadership in part to her ability to solve problems creatively—skills she developed from her interior design background. Her perspective describes these and other reasons why interior design educators should consider positions of academic authority:

> Leadership . . . what does this mean to—and for—interior design education? Is it the same as, or different from, leadership in other fields of study? Is the leadership role of academic professionals defined by

the academy or by the profession? What are the benefits of assuming leadership roles?

These are some of the key questions that face interior design educators as their careers advance and mature. There is constant tension between the requirement to be validated as a design practitioner (as defined by the professional community), the need to be recognized as a scholar (as mandated by the academy), and the call from each of these sectors to assume leadership roles. The struggle to meet these demands places interior design academic professionals in the difficult position of having to make choices about whether to accept—let alone seek out—leadership opportunities.

Over the course of my career as an academic professional I have had to make these kinds of decisions. I have never regretted that the path I chose was that of a leadership role within higher education. Early in my career as an interior design faculty member at an institution of higher education, it became evident to me that interior design was all too often seen as "beneath" other disciplines or relegated to second or third priority when decisions were made about the budget, staffing, and/or faculty recognition and awards. It also soon became evident to me that my background in interior design had provided me with the ability to creatively problem-solve and develop strategies that could address complex issues—much more so than many of the administrators I had witnessed who did not have such grounding. These realizations crystallized for me the importance of having interior designers in key leadership roles within the academy—and as perhaps the only way to ensure that interior design was "at the table" when the university made major budget decisions and laid out strategic plans for the future.

Many will choose other pathways for leadership than I have. That is as it should be. But, I would argue that, regardless of the path chosen, some form of leadership is an essential component of the success of an academic professional's career. Knowing that your choice to take on a leadership role has helped to secure the future of the profession far outweighs the sacrifices that may have to be made along the way.

My own experience has made me a true believer in the fact that leadership from interior design academic professionals is critical to the continued advancement of the discipline and profession. By assuming key leadership roles within the academy and/or the practitioner community, interior design academic professionals increase the visibility and elevate the perceived prestige of interior design to a variety of diverse audiences. Such roles provide unique opportunities to share with others the kind of scholarship that is being done—and is adding to—interior design's body of knowledge.

At this juncture in time interior design continues to suffer from stereotypes and questions from both the public and the academy about its validity as a discipline and as a profession. I am confident that over time these things will become less and less of an issue—but only if interior design academic professionals continue to take on leadership roles and are willing to make the sacrifices necessary to help lead the next generation to an even brighter future.

Avoiding Burnout

Regardless of the proportions of teaching, research, service, and leadership that make up an academic's responsibilities, the academic career is one characterized by intense, sustained effort. This fact in itself is not necessarily a problem, though it can precipitate the unpleasantness of **burnout.** Defined as "a state *not* clearly chosen or desired, one of frustration or involving a sense of defeat that persists for long periods of time, if not the remainder of a career," burnout is sufficiently pervasive to be mindful of avoiding.[38] Wise institutions and their leaders are interested in not only hiring qualified academics but presenting them with job responsibilities that keep them fulfilled, happy, and productive. However, academics themselves may be the partial or primary culprit in the case of burnout, working themselves into a state of frenzy and numbness. The following list identifies seven actions one can take to avoid the onset of burnout:

1. *Join and be an active member of an interior design professional organization.* Attend conferences, network, listen, and engage. Nourish yourself with outside ideas.
2. *Read widely in your area of interest*, or reconnect by beginning to read widely again.
3. *Define your career goals precisely and carefully.* A good goal is one you can control, not one you cannot. For example, a stated goal might be to produce a journal article for submission in six months. The initial goal does *not* include getting it accepted to avoid setting yourself up for bitterness. The next goal might be the submittal and the next the revision of a rejected manuscript.
4. *Be wary of goals that pursue academic fame at the expense of community and institution.* These can be fame-enhancing but can produce a narrow life.
5. *Look out for yourself in professional relationships.* It is necessary to learn how to withdraw gracefully from unsatisfactory professional relationships. Be attuned to patterns of others' work and be prepared to say no if the relationship has disaster written all over it.
6. *Establish micro-support networks.* A support system of colleagues at your institution who have a similar interest or a professional organization's informal network group can both nurture and challenge you professionally. If participation recharges you, it is worthwhile. If the group moves you toward inactivity or dread, do not stay involved.[39]
7. *Consider your personal capabilities, life circumstances, and institution's expectations.* Pressures on institution budgets and other problems can lead administrators to sometimes have unrealistic expectations for academics' productivity. Institutions exist that overreach, resulting in high turnover in their faculty populations. A wise job-seeker will network with other academics to identify and avoid working for such institutions.

In Conclusion

Academic responsibilities form the heart of one's satisfaction or displeasure with a given job. Teaching, research/creative scholarship, service, and leadership compose a wide collection of potential activities unique to the academic life. While institutions have much to say about one's specific activities, an eyes-wide-open approach to job selection and willingness to commit to a given set of expectations can help an academic maintain a sense of self-destiny. Critical engagement with one's academic career is an ongoing journey that can sustain interest and satisfaction for the long term.

B. CONTRIBUTIONS OF ADJUNCT FACULTY

Adjunct (or part-time) faculty represent a substantial entity within higher education and play a vital role in the learning experiences of thousands of students.

- Adjuncts augment instructional opportunities and needs that current faculty are not available to meet.
- Adjunct professors provide a diversity of viewpoint, approach, and process to the program and classroom.
- Students benefit from the employment networking connections that adjunct instructors may bring to the classroom.
- Finally, adjunct professors are generally an enthusiastic group! Infusion of this enthusiasm is welcome inside the classroom and out.

CURRENCY IN THE PROFESSION

One of the significant strengths of adjunct instructors is that they often come directly from, or are currently engaged in, practice. In the education of future professional interior designers, this attribute is highly valued. What does this currency in practice mean? It implies that oftentimes adjunct professors are in direct contact with the procedures for project management, working with representatives, talking with colleagues to compare notes, and keeping abreast of current products and trends. This is not to suggest that full-time educators are not also involved with some, if not all, of these activities, but the reality is that the primary emphasis for most full-time educators is on the education of students.

Currency in the profession is as much an attitude as it is a quantifiable attribute. Keeping current with local projects in the various phases of design, whether "on the boards" or during installations brings a sense of involvement and immediacy to the classroom. Keeping tabs on the local economic pulse and the hiring practices of firms is invaluable as students prepare for internships or permanent positions. The ability to speak directly to deficiencies noticed in recent graduates, or on the other hand, their superior abilities and attitudes, make students eager to participate with adjunct professors!

Maintaining a link to the profession provides an additional advantage to academic programs. In their paper *Interior Design Trends and Implications* for the Council for Interior Design Accreditation, Coleman and Sosnowchik cite additional implications, noting that "today's practices are expanding their employee bases to include professionals from both inside and outside the design fields. The intrinsic link between professional practice and design education necessitates the discovery of new means of communication and new methods of strengthening our leadership and value propositions."[40]

Learning Experiences Beyond the Classroom

Because they are typically involved with professional practice, the adjunct instructor often brings a wealth of examples and current experiences to bear in the classroom. These can include examples of project manuals, construction documents, specifications, presentations to clients or communications to consultants, tips on the current practitioner climate, or images of projects under construction.

Rarely does every aspect of a project proceed smoothly from initial design through to final installation of products. Examples of things gone wrong and lessons learned can provide lively discussions and memorable examples. It is helpful to remember that "the morals of the story" learned in this manner are often remembered better than through more traditional means of teaching.

As a direct result of recent or current engagement in practice, adjunct instructors may have developed good relationships with manufacturers' representatives. These are wonderful resources to bring into the classroom. When preparing learners for interaction with the manufacturers' representatives, adjunct educators should caution students to compare the information received with that from other courses and to question effectively. Many manufacturers' representatives are excellent resources for product knowledge, as well as observations regarding design and architectural firms.

Adjunct educators often have ties to projects under construction or recently completed. Field trips to these sites are invaluable, and adjunct instructors can use their experience as well as their particular knowledge of the project itself to shed light on its various aspects. The decision-making process for finishes, construction types, and particular challenges in the design's implementation are especially valuable in the educational process.

In addition to the contact opportunities outlined, adjunct educators may possess a firsthand ability to conduct firm tours. Firm tours are beneficial to students in gaining familiarity with the professional environment. These tours, along with tours of projects under construction, and visits from product representatives, can influence learner knowledge and goals well beyond a single course.

The current knowledge of professional practice and project procedures that adjunct educators bring to the classroom is an exceedingly valuable asset for student growth and understanding. The impact of an actual project document, field trip, or guest speaker that adjunct instructors make possible should not be underestimated. It is not unusual for a student, years later, to recall a certain site visit or exposure to a speaker as a preeminent influence upon their knowledge and inspiration for practice.

Challenges Faced

While adjunct educators play an important role in many interior design programs, the role of an individual educator is often limited by the nature of a part-time appointment. Challenges to the positive contributions of adjunct faculty often fall under one of several specific issues, each relating to the fundamental difference in goals between practice and higher education.

- Practice, by nature, is fast-paced and product-oriented. Education, while preparing learners to enter the practice of interior design, also has the important charge of creating high-level thinking skills, research capabilities, and creativity. Adjunct faculty do well to keep the overarching educational and curricular goals in mind when teaching a single course. For instance, students require extra time to ingest and internalize new ideas and curricula that have been designed to build learning experiences from one academic term to the next. Including project types (without regard to the overall curricular goals) that students are not prepared to address may be frustrating for faculty and student alike. Likewise, to build knowledge, future courses rely on information presented in previous courses, and it is important to comply with all of the educational goals prescribed for a particular course.
- In many cases, the role of practitioner is the most prominent role of the adjunct. The challenge is to maintain separation between the practice life and academic life while in the classroom and during office hours, even when deadlines loom. Phone calls taken during class or office hours regarding projects at the office are not necessarily consistent with a focus on the academic success of the learners. Additionally, while overhearing conversations

in an interior design office is common, in the academic realm a small teaching session or class may be interrupted by an unintentionally loud cell phone conversation with a colleague or contractor.
- Institutions typically have requirements for office hours outside of class times, even for adjunct instructors. These hours are intended to give the learner access to extra help and are an important ancillary learning time that the adjunct instructor provides.

While mentoring a team of assistant designers in a firm translates in many ways to teaching in a studio setting, it is not a direct translation. The overarching goals are fundamentally different and should be recognized. The nature of mentoring in a firm often takes the form of specific situations that, when combined, result in both more effective contributions to the design project process and potential management or leadership of teams. This mentoring assumes that basic frameworks of research and theory (and their application), as well as designers' finding their own "voice" are solidly in place. This may not yet be the case with interior design students. Adjunct faculty can bring substantial benefit to academic programs. With careful administrative leadership in the selection of adjunct faculty, a focus on the positive contributions of such, and mentoring to overcome potential drawbacks, learners (and colleagues) have the opportunity to enjoy a beneficial blend of professional interior design educators as well as professional interior design practitioners.

C. TODAY'S LEARNER

When teaching, it is common to relate current learners' experiences with that of your own educational (and extracurricular) understanding. Today's learner may be quite different from current educators in world experience, expectations, and other ways. Learners today comprehend world or local events with a frame of reference different than that of even ten years ago. To communicate effectively with today's learner, it is helpful to understand what that learner's frame of reference looks like. Examining demographics, experiences, attitudes, and the external demands common for today's learner is often helpful in understanding their particular mindset and approach to problem-solving.

Coleman and Sosnowchik's 2005 study discusses these characteristics. "Today's college students, who began using computers more than a decade ago at the age of 5, now think and process information completely differently from previous generations."[41] This presents, as they put it, "new challenges for educators who must engage students and interact with them on a whole different level and in a brand new language."[42]

Each generation of learners possesses unique characteristics and a shared set of experiences that frame their knowledge of the world. This section explores the composition of today's learners, through demographics, common experiences, attitudes, and external demands, and relates them to interior design education. For it is in knowing one's learners that the most appropriate teaching and learning situations can be designed.

DEMOGRAPHICS

According to a 1997 National Center for Education Statistics study,[43] more than 50 percent of learners enrolled in higher institutions in the second half of the 1990s were 18 to 22 years of age. However, this segment has decreased each year since 1992. On the other hand, the population of non-traditional and ethnically diverse learners has increased. Traditional incoming freshmen to the 2007–

2008 terms were typically born in 1989 and their high school years ranged from the years 2003 to 2007.

Gone are the days when a majority learner population was described as white, male, middle-class, single, 18 to 22 years old, residing on campus and working fewer than 10 hours a week.[44] According to a College Board Press Release, "The SAT takers in the class of 2007 are the most diverse group on record, with minority students comprising 39%."

- There are more African-American, Asian-American, and Hispanic SAT takers in the class of 2007 than in any previous class.
- Hispanic students represent the largest and fastest growing minority group.
- There are also more SAT takers in this year's class for whom English is not exclusively their first language learned, compared to previous years' SAT takers. In the class of 2007, 24% of students did not have English exclusively as their first language, compared to 17% in 1997, and 13% in 1987.
- Thirty-five percent of this year's class will be the first in their families to attend college.
- Females comprise 54% of SAT takers and males comprise 46%.[45]

Critical factors influencing these changing demographics in the United States include race, migration and immigration, birth rates, mortality rates and age, and gender. All of these factors ultimately affect the profile of college learners as well as enrollments.[46] The Western Interstate Commission for Higher Education (WICHE) predicted that by 2017–2018, 22.1% of high school graduates will be Hispanic as compared to 12.3% in 2002–2003. However, Black, non-Hispanic graduates will statistically remain about the same at 13.2%.[47] In a media release regarding high school graduates, WICHE documents the sometimes dramatic change in student demographics that are poised to affect college classes:

- In the graduating class of 2014, only about half of the learners are projected to be White, non-Hispanics, while half will represent a racial/ethnic minority.
- Hispanics are expected to be the fastest-growing group in the United States, representing over one-fifth of that class; Asian/Pacific Islander learners will also increase their share.
- Black, non-Hispanic numbers are expected to hold steady, and White, non-Hispanics will see their share of enrollments and graduation rates decline.[48]

Recent successive years of learners have demonstrated sometimes evident changes in these individuals' expectations and personality profiles. Current traditional college learners are considered the Millennial generation, consisting of individuals born between 1980 and 2002.[49] Howe and Strauss describe the Millennials as "special," "sheltered," "confident," "team-oriented," "achieving," "pressured," and "conventional."[50] If pursuing a traditional timeline of undergraduate college enrollment directly after high school, Millennial students entered college classrooms in 1998.

Interestingly, the descriptors are significantly different from those associated with Generation X, meaning those born between 1961 and 1981, and entering college classrooms in 1979. They have been described as "castaways," "at risk," "neglected," "aggressive," "slackers," and "alienated."[51] In her report "Changing Demographics and Generational Shifts: Understanding and Working with the Families of Today's College Students," Judy Donovan reports that Generation X learners tended to be raised in day-care, and were set aside to make room for their parents' fulfillment. She describes that they have excelled in underachievement according to all societal perceptions. The lack of societal standards amidst the major political, social, economic, and cultural turmoil of the past twenty years is considered a major contributor to the demise of Generation X.[52]

Not surprisingly, as the Millennials are characteristically different from the previous Generation X learners, the Baby Boomer parents are radically dissimilar to parents of previous generations as well. Baby Boomers, the parents of the Millennials, were born between 1943 and 1960.[53] Growing numbers of the Silent Generation[54], born between 1925 and 1942, are serving as the heads of households in the place of the Baby Boomers who are single parents or unable to raise their children for other reasons.[55] Significantly, Millennials have demonstrated a return to the Silent Generation's values and beliefs, identifying also with their grandparents' generation.[56]

Today's college learner, then, is significantly molded by numerous social and familial forces which in turn affect their learning behavior. More than anytime during the last 50 years, family plays an important role in the higher education of this Millennial generation. Parents of this group greatly vary in their own academic preparation. There are other social differences that distinguish the family backgrounds of today's college learners. These significant differences pose new challenges for colleges and universities. Older, more financially stable, and focused on fewer children, the Baby Boomer parents of today's college learners are more involved in their children's education than ever before.[57] In addition, today's college learners are more likely to be raised in a single parent household (32%), to experience living below poverty-level (23.1%), and to have a mother who works outside of the home (89.4%) than previous generations of college learners.[58]

Experiences

What is the cultural frame of reference for current traditional (those progressing directly from high school to college) 18- to 22-year-old college learners? Traditional learners today have firsthand knowledge of only two United States presidents, Bill Clinton and George W. Bush. Their experience includes the Florida ballot chad and the September 11, 2001 tragedy. They were in grade school during the 90s and were in middle school during Y2K. AIDS has always been a health risk, and DNA testing has always been a reality. Microwaves have always been standard kitchen appliances, and a cookie is not necessarily a food product. The thought of not carrying a cell phone is foreign to them. Johnny Carson has only been on the *Tonight Show* in reruns.

The O.J. Simpson chase occurred before these learners were in school. They have no recollection of him hurdling through airports. They were still in grade school when President Clinton admitted to having an affair with Monica Lewinsky and when the Columbine tragedy occurred. Computers have always fit into backpacks; stores have always had scanners at the checkout; and there have always been PIN numbers. The Millennial generation has always known seatbelts, child safety seats, and bike helmets—and is the most cared for and overprotected generation of children in U.S. history.[59]

Current families have few children; in many cases young people have one or no siblings within the household. Because of this, today's learners often lack the familial experiences to learn how to share or to develop much needed conflict resolution skills within the family structure. This is an important point for educators to keep in mind when assigning team projects.

Coleman and Sosnowchik add further definition to the Millenial student profile:

- Twenty percent of today's college learners (Millenials) began using computers between the ages of 5 and 8.
- Today's average college graduates have spent less than 5,000 hours of their lives reading, but over 10,000 hours playing video games as well as 20,000 hours watching TV.
- Millennials are known to thrive in informal and non-traditional learning environments. They prefer group study situations, real-world problems, experiential learning, and improvised study environments.
- They are deeply engaged with technology.[60]

What are the implications of this set of reference experiences?

- Spaces designed for the new generation of learners should be designed around their needs and their cognitive style of learning.
- Today's learners, kindergarten through college, represent the first generation to grow up as digital natives who think and process information fundamentally differently from their predecessors.
- Teaching digital natives requires redesigning both learning methodology and information content. In order to reach these learners, today's instructors need to communicate in a language and style that these learners understand. Legacy content (reading, writing, arithmetic) needs to be replaced with "future content"—information that is technological and digital (software, robotics, nanotechnology) and also embeds ethics, politics, and sociology.[61]
- Importantly, the rise in visual literacy and the subsequent decline in textural literacy is predicted to herald the end of the Information Age and the beginning of the Concept Age, where people will use right-brain capabilities (creativity, empathy, pattern recognition, and the making of meaning) in how they work, entertain, communicate, and educate.[62]

Attitudes

Generational attitudes are interesting to note. In Millennials Coming To College, DeBard describes a comparison of attitudes among three recent generations, as explained in Table 2.1.[63]

In their work published in ISdesigNET, interior design educators Jane Kucko, Texas Christian University, and Betsy Gabb, University of Nebraska-Lincoln, reacted to a recent UC-Los Angeles article reporting that today's college freshmen have the highest level of self-esteem of any other class for the past 30 years. Kucko and Gabb remarked that ". . . traditional college-age learners know what they want and they expect to get it! And, it is important to remember if they make a mistake, it isn't their fault. The sooner we understand this fundamental principle, the better we will 'communicate' with this generation of student."[64]

Today's learners, reacting to a perceived lack of loyalty from employers, corporations, and others in general, are more likely to view themselves as consumers of an educational experience. Consequently, learners may perceive themselves as more on par with their instructors in a variety of ways compared to previous generations and deserving of a quality education experience in exchange for their time and monetary sacrifice.

Strauss & Howe (2000) describe a Millennium generation personality using seven distinguishing traits:

- Special: possessing a sense of being vital to the nation and to their parents' sense of purpose

TABLE 2.1: ATTITUDINAL TRAITS OF DIFFERENT GENERATIONS

Views toward	Boomers	Gen Xers	Millennials
Level of trust	Confident of self, not authority	Low toward authority	High toward authority
Loyalty to institutions	Cynical	Considered Native	Committed
Most admire	Taking charge	Creating enterprise	Following a hero or integrity
Career goals	Build a stellar career	Build a portable career	Build parallel careers
Rewards	Title and the corner office	Freedom not to do	Meaningful work
Parent-child involvement	Receding	Distant	Intruding
Having children	Controlled	Doubtful	Definite
Family life	Indulged as children	Alienated as children	Protected as children
Education	Freedom of expression	Pragmatic	Structure of accountability
Evaluation	Once a year with documentation	"Sorry, but how am I doing?"	Feedback whenever I want it
Political orientation	Attack oppression	Apathetic, individual	Crave community
The big question	What does it mean?	Does it work?	How do we build it?

- Sheltered: exposed to kid safety rules, lockdown of public schools, sweeping national youth safety movement
- Confident: possessing high levels of trust and optimism
- Team-oriented: used to classroom emphasis on group learning, school uniforms, tighter peer bonds
- Achieving: held to higher levels of accountability and school standards
- Pressured: expected to excel in several different areas (athletics, music, and other extracurricular demands)
- Conventional: instilled with the idea that social rules are positive and comfortable with parents' values[65]

A consumer mentality has led to increased accountability for higher education professionals to deliver on the expectations of not only the enrolled learners but of their families as well.[66] Parents are no longer willing to allow their children to attend college in order to "find themselves." The college experience is seen as an investment rather than a time for self-discovery and growth, even though earlier generations were afforded this option. In many cases, parents see the college experience as an investment, a four-year degree being second only to the family home in terms of funds committed.[67] Clearly, today's college learners are expected to capitalize on their parents' educational investment and graduate with a job and/or specific career goals.

For a recent IIDA Perspectives article, Michelle Bowles interviewed three design educators—Beverly Brandt, Ph.D., IIDA, Professor in the College of Design at Arizona State University; Paul Eshelman, Professor in the Department of Design & Environmental Analysis at Cornell University; and Mary Ann R. Potter, Assistant Professor in the College of Human Sciences at Auburn University—to establish characteristics of current interior design learners. These educators offered their personal observations of the current college interior design learner:

- They are deadly serious.
- Overburdened and overcommitted, they work 1 to 40 hours per week.
- They're on a 24/7 schedule and expect this of faculty.
- Many are paying for their degrees.
- They still need confirmation that they have made a good career choice.
- They are risk takers and ambitious, but still young.
- They know how to keep focused on possibilities, not limitations.
- They know how to have fun.
- They are media savvy and often know about interior design only what they have seen on cable TV. After conditioning, they move from its "fun" aspect to realizing its seriousness.
- They expect immediacy in communication being accustomed to text messaging and 24/7 availability.
- They are comfortable with technology (i.e., creating a digital presentation board) but do not necessarily understand the principles of design and composition.
- They often live in a virtual world—through which they have global awareness.
- Technology allows them to work away from the studio at any time they wish, and they will likely take this expectation into the work world.
- They value safety and security (9/11).
- They care about people.
- They are aware of environmental and social issues.
- They multi-task.
- Career flexibility is important. They look for meaningful engagement, and if they do not find it, they will move on.
- They are quality- not quantity-oriented.
- They put function first.[68]

With these insights into the current college learner, it is most helpful to understand what these learners want from their college instructor. In "The Adjunct Professor's Guide to Success," Lyons, Kysilka, and Pawlas offer the following observations:

- Expectations of learner performance that are reasonable in quantity and quality and are consistently communicated.
- Sensitivity to the diverse demands on learners and reasonable flexibility in accommodating them.
- Effective use of class time.
- A classroom environment that values learners' input and protects their dignity.
- A classroom demeanor that includes humor and spontaneity.
- Examinations that address issues properly covered in class, are appropriate to the level of the majority of learners in the class, are punctually scored and returned, and are used fairly to determine final class grades.
- Consistently positive treatment of individual learners, including a willingness to spend extra time before or after class meetings to provide additional support.[69]

External Demands

Today's learners face the challenges of educational expectations coupled with increasing external demands. Kucko and Gabb offer a compelling description of this situation:

> More than 50 percent of students work at least 20 hours per week while carrying a full academic load. This blended with the pressures of being involved on campus or in professional

> student organizations creates a college student who is under pressure. The days of the student having to worry only about collegiate life are over. Faculty are faced with the challenge of maintaining high academic standards with students who have little free time to explore the intellectual challenges and life that a campus community offers.
>
> Students have to juggle more activities with less time to develop their passion for design. For most, higher education has become a means of training to get a job rather than an intellectual experience that becomes life changing. Thus, students frequently do not understand passion or a commitment to design. They have little time to explore these fundamentals in the institution that used to foster them.[70]

Many learners are often focused and very committed to their educational pursuits, but also crucially aware of the other aspects of their lives. This situation may reveal itself through the learners' concurrent high expectations of themselves and the stress of juggling school, work, and family responsibilities. While such priorities exist for all, instructors must individually judge how much leeway to allow regarding attendance and tardiness as well as the rigor of course requirements in light of these circumstances.

Almost 9,000 learners have graduated from interior design programs in the last three years. This represents a growth of about 6 to 8% annually. About one-third of learner enrollment is part-time.[71] This, too, has implications for institutions, instructors, and the design profession as a whole:

- Competition for entry-level design jobs will become increasingly fierce, thus forcing new graduates to explore multiple career opportunities in the design field instead of just that of a practitioner.
- Educators must guide learners to identify and seek out related careers that reflect their strengths.[72]

Across North America, universities and colleges face a changing learner and family constituency. Challenges posed by changing demographics, increased external pressures, and media depictions of the interior design profession exist alongside the opportunities for enriched classroom discourse brought by a non-traditional and ethnically diverse learner population. The variety of experiences and perspectives from such a varied learner population will likely increase awareness of lifestyle and culture, complementing the inherently diverse nature of the field of interior design. For instructors, such variables force flexibility, understanding, and a willingness to understand and adapt learning techniques.

D. LEARNING THEORY: THE DESIGN PROCESS AND BEYOND

Those who teach in or have practiced in the design professions are quite familiar with the studio method of teaching and learning. This method requires a high level of understanding to research, experiment, judge, analyze, effectively apply knowledge to a project, and then present it in a manner that makes it comprehensible to a given audience. High value placed on other experiential modes of learning such as internships reinforces this active learning approach. However, awareness of other means by which students learn is also useful knowledge. Therefore this chapter will present learning theories considered most relevant to interior design education.

The bottom line of each theory presented here is that not all students learn effectively in the same way. Some need visual stimuli, others learn better by hearing the information, and still others by reading it. Most retain information best when a combination of these methods is used and when the information is subsequently applied.

When deciding amongst methods for students to learn particular material in a course or throughout a curriculum, one must consider the level of desired learning compared with the level of learning reinforced through particular teaching and evaluation methods. For instance, one low level of learning skill is the ability to repeat a given answer to a question. It requires memorization. This level of learning is best reinforced through certain test questions that require students to merely remember the phrasing of a definition or the spelling of a word. Higher levels of learning require students to incorporate a variety of inputs of knowledge, evaluate that knowledge for appropriateness, perhaps interpret it in a new way, and then apply it to a particular problem. When preparing for a course, an educator must consider the level of competency required of students, as well as the instructor's capabilities in the teaching approach. One set of planning benchmarks for minimum competencies is the CIDA standards. These competencies cover the minimum level of student learning that must be addressed.

Many renowned scholars have spent their academic lifetimes examining and formulating theories related to both teaching and learning. Many educators teaching in fields other than education have no formalized instruction regarding the theories of teaching and learning. As a consequence, they typically model, for better or worse, the strategies for teaching they experienced in their own education.

Several of the most prevalent and accepted educational theories are presented here as a way of revealing ideas that may reinforce and supplement design instructors' own educational experiences. Learning styles will be discussed first, as this content is present in many of the learning theories presented in the latter half of the chapter.

LEARNING STYLES

Learning styles are the preferred manner in which an individual assimilates, organizes, and uses information to make sense of the world, whether in a classroom or in a professional job. All classes are composed of students with varied learning styles. Interior design educator Stephanie Watson Zollinger states: "Overall, the most important finding in this study was the diversity of learning styles among interior design students. Not only were all learning styles represented in the sample, but 49% of students exhibited dominance in more than one style—unlike the results of previous studies with non interior design students."[73] Material presented in a variety of methods addresses more learning styles, keeps the learners interested, and reinforces itself.

Learning styles come from three general schools of thought: Perceptual Modality, Information Processing, and Personality Models.[74]

Perceptual Modality

This learning theory suggests that learners have biologically based reactions to the physical environment and take in information in different ways, such as auditory, visual, olfactory, kinesthetic, and tactile. As the name suggests, the Vision, Auditory, and Kinesthetic (VAK) theory of learning style purports that while learners typically use all three main sensory receivers—visual, auditory, and kinesthetic (movement)—one is the dominate learning style. A learner may prefer one style of learning for one task and a combination of others for another task. Each sensory receiver style has learner consequences that make it distinct from the others.

- Auditory learners often talk to themselves and usually do better talking to a colleague or a tape recorder and hearing what was said than through reading and writing. The inclusion of "lessons learned" through storytelling can provide examples that are an effective teaching strategy in many courses, including Professional Practices, Materials, and Construction Documents among others.
- Visual learners have two sub-channels: *linguistic* and *spatial*. Learners who are *visual-linguistic* like to learn through written language tasks (reading and writing), write down directions, and pay better attention to lectures if they watch them. Learners who are *visual-spatial* usually do better with charts, demonstrations, videos, and other visual materials than with written language. Watson Zollinger addresses the issues facing students in many lecture courses: "Most people and presumably most design students are visual learners, while the information presented in almost every lecture course is overwhelmingly verbal—written words and formulas in texts and on the chalkboard, spoken words in lectures, with only an occasional picture or demonstration breaking the pattern."[75]
- Kinesthetic learners do best while touching and moving. The kinesthetic modality also has two sub-channels: kinesthetic (movement) and tactile (touch). These learners tend to lose concentration if there is little or no external stimulation or movement. When reading, they like to scan the material first and then focus on the details so that they understand the big picture first. They typically take notes by drawing pictures, diagrams, or doodling.

Using Perceptual Modalities in Interior Design Education

Interior design instructors can use the concepts of perceptual modalities to design teaching and learning activities that address each of the modes: visual, auditory, and kinesthetic.

- *Auditory learners.* Instructors can provide opportunities to talk with others, record, and listen, and offer information through verbal story-telling or narratives.
- *Visual learners.* Instructors can provide opportunities for written language tasks (reading and writing) and visual lectures. Supplementing lectures and course materials with charts, demonstrations, videos, and other visual materials can also be helpful.
- *Kinesthetic learners.* Instructors can provide opportunities to experience movement or tactile sensation. The encouragement of note-taking during lectures, color-coding information, diagramming and doodling, passing materials around, and shifting chairs to actively collaborate can facilitate learning.

Information Processing

This second learning style theory distinguishes between the ways people think, solve problems, and remember information—in other words, the way the brain processes information. Kolb's Learning Styles Theory fits within this general category of learning styles. A 1999 paper by Kolb and colleagues ". . . suggests that learning requires abilities that are polar opposites, and that the learner must continually choose which set of learning abilities he or she will use in a specific learning situation. In grasping experience some of us perceive new information through *experiencing the concrete*, tangible, felt qualities of the world, relying on our senses and immersing ourselves in concrete reality. Others tend to perceive, grasp, or take hold of new information through symbolic representation or *abstract conceptualization*—thinking about, analyzing, or systematically planning, rather than using sensation as a guide."[76] Kolb views the learning process as a combination of choices based on heredity, particular past life experiences, and the demands of the present environment. He notes that the conflict presented between concrete and abstract, and between active or reflective modes, is resolved individually in some patterned, characteristic ways, called "learning styles."[77]

Kolb identified four prevalent learning styles: Diverging, Assimilating, Converging, and Accomodating.

- *Diverging:* dominant learning abilities are Concrete Experience (CE) and Reflective Observation (RO). These learners perform well in situations that call for the generation of ideas, such as brainstorming sessions. They typically have broad cultural interests, like to gather information, and tend to be imaginative and emotional. They prefer working in groups, listening with an open mind, and receiving personalized feedback.
- *Assimilating:* dominant learning abilities are Abstract Conceptualization (AC) and Reflective Observation (RO). These learners can understand a broad range of information and put it into a concise, logical form. They are generally less focused on people and more interested in ideas and abstract concepts. Readings, lectures, and exploring analytical models are preferred by these learners.
- *Converging:* dominant learning abilities include Abstract Conceptualization (AC) and Active Experimentation (AE). These learners find practical uses for ideas and theories. They prefer to experiment with new ideas, simulations, and practical applications. They have the ability to solve problems and make decisions based on finding solutions to questions or problems.
- *Accommodating:* dominant learning abilities are Concrete Experience (CE) and Active Experimentation (AE). These people learn through hands-on experiences. They rely more heavily on people for information than on their own technical analysis. They typically prefer to work with others and enjoy involving themselves in new and challenging experiences.[78]

Using the Kolb Learning Styles Theory in Interior Design Education

An instructor can structure teaching and learning activities in class to respond to each of the learning styles identified by Kolb.

- *Diverging.* Because Divergers like to gather information and work in groups, provide opportunities for small group brainstorming sessions, where imaginative solutions are valued.
- *Assimilating.* Because Assimilators are very interested in ideas and concepts, provide opportunities to summarize lectures or readings in a concise and logical form.
- *Converging.* Because Convergers like to find practical uses for ideas and theories, present concrete examples of the application of theory during lecture and create assignments that ask students to invent a product or suggest potential solutions.
- *Accommodating.* Because Accommodators like experiential learning, provide plenty of opportunity for hands-on activities, such as working on a Habitat Home as a group or partnering learners to develop activities to teach K-12 students about interior design.

Personality Models

This third learning style theory is based on the way people interact with their surroundings. Each person has a preferred, consistent, distinct way of perceiving, organizing, and retaining information. Three general theories support Personality Models as a way of addressing learning styles: Kolb's Learning Style Inventory (which bridges both the information processing and personality models categories), Myers Briggs Type Indicator, and Howard Gardner's Multiple Intelligence Theory.

- Kolb's Learning Styles are described in the preceding section on information processing.
- Myers Briggs is a personality test in which results are a series of personality descriptors that can then be responded to with teaching and learning strategies. These descriptors include
  - *Extroversion (E) versus Introversion (I):* indicates whether a learner prefers to direct attention toward the external world of people and things or toward the internal world of concepts and ideas. Extroverts prefer interaction with others and tend to be action-oriented. They tend to think on their feet and talk more than listen. Extroverted learners learn by teaching others. Introverts can be social but prefer the inner world of ideas, concepts, and abstractions. They want to understand the world; they concentrate and they tend to be reflective thinkers. They think more than talk. Introverted learners want to develop frameworks that integrate or connect the information that they learn.
  - *Sensing (S) versus iNtuition (N):* indicating whether a learner prefers to perceive the world by directly observing or through impressions and imagining possibilities. Sensing people choose to rely on their five senses. They are detail-oriented, they want facts, and they trust them. Intuitive people seek out patterns and relationships among the facts they have gathered. They trust hunches (their "sixth sense") and their intuition and look for the "big picture." They also value imagination and innovation.
  - *Thinking (T) versus Feeling (F):* indicating how a learner makes decisions, either through logic and fairness or human values. Thinkers decide things impersonally based on analysis, logic, and principle. They value fairness, place great weight on objective criteria in making a decision, naturally see flaws, and tend to be critical. Feelers focus on human values and needs as they make decisions or arrive at judgments. They value empathy and harmony. They tend to be good at persuasion and facilitating differences among group members.
  - *Judging (J) versus Perceptive (P):* indicating how a learner views the world, either as a structured and planned environment or as a spontaneous environment. Judging people are decisive, self-starters, and self-regimented. They focus on completing the task, knowing the essentials, and taking action quickly. Perceptive people are curious, adaptable, and spontaneous. They start many tasks, want to know everything about each task, and often find it difficult to complete a task, as they prefer to leave their options open.

Using the Myers Briggs Personality Types in Interior Design Education

An instructor can use the Myers Briggs Personality Types theory in design learning to impact a range of personality types.

Extroversion (E) versus Introversion (I). Extroverted learners learn by teaching others, so problem-based learning and collaborative learning are good teaching techniques for this group. In-class or outside-of-class group exercises and projects are also effective. For example, learners identified as extroverted could be grouped together and engaged in a problem-solving scenario in a business practices class.

For Introverted learners, educators should teach how to *chunk*, or group and interconnect, knowledge; this might include how to build a compare and contrast table, flowchart, or concept map. For example, grouped introverted learners in a beginning Introduction to Interior Design class could be tasked with creating a flowchart that details the stages of the design process.

Sensing (S) versus iNtuition (N). Sensing students prefer organized, linear, and structured lectures and systematic or step-by-step instruction. Interior design students in this learner category might respond to a lecture on calculating lumen levels in lighting that also employed a fill-in form.

Intuitive learners prefer various forms of discovery learning and must have the big picture (metaphors and analogies) or an integrating framework in order to understand a subject. Concept maps or compare-and-contrast tables are helpful teaching tools for this group. Intuitive-style interior design students might be highly engaged in an exercise that challenges them to design a waiting room inspired by the qualities of an egg or a leaf, for example.

Thinking (T) versus Feeling (F). Provide clear goals and objectives for the Thinking learners. They want to see precise, action-oriented objectives. They also want to know what they have to do to learn the material. Feeling learners enjoy small group exercises, especially in harmonious groups.

Judging (J) versus Perceptive (P). Provide tools that help Judging learners to plan their work and guides that give quick tips. Because Judging learners often focus on completing the task and taking quick action, provide mechanisms for a second look at work, whether through individual or group activities.

For Perceptual learners, break down a complex project into a series of subassignments and provide interim deadlines to keep them on target.

- Howard Gardner's Multiple Intelligences looks at learning styles as a variety of "intelligences." Multiple intelligence theory states that there are at least eight different ways of learning anything, and therefore these "eight intelligences" describe the great variability in taking in information:

  - Body/kinesthetic (moving)
  - Interpersonal (socializing)
  - Intrapersonal (solitary)
  - Logical/mathematical (questioning)
  - Musical/rhythmic (music)
  - Verbal/linguistic (words)
  - Visual/spatial (pictures)
  - Naturalist (interaction with nature)

According to multiple intelligences theory, not only do all individuals possess numerous mental representations and intellectual languages, but individuals also differ from one another in the forms of these representations, their relative strengths, and the ways in which (and ease with which) these representations can be changed.

Using Gardner's Multiple Intelligences in Interior Design Education

Multiple Intelligence theory can be applied in Interior Design curricula, enabling an instructor to design learning to impact a variety of intelligences.

- *Verbal/linguistic Intelligence:* Use activities that involve hearing, listening, impromptu or formal speaking, oral or silent reading, documentation, creative writing, or journaling. For example, interior design students with verbal linguistic intelligence would benefit from a web blog assignment.
- *Logical/mathematical Intelligence:* Use activities that involve abstract symbols or formulas, outlining, graphic organizers, numeric sequences, calculation, or problem solving. For example, developing a matrix to organize and evaluate the relative importance of programming information for a studio project would involve logical-mathematical intelligences.
- *Musical/rhythmic Intelligence:* Use activities that involve recordings, environmental sounds, or rhythmic patterns. When discussing the design principle of rhythm, tap out the rhythm or encourage students to tap the rhythm on their tablets. Include supplementary material in the form of audio downloads or other recordings in addition to readings.
- *Visual/spatial Intelligence:* Use activities that involve art, images, sculpture, drawing, doodling, mind-mapping, patterns and designs, color schemes, active imagination, and imagery. Include diagramming exercises in each course. Create a pause at particular points during a lecture and encourage a doodle or diagram in the margin of notes.
- *Body/kinesthetic Intelligence:* Use activities that involve role playing, physical gestures, inventing, and body language. In a professional practices course, role playing may be easily included to understand client-designer relationships or working through ethics situations. With programming, one student might serve as a client performing a hobby (such as playing a musical instrument), while other students observe and record.
- *Interpersonal Intelligence:* Use activities that involve group projects, division of labor, collaboration skills, and receiving or giving feedback. Nearly all classes can make use of group projects, whether in preparing a student-led presentation of research or in small group critique situations.
- *Intrapersonal Intelligence:* Use activities that involve emotional processing, silent reflection methods, thinking strategies, concentration skills, and higher-order reasoning. For example, read a descriptive passage from a novel and ask students to envision and describe the physical qualities of the space that would support such a description.
- *Naturalist Intelligence:* Use activities that involve bringing the outdoors into class, relating to the natural world, and mapping changes. An example particularly suited to interior design education could involve descriptive journaling over time a particular exterior space that has the qualities of an interior room (for instance, as defined by natural borders such as a tree canopy).

Active Learning

Research also indicates that learning occurs more efficiently when the learner is actively engaged rather than passively participating. Active learning almost always engages the learner in creating learning-based outputs that, in turn, result in receiving performance-based feedback. In interior design education, this active learning often involves projects located in studio courses, with the performance-based feedback in some form of critique. This is not, however, the only occurrence of active learning in interior design curricula. Many courses (and nearly all excellent courses) engage students in activities that require their kinesthetic, mental, and emotional involvement directly in the learning and assessment activities.

Anderson's Idea of a Learning Continuum

In "Tailoring Assessment to Student Learning Styles: A Model for Diverse Populations" Dr. James Anderson proposes that learning styles can be characterized by how one prefers to learn, such as

- The Type of Information One Receives: Sensory vs. Intuitive
- How Information is Perceived: Visual vs. Verbal
- How Information is Organized: Inductive vs. Deductive
- How Information is Processed: Actively vs. Reflectively
- How Information is Understood: Sequentially vs. Globally[79]

Anderson suggests that learning is not bipolar. That is, students are not either visual learners or not, reflective processors or not, but rather all learners fall into a continuum for each of these categories. Often students know how they learn information best, based on years of experience. By designing a course to include a variety of learning experiences, requiring more than one learning style, that course will successfully impart knowledge to a broader array of students. Examples have been provided with each theory of learning styles that encourage this variety within interior design courses. As a means of weaving together experiences through teaching and learning, there are several predominant theories that have been developed and are widely accepted.

LEARNING THEORIES AND TEACHING STRATEGIES

In addition to knowledge of learning styles, an understanding of general learning theories can be helpful to developing teaching strategy. This section will examine several prominent theories that interior design educators may find particularly relevant to their learners:

- Multiple Intelligences, as put forth by Gardner
- Kolb's Experiential Learning Theory
- Bloom's Taxonomy, a classification of intellectual behavior levels important in learning
- Interactive Compensatory Model for Learning (ICML), which regards prior knowledge as the best predictor of success with new learning
- Comprehensive Unified Learning Model, which adds learner confidence to the ICML

Each theory builds upon the idea of learning styles addressed earlier.

Multiple Intelligences

Educational theorist Howard Gardner has questioned the idea that intelligence is a single entity, that it results from a single factor, and that it can be measured simply via IQ tests.

> In the heyday of the psychometric and behaviorist eras, it was generally believed that intelligence was a single entity that was inherited; and that human beings—initially a blank slate—could be trained to learn anything, provided that it was presented in an appropriate way. Nowadays an increasing number of researchers believe precisely the opposite; that there exists a multitude of intelligences, quite independent of each other; that each intelligence has its own strengths and constraints; that the mind is far from unencumbered at birth; and that it is unexpectedly difficult to teach things that go against early "naive" theories or that challenge the natural lines of force within an intelligence and its matching domains.[80]

Kolb's Experiential Learning Theory

Most people have the ability to develop skills in each of the intelligences and to learn through them. David Kolb puts forth a learning styles model based on two axis lines, or continuums: one's approach to a task (whether the individual's preference is to do or watch), and one's emotional response (whether an individual prefers to think or feel). Kolb's learning theory sets out four distinct learning styles (described earlier) based on a four-stage learning cycle. This model offers a way to understand people's different learning styles and also provides an explanation of a cycle of experiential learning.

The cycle of learning is a central principle in Kolb's experiential learning theory. It is typically expressed as a four-stage continuum of learning, where immediate or concrete experiences provide a basis for observations and reflections. These observations and reflections are assimilated and distilled into abstract concepts, producing new implications for action that can be actively tested, in turn creating new experiences.

Kolb's theory purports that ideally this process represents a learning cycle of experiencing, reflecting, thinking, and acting. The model works on two levels and represents a four-stage cycle:

1. Concrete Experience (CE)
2. Reflective Observation (RO)
3. Abstract Conceptualization (AC)
4. Active Experimentation (AE)

Kolb's Experiential Learning Inventory theory proposes a model with the horizontal axis called the Processing Continuum (how one approaches a task), and the vertical axis called the Perception Continuum (one's emotional response). The four resulting quadrants of the diagram are described as Accommodating, Diverging, Assimilating, and Converging. Refer to Figure 2.3 for an illustration of Kolb's theory.

- *Accommodating:* doing and feeling preferences, or "concrete-active"; relies on intuition rather than logic, uses other people's analysis, likes a practical, experiential approach and active experimentation.
- *Diverging:* watching and doing, or "concrete-reflective"; looks at problems from different perspectives, is sensitive, engages in reflective observation, gathers information, and uses imagination to solve problems.
- *Assimilating:* watching and thinking, or "abstract-reflective"; employs a concise, logical approach, abstract conceptualization, a preference for ideas and concepts over people; requires good, clear explanation rather than practical opportunity.
- *Converging:* thinking and doing, or "abstract-active"; can solve problems and will apply learning to find solutions to practical issues, prefers technical tasks, is less concerned with people and interpersonal aspects.

Bloom's Taxonomy

In 1956, Benjamin Bloom led a group of educational psychologists who developed a classification of levels of intellectual behavior important in learning. This evolved into a taxonomy that includes three overlapping domains called the cognitive, psychomotor, and affective. Of these, the cognitive portion has received the most attention and is the most recognizable in the literature.

Cognitive learning is demonstrated by knowledge recall and intellectual skills identified as

- Comprehending information
- Organizing ideas
- Analyzing and synthesizing data

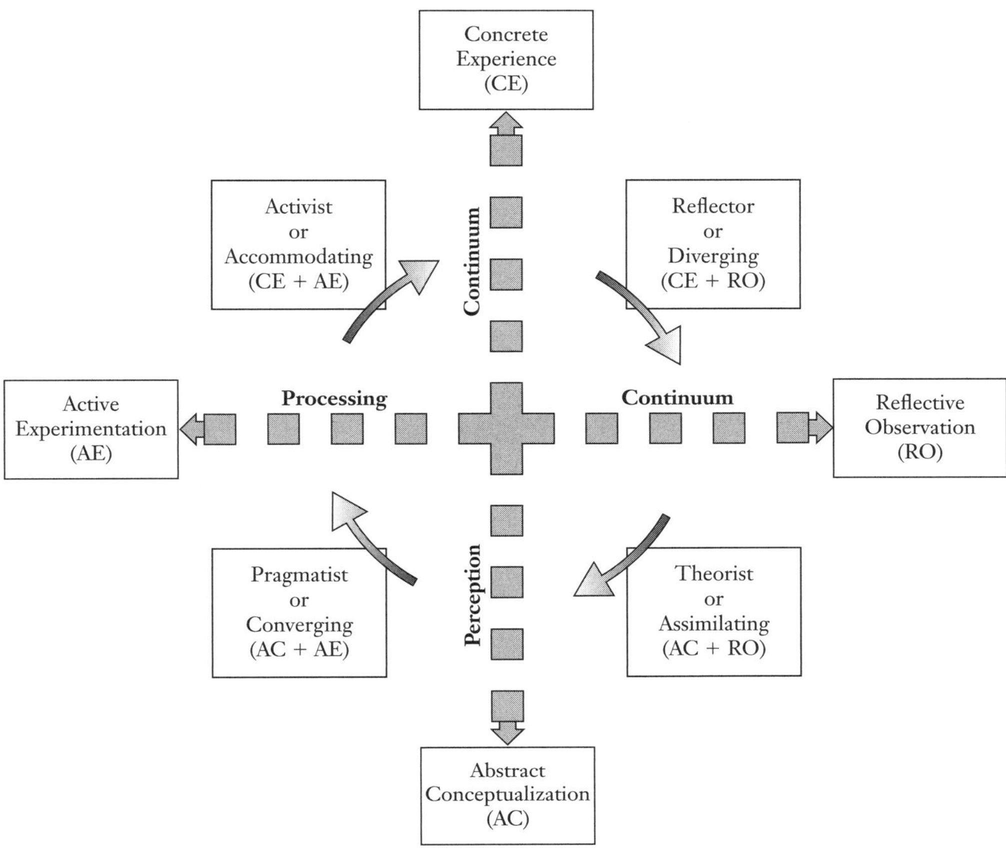

Figure 2.3 Kolb's process represents a learning cycle of experiencing, reflecting, thinking, and acting.

- Applying knowledge
- Choosing among alternatives in problem-solving
- Evaluating ideas or actions

Bloom identified six levels, from the simple recall or recognition of facts as the lowest level, through increasingly more complex and abstract mental levels, and culminating in the highest order, which is classified as evaluation. Figure 2.4 describes actions associated with this ascending scheme of learning. These actions are often expressed through course objectives and exam questions. Instructors should seek agreement between the level of learning students experience in lecture and discussion, and the level of question they are asked to respond to on an exam.

Interactive Compensatory Model for Learning

The Interactive Compensatory Model for Learning relies on the belief of most educators that there are three ingredients to successful learning:

1. Prior knowledge: what the learner already knows
2. Ability: how smart the learner is
3. Motivation: how engaged the learner is

There is widespread agreement that prior knowledge is the most significant of these factors in successful new learning. The Interactive Compensatory Model for Learning (ICML) includes these three components (prior knowledge, ability, and motivation) as its central core.[81]

Bloom's Taxonomy		Level	Classification of Learner Abilities	
Evalution	Judge appropriateness for a specific purpose.	6	Synthesis	Produce new, unique, or creative solution to problem.
Synthesis	Put together parts to form a new whole.	5	Analysis	Recognize a problem and solve it.
Analysis	Break an item into its constituent elements or parts.	4	Application	Apply principles to solve a given problem.
Application	Apply abstract info in a concrete situation	3	Interpretation	Recognize correct and incorrect application; predict correct application.
Comprehension	Translate, apply rules, recognize unknown examples; use without relation to other material	2	Translation	Distinguish between examples and non-examples.
Knowledge	Recall isolated and specific	1	Memory	Define or state a concept or principle.

Figure 2.4 Bloom's Taxonomy of Cognitive Learning represented as a scale of knowledge acquisition.

Prior Knowledge: The First of the Three Components

To be useful, prior knowledge must be accessed by the learner, delving into the realm of memory. Working memory is a term referring to the amount of input and long-term memory a learner can access and activate at any given time. Through learning and practice, the capacity of working memory appears to change, explained in terms of chunking (or schemata formation). The ability to chunk subtasks into larger tasks is sometimes referred to as forming schema.[82]

Ability of the Learner: The Second of the Three Components

Recent research in the ability of the learner proposes two constructs. The first is called fluid intelligence, a rather fixed entity that deals with overall capacity, and the second is called crystallized intelligence, a malleable entity that can grow through effort and experience. Researchers have suggested that working memory capacity is the same construct as fluid intelligence.[83] The schemata or chunks, especially when they are large, are thought to be a part of crystallized intelligence.

Learner Motivation: The Third of the Three Components

The third component in the ICML model of learning addresses the motivation of the learner. Brooks indicates that motivation is essentially paying attention. There are degrees to which a learner can pay attention, dictated by environmental conditions or attention span. Therefore, a more workable definition may be "motivation is the conscious or subconscious allocation of working memory to a life task."[84] With this definition, it follows that a fully motivated learner cannot give more to a learning activity than his or her full ability, which means their full working memory.

In summation of ICML theory, *prior knowledge* is stored in long-term memory;

ability limits how much prior knowledge can be activated at once; and *motivation* determines how much prior knowledge is activated at a given moment. Chunking (schemata formation) permits individuals of different ability levels to succeed at the same complex tasks.[85]

ICML Theory's Application to Interior Design Instruction

Interior design researchers are beginning to examine ICML theory in relation to the unique nature of interior design instruction. In her presentation "Are There Lasting Effects of a Schema-based Learning System in the Interior Design Studio?" Brunner found that introducing a schema-based learning system in the design studio (that is, one that chunks subtasks into larger tasks) "assisted novice designers in a structured, purposeful process, where they began to see patterns of information and [to] use these patterns to develop and refine their design solutions."[86] She described that schema-driven strategies involve the use of chunking in performing complex cognitive tasks, such as (a) Categorizing information by concept domains; (b) Developing conceptual hierarchies for information that is processed; and (c) Forming relationships between concepts.[87] Each of these tasks is present during the initial design phases of a project.

In her study, a customized database environment was developed, emphasizing the problem-solving process. The database provided an expert-like structure by including categories or ways to organize, sort, and build relationships between various student-developed cards into meaningful patterns of information. Most would agree that the initial phases of a design project are largely composed of successful exploration of these activities related to spaces, objects, and/or functionality.

Comprehensive Unified Learning Model

While the Interactive Compensatory Model for Learning addresses prior knowledge, learner ability, and motivation, the Comprehensive Unified Learning Model[88] additionally includes learner confidence. Sometimes, the most difficult challenge facing an interior design instructor is in developing a framework of trust, knowledge, and respect for each individual and their ideas. Within such a framework, the sharing and integration of knowledge empowers students and allows high achievement. Belief that each student possesses individual strengths and providing opportunities for student discovery, recognition, and development of these unique strengths contribute to student confidence. Whether in sports, medicine, or the design fields, a substantial amount of hard work, coaching, encouragement, and a particular kind of practice (deliberate practice) is involved in creating an expert (that is, someone fluid in their knowledge and the practice of that knowledge).

Deliberate practice refers to time spent focused on some aspect of a more complex performance. To function effectively as an expert, full access to working memory is required. To improve, a learner must make use of self-regulatory chunks (schema) that take up a working memory slot or two and free up other capacity for learning. One goal of chunking is to achieve what is called *automaticity*, the ability to do things using a minimal amount of working memory. Achieving automaticity usually involves deliberate practice of parts of an expert performance.[89]

Working memory can sometimes be extended by writing notes or making sketches while working on a task. Working in groups may also extend working memory. Sometimes a chunk (a thought) is kept activated by one member of a group so that it can resurface during a group exchange. Thus one learner takes advantage of a working memory slot that is within the mind of another group member (learner), rather than taking up all of their own slots. The most important extension, however, potentially comes from a teacher, coach, or tutor. An expert tutor (or educator) can realize which chunk is missing for a learner and "fill" that chunk. This is by no means an automatic or straightforward matter. Especially for complex learning, the learner needs to make his or her own sense of the content. While an instructor can recognize the missing chunk that will help this process, the instructor cannot simply transfer a chunk or schema intact to the learner.[90]

Automaticity and Chunking Theory and Its Application in Interior Design Education

Automaticity theory's application to artistic activities such as drawing may have relevance to interior design education as well. For example, practicing quick perspective sketching using timed exercises can in effect strengthen the brain's ability to "automatize" certain arm gestures, releasing the brain from the need to command conscious thought for these gestures. This is important to interior designers, as the brain is now freed up to turn its attention to creatively designing a space rather than just concentrating on the physical gestures needed to draw it. The end results of the "automatized" ability to sketch are faster and more accurate perspective sketches. Therefore, it may produce superior results if interior design students work through timed sketch exercises working with a partner, explaining their emerging design as they draw.[91]

The Seven Principles of Good Practice in Undergraduate Education

Finally, while not a specific learning theory, the Seven Principles of Good Practice in Undergraduate Education by Chickering and Gamson[92] provide guidelines for quality in education delivery. They have been applied to traditional as well as online education models. They seem like good common sense, and they are—because many teachers and students have experienced them and because research supports them. Good practices hold as much meaning for professional programs as for the liberal arts. They work for many different kinds of students—White, Black, Hispanic, Asian, rich, poor, older, younger, male, female, well-prepared, underprepared.

1. *Encourages Contact between Students and Faculty.* Frequent learner-instructor contact in and out of classes is the most important factor in learner motivation and involvement. Faculty concern helps learners get through rough times and keep on working. Knowing a few faculty members well enhances learners' intellectual commitment and encourages them to think about their own values and future plans.
2. *Develops Reciprocity and Cooperation among Students.* Learning is enhanced when it is more like a team effort than a solo race. Good learning, like good work, is collaborative and social, not competitive and isolated. Working with others often increases involvement in learning. Sharing one's own ideas and responding to others' reactions sharpens thinking and deepens understanding.
3. *Encourages Active Learning.* Learning is not a spectator sport. Learners do not learn much just by sitting in classes listening to instructors, memorizing prepackaged assignments, and spitting out answers. They must talk about what they are learning, write about it, relate it to past experiences, and apply it to their daily lives. They must make what they learn a part of themselves.
4. *Gives Prompt Feedback.* Knowing what you know and don't know focuses learning. Learners need appropriate feedback

on performance to benefit from courses. When getting started, learners need help in assessing existing knowledge and competence. In classes, learners need frequent opportunities to perform and receive suggestions for improvement. At various points during college, and at the end, learners need chances to reflect on what they have learned, what they still need to know, and how to assess themselves.

5. *Emphasizes Time on Task.* Time plus energy equals learning. There is no substitute for time on task. Learning to use one's time well is critical for learners and professionals alike. Learners need help in learning effective time management. Allocating realistic amounts of time means effective learning for students and effective teaching for faculty. How an institution defines time expectations for learners, faculty, administrators, and other professional staff can establish the basis of high performance for all.
6. *Communicates High Expectations.* Expect more and you will get more. High expectations are important for everyone—for the poorly prepared, for those unwilling to exert themselves, and for the bright and well motivated. Expecting learners to perform well becomes a self-fulfilling prophecy when teachers and institutions hold high expectations for themselves and make extra efforts.
7. *Respects Diverse Talents and Ways of Learning.* There are many roads to learning. People bring different talents and styles of learning to college. Brilliant learners in the seminar room may be all thumbs in the lab or art studio. Learners rich in hands-on experience may not do so well with theory. Learners need the opportunity to show their talents and learn in ways that work for them. Then they can be pushed to learn in new ways that do not come so easily.[93]

In Summary

The challenge to educators also profoundly impacts students' learning. Watson sums up the challenge of teaching and learning strategies thusly: "Students whose learning styles fall in any of the given categories have the potential to be excellent designers. Instructors need to balance their instructional plan by selecting strategies and resources that cater to a variety of styles. This means moving beyond only those with which the instructor is comfortable to include the range of activities that meets the learning needs of others. Specifically, this means planning every instructional episode (presuming there are learners with varying styles) to include a variety of instructional strategies. For example, suppose an interior design educator is introducing the design process. The educator may begin by describing the components that make up the process (intuitive, sequential) and explaining why these components are important and how the design process is used in design practice (sensing, global). Next, he/she demonstrates through scenarios how the design process works (inductive). A discussion follows on how these components are used, and how they may be modified (verbal). Students are then given a scenario and work individually or in small groups (active, reflective). The instructor moves around to help individuals as they request or appear to desire assistance. Finally, the instructor provides written materials that summarize the content of the lecture (visual). This type of varied presentation is likely to be effective because it builds on the principles of how students learn and the ways in which students learn best."[94]

ENDNOTES

1. Niederhelman, M. (Summer 2001). Education Through Design. *Design Issues* 17(3): 83–87.

2. See Sim Van Der Ryne's recounting of the various "epochs" of human civilization. He suggests Western culture is on the edge of entering the "integrated" age characterized by collaboration, network, personal empowerment, and decentralization. Van der Ryne, S. (2005). *Design for Life*. Layton, UT: Gibbs Smith.
3. Vischer, J. & Poldma, T. (2003). Growing a Discipline: Evolving Learning Practices in Interior Design. *IDEA Journal*. Retrieved 9/30/07 from http://www.idea-edu.com/alt_content/pdf/2003/Dr_Jacqueline_Vischer_and_Dr_Tiiu_Poldma.pdf.
4. Anderson, B., Honey, P. & Dudek, M. (2007). Interior Design's Social Compact: The Missing Aspect of our Quest for Professional Legitimacy. *Proceedings of the International Interior Design Educators Council Conference*, Austin, TX, pp. 91–98.
5. Wallis, C. & Steptoe, S. (December 18, 2006). How to bring our schools out of the 20th century. *Time*, pp. 49–56.
6. See Nair, Prakash. (January 2003). Imperatives for Change in Higher Education. *DesignShare: The International Forum for Innovative Schools*. Retrieved 7/1/07 from http://www.designshare.com/Research/Nair/HigherEd/imperatives. Also Snyder, D.(January/February 2006). Big Change on Campus *Facilities Manager*. Retrieved 6/30/07 from http://www.appa.org/FacilitiesManager/article.cfm?ItemNumber=2550&parentid=2540; Fisher, J. & Miller, S. (January 2000). From Here to 2010. *College Planning and Management 3*(1). pp. 24–35. Retrieved 7/1/07 from http://www.peterli.com/archive/cpm/35.shtm.
7. For example, the New Commission on the Skills of the American Workforce was released in December of 2006. This consensus document produced by educators and businesspersons discusses reforms needed to maintain global competitiveness. In Wallis & Steptoe (2006).
8. The Western business model's influence on education is clear to see here: these skills are less able to be outsourced overseas.
9. Anderson, D., Honey, P. & Dudek, M. (2007). Interior Design's Social Compact: The Missing Aspect of Our Quest for Professional Legitimacy. *Proceedings of the International Interior Design Educators Council Conference*, Austin, TX, pp. 91–98.
10. Kellogg, C. (January 2006). Learning from Studio. *DesignIntelligence 4*: 15–16.
11. Perlstein, R. (n.d.). What's the Matter with College? *New York Times Online*. Retrieved 7/20/07 from http://nytimes.com/marketing/collegeessay/essay.html.
12. From the Council of Arts Accrediting Associations. (October 2, 2006). Achievement and Quality: Higher Education in the Arts: A working draft for the NASAD 2006 Annual Meeting, p. 22: "Under real/operational conditions, quality is always defined and evaluated in terms of something . . . . It is possible to believe in a single indicator. In this approach, almost any indicator will do. However, in a teaching and learning institution . . . such an approach is so far removed from the realities of developing and producing achievement and quality that it is fundamentally useless. Too many factors have an influence on quality, and it is imprudent to pretend otherwise. It would certainly be more convenient if the issue of quality could be expressed mathematically with a small number of measurable indicators. However, achieving quality is far broader than hitting a set of targets, especially if they are expressed only in mathematical terms. Quality comes from a complex interaction."
13. Snyder, D. (January/February 2006). Big Change on Campus. *Facilities Manager*. Retrieved 6/30/07 from http://www.appa.org/FacilitiesManager/article.cfm?ItemNumber=2550&parentid=2540.
14. Fisher & Miller (January 2000).
15. Gibney, F. & Luscombe, B. (March 20, 2000). The Redesigning of America. *Time*. Retrieved 7/1/07 from http://www.time.com/time/magazine/article/0,9171,996372,00.html.
16. Waxman, L. & Clemons, S. (2007). Student Perceptions: Debunking Television's Portrayal of Interior Design. *Journal of Interior Design 32*(2): v–ix.
17. Adapted from Rittel. H. & Webber, M. (1973). Dilemmas in a General Theory of Planning. *Policy Sciences, 4*(2): 155–169. Applied to architecture in Mann, T. (2004). *Time Management for Architects and Designers*. New York: Norton.
18. Hall, D. (2002). *The Academic Self: An Owner's Manual*. Columbus, OH: Ohio State University Press, pp. xii–xiii.
19. Kalwarski, T., Mosher, D., Paskin, J. & Rosato, D. (May 1, 2006). 50 Best Jobs in America. *Money Magazine*. Retrieved 7/20/07 from http://money.cnn.com/

magazines/moneymag/moneymag_archive/2006/05/01/8375749/index.htm.

20. This session included representatives of the Interior Design Educators Council (IDEC), the Council for Interior Design Accreditation (CIDA), the American Society of Interior Designers (ASID), the International Interior Design Association (IIDA), and the Association of Registered Interior Designers of Ontario (ARIDO).
21. Interior Design Educators Council. (2006). *Defining Graduate Education in Interior Design*. A white paper produced by the IDEC Graduate Education Committee. (Available from the Interior Design Educators Council, 150 Winton Drive, Suite 300, Indianapolis, IN 46268; www.idec.org).
22. Retrieved 6/24/07 from University of Wisconsin, Academic Programs and Resources, at http://www.wisc.edu/about/facts/acprograms.php.
23. Adapted from Hall (2002), p. 31.
24. McCoy, J., Guerin, D. & Portillo, M. (2006). Who Are We? Beginning Markers of Accredited Interior Design Programs. *Proceedings of the 2006 International Interior Design Educator's Conference*, Scottsdale, Arizona, p. 82.
25. Ibid., 2006, p. 83.
26. Hall, D. (2002), p. 23.
27. Richardson, J. (1999). Tenure In The New Millennium: Still A Valuable Concept. *National Forum, The Phi Kappa Phi Journal 79*(1). Retrieved 10/5/07 from http://wolfweb.unr.edu/homepage/jtr/tenure.html.
28. Ibid.
29. Benjamin, Ernst. (1998). Declining Faculty Availability to Students Is the Problem—But Tenure Is Not the Explanation. *American Behavioral Scientist 14*: 716–735.
30. Notre Dame, University of Pennsylvania, and several institutions in California have graduate student unions that serve as watchdog organizations for tuition, fees, and healthcare issues. The National Association of Graduate-Professional Students (http://www.nagps.org) is a non-profit organization dedicated to improving the quality of graduate and professional student life in the United States.
31. Hall, D. (2002), p. 9.
32. Ibid., pp. 10, 13, 31.
33. Ibid., p. 9.
34. Carroll, S. (January 18, 2007). Teaching Excellence Series: Enhancing Interaction. Seminar at Florida State University, Tallahassee, FL.
35. Carnegie Foundation for the Advancement of Teaching. (1989). *The Condition of the Professoriate: Attitudes and Trends, 1989*. Princeton, NJ: Carnegie Foundation for the Advancement of Teaching. Curiously, this has not always been so. Prior to World War II, preparing outstanding lectures came first for even the most famous research faculty at Berkeley, as R. Nisbet relates in Blackburn, R. & Lawrence, J. (1997). Faculty Research. In Philip Altbach, ed., *Contemporary Higher Education: International Issues for the Twenty-First Century*. New York: Garland, p. 216. The need for war research in the 1940s and the current environment of global competition have conspired to keep the spotlight, recognition, and accompanying rewards with research.
36. Hall, D. (2002), p. 36.
37. Ibid., p. 36.
38. Ibid., p. 55.
39. Ibid., p. 56–65.
40. Coleman, C. & Sosnowchik, K. (September 2006). *Interior Design Trends and Implications*. Grand Rapids, MI: Council for Interior Design Accreditation.
41. Ibid., p. 6.
42. Ibid.
43. Levine, A. & Cureton, J. S. (1998). What We Know about Today's College Students. *About Campus 3*(1): 4–9.
44. Ibid.
45. Retrieved 10/5/07 from http://www.collegeboard.com/press/releases/185222.html.
46. Gohn, Lyle A. & Albin, Ginger R., eds. (2006). *Understanding College Student Subpopulations*. Retrieved 10/5/07 from National Association of Student Personnel Administrators (NASPA), Inc., at http://naspa-webmail.naspa.org:3301/ftp/Understanding_College_Student_Subpopulations.pdf, p. 25.
47. Knocking at the College Door: Projections of High School Graduates by State, Income, and Race/Ethnicity. (2003). Press release, Western Interstate Commission for Higher Education, available at http://www.wiche.edu/policy/Knocking/press_release.pdf.
48. Gohn & Albin, eds. (2006). The Educational Testing Service (ETS) addressed the changes, challenges, and opportunities these new learners (often from underrepresented populations) bring to campuses across the nation in a study entitled *Crossing the Great Divide: Can We Achieve Equity When Generation Y Goes to College?* (2000). See http://www.eric.ed.gov/ERICDocs/data/ericdocs2sql/

content_storage_01/0000019b/80/16/5d/a5.pdf.

49. Some researchers put the Millennial generation birthdates between 1980–2000, others as 1982–2002. See the Intercampus Community of Practice website at http://www.uwsp.edu/education/lwilson/icop/millennials.htm for a host of links relating to the Millennial generation.
50. Howe, N. & Strauss, W. (2000). *Millennials Rising: The Next Great Generation*. New York: Vintage Books, 2000, pp. 43–44.
51. Ibid., pp. 44–50.
52. As reported by Donovan, Jody. (2003). Changing Demographics and Generational Shifts: Understanding and Working with the Families of Today's College Students. Retrieved 6/23/07 from http://www.colostate.edu/Depts/SAHE/JOURNAL2/2003/Donovan.htm. Jody Donovan is the Assistant to the Vice President for Student Affairs at Colorado State University.
53. Zemke, R., Raines, C., Filipczak, B. (2000). *Generations at Work: Managing the Clash of Veterans, Boomers, Xers, and Nexters in Your Workplace*. New York: AMACOM.
54. Termed thus to reflect that they felt they were a generation without a cause. Remembering World War II from their childhood, many Silents were looking for a cause. Some found the Peace Corps, founded by John Kennedy, as a way of achieving a generation bond. The vast majority of this generation wanted the job security offered by big corporations. Only 2% took the risk to be self-employed. Born mostly during an era of depression and war, the Silent generation knew hardship and knew how to struggle through tough times. See http://library.thinkquest.org/23440/silent.html for more information.
55. Howe & Strauss. (2000).
56. Zemke, R., Raines, C., Filipczak, B. (2000).
57. Johnson, H. E. & Schelhas-Miller, C. (2000). Don't Tell Me What To Do, Just Send Money: The Essential Parenting Guide to the College Years. New York: St Martin's Griffin.
58. AAHE-Bulletin Teaching Ideas #8. (November 1998). Essential Demographics of Today's College Students. Available at http://www.Emporia.edu/tec/tchid08.html.
59. Howe & Strauss. (2000).
60. Coleman & Sosnowchik. (2006)., p. 44. Sources cited within the quote: (1) Carlson, S. (July 2006). Campus Planners Have a Tech-Savvy Generation's Needs to Consider (Today's News). *The Chronicle of Higher Education*. Available at www.chronicle.com/daily/2006/07/2006071102n.htm; (2) Selingo, J. (July 2006). Education and Entertainment Merge in One Whimsical View of College's Future (Today's News). *The Chronicle of Higher Education*. Available at www.chronicle.com/daily/2006/07/2006071104n.htm; (3) Prensky, M. (2001). *Digital Natives, Digital Immigrants on the Horizon*. NCB University Press, vol. 9, no. 5; (4) Fallows, D. Pew Internet and American Life Project. The Internet and Daily Life. (2004). Available at www.pewinternet.org; (5) Bleed, R. (2005). *Explorations: Visual Literacy in Higher Education*. EDUCAUSE Learning Initiative. Available at www.educause.edu/SEARCH/606.
61. Prensky, M. (2001).
62. Coleman & Sosnowchik. (2006), p. 44.
63. DeBard, R. (Summer 2004). New Directions for Student Services, no. 106. New York: Wiley Periodicals, pp. 33–45.
64. Kucko, J. & Gabb, B. (May 2000). Students Today and Professionals Tomorrow: A Sometimes Challenging Position. *Interiors & Sources*. Cedar Rapids, IA: Stamats Business Media.
65. Howe & Strauss. (2000).
66. Scott, B. R. & Daniel, B. V. (2001). Why Parents of Undergraduates Matter to Higher Education. In B. V. Daniel & B. R. Scott, eds., *Consumers, Adversaries and Partners: Working with the Families of Undergraduates*. New Directions for Student Services, no. 94. San Francisco: Jossey-Bass, pp. 83–89.
67. Oluwasanmi, N. A. (September 2000). Tuition: Impossible. *Smart Money*, pp. 146–154.
68. Bowles, M. (2007). Design: The Next Generation. *IIDA Perspective* (Winter): 26–31. Access the full article at http://www.designmatters.net/pdfs/0107/DesignGeneration.pdf.
69. Lyons, Kysilka, & Pawlas. (1999). *The Adjunct Professor's Guide to Success*. Needham Heights, MA: Allyn and Bacon.
70. Kucko & Gabb. (May 2000).
71. Who We Are: Beginning Markers of Accredited Interior Design Programs, as reported in Coleman & Sosnowchik, (September 2006). p. 47.
72. Ibid.
73. Watson, S. & Thompson, C. (2001). Learning Styles of Interior Design Students as Assessed by the Gregorc Style Delineator. *Journal of Interior Design* 27(1): 12.

74. Retrieved 8/17/07 from http://www.learnativity.com/learningstyles.html.
75. Watson, S. (2003). Retrieved 10/3/07 from http://scholar.lib.vt.edu/ejournals/JDC/Spring-2003/learningstyles.html.
76. Kolb, D. A., Boyatzis, R. E., & Mainemelis, C. (2000). Experiential Learning Theory: Previous Research and New Directions. In R. J. Sternberg & L. F. Zhang, eds., *Perspectives on Cognitive, Learning, and Thinking Styles.* Mahwah, NJ: Lawrence Erlbaum.
77. Ibid.
78. Adapted from Kolb et al. (1999).
79. Anderson, James. (2000). Tailoring Assessment to Student Learning Styles. *AAHE Bulletin.* Available at http://aahebulletin.com/public/archive/styles.asp.
80. Gardner, Howard. (1993). *Frames of Mind: The Theory of Multiple Intelligences.* New York: Basic Books, p. xxiii.
81. Adapted from Brooks, David. (2007). Integrated Learning Theory: Applications in Teaching. Entire discussion may be accessed at dwb4.unl.edu/dwb/Research/TheoryPaper/CompTh.html.
82. Ibid.
83. Ibid.
84. Adapted from Brooks, David. (2007).
85. Ibid.
86. Brunner, Lori. (2006). Are There Lasting Effects of a Schema-based Learning System in the Interior Design Studio? *Proceedings of the 2006 International Interior Design Educators Council Conference*, Scottsdale, AZ, p. 138.
87. Ibid., p. 139.
88. Adapted from Shell, D. & Brooks, D. (forthcoming). The Unified Learning Model: Implications for Learning and Teaching, Available at http://dwb4.unl.edu/dwb/Meetings/BostonACS/ULM-Submit-7-3-07.pdf, pp. 1–35.
89. Ibid.
90. Ibid.
91. Pable, J. (2000). *Sketching Interiors at the Speed of Thought.* New York: Fairchild.
92. Chickering, Arthur W. & Gamson, Zelda F. (1987). Seven Principles for Good Practice in Undergraduate Education, *AAHE Bulletin 39*(7): 3–7.
93. Ibid.
94. Watson, S. (2003). Retrieved 10/3/07 from http://scholar.lib.vt.edu/ejournals/JDC/Spring-2003/learningstyles.html.

SECTION TWO

Fostering Successful Learning

CHAPTER 3

Course Preparation

A. MANAGING TIME AND THE DEMANDS OF TEACHING

Assistant professor Jan Adler was late again to her 2 o'clock Thursday history class. As she scurried down the hall with her laptop and notes in hand, Jan glumly realized this had been a recurring problem, and last semester's student evaluations reported that she often seemed disorganized and stressed and returned their work in a late fashion. Today's problem revolved around her research project which had hit a snag—the human subjects approvals were not going to be back in time to start the student interviews as she had hoped. Because of grant deadlines, she sadly realized that this probably meant she was going to have to miss her anniversary dinner with her husband the next evening.

Jan had meant to update her lecture on Egyptian styles, incorporating student discussion questions to make the session more interesting. She had gotten started with these improvements but ended up looking through a fantastic new digital image collection she came across on the Internet. It didn't help that she had to download new software for her computer to read the digital images. Before she knew it, it was three minutes before class, partly because students were stopping by nearly constantly with 'got a minute?' questions. She also missed lunch again. When she got to class, Jan realized to her horror that she had forgotten to make copies of today's quiz for the students, who had studied diligently to make the most of this grade opportunity.

DO DESIGNERS STRUGGLE WITH TIME MANAGEMENT FOR CERTAIN REASONS?

Consistently, lack of time is near the top of the list of instructor concerns. Shrinking budgets and salaries coupled with reduced staff support do not relieve the situation. Consequently, it is very important that time is managed effectively because teaching responsibilities nearly always take more time than one anticipates.

The book *Time and Its Use* describes possible symptoms of poor time usage by teachers.[1]

- Uses vacation days and weekends just to catch up
- Feels he or she is the only one that can do the job right
- Stays at school long after hours
- Uses obsolete handouts and visuals in class
- Has an extremely disorganized office or desk area
- Has a home life in which school work dominates
- Is behind in grading, reports, and record keeping
- Shows significant signs of stress

Most instructors experience one or more of these symptoms as a result of teaching responsibilities, at least from time to time. Not surprisingly, full-time instructors report that a nine-hour undergraduate workload (typically, three 3-hour credit classes) equates to 37½ hours of teaching-related activities per week, according to a 2002 survey at a midsized private university.[2] This often comes as a surprise to educators, who rarely analyze their time usage (or perhaps do not perceive they have time to do so!).

In his book *Time Management for Architects and Designers*, Thorbjoern Mann explains that there are certain characteristics of design that make its practitioners particularly prone to disorganized time usage:

- By its nature, design is complicated and time-consuming.[3]
- Design is often accomplished by teams of people, increasing the complexity and time requirements for decision making.[4]
- Design is inherently chaotic and creative, prone to an almost exponentially expanding number of possibilities for solutions.

Teaching the intricate content of design adds another layer of complexity and potential for disorganized, unproductive time usage. Instructing others in design often means immersion in what education theorist Benjamin Bloom calls the high levels of cognitive processing, such as analyzing ideas and synthesizing new solutions. Studio classes, for example, often challenge students to "keep many juggled balls in the air at once." This makes it quite easy for instructor and/or student to get overly immersed in details without confronting the project's main points.

Typical reasons for time management problems often include

- Taking on too many responsibilities
- Not anticipating all costs of a task
- Beginning a task too late
- Insufficient knowledge to take on a task
- Not fully defining the parameters of a task[5]

Expectations of Class Preparation Time

While rules of thumb vary, instructors can generally expect to spend at least three hours of preparation for each hour of lecture and seminar class time, especially when developing a course for the first time. It is easy to underestimate the time required for thoughtful grading feedback, lecture preparation, student project development, and in-class exercise development, for example. Subsequent offerings of a course can sometimes shave down preparation time to one to two hours per hour of class time. This, of course, will still mean three hours of class preparation for a class that meets three hours per week.

Equally important but less discussed is the mental toll that teaching exacts. This varies widely, but often an advanced course is more energy-exacting in its teaching strategies and content than one discussing foundation skills or comprehension-level material.

Working Smarter

Often instructors are so excited about the teaching experience that the "big picture" of life is set aside. Keeping teaching and life in balance requires an active protection of one's well-being. It is helpful to keep the following three statements in mind.[6]

1. *Instructors are expected to do a good job, not a perfect job.* Instructors are often, by nature, academic high achievers and set very high standards not only for their students but for themselves. Perfectionism, taken too far, can be destructive to self-esteem and counterproductive. An instructor will likely not be fired for occasionally forgetting a fact in lecture or showing a less-than-perfect visual. Resigning oneself to doing a good-enough job in certain tasks can be quite liberating.
2. *Instructors deserve a fair wage.* Like all life initiatives, there are both costs and benefits to teaching. It is likely that people choose to teach because they value the giving aspect of the profession and the chance to shape young professionals. However, instructors must evaluate their assessment of the salary offered for teaching plus the intangible aspects to decide if it is worth the time and devoted energy. It is not out of the question that, at times, a teaching opportunity will not pay well enough to suit life circumstances, especially if one is an adjunct instructor. In such cases, a person will do him- or herself, the institution, and the students a favor by declining, rather than offering substandard, distracted, or rushed instruction.
3. *Instructors deserve a life outside of teaching.* First and foremost, an instructor is a person with a diversity of needs and gifts. While a teaching life is eminently valuable and a means to a living, it is not the *entirety* of a person. In the long run, those who immerse themselves in teaching and only teaching are prime candidates for burnout, dissatisfaction, and even divorce. (See Chapter 2 for tips on avoiding burnout.) Society today provides many temptations to define oneself solely by one's profession; however, by resisting this temptation and maintaining a well-rounded, balanced life, an instructor stands the chance of offering more to students, friends, and loved ones as well.

Specific Time-Saving Tips

There are many areas of academic life that may contribute to a sense of too little time. Seemingly small issues can build to an overwhelming point, but simple suggestions to manage time more effectively may provide liberation. Specific tips related to several areas of time investment are offered in the sections that follow.

Class Preparation

- *Set aside a weekly planning session.* Provide room in your weekly schedule to look ahead to the following week. This is the opportune time to send guest speakers a friendly reminder, update an in-class quiz, or review the assigned textbook content. Be realistic with extra time that might be required when learning new software or trying a new strategy. Avoid scheduling office hours immediately before a class, and reserve this time to achieve the right teaching mindset. This way you will enter the class with a calm and purposeful demeanor and with an optimistic attitude.
- *Create a test bank of questions for quizzes and exams.* Add questions to it after each weekly class. This will make exam development much faster and the content will be fresh on your mind after teaching it that week. Many texts come with an instructors' guide that offers good quality questions that can be altered or reworded.
- *Book and arrange all guest speakers and field trips before the semester starts.* You will

find economies of scale in grouping these phone calls, arrangements for campus parking passes, and invitation emails. Insert these into your semester schedule so you can plan activities around them.

- *Create a binder of your personal "just-in-time" creative teaching ideas.* All instructors sometimes hit a brick wall when trying to inject new life into a course or determine a way to get past a particular student learning challenge. When attending conferences, make a list of ideas you hear about that you'd like to try. In times of last-minute need, the binder will be there for you to consider a new solution.
- *Stagger due dates so that you are not buried in grading at any point during the semester.* Consider requiring a project that is due the week before the usual examination times so that students can clearly reflect and learn your material. This is especially effective if the students' other classes require traditionally timed final exams.
- *Take photos of notable student projects when permissible so that future students might model their behavior on positive examples.* Over a series of years, you will see learners continue to meet and exceed expectations and quality will be elevated. These images can also contribute to your teaching portfolio. A teaching portfolio is a useful (and sometimes institution-required) tool to seek tenure, promotion, or a different teaching position at another institution.
- *Do not try to be an expert on everything.* For example, instead of spending evening hours on a topic you know nothing about, arrange to bring in a speaker that is an expert on this material. Students appreciate learning information from a variety of sources.

Meetings and Administration

- *Set time schedules and stick to them.* If Monday afternoons are your private time to prepare for your evening class, do not make yourself available for drop-in questions. Establishing such a schedule at the beginning of the semester will allow others to know your consistent availability and may also show the right people the amount of work you are taking on.
- *Handle paper as little as possible.* Institutions are often guilty of needless paper in endless publications, requests, and committee announcements. Dispose of junk mail right by your mailbox. Seek to handle, file, or pass an item on to the appropriate person immediately.
- *If possible, meet with others in their office.* This will allow you the flexibility to leave on your schedule instead of waiting for the person to leave your office. If you are running the meeting, have an identified agenda in advance and stick to it. People often dislike meetings and will appreciate your respect of their time by keeping meetings to the point.
- Meetings rarely start on time. *Bring tasks with you that you can work on before everyone is present.*
- *Constant disruptions to your office schedule can keep you from completing tasks.* Apart from required office hours, consider keeping other times safe from interruption.

  - If your office is *too* available, consider creating a sign that you can place on the door: Thanks for coming by. If the door is closed, please leave me a note on the bulletin board, and I will get back to you as soon as possible.
  - In extreme cases, be less available. You might locate a faculty study room in the library or a nice picnic table outside that you can retreat to.
  - If someone does drop by, you might nicely let them know before the conversation starts that you only have two or three minutes.
  - If you are often plagued by others that

require your office time and you have a sympathetic colleague nearby, you might pre-arrange that your colleague come by to let you know that "the meeting is starting now," thus giving you an excuse to get rid of the drop-in person.

Classroom Time

- *During the first class session, have students find at least one or two "buddies" in class that they can exchange information with.* Announce that buddies are the source for needed handouts and class announcements should someone have to miss class. This will reduce the burden on you for requests of these materials.
- If appropriate, consider letting students review your lecture presentation notes prior to class. This will help prepare them for the content and may reduce needless questions along the way.
- *Creating email groups from your class lists will prevent endless individual emails sent to you by students.* This will allow you to send out blanket messages to all class members at one time to clarify a point of information or remind the class of an upcoming deadline.
- *Let students correct each others' work when appropriate.* This will reinforce the content for them and reduce your grading burden. Students often learn well in teams, and this strategy may increase the collegiality of class members. Consider that not all exercises have to have an assigned grade for the gradebook.
- *As appropriate, seek to delegate.* Enlist students to clean the classroom at the end of each session instead of doing it yourself. Students should be learning to take initiative themselves anyway, and assigning general responsibilities is a helpful nudge. This also pertains to students helping each other, as you cannot be everywhere at once.
- *In the case of large classes, it is much faster to hand back projects and papers if they are filed in an expandable file box organized alphabetically.* This will allow students to retrieve their own work rather than you having to pass it back yourself.

The most valuable current commodity is not time but one's full and undivided attention to a task.[7] However, the only way to give that full attention is to know that one has adequate time to devote to that activity. In general, instructors are the guardians of their time, thoughts, and energy. A consistent truth is that people are best able and willing to look out for their own sanity. It is often said that entrepreneurs should pay themselves first before others get paid—this is a good guideline for the use of instructors' valuable time as well.

B. MATCHING COURSE GOALS TO MEASURABLE OUTCOMES

Biographies of seemingly "successful" people have one thing in common: goals. Goals provide a broad-stroke glimpse of what to strive for. To achieve goals, experts describe the importance of a series of objectives, or steps that break the goal down into achievable portions. Outcomes provide the means by which success is measured. *Goals, objectives, and measurable outcomes* provide a destination and compass, means of transportation, and the arrival gate, respectively. This section provides discussion as well as practical tips on establishing and writing successful goals, objectives, and measurable outcomes.

Just as goals set expectations for design projects, goals can set expectations in academic courses to establish a common understanding of content to be covered and learning expectations. Objectives are closely linked to goals in that they are the individual steps or actions needed to accomplish the goal. While goals tend to be lofty and are often far reaching, objectives provide a description of the concrete means by which the goal is realized. Outcomes serve as the means of assessing whether the objectives, and ultimately the goals, are achieved. As a measuring instrument, outcomes are best assessed when tangible accomplishments can be ascertained.

GOALS

Goals for an existing course usually will already be established when one agrees to teach and may be set by others. In some cases, especially with new courses, instructors will have the opportunity to decide on course goals themselves or in collaboration with colleagues involved in curricular planning for the program. Within each program of study, there are both required and optional courses that fulfill university and/or college requirements. Each course fulfills a particular niche within the program and can be located on a curricular "map." Curricular maps allow students to review their progress through the curriculum and also serve as a tool for faculty to plan the sequential development of knowledge deemed necessary in the profession or required by accreditation standards. For instance, the Council for Interior Design Accreditation (CIDA) outlines distinct categories of knowledge that accredited programs of study must provide. Each category could conceivably be used to follow a curricular map of knowledge development through courses within a program.[8] Programs often use a curricular map to identify when and where specific goals and outcomes will be achieved during the students' academic career.

Curricular goals are important to the program of study as a whole. Course goals are more local and represent one of the fundamental elements of a syllabus that provides a framework for learning strategies. Carefully and thoughtfully articulated course goals are helpful because they provide a common understanding among all constituents of intended learning in each course. Written course goals establish which parts of courses are expected to address particular issues within a curriculum of study. Course goals allow academic freedom in approach and course content while expressing an overall aspiration for learning.

Guidelines for Establishing Goals

Goals are general, broad, and often abstract statements of the results desired from the learning process and can relate to the mission of the university, college, and program. In establishing goals for a course, it is important to determine if there is internal consensus on particular program goals to be exemplified in each course. Goals are written in broad, global, and sometimes ambiguous language; they are statements of what learners should be able to do at the conclusion of instruction.

Goals may address student outcomes and/or instructional practices. For example, Indiana State University's reference guide *Instructional Design and Teaching Styles* states that goals are typically derived from three sources:

1. External factors
   - Society's expectations
   - Accreditation agencies
   - Disciplinary norms and research
2. Internal factors
   - Priorities of peers, department, school/college and university committees
   - Evaluations
   - Student characteristics
   - Available resources
3. Personal factors
   - Instructor's personal values, commit-

ments, beliefs, abilities, qualifications, and experiences[9]

Goal statements are often created by considering how a student will be different as a result of the course. Goals may be discipline-specific, or cross-disciplinary in nature. A single goal will often have several objectives associated with it. Common action-style verbs are used to express goals as these abbreviated statements show:

- Students will understand . . .
- Students will learn . . .
- Students will recognize . . .
- Students will develop . . .

One example of a general goal expressed on a syllabus for, say, a Systems and Codes course might be

> Through this course, students will understand the basic environmental interior support systems in a building and the impact of building, life safety, and accessibility codes.

Similarly, an example of a general goal expressed on a syllabus for a seminar course entitled Evolving Issues in Interior Design might be

> This course will provide an understanding of the issues facing the contemporary interior design professional.

Such goals portray, in broad strokes, what the instructor hopes students will gain from each course. Without the objectives and measurable outcomes discussed next, however, it would be very difficult to ascertain if the goal for either course was actually met.

Objectives

Objectives are the results or consequences expected of instruction or learning and are typically specific, demonstrable, and focused on student performance. Objectives are often written from a "teaching" intention and address subject contents. Additionally, they provide the conceptual scaffolding for the course, outlining the components necessary to accomplish the overall course goal.

Objectives describe, in performance terms, observable and measurable behaviors. Objectives include the topics to be covered and how students will be engaged in processing the course content. As such, educational objectives are included in the course syllabus and are often found on project or assignment descriptions as well. Objectives lead to specific student learning outcomes that define successful accomplishment of the goals.[10]

Objectives can be classified and written in a variety of styles according to cognitive, affective, or skill and performance dimensions.

- Cognitive objectives describe thinking (knowledge) skills and include particular knowledge of subject matter.
- Affective objectives refer to attitudinal, personal, and social dimensions of outcomes.
- Skill and performance objectives such as writing, speaking, drawing, and computer skills address the means by which knowledge is acquired.

Objectives can also be classified according to the expected level the learner should achieve. Two common classifications include

- Those that describe minimum performance essentials (mastery objectives). This classification is particularly appropriate when describing basic skills or knowledge that beginning design students must master.
- Those that describe degrees of progress (developmental objectives). These objec-

tives describe a higher level of learning and recognize that some knowledge and the application of that knowledge must be progressive and will not happen entirely within one course.

Writing clear objectives can help the instructor design and deliver lessons that are easier for the student to comprehend and the instructor to evaluate. A properly written objective describes the specific knowledge, skill, or attitude desired, along with the method of instruction and criteria for learner achievement. Writing clear course objectives is important because objectives define what the students will do and provide an important link between expectations, instruction, and assessment (grading).

Guidelines for Establishing and Writing Objectives

Learning objectives should state the outcome of the activity and not merely the activity itself. Most instructional design sources agree that objectives should address the cognitive, psychomotor, and affective domains for learning. (See Chapter 2, Learning Styles for more information on these domains.) They further agree that the most effective learning objectives focus primarily on learners and their behaviors rather than on instructor behaviors or methods. Objectives describe

- What the student will learn, or what the change in knowledge or skill will be
- What depth of understanding or mastery is expected
- How the learning will occur

When developing objectives, consider particular verbs that "operationalize" the learning activity. Levels of expected performance are frequently described in terms of Bloom's cognitive taxonomy (knowledge, comprehension, application, analysis, synthesis, and evaluation[11]). It may prove helpful to categorize objectives in a matrix with the course goals along one axis and levels of learning outcomes along the other. Especially effective objectives are articulated using particular operation verbs such as translate, evaluate, diagram, summarize, compose, and predict.

As illustrated in Table 3.1, an example of educational objectives for the Systems and Codes course noted earlier (refer to the goal example) might read as follows: As a result of this course, students will be able to

1. Predict the implications of structural systems on the initial space planning design of interior spaces
2. Demonstrate an understanding of light frame construction through model and drawing form for new and existing construction with 80% accuracy
3. Explain implications of plumbing, electrical, and HVAC systems on the design of interior spaces to avoid conflicts
4. Contrast lighting systems according to their integration into the built environment and present the information in a usable fashion
5. Recognize acoustical principles related to design and control in given interior environments
6. Apply building and life-safety codes and accessibility standards to design projects in initial design and in checking existing spaces for proposed uses

The ABCD Method of Objective Writing

The ABCD method can serve as an excellent starting point for writing objectives and consists of the following components:

TABLE 3.1: LEVELS OF LEARNING OUTCOMES (ACCORDING TO BLOOM'S TAXONOMY)

Goal	Knowledge	Comprehension	Application	Analysis	Synthesis	Evaluation
Through this course, students have an opportunity to understand the basic environmental interior support systems in a building and the impact of building, life-safety, and accessibility codes.	Recognize acoustical principles related to design and control in given interior environments	Explain implications of plumbing, electrical, and HVAC systems on the design of interior spaces to avoid conflicts	Demonstrate an understanding of light frame construction through model and drawing form for new and existing construction with 80% accuracy	Contrast lighting systems according to their integration into the built environment and present the information in a usable fashion		
			Predict the implications of structural systems on the initial space planning design of interior spaces	Apply building and life-safety codes as well as accessibility standards to design projects in initial design and in checking existing spaces for proposed uses		

- *A* = *Audience*: the group of learners the objective is written for
- *B* = *Behavior*: a verb that describes what the learner will be able to do after the instruction
- *C* = *Conditions*: description of the circumstances under which the objectives must be completed
- *D* = *Degree of mastery needed*: a standard that the learner must meet to reach acceptable levels of achievement[12]

An objective should include each of the components, although not necessarily in any defined order. Thus, in the stated objective "Students will be able to demonstrate an understanding of light frame construction through model and drawing form for new and existing construction with 80% accuracy on a written test" the Audience is "Students"; the Behavior is "demonstrate an understanding of light frame construction through model and drawing form"; the conditions are "for new and existing construction"; and Degree of mastery is "with 80% accuracy on a written test."

In addition to providing a framework when writing new objectives, the ABCD method provides excellent guidance when reviewing the stated objectives in existing courses. Additionally, instructors are encouraged to

- Use action verbs that specify definite, observable behaviors
- Use simple language
- Describe student behaviors (not instructor behaviors)
- Describe learning outcomes (rather than processes)
- Keep the scope of each objective to one outcome
- Ensure the objective is clearly associated with a goal
- Ensure the objective is attainable

Once the behaviors, conditions, and degrees of mastery for each objective are established, they can be used to determine the types of assignments, tests, and projects to include within the course. (Chapter 4 includes advice on writing tests that address the learning objectives of the course.)

Measurable Outcomes

While *objectives* define the intended results or consequences of instruction and learning, *outcomes* are the actual evidence of learning that took place. Objectives specify what is expected and describe what should be assessed; outcomes are behaviors and products generated by students after instruction and are the objects of assessment. Thus, an outcome is often referred to as a *measurable outcome*, since one may evaluate whether it was in fact achieved or not, and to what degree. Sometimes, the outcomes are referred to as Student Learning Outcomes (SLOs).

Learning outcomes are one way in which programs evaluate their success in providing the overall educational goals and objectives for their graduates. In addition to assessing the effectiveness of the sequence of courses in a curriculum, outcomes provide a means for assessing an individual student's progress through a program.

In interior design education, as with all educational programs of study that have an accreditation process, outcomes are also used to determine the basis for awarding accreditation. They serve as the basis on which accreditation boards assess competency and on which accreditation standards are written.

Outcomes for particular learning objectives may be included in the syllabus but more often are not seen by students. Often curricular planning devices, outcomes are designed to assure the appropriate scaffolding of knowledge and skills within the educational curricula.

Outcomes are very specific, narrow, and measurable results expected subsequent to a learning experience. Learning outcomes are clear and measurable statements that define what a student is able to *do* or *demonstrate* at the completion of a course or program. These outcomes may involve knowledge (cognitive), skills (behavioral), or attitudes (affective behavior) that display evidence that learning has occurred, at a specified level of competency, as a result of a course or program.

Guidelines for Establishing Outcomes

Before appropriate outcomes can be defined, and assessment tools and procedures can be selected or designed, the objectives of the course must be clear. At a minimum, objectives should describe student behaviors and products that faculty would accept as evidence that the learning outcomes had been achieved. Goal statements are helpful but are usually too general, broad, or vague for developing specific assessment tools.

To be measurable, an outcome must contain reference to each of the following:

- Identification of the knowledge, skill, or attitude to be learned
- The level of learning to be achieved (which may be stated based on language in accreditation standards or on readily understandable achievement scales such as "awareness," "understanding," or "competency")
- The conditions in which the learning will be demonstrated

A common way of both thinking about and phrasing measurable outcomes is to begin each statement with "The student will." For example, a measurable outcome for a materials course might be stated thusly:

> When provided with a copy of the Life Safety Code, a student will be able to specify code-compliant carpet for the lobby of an elder care center and demonstrate compliance by citing specification documentation.

When developing measurable outcomes from the goals and objectives established for a course, develop a list of the knowledge and skills the students should display upon completion of the course. Cross-reference this list with the goals for the course to be certain that the defined goals are inclusive. Next, translate the list into measurable actions. An illustration of the relationship is found in Table 3.2.

Bloom's classification of cognitive skills is widely used in instruction planning and provides a workable framework when writing outcomes. Use of this or other classification systems is recommended to safeguard against a tendency to focus on content coverage and to ignore what the students should learn to do with content. The resulting outcomes may be assessed to determine the effectiveness of learning activities. Table 3.3 relates common action verbs to examples of outcomes, using the overarching framework of Bloom's Taxonomy of learning.

TABLE 3.2

Goal	Objective	Measurable outcome
Advance the study of color theories and their application to the built environment	Demonstrate an understanding of the historical use of color and its contribution to contemporary color usage	Identify color use in an historic period and apply it accurately in a studio project

A distinct relationship is present between goals, objectives, and measurable outcomes.

TABLE 3.3: EXAMPLES OF MEASURABLE LEARNING OUTCOMES BASED ON BLOOM'S TAXONOMY

	Knowledge	Comprehension	Application	Analysis	Synthesis	Evaluation
Definition of classification	Recalling or remembering something without necessarily understanding, using, or changing it (particularly terminology)	Understanding something that has been communicated without necessarily relating it to anything else	Using a general concept to solve problems in a particular situation; using learned material in new and concrete similar situations	Breaking something down into its parts; may focus on identification of parts, analysis of relationships between parts, or recognition of organizational principles	Creating something new by putting parts of different ideas together to make a whole	Judging the value of material or methods as they might be applied in a particular situation; judging with the use of definite criteria
Related behaviors (action verbs)	Define, describe, identify, label, list, match, memorize, point to, recall, select, state	Alter, account for, annotate, calculate, change, convert, group, explain, generalize, give examples, infer, interpret, paraphrase, predict, review, summarize, translate	Apply, adopt, collect, construct, demonstrate, discover, illustrate, interview, make use of, manipulate, relate, show, solve, use	Analyze, compare, contrast, diagram, differentiate, dissect, distinguish, identify, illustrate, infer, outline, point out, select, separate, sort, subdivide	Blend, build, change, combine, compile, compose, conceive, create, design, formulate, generate, hypothesize, plan, predict, produce, reorder, revise, tell, write	Accept, appraise, assess, arbitrate, award, choose, conclude, criticize, defend, evaluate, grade, judge, prioritize, recommend, referee, reject, select, support
Example of measurable outcome	Multiple choice test questions, matching terms test questions, list test questions, vocabulary assignments	Calculating material amounts, converting imperial to metric measurements, paraphrasing narratives	Assembling a collection of similar artifacts demonstrating a single design principle	Analyzing a series of spaces with a diagram based on particular zoning requirements	Choreographing a series of spaces related by functional or other characteristics	Peer critique of design project or presentation

When the measurable outcome has a time relationship to students' progress through an educational program, it is considered a benchmark outcome. Benchmark outcomes measure students' knowledge and skills at various times across their program experience. This might occur at initial entry to the program, at progress gates (such as portfolio reviews), at exit (graduation), and at follow-up times (professional exams). To create benchmark outcomes, a target date or other time reference is added to standard measurable outcome components.

In summary, whether planning the overall curriculum of a program or designing the direction and emphasis of a single course, it is imperative to include goals, objectives, and measurable outcomes. Goals define the direction to go, objectives describe how to get there, and outcomes are proof of arrival. Each plays a critical part in providing a common ground for planning and assessment.

C. BASIC COURSE CONSTRUCTION AND SYLLABUS PREPARATION

Third-year student Maria particularly looked forward to taking classes with Mr. Bonner. She noticed she felt comfortable with him in part because he always seemed to start the course off on the right foot with an easy-to-understand syllabus. On the first day of class he seemed to have a clear vision for the skills and knowledge students would come away with at the course's conclusion, and why those skills were important. She had so many courses to take and she appreciated receiving a course schedule that allowed her to get a grip on upcoming due dates and generally get organized. From experience, Maria understood from past classes that if she knew how she would be assessed from the start, she usually grew less stressed during the semester.

PLANNING A COURSE

Creating a new course can be an exhilarating and exhausting undertaking. On one hand, creating a new course opens wide the possibilities of offering one's areas of design passion or expertise to learners—an exciting prospect. On the other hand, designing a course that fulfills educational objectives placed on it by accreditation, university, and curriculum objectives and also covers the content in a refreshing, interesting fashion can be a challenge.

One of the most commonly reoccurring frustrations educators face when planning a new course or tweaking an existing one is how to effectively insert all of the content into it that "must" be covered. It is easy to talk oneself into the idea that "I'll lecture faster" or "students can skim pretty quickly" when evaluating content quantity.[13] Learners (and educators!) may feel uninterested or exhausted at the prospect of covering too much material in a rushed fashion. Information must be winnowed down to create a meaningful learning experience. It is helpful to recall that it is not the amount of content going out—it is the nature of the content *retained* that counts. Filene's four-step process is adapted here to the specifics of interior design course preparation to help manage the many choices that arise when planning a new course[14]:

1. *Covering.* With course goals and objectives close at hand, brainstorm all the topics the course will include, translating these into specifics. *Do not get overly attached to any of them.* This is the time to double-check content with needed accreditation and other required standards. Pair these goals and objectives with the available days in the semester or quarter, estimating the amount of time each will take. This will illustrate the quantity of

ideas that will go untaught due to time constraints.

2. *Uncovering.* Consider the sequence of topics. Is the content best discussed chronologically, building in complexity, or in some other order? Should it present theory and then move toward application? To help reduce topics, think about what must be learned now and what can be deferred until later. If appropriate, assign units to chunks of the content, then do a quick check on how much time is devoted to each unit—is it enough? Too much? Sometimes experience will be a guide to estimating time requirements. If the content is entirely new, particularly abstract, or highly interactive, allow more time. Team exercises will usually require more time as well. Now be ruthless—what can be cut and still fulfill the promises of the course goals?
3. *Adding.* Now consider the learners, and think about what learning strategies are best to introduce, reinforce, or master the topics. Refer back to the course goals and objectives as you reflect on this. Activities that include learning strategies such as discussion, interactive exercises, guest speakers, and field trips can be woven together within the overall course. Again, certain strategies will take more time, and this is especially true of discussion and studio activities. Build in necessary assessments such as tests and critiques. Also consider the load and timing for grading and providing feedback, plus the timing of assessments with other courses the learners will be taking simultaneously. Factoring in "celebration time," to acknowledge learners' achievements with a brief party or other recognition to maintain motivation, can also be time well spent. It may be necessary at this stage as well to eliminate content based on your time estimates for covering critical information. It is sometimes helpful at this point to begin creating a "back of house" course schedule only you will see to organize content and time allotments. An example of a back of house schedule is shown in Figure 3.1.
4. *Modulating.* Consider the ebb and flow of learner energy and potential for distraction, as students may be taking three or four other courses simultaneously. Do you notice a drain in enthusiasm as the semester moves on? It may be better to strategically place particularly taxing information or tasks early to accommodate this phenomenon. Also consider diversifying the tasks in class—most people like variety. Consider mixing up class activities with a debate, role playing, or other case study analysis.[15] Varying the due dates of tests and projects (sometimes Monday, sometimes toward the end of the week) can bring fairness to learners, some of whom work weekends and others weekdays.

Daily Course Session Planning

Once the overall course structure is in place, it is fairly straightforward to plan out each class meeting's sequence of topics and/or activities. One's back of house course schedule can provide general guidance on the necessary flow of content. Many educators additionally use a daily course session planning sheet like the one shown in Figure 3.2 to guide their minute-to-minute activities. This sheet provides the educator an at-a-glance reference to make sure daily objectives are accomplished. Effective and thorough course planning at both the course level and the daily level is an essential exercise *before* a course syllabus is written.

Tentative Schedule
ID 345 History of Housing
Revised 12/3/05

Spring 2006

Class Meeting	Topics	Readings	Due	Instructor Overview Notes
History of the Home				
1 Jan 24	• Introduction • The Idea of Comfort	• Rybczynski: Home: A Short History of an Idea: ch. 1 & 10. • Focus Questions: ch. 1-3, 10 • Plagiarism exercise	Gather books and supplies. Locate book for report project.	"What is a House" video
2 Jan 31	• The Middle Ages • Renaissance • The Holland experiment	• Rybczynski: Home: A Short History of an Idea: ch. 2 & 3. • "Why Study History" • Focus Questions: Holland	Focus Questions: ch. 1-3, 10 Focus Questions: Holland Plagiarism exercise	Quiz
3 Feb 7	• English Country Houses • Victoriana • Downing • Voysey	• Rybczynski: Home: A Short History of an Idea: ch. 5. • Focus Questions: "Georgian and English Country Houses" • Focus Questions: "Downing, Voysey, etc."		Childhood Place exercise. Begin Pattern project.
4 Feb 14	Early 20th c.: • Mechanization • Arts & Crafts • Beecher • Bungalows	• Rybczynski: Home: A Short History of an Idea: ch. 7. • Focus Questions: "Mechanization of the Home" • Focus Questions: "Think & Compare" • Beecher: The American Woman's House: pp. 23-42. • "Suburban Paradise: The Fab Forties Were an Antidote to Early City Life." • "A Glossary of Bungalow Terms"		Guest Speaker: Jim Phillips, Bungalow Heritage Association. Call him at home to firm: 555-3434. Also he has info on mechanization & marketing of bungalows. **Confirmed for 10am. Call 1 week in advance.** Do grade check: last day to drop is March 1.
The 1950's				
5 Feb 21	20th century: • Flight to suburbia/sprawl	• "The Suburban House." In Housing: Symbol, Structure, Site. pp. 72-73.	Pattern project	Collect, discuss Pattern project.

Figure 3.1 A "back of house" course schedule helps determine how content is sequenced and time allotted to each topic.

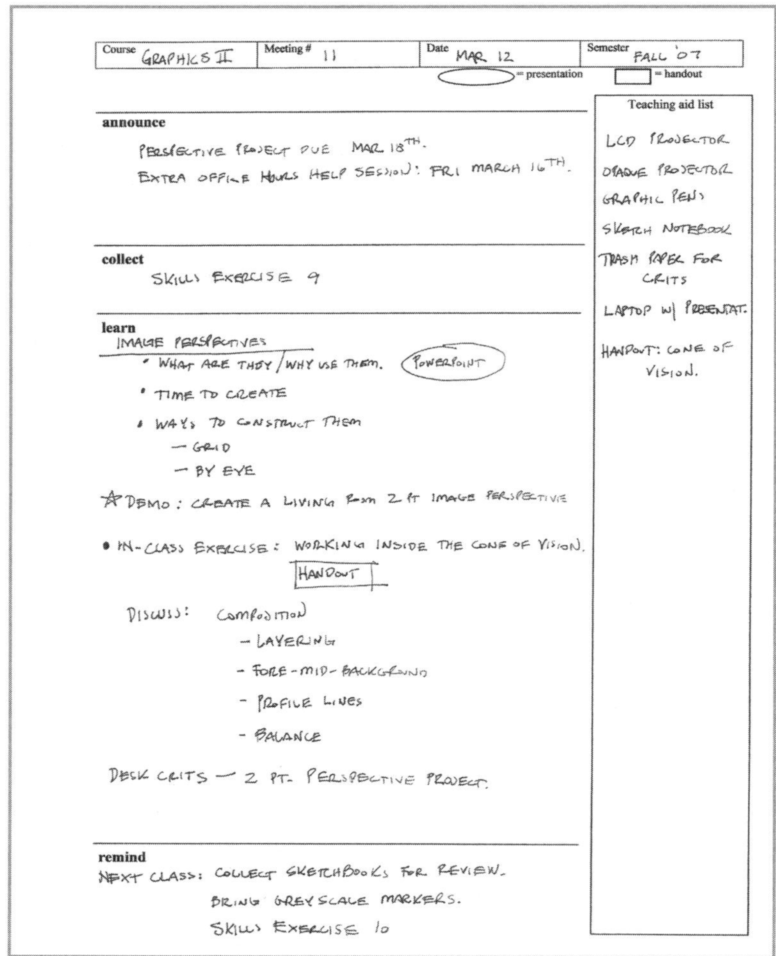

Course GRAPHICS II	Meeting # 11	Date MAR 12	Semester FALL '07

= presentation = handout

announce
PERSPECTIVE PROJECT DUE MAR 18TH.
EXTRA OFFICE HOURS HELP SESSION: FRI MARCH 16TH.

collect
SKILLS EXERCISE 9

learn
IMAGE PERSPECTIVES
- WHAT ARE THEY / WHY USE THEM. (POWERPOINT)
- TIME TO CREATE
- WAYS TO CONSTRUCT THEM
  - GRID
  - BY EYE

☆ DEMO: CREATE A LIVING ROOM 2 PT IMAGE PERSPECTIVE

- IN-CLASS EXERCISE: WORKING INSIDE THE CONE OF VISION. HANDOUT

DISCUSS: COMPOSITION
- LAYERING
- FORE-MID-BACKGROUND
- PROFILE LINES
- BALANCE

DESK CRITS — 2 PT. PERSPECTIVE PROJECT.

remind
NEXT CLASS: COLLECT SKETCHBOOKS FOR REVIEW.
BRING GREYSCALE MARKERS.
SKILLS EXERCISE 10

Teaching aid list
LCD PROJECTOR
OPAQUE PROJECTOR
GRAPHIC PENS
SKETCH NOTEBOOK
TRASH PAPER FOR CRITS
LAPTOP W/ PRESENTAT.
HANDOUT: CONE OF VISION.

Figure 3.2 A daily course session planning sheet provides a detailed reference to guide each class meeting's activities.

The Syllabus

One of the most comprehensive and important documents an educator creates is a course syllabus. Part legal contract and part learner aid, this document is nothing less than a means to link the students' learning with the larger mission statements of the department and university or college.[16]

The Many Purposes of a Syllabus

A syllabus potentially serves many purposes:

- It can be used to establish the philosophical bent an educator takes in a course and the level of thought expected of learners from the first day.
- Learners who are unsure of their readiness for a course can often quickly assess their standing by reviewing an information-rich syllabus. A syllabus can also communicate to learners the related financial costs of the course with regard to books and supplies.
- It is the first point of contact and connection between learner and educator, and portrays much about the educator in its writing style and content.
- A well-constructed syllabus can establish the meaning and credibility of the course in the wider context of the design profession.
- It can serve as a literal or figurative contract or memorandum of understanding between the learner and educator.[17]
- A syllabus forms a record of a course.

This record may be used during the accreditation process, in program planning, or for incoming faculty to use as a starting point for teaching the course at a future time. The syllabus is a documentation of the goals, objectives, and requirements of a course. Importantly, while the syllabus tells what a course is, it does not specify how one should teach it.

Viewing the syllabus as essentially a set of promises and agreements that an educator makes with learners has several advantages:

1. It tends to make the syllabus easier for the educator to commit to when viewed as a local agreement.
2. It keeps the syllabus realistic, as it focuses on learners exiting the course with identifiable skills.
3. It prompts rich integration between teaching and learning.[18]

A Syllabus Example

Each syllabus is inherently different, as is every educator and learning situation. The Appendix to this chapter provides a sample syllabus with explanations of its various components. Educators may find that not all of the information in this example is required or that other information is necessary to customize a syllabus to their approach. Additionally, some design programs have syllabus templates that should be used for consistency across the design curriculum.

Further Tips for Course Construction and Syllabus Writing

Consider this additional advice from seasoned educators when developing a syllabus (and designing the learning opportunities presented to students):

- Provide the course's "guiding questions" in the syllabus, then give these questions to the learners on the final exam, assuring that goals match outcomes effectively.
- Assign only a quantity of reading that you as the educator would be capable of digesting. If it is difficult to give up some readings, assign some as supplementary, giving interested learners sources for further information.[19] Readings may be further delineated with terms such as *peruse* and *focus*. For example, "Peruse pages 165–193, focusing on the concepts presented on pages 177–8."
- Using the second person voice in the syllabus can establish a friendly tone with learners, beginning the process of relationship building. Education author Filene discourages writing syllabi in the third person because "no one is speaking. By writing that 'the course seeks to develop' for 'students,' the teacher has deleted his presence and depersonalized his audience."[20]
- Leave one or more "To be announced" sessions in the schedule, especially if the course is new or you are otherwise unsure what to expect as the semester progresses.

The Course Schedule

Learners can plan their schedules effectively when they have an understanding of the time requirements a course will involve. A course calendar or schedule should be provided to learners that includes the dates for critiques and exams as well as comprehensive project due dates. Many educators find it helpful both for their learners and themselves to fully outline the course in a schedule. This approach lists the topics to be addressed in lecture, lab, or other daily activity (field trip, guest speaker, presentation, etc.). Some educators provide an expanded outline indicating sources to be read and assignments to be completed on particular days. In other cases, it makes sense to keep a syllabus fluid and less specific, especially if changes are anticipated

Tentative Schedule
ID 345 History of Housing
Revised 12/3/05

Spring 2006

Class Meeting	Topics	Readings	Due
1 Jan 24	• Introduction • The Idea of Comfort	• Rybczynski: Home: A Short History of an Idea: ch. 1 & 10. • Focus Questions: ch. 1-3, 10 • Plagiarism exercise	Gather books and supplies. Locate book for report project.
2 Jan 31	• The Middle Ages • Renaissance • The Holland experiment	• Rybczynski: Home: A Short History of an Idea: ch. 2 & 3. • "Why Study History" • Focus Questions: Holland	Focus Questions: ch. 1-3, 10 Focus Questions: Holland Plagiarism exercise
3 Feb 7	• English Country Houses • Victoriana • Downing • Voysey	• Rybczynski: Home: A Short History of an Idea: ch. 5. • Focus Questions: "Georgian and English Country Houses" • Focus Questions: "Downing, Voysey, etc."	
4 Feb 14	Early 20th c.: • Mechanization • Arts & Crafts • Beecher • Bungalows	• Rybczynski: Home: A Short History of an Idea: ch. 7. • Focus Questions: "Mechanization of the Home" • Focus Questions: "Think & Compare" • Beecher: The American Woman's House: pp. 23-42. • "Suburban Paradise: The Fab Forties Were an Antidote to Early City Life." • "A Glossary of Bungalow Terms"	
The 1950's			
5 Feb 21	20th century: • Flight to suburbia/sprawl	• "The Suburban House." In Housing: Symbol, Structure, Site. pp. 72-73.	Pattern project

Figure 3.3 **The course schedule can be a simplified version of the "back of house" course schedule explained earlier in this chapter.**

(such as in new courses) or uncertainty exists about the learners' ability levels. Regardless of course characteristics, it is usually prudent to include a statement indicating that the schedule is tentative and subject to change throughout the term. Figure 3.3 provides an example of a course schedule.

The Learners' Experience of the Syllabus and Schedule

Finally, recognize that a discussion of the syllabus and schedule is often the first topic covered in a course. Educators who have thoughtfully considered the course goals and objectives, type and sequence of activities to accomplish learning, and the timing of learning and assessment will exude a sense of confidence and ease in leading this discussion. When one recognizes that learners are presented with perhaps four or five syllabi from their other courses simultaneously, it is easy to see how learners can feel overwhelmed with responsibilities. Some educators opt to include a short paragraph that reminds the learner that everyone desires the same outcome: quality education and the gaining of knowledge and skill. This can serve to relieve initial class tensions and set a positive tone for educator-learner engagement.

An effectively designed course syllabus and schedule can help learners come to grips with the task ahead of them, much like a road map is helpful for travel. A well-constructed learning experience is in effect a gift the instructor gives to the learner—a gesture many learners feel obligated to return in the enthusiasm and positive energy they inject into the class.

D. SELECTING AND CREATING COURSE RESOURCES

Carl Menotti's studio class involved learners in the design of a fusion-style restaurant. The nature of the assignment usually generated much interest, and this was due in part to the programming research Carl required of class members. Carl typically immersed the class in examining projects by a single targeted interior design firm to introduce them to the realities of restaurant design. Several case study articles of the firm's restaurants published in trade journals helped make his teaching points clear. Carl additionally came to see the power of well-placed course reference material when one of his learners, thoroughly taken by the targeted design firm's philosophy, made contact with the firm and was eventually hired to pursue restaurant design as her career.

SELECTION OF MATERIALS

Course references that supplement class activities are among the most important decisions an instructor makes, in part defining how students will come to integrate class content into their personal perceptions. As the preceding scenario suggests, background references can also ignite a spark in learners that can lead to career-influencing decisions. The task of selecting these learner references has grown increasingly complex in recent decades because access to information is undergoing dramatic, fast-paced change. Expectations of quick access, low cost, and content timeliness have often caused instructors to embrace but also move beyond the traditional textbook. This section will discuss criteria for selecting course resources, address issues of copyright and fair use, and explore several options for technology-assisted information access for learners.

The appropriate selection of course materials is a task that is important for several reasons. First, course materials should support the goals and objectives of the course. Second, course materials come into play at the department curricular level as well:

1. Course materials must naturally support the larger objectives of the curriculum, including level of content, pace of content introduction, and overlap of material between courses.
2. Course materials may be duplicated over multiple courses. At times, this can provide needed reinforcement for learners. For example, some reference books are relevant and necessary at multiple points in the curriculum. If course material re-use is overdone, however, learners may perceive a lack of curricular planning that wastes their time and funds.
3. Faculty at some institutions require a vote of approval for new course resources so that all can be aware of the curricular content.

In some cases, course resources have already been selected, and a new instructor can enter into teaching with this task already completed. Other situations require the updating of course resources or the development of resource collections for new courses.

Choosing Amongst Resource Types

The variety of course references can make development of a collection both exciting and intimidating, especially for new instructors. Print, image, and video are only three of many different formats to choose for class background information and in-class presentation. Human cognition research offers some guidelines on making these decisions. For example, multiple intelligence theory suggests that learners ingest material in multiple and different ways which lends justification to choosing a variety of resource formats within a single course. Resource formats also have individual characteristics that suggest it is not just about how content is presented but also how learners can respond to it and ingest its meaning:

- Text is processed by learners from left to right, one piece at a time. This prompts learners to focus on individual ideas rather than putting them together.[21] However, reading lets learners proceed at their own pace and re-read difficult sections.[22] Note-taking for personal decoding is fairly straightforward.
- Audio and video are real-time formats and simulate life experience more thoroughly than text. However, note-taking can be rushed unless a pause feature or other asynchronous control is available.
- Graphic images are information rich and can transcend the linear nature of text. They offer learners the chance to link disparate concepts together to observe interactions and consequences.[23] Note-taking or learner image-making from provided graphics can be a way for interior design educators to simulate the spatial thinking of professional practice.

Considerations in Making Course Material Selections

The wide availability and benefits of gaining knowledge through reading dictate that many course references will be in text form. It is fairly obvious that a reference first and foremost should offer support of the course's goals and objectives. Beyond this, there are other helpful criteria to consider when making textbook and other resource selections:

Adopting a comprehensive reference such as a textbook. An entire textbook is rarely used exclusively chapter by chapter for a course. The academic program emphasis and curriculum structure may demand that only portions of textbooks are used, and often the textbook that best suits the *majority* of the class content is selected. This textbook is then supplemented with additional course materials such as handouts, custom course packet materials, and other readings.

Cost of the resource. With the financial demands books, projects, and technology exert on student budgets, many instructors examine the cost of the required references to be certain that references sufficiently support the class objectives. Rather than requiring several costly textbooks for purchase and then using only portions of each for a course, educators can examine alternate ways for students to access the information, such as online, provided that copyright laws are respected.

A separate course packet of materials is another possible textbook supplement. Print vendors usually gain necessary permissions for use from an instructor-generated reference list and determine the sale price of the course packet.[24] It is important to recognize that it may take four to six weeks for copyright permissions to be gathered and course packets printed. Print vendors are also good resources for gaining permission and replicating out-of-print resources.

Currency of the information. Some intellectual content is never dated while other information changes quickly, such as technology, building codes, and product specifications. Due to the extended process of their production, print textbooks can be outdated shortly after their publication, making a spot check of time-sensitive information a good idea.

Diversity of viewpoint. Quality higher education demands that learners consider a variety of human perspectives in order to make informed decisions. A solitary viewpoint in course references can offer learners an incomplete picture of reality. However, teaching author McKeachie recommends that instructors choose primary resources that match their own point of view. This avoids learners becoming confused or annoyed if the instructor expresses disagreement with the text.[25] Alternative viewpoints can provide counterpoint to the text through additional readings, handouts, videos, or guest speakers.

Level of challenge. Course materials should match the level of learner ability. Well-chosen materials challenge learners but do not overwhelm them inappropriately. In the case of a wide variety of learner abilities in a class, some instructors provide supplementary materials that accommodate the advanced class members.

Coherence. Resources can vary considerably in ease of understanding for learners. "Inconsiderate" texts cause comprehension problems due to their structural deficiencies. Conversely, the "considerate" text can be read and understood with minimal effort. Educational researchers identify text features that foster easy comprehension:

- Topics are organized with a top-level heading structure that allows concepts to relate both to each other and to the overall structure.[26]
- The text includes "directives" that help learners determine if they are internalizing the content.[27] Examples of directives include objectives at the beginning of chapters and questions at the end or throughout a chapter.
- The text includes "signals" that show how the information is connected or organized and help prioritize the importance of information. These include font cues such as underlining, bolding, color changes, and size variations. In-text phrases like "this is important because" help learners detect key points. Bulleted and numbered phrases coupled with heading levels help learners stay organized as they construct their personal framework of understanding.[28]
- The text includes graphic aids that help learners discover relationships across concepts, transcending the one-dimensional format that words alone offer.[29]

Copyright and Fair Use Laws

Teaching almost always involves the use of others' ideas to provide comprehensive instruction. There is implicit ownership involved in all work, and copyright refers to the "ownership" of the intellectual property contained in the work, regardless of whether the work is published on paper, via the Internet, or in a video or movie format. A copyright symbol (©) does not need to be present for work to be copyrighted. Therefore, instructors must be aware of lawful ways to provide access to content. Fortunately, federal Fair Use guidelines allow a portion of many works to be used for academic purposes, allowing educators to legally use copyrighted materials. Fair use guidelines are fairly extensive in length. A helpful summary can be viewed at www.umuc.edu/library/copy.shtml#teacher.

Educators can determine fair use by considering four aspects of the target resource.

1. The purpose and character of the use:
   - If the resource will be used for non-profit/educational use, it is more likely to fall under fair use.
2. Nature of the copyrighted work:
   - If the work is creative rather than factual, it is less likely to be called fair use.
   - If the work is out of print, it is more likely to be called fair use.
3. The amount of the original work used:
   - If the desired resource excerpt approaches 50% of the original work, it is less likely to be called fair use.
   - Text source quantities considered fair use: up to 10% or 1000 words.
   - Image quantities considered fair use: no more than 5 images from one artist or 10% or 15 images from a collection, whichever is less.
4. Effect of use on the work's potential market:
   - If the new work contains its own original content in addition to the copyrighted work of others, it is more likely to be called fair use.[30]

A 2002 addition to copyright law called the TEACH Act defines copyright reproductions in online and technology-based learning situations and gives educators at accredited non-profit institutions greater leeway in using copyrighted materials. The TEACH Act permits the display of works during online instruction without the consent of the copyright owner permitting that

1. The online instruction is mediated by an instructor.
2. The materials are intended only for those officially enrolled in the course.
3. The institution puts in place measures that prevent users from accessing the work beyond the length of the course.
4. The institution takes steps to limit the distribution of the material only to those officially enrolled in the online course and takes steps "to the extent technologically feasible" to prevent retention and redistribution of the content "downstream".

The full text of the TEACH Act can be viewed at www.copyright.gov/legislation/pl107-273.html#13301. A helpful summary of the TEACH Act is available at learningforlife.fsu.edu/ctl/explore/bestPractices/docs/TEACHAct.pdf.

Textbook and Resource Availability for Instructors

Thankfully, most textbooks are available to instructors at reduced or no cost. **Desk copies** of textbooks, workbooks, and other required references can often be ordered directly from publishers. Many publishing houses offer this service from their website or toll-free phone number. Instructors often must prove valid association with their institution either through a letter from the chairperson or by having the materials sent to a legitimate institution that the publisher recognizes. It is also helpful to know that publishers are also willing to send **evaluation copies** of textbooks that instructors might consider adopting in the future.

Textbook Sources

Interior design education is fortunate to have a growing number of dedicated textbooks and other resources available on many topics. This situation is different from the past, when instructor reliance on architecturally focused textbooks were the main viable option. Texts are currently available or in production on such specialized topics as environmental psychology, interior design theory, writing for interior designers, construction documents, and quick perspective sketching.

See Table 3.4 for a list of interior design textbook publishers as of 2007. Publisher contact information is included so that instructors can request desk copies.

Making Resources Available to Learners

Effective research and selection of resources in the initial stages allow course and lesson planning to proceed smoothly. The next consideration is how students will access the resources. If possible, make resource selections known to learners prior to the beginning of the course. Posting information on Blackboard or similar online course management systems is one solution.

Making Resources Available Through a Local Bookstore

Calls for instructor textbook selection often occur during the semester or quarter prior to the target term. Bookstores need a reasonable amount of time to respond to textbook requests, so ordering promptly assures that books will arrive in the university or local bookstore in time. Using a bookstore as the access point for learners to order course materials ensures that sufficient copies will be available locally when needed. However, some instructors and learners complain of high bookstore prices. Bookstore availability can also encourage less committed learners to sell back their textbooks, an action some instructors would rather not occur.

Online Orders

As an alternative to bookstores, some instructors suggest or require that their learners obtain course texts from Internet sources. This both solves and raises several issues. On the positive side, instructors do not have to alert Internet booksellers to their learners' needs in advance. Internet bookseller prices can also be quite competitive, especially if learners locate used copies, and delivery is rapid. However, it is possible that textbooks will be sold out at the precise time when learners need them.

Reserve Reading

When only limited copies of resources are available, instructors can choose to place them on reserve in an institution's library for learner checkout or digital access. This strategy works well for making an instructor's personal copy of a reference accessible to learners, for example. Some institutions will also place reference materials that are not permitted to be removed from the library on reserve for in-room learner checkout.

The instructor's decision regarding length of checkout for print materials must consider the number of learners who will be using the materials during the needed time period. For example, if thirty learners need access to one resource on library reserve and knowledge of its contents will be determined through a scheduled examination, then the instructor might choose a two-hour checkout

TABLE 3.4: A SELECTION OF INTERIOR DESIGN TEXTBOOK PUBLISHERS

Publisher	Address	Phone	Website
Crisp Learning Inc.	Acquired by Thomson Learning	203-539-8000	http://www.thomsonedu.com
Fairchild	750 Third Avenue New York, NY 10017	800-932-4724 212-630-3880	http://www.fairchildbooks.com
Harper Collins	10 East 53rd Street New York, NY 10022	212-207-7000	http://www.harpercollins.com/
Insight Media (visual media)	2162 Broadway New York, NY 10024-0621	800-233-9910 212-721-6316	http://www.insight-media.com
McGraw Hill	7500 Chavenelle Road. Dubuque, IA 52002	877-833-5524	http://catalogs.mhhe.com/mhhe/home.do
Norton	500 Fifth Avenue New York, NY 10110	800-233-4830 212-354-5500	http://www.wwnorton.com/
Prentice Hall	One Lake Street Upper Saddle River, NJ 07458	800-282-0693	http://vig.prenhall.com
Professional Publications	1250 Fifth Ave. Belmont, CA 94002	800-426-1178 650-593-9119	http://ppi2pass.com

Rizzoli	31 West 57th Street New York, NY 10019	(800) 52-BOOKS (212) 759-2424	http://www.rizzoliusa.com/
Rockport	100 Cummings Center Suite 406-L Beverly, MA 01915	978-282-9590	http://www.rockpub.com/
Taunton	63 South Main St., PO Box 5506 Newtown, CT 06470-5506	203-426-8171	http://www.taunton.com/
Van Nostrand Reinhold	115 Fifth Avenue New York, NY 10003	606-525-6600	
Whitney Library of Design (Watson Guptill)	770 Broadway New York, NY 10003		http://www.watsonguptill.com/
Wiley	10475 Crosspoint Blvd. Indianapolis, IN 46256	877-762-2974	http://www.wiley.com

period with in-library use only. This allows each learner equal access to the information. If, in the same situation, the time cited for a single learner's checkout is 24 hours, not all learners will have equal access to the necessary information. To help in such situations, some libraries will make multiple copies of a resource available for learner checkout.

Online Materials

Placing materials online provides another access option for learners. Institutions often make course management software packages such as Blackboard, WebCT, or others available to their educators to manage resource availability as well as communications and grading. These can be effective ways to assemble non-traditional materials for class and exploit web links to identified sources, and expands the variety of learning resources to include video, audio, computer-aided drawings, blogs, and other formats. TEACH Act 2002 copyright laws apply to online instruction, and instructors should check with their institution for further information on these regulations.

An Interior Design Education Example. The growing number of Internet-based resources makes possible customized "virtual textbooks" that provide in-depth information to

Virtual Textbooks: Alzheimer's Care Unit Design

Project Objective:
Develop an understanding of Alzheimer's Disease and related behavioral problems
Develop an awareness of design for special needs
Develop the basic skills for interpreting and applying information in the design process for novel problems
Exhibit understanding of above concepts through a design problem and solution

Course Topics:

Week One
General Healthcare Design
Environment Linked to Medical Outcomes, *ISmagazine*, March 97
http://www.isdesignet.com/Magazine/Mar'97/TakeNote_1.html
Environments that Support Healing, *ISmagazine*, July 96
http://www.isdesignet.com/Magazine/J_A'96/EnvSupHeal.html
Safety First in Health Care Facilities, *ISmagazine*, October 98
http://www.isdesignet.com/Magazine/Oct'98/Slips.html
Design in Nursing Homes: Environment as a Silent Partner in Caregiving.
Eunice Noell, *Generations*, 19, (Winter 95/96).
http://firstsearch.ocle.org (available through U of A Library Home Page)

Week Two
Alzheimer's Disease and Behaviors
Alzheimer's Disease, *Mosby's Medical, Nursing and Health Dictionary*, (1998).
http://web4.infotrac.galegroup.com (available through U of A Library Home Page)
What Is Alzheimer's Disease, Clinical Reference Systems, (July 99).
http://web4.infotrac.galegroup.com (available through U of A Library Home Page)
Treatment of Alzheimer's Disease, ElderSearch Library
http://secure.www.comm.com/eldersearch/elderlibrary/right
Behavior Problems Associated with Alzheimer's Disease, Clinical Reference Systems, (Jul 99).
http://web4.infotrac.galegroup.com (available through U of A Library Home Page)
A Biopsychosocial Perspective on Behavior Problems in Alzheimer's Disease
Wayne Caron and Darryl Goetz, Geriatrics, 53, (Sep 98 supp 1).
http://firstsearch.oclc.org (available through U of A Library Home Page)
Management strategies for Problem Behaviors in the Patient with Dementia
Frank Lehninger, Vijaya Ravindran and Jonathan Stewart, *Geriatrics*, 53 (4), (Apr 98).
http://firstsearch.oclc.org (available through U of A Library Home Page)

Figure 3.4 Excerpt from interior design educator Jennifer Webb's "Virtual Textbooks: Alzheimer's Care Unit Design" online reference list for a studio course. From J. Webb (2000), Virtual Textbooks: Creating a Supplemental Text for Interior Design Studios. Unpublished handout distributed at the 2000 International Interior Design Educator's Conference, Calgary, Alberta, Canada, March 29–April 1, 2000.

learners for class assignments. Interior design educator and associate professor Jennifer Webb has explored this option, creating a class home page that features a comprehensive collection of electronic resources.[31] These references guide learners through the sequential stages of a studio project, as the excerpt shown in Figure 3.4 shows.

Webb provides recommendations gained from her experience with electronic resource management:

- Check links regularly for functionality. The deeper the page within a site's hierarchy, the more volatile that page may be.
- Use a variety of sites for multiple viewpoints.
- Make sure learners have the necessary technical knowledge, software, and hardware to access the materials.
- Be conscious of any accessibility restrictions to sites. Some sites are public domain while others may be restricted or fee-based.
- Arrange for learners' group ID numbers and passwords in advance if necessary.
- Make learners aware of the potential for bias on corporate or sponsored websites.
- Include study questions and other tips.
- Add learner discoveries to the content to encourage others to share and update the information.[32]

Ethics and Conflicts of Interest in Learning Resources

Some educational institutions do not allow faculty or departments to sell textbooks or course materials directly to learners so that monetary exchange does not influence the educator-learner relationship. Some educator/authors who require their learners to purchase their textbooks elect to donate their profits on those materials to their student organization or other source to avoid the appearance of conflict of interest. It is also unethical for instructors to sell free desk copies of textbooks to learners or textbook buy-back companies, as this dilutes the economic return to publishers and their authors.

In Conclusion

Course materials may be selected by an instructor as teaching tools to supplement lectures, accentuate a point, provide diversity of viewpoint, supplement their expertise, or punctuate knowledge. Educator-selected course materials can also be important additional learning resources for students outside of class time. Therefore, these materials play an important role in supporting a course's goals and objectives. Thoughtful selection of both content and method for transmitting the materials to learners can make these resources a dynamic, inspiring vehicle to connect new ideas with learners' current framework of understanding.

E. APPENDIX

An example syllabus for an interior design course.

DEPARTMENT OF INTERIOR DESIGN **Anywhere University**

IND 4236 Interior Design Studio II **Term Fall 2xxx**

Check to see if your department has a standard syllabus layout.

Instructor: Jane Doe
Office Number: 345 Anywhere Building
Office Hours: Please see my door for the current schedule. I am also available by appointment.
Phone: xxx-xxxx
Email: xxx@xxxx.edu
Department Main Office: 225 Anywhere Building: 8:00 AM – 4:00 PM Monday-Friday
Department phone: xxx-xxxx
Department FAX: xxx-xxxx

Choose office hours that are not in conflict with the likely course schedule of your students if possible.

Course Schedule
Wednesdays 11:45 – 2:00 & Fridays 11:45 – 2:45

If students are to turn in assignments or other work to you outside of regular class hours, be sure to specify that location here as well.

Course Location
Room 134 Anywhere Building. We will also travel to several field trip destinations.

Course Description and Purpose
Advanced non-residential projects in creative problem solving with emphasis on programming, spatial analysis and open-office systems.

Include the course description as it is written in the bulletin or catalog of classes.

Course Goals and Objectives

Goals

- Develop understanding of the design processes for specific non-residential environments including space planning, use of elements and principles of design, spatial and functional relationships and the specifications of materials, finishes, furniture, and textiles.
- Acquire knowledge regarding the design of contract facilities with regard to application of building and accessibility codes.
- Recognize the potentials within and specification of open office systems.

See the section on Goals and Outcomes for writing these statements.

Objectives

As a result of this course, students will be able to

1. Apply building and accessibility codes in the creation of a compliant design for an office project, demonstrating compliance through reference to code statutes.
2. Identify and record the client program through research and interviews.
3. Synthesize client needs for space planning, furnishings, fixtures and equipment into a program-fulfilling, code-compliant solution.

4. Demonstrate proficiency with communication skills through effective graphic and verbal presentation of design solutions.

Prerequisites/Co-requisites: IND4435, IND4235 (studio).

Also explain any necessary instructor permissions here if appropriate.

Class Procedures

The studio course environment can be a stimulating, positive aid to your creativity and progress. In order to ensure this occurs, you are expected to be prepared to work in class unless we are experiencing a field trip or other activity. It is necessary to arrive to class with required activities completed to avoid being counted absent for class.

Working in class is an important part of a studio class experience. Ideas are exchanged and questions raised by one student benefit everyone. Exercise and projects will span longevities of a few days to several weeks, followed by a class critique or presentation, as suitable to the project.

Textbooks

- Required course packet available at Express Copy Shop, 635 W. Alfred Street, Anywhere, State. 890-456-5554.
- The course has a Blackboard website with significant resources that you will reference. Please secure access to a computer with Internet browser connection as soon as possible.
- Interior Graphics and Design Standards, 1st Edition, S.C. Reznikoff, Watson-Guptill Publications, Inc., New York, 1986.
- Americans with Disabilities Act (ADA) regulations. (Available online at the course Blackboard site)
- You will refer to other previous textbooks and resources such as those for lighting, graphics, and design presentation.

If possible, provide an estimate of book price for students. Including ISBN numbers can help students order books online.

Be clear here about the required or supplementary status of books.

Materials and Equipment

You are likely familiar with supplies that help you to create projects at this point in your coursework. Depending on your working style, the following is a list of items you might need to complete your projects for this class. Unless otherwise noted, you are also permitted to complete projects digitally using Photoshop, Illustrator, AutoCAD or other programs.

Required Programming equipment.

- Metal tape measure for field measuring
- Camera, preferably digital.
- Project Journal: Blank Bienfang Note/Sketch Book. They are available at Studio Art.

Not required, but helpful if you have one.

- Video camera
- Portable cassette recorder for recording interviews.

It's very helpful for students with limited budgets to get a feeling for required expenditures as soon as possible.

If appropriate, it may be worthwhile to have a local bookstore bundle certain materials together for students' easy purchase.

This list may vary depending on your preferred method of design development—via hand drawings or CAD.

- Pencil or mechanical pencil and extra leads
- Pencil sharpener, if necessary
- Triangles: 30-60-90 and 45. Tape dimes to the backs of them to raise them above your drawing surface-- prevents smearing.
- Black felt tip pen for sketching- a Pilot Precise V5 or V7 works well.
- A pad of ¼" quadrille ruled paper for creating to-scale sketches
- Bathroom and furniture templates
- Architect's scale
- Appropriate paper for design development drawings and final submittals.
- Drafting tape (or better yet, dots)
- Design Applique Film: also called 'stickybacks'. Used to create transparent labels that are word processed. Available at Design Store for $1/sheet. Don't buy these until you need them.
- Color media—color pencils and/or design markers or other
- Roll of white or yellow 24" trash paper (also called 'bumwad' or tracing paper, but note: this should be an inexpensive purchase)
- Mat board and/or foamcore board for various purposes. Don't buy this now--wait until you know what you need. Sizes shall be discussed.
- Eraser-- I like the Pentel Clic eraser. Kneaded erasers are also suitable.
- Eraser shield.
- 3 technical graphic ink pens; one each of .7, .5 and .3 line widths.
    Suggestions for these: Pilot Razor Point, Expresso disposables. If you can't find these specific brands, there are many others that might be suitable as well. Make sure that the pens you select share the approximate same color of black ink and that the ink does not take an inordinate amount to time to dry (smearing is no fun).
- 1 medium width black marker for drawing presentation borders (A Sanford Sharpie does nicely)
- An architect's scale.
- Pair of inexpensive scissors
- T-square (for out-of-classroom use only if necessary)
- A bottle of SOBO brand white glue or Elmer's School Glue Gel-style
- Inexpensive fishing tackle box or tool box to keep all of these supplies in.
- Aspirin or ibuprofen- or whatever headache relief preparation you prefer.
- Calculator
- Post it notes or other bookmark material
- Two two-inch three-ring notebooks for project documentation

We will also build models in this class. While supplies will vary depending on your needs, the following are items you will likely use.

- Exacto knife with extra blades.
- Various sizes/thicknesses of planar media. These can be balsa wood, foam core, illustration board, card stock or other.

- Stick pins or dressmaking pins to hold study models together
- Scotch tape
- Use gesso (a thick paint available in art stores) for smoothing edges of foamcore
- Fine sand paper
- Various model parts, depending on your design
- Spray glue
- A metal ruler or yardstick or metal straightedge such as a triangle to cut with.
- 'Found' items that can be used as materials for your particular situation.

Class Communication

As this is an advanced studio, out-of-class communication is vital so that I can inform the class of schedule changes or make clarifications. It is important that you supply to me a valid and current email address and check it at least every other day. Note that information distributed via email constitutes informing you of course changes and updates. At times we will also communicate via the class's Blackboard site. All details in this syllabus are subject to revision. Any necessary revisions will be announced in class. Such announcement will constitute adequate notification to all class members whether present or not. Please be aware it is your responsibility to remain appraised of all class matters.

Clear standards about class communication are important, including out-of-class communication and policies on technology.

In the event of an emergency which will force you to miss class, please call me at xxx-xxxx and leave a message. In case of inclement weather, refer to Anywhere University's weather line at xxx-xxxx to determine the status of class meetings.

Please silence all cell phones and other devices while in class. You are expected to work only on your class project while using your laptop in class. Text messaging is not permitted in class at any time.

When corresponding with me via email, please understand it may at times take 48 hours for me to respond. I make every effort to check my email one time per day. It is my intention to provide feedback and grades within two weeks of the submission of work.

Students benefit from a clear understnanding of feedback turnaround time, especially if that feedback is electronically based.

Grading Standards and Evaluation Criteria

Project 1: The Emergency Operations Center	50%
Project 2: A Monograph Museum	40%
Attendance/Attention/Attitude/Professionalism	10%
Total	**100%**

An overall snapshot of grade distribution shows topic emphasis and deemphasis for students.

Please note that full credit for attention, attitude and professionalism is awarded for receptivity to ongoing feedback, maintenance of positive outlook and active response to feedback and adherence to deadlines. Active participation in

Specific information on participation expectations aids in accountability at grade time.

critiques is a course requirement.

The **Grading Scale** for the Department of Interior Design is as follows:

95 - 100 = **A**	83 - 86.99 = **B**	73 - 76.99 = **C**	63 - 66.99 =**D**
90 – 94.99 = **A-**	80 - 82.99 = **B-**	70 - 72.99 = **C-**	60 - 62.99 = **D-**
87 – 89.99 = **B+**	77 - 79.99 = **C+**	67 - 69.99 = **D+**	Below 59 = **F**

Some instructors include a descriptive written statement with the letter grade. For example, a B+ may represent points in the 87-89.99% range, and may be described as: "Represents very high achievement as a result of ability and effort. It shows the student has a very good understanding of the material and is developing a very good comprehension of its application."

It is helpful to keep in mind these letter grade descriptors.

A = Outstanding
A- = Very good
B = Good
C = Satisfactory
D = Weak
F = Unacceptable

A 'reality check' on the true meanings of letter grade levels can help alleviate grade inflation.

Attendance

Success in this class requires attendance. Everyone is responsible for signing their names to the role sheet each day. You are permitted two (2) unexcused absences; the grade for a course will be reduced by one-third grade level for each unexcused absence in excess of one week's equivalent class meetings. Four other absences may be excused with a doctor's note or other documentation of an emergency.

If you reach six absences you will fail the class. Arriving more than 15 minutes late or leaving early is considered an absence, so please be aware of your quantity of absences. Ask if you are unsure of your current quantity.

You may be required to drop a course if you do not attend the first class meeting or make prior arrangements with the instructor. Information missed due to tardiness or absence is your responsibility of the student. Unfortunately, there is no time to repeat missed information, so please speak with a class buddy to obtain this content.

Attendance at project critiques, charettes and presentations is required even if they are held outside of the usual class meeting times. Please consult the schedule or class updates for these times.

Handling attendance is often institution-specific--- be sure to check about any standards that should be used. One time-tested solution is to allow students a certain small number of absences without penalty, to allow for sickness, death in the family and other understandable events. This relieves you, the instructor, of the need to check endless doctor's notes upon each absence and trains students to keep a close watch on their attendance behavior.

Incompletes will be given only in classes of serious illness or hospitalization (written notification from doctor is required), or in cases of death in the immediate family. It is your responsibility to make sure that any incompletes are removed. This must be done no later than the first week of classes of the following semester unless other arrangements have been made between us.

Late or Missing Project Policy

- In-class assignments

In-class exercises must be completed together as a group. Therefore, they cannot be made up at a later date. Other arrangements will be considered in the case of a medically excused absence/death in the family. The simplest way to avoid problems is to never miss or be late to class.

- Incremental Class Reviews

Pinup review dates will be announced in class or in the schedule. It is your responsibility to know when these reviews will occur and it is possible they will change depending on how the class is proceeding. *The class participation grade will be based in part on providing and presenting the required materials at reviews in class or with outside critics. Note there is no opportunity for late pinup submittals.* Compliance or non-compliance with review dates can mean the difference of a letter grade.

- Final Due Dates and Presentations

Presentations of projects are a vital part of the project grade. Failure to present the project as required may have serious consequences on the course grade. Projects are due at the start of class on the day they are due. If an assignment is turned in after class has started on the day they are due, they are still late. If an assignment is turned in late, a penalty of 5% of the grade will be applied for each day late, including weekends. Late assignments may be turned in to my box in the office. When turning in a late assignment please have office staff mark it with the date and time it was turned in; otherwise I will assume it was turned in at the time I find it.

Projects that are late must still be presented on presentation day in their current state. Failure to do so will seriously affect the project grade. The final opportunity for late submittal of the final project is <u>the announced project due date</u> at conclusion of class. <u>Final projects will not be accepted after this date</u> so that I have sufficient time to grade them prior to grade deadlines.

Field Trip Policy

Be aware that we will enjoy several field trips this semester. These experiences are required and I must collect your signature on several university forms for you to participate. Absence from a field trip will be counted as a normal class meeting absence.

This course is demanding… but is as exciting and fulfilling as you are willing to make it.

This course is a advanced-level studio experience—its nature requires you to apply information you have accumulated from previous courses such as lighting, presentation, drawing, space planning, and graphics. It is demanding in that you are analyzing, critiquing and designing intricate spaces based on

State if and how late work will be accepted as well as any penalties. If classes are large, note that handling grading for late projects can become a problem, as well as accounting for whose work was late or on time. To manage this issue, some instructors permit late submittal up to one week that incurs an automatic percentage grade penalty. Installing a policy where work more than one week late is not permitted keeps late submittals manageable.

It is advisable to have a policy governing if and when tests can be made up in the case of documented absence. Some institutions have on-campus test proctoring services. It is a good idea to inform students of any associated fees. You should also inform students where to submit missed assignments in your absence. If permitted, the department's main office might datestamp late work for verification of when the assignment was turned in.

many parameters. It is also complex in that you must at times operate in a team environment, much like you will in your career. All of this means that the course can be as fulfilling and challenging… or as grueling and torturous… as you are willing to make it. The key is to be open to ideas, be a cooperative and contributive team member, do your homework, work hard, and let it happen.

Instructor biography

Welcome to IND 4236 Studio II! I am interested in you having a positive learning experience that helps prepare you for your professional career. I have undertaken preparation in my own background to help this happen. After graduating from Somewhere University in 19xx, I practiced interior design with the XTZ Studio for six years. Having then realized that teaching was my true passion, I returned to There University and completed my Masters of Interior Design degree in 2xxx. I am NCIDQ certified and am licensed within the state of Zeb. I believe I bring an effective combination of practice reality to design theory to our classroom, and my goal is to impart some of what I have learned along the way to your understanding of our profession. I look forward to getting to know you and being of assistance to your career development.

By its nature a syllabus is broad-scope and sometimes intimidating document for students. Some instructors elect to personalize it by including background inforamtion on themselves as well as information that begins to build the instructor-student relationship.

Many instructors prefer the friendly tone of a second-pesron writing style ("you will experience...") in a syllabus to break the ice.

I am here to help you

Design hurts. You will likely encounter 'designer's block' or issues regarding team dynamics. These situations are typical, so know that you can handle them and they will resolve. Do come and talk to me about how things are going, especially if you foresee things you are concerned about, and don't let them mount up! It is best to confront issues as they arise, rather than reacting to them after they are a problem.

Americans with Disabilities Act (ADA)

If you require accommodation due to a disability, please bring it to my attention. University policy requires that you: (1) register with and provide documentation to the Student Disability Resource Center; (2) bring a letter to me indicating the need for accommodation and what type. This should be done during the first week of class or within one week of the onset of the disability as possible.

For more information about services available to Anywhere University students with disabilities, contact the Student Disability Resource Center 97 Sanford Avenue, Anywhere University, Anywhere, State. 2345-3254 (206) 353-3434 (voice) (206) 353-6565 (TDD) sdrc@admin.any.edu http://www.any.edu/~staffair/dean/StudentDisability/

This syllabus and other class materials are available in alternative format upon request.

Academic Honor Code

Students are expected to uphold the Academic Honor Code published in The Anywhere University Bulletin and the Student Handbook. The Academic Honor

System of Anywhere University is based on the premise that each student has the responsibility (1) to uphold the highest standards of academic integrity in the student's own work, (2) to refuse to tolerate violations of academic integrity in the university community, and (3) to foster a high sense of integrity and social responsibility on the part of the university community.

Please see the following web site for a complete explanation of the Academic Honor Code. http://www.any.edu/Books/Student-Handbook/codes/honor.html http://www.any.edu/Books/Student-Handbook/

Plagiarism

Definition: To take and use as one's own the concepts, ideas or writings of another. Although all designers are inspired and influenced by the work of other artists and designers; their ideas, concepts and images MUST NOT be directly or recognizably be utilized in student work without written or verbal attribution. Penalties for plagiarism range from failing the course to dismissal from the program and/or the University.

With the ease and availability of internet resources, plagiarism be an issue. Some instructors choose to address academic dishonesty in the syllabus, and then supplement the information in class, providing examples and making clear what constitutes plagiarism. Others may include a more lengthy discussion in the syllabus including guidelines and examples.

Extra university help

I am interested in you performing your best within this class and your career. Please be aware of these campus resources:

The Writing Center

Help with writing of all types. Will proof student drafts at no charge. Xxx-xxxx.

Student Counseling Services

Confidential counseling for all matters personal including stress, family matters and substance dependencies. xxx-xxxx. Located at the Student Health Center.

Lab Fees

You are assessed a lab fee for most courses in the program. The lab fee of $10.00 for lecture courses helps defray the costs of supplying and maintaining the library with resources and consumable supplies. You will not be charged for making copies from the resources held in the department library. Studio based courses and courses involving the use of CAD for instruction or individual study are assessed a fee of $15.00.

These fees do not, in fact, cover those expenses and your cooperation is appreciated in keeping those costs to a minimum. Certain CAD courses may restrict the amount of duplicating or plotting per student. If equipment is broken or off-line for any reason you may need to seek duplicating and plotting services elsewhere. Every effort will be made to resolve such problems within a reasonable amount of time.

Department Resources

Resource and Equipment Rooms: Policies and procedures for use of the Resource and Equipment rooms are posted in the room. Please follow them at all times. The CAD Computer Lab: (Room 231) is available only to students enrolled in CAD classes or CAD Directed Independent Study courses. Students may use the CAD lab to check e-mail when classes are not in session. Other computers are available in main floor library for word processing. *To avoid viruses, students must never load any software on to any department computers. Please, no smoking, food, drink or pets in the office or classrooms.*

University Policy on Student Project Use

The University possesses the right to retain a student's original writings or graphic expression for use in accreditation, research or teaching activities for a period of one year. After this time, the Interior Design Department has the option to 1) return your original project to your possession; or, 2) offer you a high-quality digital representation in exchange for the department's permanent retaining of your work. Please understand that this policy is very important in the progression of learning and the interior design profession as a whole, as innovation supports and spurs on new techniques and ideas. It is very likely this policy will impact you only minimally anyway, as you will be engaged in photographing your work for your digital portfolio.

Many accreditation bodies require that departments retain student work as proof of learning. It is important to communicate your department's policy on the retaining and use of their original work early to avoid difficulties.

Grading Rubric

General Descriptions of Grade Assignments for Presentation Projects

You might elect to expand the explanation of letter grades by including a grading rubric that describes a typical course project and expectations for standards of excellence assigned to a letter grade of A,B,C, etc.

The following are general descriptions of an example project that would receive a grade of A, B, C, or D. Each project you will complete will have its own specific set of requirements. Every student's project and in fact, every student's situation, is, of course, different as well. Therefore, chances are good that your project and actions will not exactly correspond to any of the following descriptions—they are not supposed to. Instead, the following descriptions are offered to you as a general documentation of an imaginary project's successes and failures and the grade resulting from it.

In GENERAL, a project receiving an A for a grade might possess the following characteristics:
Student proposes a uniquely creative and functional solution and fully takes into consideration program requirements. Graphic conventions are effectively manipulated to produce an easily understood interior solution, either in blackline or with renderings as required. Text is easily readable and accurate in content. Color palette is balanced and realistic and a knowledge of focus and contrast is demonstrated in the case of either line quality and/or color. Student took initiative to exceed the required minimum guidelines through extra drawings, renderings, or other means. Presentation is consistent and in keeping with the approach of the solution. All required elements are included. The verbal presentation is obviously rehearsed and the student, while perhaps nervous, is knowledgeable in the project solution and can justify decisions made. Student has consistently attended and interacted in class and has taken constructive criticism into account. Project is handed in on time or ahead of due date. *The project represents the student exceedingly well in a portfolio and would likely be assessed as the work of a beginning professional by a client or design employer.*

In GENERAL, a project receiving a B for a grade might possess the following characteristics:
Student has clear grasp of project parameters and other impacting elements. Resulting space planning shows this knowledge, with a few minor flaws in some areas. There is evidence of creativity in the solution. Graphic conventions are basically sound, but lack fine-tuned refinement. Small notations may be missing, inadequate, or incorrect. Project in its final presentation form shows clear thinking as it evolved into its final form, but may possess small flaws that are distracting in minor ways to the overall design communication. The verbal presentation shows competence in the overall solution, but a short or incomplete explanation in the project shows little rehearsal. Student has consistently attended class and interacted with others. Project is handed in on time. *The project represents the student fairly well in a portfolio and would likely be assessed as a competent and*

adequate student project by clients and design employers.

In GENERAL, a project receiving a C for a grade might possess the following characteristics:
Student has been attentive in class to lecture, but lacks a definitive grasp of space planning and/or program requirements. The project may lack creativity. Elements of the given program may be missing, ignored or underestimated. Interior elements are not drawn to scale and space planning traffic flow presents some major problems to the project's overall success. Adjacencies and clearances are insufficient. Final drawings may appear ordinary or even boring through repetitive use of the same ideas, line weight or lack of value variety. Some lines may appear to have been 'free-handed' in inappropriately. Text is inconsistent and distracting. Notations such as scale are missing. Presentation lacks consistency and rendering shows lack of time investment. Verbal presentation is marked with stammering or presentation is missed altogether. Project is handed in on time. *The project does not represent the student particularly well in a portfolio and would likely be assessed as a beginning student project by clients and design employers.*

In GENERAL, a project receiving a D for a grade might possess the following characteristics:
Through absences from class or aversion to reading, listening, or studying, student has not grasped the project requirements. The project clearly lacks a direction and space planning is inconsistent. Requirements are largely ignored or incorrectly applied. Some of the drawings, through lack of time, may appear to be quickly free-hand drawn. Text is inconsistent or entirely unreadable. Elements of the project are missing. Prior constructive criticism is either received with hostility or ignored. The verbal presentation is obviously hurriedly assembled with little or no prior rehearsal. Class attendance is spotty and missed handouts are frequently requested of fellow students. Project is handed in late, resulting in a lowered grade. *The project does not represent the student well in a portfolio and should not be included as an indicator of their work.*

IND 4236 Interior Design Studio II
Term Fall 2xxx

Student Agreement

I, ______________________________________
have read the syllabus completely.

Understanding the considerable impact this course has upon the quality of my design portfolio and ultimate employability, I agree to perform to the best of my ability during every class and will make and demonstrate continual and consistent progress on projects.

I will do my best to support my team members and will be a willing and active participant in decision-making and recognize that they will be required to react to my participation or non-participation.

I recognize that the strength or weakness of my resulting projects is dependent upon my willingness to take initiative and perform well.

Date ____________________________

Signature _______________________

Some instructors have found that treating a syllabus as a professional agreement integrates well with discussions of projects, deadlines, and general professional behavior. For this reason, some instructors include a final page of the syllabus that is literally an agreement signed by the student. This tends to formalize the class responsibilities and sends the message to take requirements seriously.

ENDNOTES

1. Drawbaugh, C. (1984). *Time and its Use: A Self-Management Guide for Teachers.* New York: Teachers College Press. p. 26.
2. Hinrichsen, B., et al. (April 1–5, 2002). *A Study of Faculty Workload as a Means of Improving the Student Learning Environment.* Paper presented at the Annual Meeting of the American Educational Research Association, New Orleans, LA.
3. Mann, T. (2004). *Time Management for Architects and Designers.* New York: Norton, p. 17.
4. Ibid., p. 62.
5. Mann, T. (2004).
6. Wachter, J. & Carhart, C. (2003). *Timesaving Tips for Teachers,* 2nd ed. Thousand Oaks, CA: Corwin Press, p. 1.
7. Goldhaber, M. (April 7, 1997). The Attention Economy and the Net. *First Monday: Peer Reviewed Journal on the Internet 2*(4). Retrieved 7/30/07 from http://www.firstmonday.dk/issues/issue2_4/goldhaber/.
8. CIDA may be accessed at http://www.accredit-id.org/.
9. Indiana State University's *Instructional Design and Teaching Styles* reference guide (1998). As is the case with many universities, Indiana State University maintains an active array of current information for instructors at http://web.indstate.edu/oit/cirt/pd/styles/tstyle.html for information regarding teaching styles.
10. Adapted from http://www.assessment.uconn.edu/docs/HowToWriteObjectivesOutcomes.pdf.
11. Adapted from Bloom, B. S., et al. (1956). *Taxonomy of Educational Objectives Handbook 1: Cognitive Domain.* London: Longman.
12. Adapted from Heinich, R., et al. (2002). *Instructional Media and Technologies for Learning,* 7th ed. Englewood Cliffs, NJ: Prentice Hall.
13. Ramsden, P. (1984). The Context of Learning. In F. Marton, D. Hounsell & N. Entwistle, eds., *The Experience of Learning.* Edinburgh: Scottish Academic Press.
14. Filene, P. (2005). *The Joy of Teaching.* Chapel Hill, NC: University of North Carolina Press. pp. 35–46.
15. Ibid., pp. 35–46.
16. Woolcock, M. (2007). *Constructing a Syllabus.* The Harriet W. Sheraton Center for Teaching and Learning, Brown University. Retrieved 3/2/2007 from http://www.brown.edu/Administration/Sheridan_Center/publications/syllabus.html.
17. Adapted from Grunert, Judith. (1997) *The Course Syllabus: A Learning-Centered Approach.* Bolton, MA: Anker Publishing. Accessed through Center for Teaching Effectiveness. Also see *Designing a Learner-Centered Syllabus.* University of Delaware. Retrieved 3/2/07 from http://cte.udel.edu/syllabus.htm.
18. Filene. (2005), p. 24.
19. Woolcock, M. (2007).
20. Filene. (2005), p. 29.
21. Mayer, R. (1985). Structural analysis of science prose: Can we increase problem-solving performance? In B. Britton & J. Black, eds., *Understanding Expository Prose.* Hillsdale, NJ: Erlbaum, pp. 65–87.
22. Robinson, D. (1994). Textbook Selection: Watch Out for "Inconsiderate" Texts. In Pritchard, K & Sawyer, R., eds. *Handbook of College Teaching.* Westport, CN: Greenwood Press, pp. 415–422.
23. Ibid., p. 419.
24. This author recently had a custom course packet assembled from numerous outside references to prevent learners from buying multiple textbooks. Due to copyright fees, the course packet itself unexpectedly ended up costing learners $68.00. It pays to obtain a cost estimate prior to committing a print shop to production.
25. McKeatchie, W. (1986). *Teaching Tips: A Guidebook for the Beginning College Teacher.* Lexington MA: Heath.
26. Anderson, T. & Armbruster, B. (1984). Content area textbooks. In R. C. Anderson, et al., eds., *Learning to Read in American Schools: Basal Readers and Content Texts.* Hillsdale, NJ: Erlbaum, pp. 193–226.
27. Alvermann, D. (1986). Graphic Organizers: Cueing Devices for Comprehending and Remembering Main Ideas. In J. F. Baumann, ed., *Teaching Main Idea Comprehension.* Newark, DE: International Reading Association, pp. 210–255.
28. Lorch, R. (1989). Text-signaling Devices and Their Effects on Reading and Memory Processes. *Educational Psychology Review* 1: 209–234.
29. Robinson. (1994), p. 419.
30. Excerpted from Information and Library

Services. (2007). Copyright and Fair Use in the Classroom, on the Internet, and the World Wide Web. University of Maryland University College. Retrieved 7/19/07 from http://www.umuc.edu/library/copy.shtml#teacher.

31. Webb, J. (2000). Virtual Textbooks: Creating a Specialized Text for Interior Design Courses. *Proceedings of the 2000 International Interior Design Educators Conference.* Calgary, Alberta, Canada.
32. Ibid.

CHAPTER 4

Managing and Guiding Learning

A. TECHNIQUES FOR LEARNING

John Richards had always enjoyed serving as instructor for Introduction to Interior Design, the freshman students' first interior design–specific class. However, this large lecture-format class made discussions somewhat intimidating, especially since the students did not know each other well.

He noticed that the students were often drawn to the major through their exposure to various reality television shows that sometimes portray the profession inaccurately. In an exploration of engaging the students from the point of view of their current knowledge, Richards obtained several short video segments that depicted the television show's interior designer explaining a residential makeover solution to the client, who had been kept entirely out of the collaborative process. He then played the segments and asked the students to count the number of times the interior designer said "I," or otherwise referred to him- or herself, and the number of times the interior designer said "you" or "your." After students had counted their totals, Richards used this information to draw students into a discussion about client-centered design. He found this simple counting procedure engaged the students in a low-stakes quantitative observation of human interaction that lent credibility to his lecture and prompted a lively classroom discussion about the purpose of design. At the end of the class session, Richards had students summarize the main points of the discussion in writing for two minutes, then share their comments with the class colleague sitting next to them.

Choosing the means by which students learn is among the most challenging and exciting decisions educators make. Greek philosopher Heraclitus captured the complexity of this task in his saying "No man ever steps in the same river twice, for it's not the same river and he's not the same man."[1] The same could be said of teaching—an educator will never teach the same class twice for reasons that include a changing student population, evolving content, and fluctuations in the physical learning environment. Constant variability like this calls for educators to approach their decision making with humility. In the words of educational reformer John Dewey, educators are themselves "pupils of the students' minds."[2] In the end, it matters less what the educator "knows" and more what students learn and retain.

ESTABLISHING AN EFFECTIVE CLASSROOM LEARNING ENVIRONMENT

The first day of class offers educators the opportunity to affect learners' initial impressions of the course and their perceived probability of success. These first signals are important for they can set the tone for successful learning and are often expressed either literally or overtly through syllabi, course activities, and educator demeanor.

Florida State University Teaching Excellence Scholar Pamela Carroll identifies pertinent questions and statements that educators should consider as they structure their class and seek to offer an accurate and positive first impression:

- Do learners feel the educator wants to be there?
- Do learners feel the educator is on their side?
- Does class structure and content set learners up to succeed?
- Do learners understand the educators' expectations and feel they can and should rise to meet them?[3]

Establishing a successful working relationship with learners early is key to effective learning both inside and outside the physical classroom. The arts are known for their casual, friendly working environments. However, learners require known boundaries for smooth interactions with faculty. Clear department policies on how faculty should be addressed, for example, can help learners navigate the waters of professional relationships. It is helpful to keep in mind that learners do not need a buddy but rather a trusted adult guide that can direct their progress. On the other hand, a distant, automaton-like authority figure can be intimidating and discourages learner/educator rapport.

Gestures in addition to typical class meetings can lend an air of humanity to an educator without sabotaging boundaries of respect. Inviting students to conference presentations demonstrates an educator's interest in their betterment. Some educators even share their own letters of rejection with learners so students recognize that everyone struggles with their own learning journey.[4]

The Four Elements of Successful Learning

Successful learning is dependent upon a "four-legged" support structure, much like a chair. First, the educator must be capable and prepared to facilitate learning, and second, learners must be ready and motivated to interact with information. Third, the nature of the activities must support the learning transaction. Last, the nature of the virtual or physical learning environment can figure heavily into the success or failure of a learning experience. The first three of these will be considered here. Learning environments are discussed in Chapter 10.

Educator Effectiveness

The first of these support structures, educator capability, is obviously a broad subject that varies widely by educator demeanor and subject matter. However, common threads can be found in educational research that transcend discipline and university setting. Educator Edwin Ralph synthesized current research literature on effective postsecondary pedagogy and identified factors that characterize effective teaching. Effective educators:

- Appear confident and efficient in their actions and processes
- Demonstrate organization and preparation for learning activities
- Show they are clearly in charge through their composed, assured manner, yet are not dictatorial
- Handle difficulties or classroom disruptions in an objective fashion without undue emotion or irrationality
- Are friendly and accessible, yet maintain their professionalism in learner/educator relationships
- Appear deserving of the authority they command and have the trust of those they work with.
- Are living models of the behavior they seek to instill in their learners[5]

Understandably, it is difficult to embody all of these characteristics all of the time. However, by living these guidelines as the rule rather than the exception, educators will more likely enjoy the respect of their learners.

The Element of Risk

While respect is a key ingredient in the teaching and learning environment, it is by no means the only one. Because of the many variables that can affect the learning experience, choosing the right teaching strategy is often a process that starts by preliminary research followed by a straightforward plunging in to the fray. Trial and error often marks the evolution toward success, as does taking on risk in this experimentation. However, there may be a educator-learner relationship payoff in doing so: "effective teachers—by [their] willing[ness] to take such risks—signal to learners that confidence and competence does not emerge fully perfected, but that in a psycho-social environment characterized by mutual respect and acceptance, both learners and teachers can learn from one another."[6]

Risks in teaching can take various forms. Some learning techniques by their nature place the educator on the sidelines in the learning process. These "learner-centered" class techniques can quickly make the educator aware of two possible contrasting outcomes. Explains Peter Filene in *The Joy of Teaching*, "the more room you leave for students to define the direction and outcome, the more they may delight you with how much and creatively they learn."[7] On the other hand, they may bicker, be apathetic, or let others do the lion's share of team projects. Educators must constantly facilitate, encourage, nudge, set deadlines, and monitor progress to mitigate these potential problems.

In order for risk taking to occur, an academic environment must exist that understands and accommodates the possible outcomes of this behavior. An educator's comfort level within this environment is central to his or her readiness to experiment. Unfortunately, the centrality some institutions place upon learner course evaluations can dissuade an otherwise willing educator from experimenting and improving teaching strategies. Some relief can be realized upon the achievement of tenure, but the two-way tug between the safety of the tried and true and experimentation is an ongoing struggle.

Student Motivation to Learn

The second support structure of student motivation embodies learners' readiness to accept new ideas and allow their incorporation into their existing understanding. Part of this readiness is reliant on intrinsic motivation that has little to do with educators' actions. However, educators can present learning opportunities that permit a sense of community and promote self-esteem within which learner motivation can grow. Broadly speaking, research suggests that students will be motivated to learn if they (1) believe the experience will help them meet their goals; (2) comprehend the value of the material; (3) have expectations that they can learn the content; and, (4) believe they can succeed in putting the content to use.[8]

In his meta-analysis of higher education research studies, Edwin Ralph's summary describes specific educator actions that instill motivation within learners:

- Link learning objectives to both classroom activities and grading.
- Use a variety of learning strategies.
- Choose strategies that learners will find stimulating from their current point of view.
- Keep presentations clear and focused.
- Include learner interaction activities and group experiences.
- Demonstrate enthusiasm for the content.
- Encourage learner contributions and use their ideas to add depth and meaning.
- Stay flexible and pursue an occasional tangent that may arise without sacrificing an entire class session.
- Become comfortable with uncertainty.
- Learn to capitalize on both educator and learner mistakes, turning them into "teaching moments" and a means to improve the learning experience.[9]

Learning Strategies

The third essential element of effective learning lies in the nature of the pedagogical strategies themselves. The choice of learning strategy is contingent on many variables that educators typically encounter, such as

1. Learner age and maturity level
2. Learner ability levels
3. Level of the course
4. The learning goals and objectives
5. Style of learning environment, including flexibility in moving seating and tables, ability to adjust lighting, and acoustic considerations
6. Number of learners enrolled in the class
7. Extent of educator's teaching experience
8. Availability of learning resources, including technology and teaching aids
9. Length of the class period
10. Length of the semester
11. Nature of the content

Six of the most common learning strategies are discussed in the following section. Each can be used in numerous different ways depending on the classroom situation. It is often a good idea to combine the strategies for several reasons:

- Varying teaching strategies keeps class time interesting. Some educators incorporate "stimulus variation," changing the activity every 20 to 30 minutes.[10] For example, a lecture can be interspersed with discussion or a writing activity.
- Research suggests that students learn in different ways. Offering various paths to understanding may bring more learners along than offering only one.[11]

LEARNING STRATEGIES: DEFINITIONS AND EXAMPLES

The broad range of interior design content and the divergent nature of the design process often challenge instructors to employ a variety of learning strategies. Familiarity with not only the use of the following strategies but also the knowledge of *when* to use them marks the experience of a seasoned, empathetic educator.

Lecture

Among the many learning strategies, lecture is among the oldest and most disparaged. By its nature, the lecture method concentrates on the "star" quality and personality of educators. Interestingly, some researchers suggest that learners will opt for a lecture instructor who possesses wit and a sense of humor over one with significant intelligence.[12] The historic popularity of lecture is due at least in part to its cost efficiency in large class-size situations. However, to discount lecture's potential is to disavow the value of a political stump speech or religious sermon. The problem for lecture in higher academia is that few educators have received training in its methods.[13] Used by itself, "pure lecturing is tolerable only for learners who are intrinsically motivated and who are skilled note-takers and synthesizers; the remainder become increasingly passive, detached and unmotivated."[14] The lecture, nonetheless, continues to endure, and offers distinct advantages to other methods:

- The timing, order, content, and points of emphasis can easily be controlled by the educator.
- Mundane material can be made more interesting by humor, drama, or personality.
- The educator can explain a difficult point instantaneously by responding to questions.
- Lectures can often include more timely information than that offered in written formats.[15]
- Lecture's formal nature implies that the information is competent and credible.[16]

The lecture method also has disadvantages:

- It is difficult to maintain learner interest and attention for a full hour of lecture.
- Lecture information is forgotten quickly, during and after the lecture.
- Because they are a passive activity for learners, lectures can be boring, especially if a room is dimmed for visual images.
- Lecture typically emphasizes low-order thinking, such as knowledge and comprehension.
- There is little accommodation of students' various learning styles.[17]

Lecture lends itself well to certain situations, such as when

- The material is not readily available to learners or is widely dispersed among many sources.
- A subject is entirely new to the learners.
- The content includes procedures that must be explained.
- The material needs to be organized in a particular way.
- Different points of view need to be communicated. However, lecture is not effective for changing existing opinions.[18]

For example, lecture might be a logical choice when introducing the procedure for using the lumen calculation method in a lighting class. This content is sufficiently difficult and distinctly linear in its structure to pose challenges to learners in formats other than lecture.

Anatomy of a Lecture

In his 1994 article "The Lecture Method," William Ekeler describes how to lead an effective, organized lecture:

1. Set the tone and get learners' attention. Ask a rhetorical question, provide an odd example, or present contradictory information.
2. Tell them what you're going to tell them. Let learners see the destination.
3. Present the guts of the argument. Associate the content with where the learners currently are, adding to their existing framework.

4. Prompt learners to apply the information through active discussion or otherwise taking action.
5. Evaluate the learner's understanding through written reflection or other means.[19]

These components of a good lecture are critical within the structure of the lecture itself. In addition, the ideas that follow offer many strategies that will enable even the most timid lecturer to be successful.

Strategies for Giving a Good Lecture

- Be well rested. Take fifteen minutes and reflect on the topic prior to class time.
- Make frequent eye contact with learners. If using a writing surface, square the shoulders toward the learners as often as possible.
- Never use absolutely complete lecture notes. Structure notes so that you can make eye contact and expand on a point without looking down.
- Prepare buzzwords or other techniques to capture learners' attention and emotions.
- Include multiple examples to illustrate concepts.
- Circle around frequently, reviewing and repeating key points.
- Indicate a hierarchy of ideas through voice inflection or repetition.
- Raise an occasional question, and be sure to pause for learner reflection time and responses. (For example, "Have you ever seen an exotic wood used in an interior?")[20]
- Don't always play the expert. The expert lecturer briefly relinquishes dominance on occasion to stimulate discussion and interest.
- Never quite complete a lecture. Leaving material unresolved keeps it fresh.[21]
- Provide learners with handouts of the lecture's headings, leaving room for them to fill in detailed notes.
- Use arousal to build interest:

  - Use novelty: Come to class dressed as Thomas Chippendale for a lecture on 18th century furniture making, for example.
  - Use surprise: Facetiously propose that learners never take a design project on so that they are never disappointed with the outcome.
  - Include unexpected activities: Have learners write questions that may be included on the exam.
  - Incorporate learner discovery within lecture: For example, have learners bring in a tape measure and measure the distance from their navel to the top of their heads and from their navel to the floor to facilitate a discussion on the golden mean proportion (i.e., if the distances are averaged over the entire class, they come out to about 1 to 1.6).[22]

Building Interactive Learning into Lectures

By its nature, lecture is a passive activity for learners and not always likely to result in retained understanding. Therefore, an educator should seek to engage learners in activities beyond merely writing notes and listening. Table 4.1 provides examples of active learning that can be used alongside traditional lecture.

There are many possible activities that can help illustrate or enliven lecture material, especially if technology is added to the mix. For example, Bowman, Hodges, Allison, and Wineman report that when a lecture on zoo habitat design was complemented by a virtual digital habitat simulation with embedded text and audio, learners scored higher on a test than learners that had attended only the lecture.[23]

TABLE 4.1: IDEAS FOR INTEGRATING ACTIVE LEARNING STRATEGIES INTO A LECTURE

Strategy	Interior design learning example
Oral question/answer episodes	Play "Renaissance Jeopardy": learners respond to an answer such as "This bronze sculptor's Gates of Paradise on the Baptistry of Italy's Florence Cathedral represented the high point in early Renaissance bronze work." The learner with the response "Who is Lorenzo Ghiberti?" (and it must be phrased as a question!) wins points leading to a "Renaissance Jeopardy Champion" certificate.
Paired problem solving: "Think, pair, share"	Learners pause during a lecture on fabric construction to compare two textile fabric swatches, deciding which is a twill weave.
Short discussions	The instructor switches from lecture on place attachment to group discussion on the "sense of place" within dorm rooms.
Resource-based exercise (supply students with a stimulus, then get them to resolve a problem)	The instructor pauses during a lecture on lighting fixture design and gives learner teams index cards, scissors, and a flashlight. Each team constructs a light filter exploring light cutoff and light/shadow pattern.
Brief independent study activities	The learners consider two office space plans for 10 minutes to understand their circulation patterns before lecture is resumed.
Minute papers	The instructor pauses after 20 minutes of lecture and asks the students to write their answer to the question "What was Mies van der Rohe's main contribution to interior design?"

Adapted from Ralph, E. (1998). *Motivation Teaching in Higher Education: A Manual for Faculty Development.* Stillwater, OK: New Forums Press Inc., p. 125.

Discussion

Leading an effective, thought-provoking discussion in a classroom setting can be among the most challenging learning methodologies. The potential pitfalls are many:

- An opening question elicits only silence.
- A discussion quickly digresses into distracting minutiae.
- Some shy learners never participate, and others aggressively dominate the exchange.
- Learners blurt out inappropriate statements that anger or alienate others.
- The discussion leads into content unfamiliar to the educator.
- The educator loses control over the discussion.[24]

While discussion can be a risky undertaking, especially for the new educator, research suggests that discussion can be more effective than lectures in promoting high levels of learning such as analysis, synthesis and critique.[25] Discussion can also promote learners' speaking skills and ability to extemporaneously form and express an opinion. It can also promote a flexible world view.[26]

Ralph suggests that discussion is an appropriate learning technique if certain conditions are met:

- Learners must learn to develop and defend their point of view logically.
- Learners need to examine multiple perspectives on a subject.

- Interacting with others on the subject will lead to new insights.
- Learners have prior background knowledge on the subject.
- The topic is somewhat controversial or otherwise interesting.
- The educator feels very prepared and knowledgeable in the subject matter.[27]

For example, the interior design topic of designing for the homeless might yield a fruitful discussion. Interior design learners have at least a cursory exposure to homelessness through the media or other outlets, and the topic can be controversial when multiple factual and personal points of view are shared.

Strategies for Ensuring Effective Class Discussion

The primary goal of discussion is to make learners feel heard and therefore, empowered. Participation lies at the heart of enduring understanding. There are many strategies that help discussion facilitate learning:

1. Make sure the text is appropriate, but in ways beyond content. That is, course references should validate learners' life experiences, such as identity, autonomy, self-esteem, relationships, and career aspirations. The references should make the connection with learners that this content is important to them, even right NOW.
2. Both educators and learners should be prepared for the discussion in advance. Readings should help provide learners with "ammunition" for forming their opinions so that discussions do not disintegrate into the "blind leading the blind." For example, the educator tells learners that next Friday everyone will discuss the role of open office systems in promoting corporate creativity.
3. Educators must enter the discussion with a clear purpose and an identifiable question or problem to tackle. Writing ideas on the board can help remind learners of this focus.
4. Discussions must be well organized to be logical and understandable. Many effective discussions move from the concrete to the abstract. For example, a discussion that starts with the question "What was in the living room of Catherine Beecher's ideal house that was so unusual?" might later move toward the question "How did Beecher's ideals for home design impact women's rights?"
5. The best discussions capture all participants and make contributing safe. If learners contribute early, they are more likely to keep participating. Some educators begin a discussion with an ice-breaking verbal group exercise, such as having learners call out personal adjectives they associate with a particular interior environment. A brief writing assignment at the beginning is another tactic that allows everyone to collect their thoughts.
6. It is important to address the potential for monopolization of the discussion. One effective strategy is that people who have spoken twice before must wait until two people have spoken on a question before they can. A hand-raising policy can offer openings for shy learners to participate and lets the educator control who is participating.
7. Visuals can be a tool to stimulate focus. Alternately, learners can create the visuals themselves. For example, the educator prompts the learners to draw the strongest furniture joint they can think of. This activity sets the tone for a discussion of appropriate specification of restaurant chairs.
8. The educator must bring the group back together from time to time, interrupt-

ing the flow of conversation to regroup. Asking "Where are we at this point?" or "What have we learned?" can help bring clarity to the discussion.

9. Effective discussions have a satisfying conclusion. Summarizing the main points at the end can help learners assess what they have gained from the experience.
10. If assigning a part of the learner's grade to "participation," it is important to define the desired behavior. Some educators keep track of questions posed to learners, making sure to ask each learner two or three questions per semester, and factoring the thoughtfulness and preparedness of these responses in with other grading components. This strategy represents "high stakes" participation that may either intimidate or motivate some learners and should be used with awareness and care.[28]

Discussions can take various forms. For example, a discussion does not have to involve the entire class. Woolcock describes an effective strategy that can heighten individual learner participation through small groups:

> An important instructional goal, particularly in discussion sections, is to maximize the amount of "time on task" of each student, or less formally, to ensure that the time that instructors and students have together is as productive as possible. A simple strategy to this end, especially at the start of semester when everyone is a stranger, is to break class discussion up into small groups: it uses peer pressure to ensure that students actually do the readings (thereby lowering the familiar "free-rider" problem) while simultaneously helping students get to know each other. In a large discussion group each student may get to say one or two things in a fifty minute section; in a small group discussion lasting thirty minutes, the same student gets to discuss perhaps five or six issues, leaving fifteen minutes for a more lively general feedback session. Notice here that the role of instructor also changes profoundly, from being leader to facilitator. During discussions, move from group to group answering questions where necessary, while gauging the quality of analysis within each. When it is time for feedback from each group, get the groups to respond in ascending order of strength so that the stronger groups have to go beyond the more mundane remarks made by the earlier groups.[29]

Discussion holds much potential for interior design education, especially because interior design so often involves high-level synthesis of information into design solutions that command an understanding of complex human behavior. Educator Lisa Waxman has found discussion to be an important part of her Social and Psychological Issues in Interior Design class, and regularly incorporates current events quizzes and news stories into in-class discussion. Web-based discussion board participation is also a course requirement, and Waxman reports that this mode of discourse helps shy learners participate, stimulates in-class follow up discussion, and appears to enhance the class's sense of community.[30]

Team Learning

Learning in groups has long been a means to creative outcomes for the interior design profession as well as architecture. A 2007 questionnaire on visual communication practices distributed to professional interior designers suggested that 72% of respondents produced brainstorming sketches with other design team members present some of the time, often, or quite a bit.[31] The Council for Interior Design Accreditation accordingly mandates that teaching and learning methods must incorporate both "team approaches to design solutions" and "experiences that provide interaction with multiple disciplines representing a variety of points of view and perspectives on design problems."[32]

In addition to modeling group behaviors they will experience in their later careers, team learning also offers benefits in college-level collaboration, often manifested in the form of team projects of various lengths:

- Team projects can increase motivation, especially if there is an industry or real-world connection.
- Team projects may be a more comforting way to introduce the vagueness and ambiguity of real-world projects to learners than projects where learners work alone.[33]
- Collaboration prompts learners to accept more responsibility than other learning strategies such as lecture and empowers them to be masters of their own learning.
- Team work can help overcome stereotypes and can assist international learners in building social networks.
- Group projects offer learners experience with managing group dynamics and can build leadership skills.
- Collaboration can build respect for the results of team thinking and can help learners see beyond the "diva" way of designing projects.
- Long-term team projects (of longer than one class period in duration) allow learners to get feedback from each other that can help mitigate individual weaknesses that learners might hesitate to share with educators.

Team learning offers several advantages to the educator as well:

- Team collaboration can offset the anonymity of large classes and can get learners interacting at higher cognitive learning skills than are otherwise possible. It is difficult at times, however, to be sure all are working equally diligently.
- Group-based teaching moves responsibility for excitement and enthusiasm for teaching from the instructor to the teams, thus avoiding premature instructor burnout.[34] (For more information on burnout, see Chapter 2.)

There may be evidence that interior design learners themselves recognize that group thinking has its benefits. In a 2002 study by Park-Gates and colleagues, interior design learners reported that while they found it more difficult to generate ideas in a group, they simultaneously believed that doing so would generate more ideas than working alone.[35]

Characteristics of Effective Team Learning Activities

Given the probable benefits of team learning, educators should strive to integrate collaboration into learning situations where it makes the most sense to do so. The best collaborative assignments (1) promote learning of identified concepts; (2) build the group's cohesion; (3) ensure individual accountability; and, (4) demonstrate the value of group interaction.[36] Beyond these general goals, Michaelsen identifies six concrete characteristics of effective group assignments:

1. The task should produce a tangible output so the group sees its effectiveness.
2. It should be impossible to create the output without understanding of course concepts—so learners see the content's worth.
3. The task must be sufficiently difficult that it takes a team to accomplish it.

Otherwise only a few group members will bear the burden.

4. The group assignment should include both solitary activities (such as background research) and group activities (for example, discussion and choosing the plan of attack).
5. It should be easy for learners to see how the project translates to later career activities.
6. The group assignment should be interesting to the learners.[37]

An interior design instructional case study illustrates these points. In a materials and methods class, learners must learn how to conduct background research on materials to ensure their appropriateness for commercial application. This information is equally valuable to working design professionals. Hence, a three-person team project was created with the goal of providing needed background research on new interior design materials to practitioners. In order of the six characteristics discussed: (1) the tangible output of the team project was a verbal and digital visual presentation and a brochure for their "adopted" practitioner; (2) and (3) the required background research and time to develop the output products was sufficiently complex to involve all three team members; (4) the team project involved solitary background research and brainstorming meetings to create the presentations and brochure; (5) the worth of the activity was clear to the learners as they received immediate appreciative feedback from the practitioners and generated networking contacts; and, (6) the background research was, in most cases, inherently interesting to the learners who were not previously knowledgeable about the materials.[38]

Managing Team Projects Effectively

Like any learning strategy, educators can present and manage interior design team projects well or poorly. Due to their human dynamics orientation, team projects have special aspects that make some educators shy away from their use. Anderson and colleagues describe that this wariness is due to educators' lack of successful methods in (1) creating teams; (2) guiding and monitoring teamwork toward positive outcomes; and, (3) evaluating team outcomes effectively.[39] The discussion that follows presents strategies that confront these issues.

Team Creation. Educators face their first dilemma in a team project as they guide learners into workable team units. One obvious choice is to allow learners to gather themselves into teams. However, this typically results in a homogenous membership who typically get along well at the beginning, yet "lack a range of perspectives which may assist in error cancellation and the development . . . of discussion which can promote innovative ideas."[40] Allowing self-selection into groups can also stir feelings of discontent for those who have been left out.[41]

Interestingly, effective teams often follow the model of "forming, storming, norming and performing".[42] Groups that have sufficient diversity to "storm," (i.e., disagree) in their early formation often exhibit enhanced creative outcomes.[43] This would support the educator choosing team members and also mirrors the autocracy of team makeup in the interior design profession. Educator choice has the added benefit of loading teams to maximize diversity in ability, culture, interests, age, gender, or other criteria. However, there seem to be few guarantees for success. For example, Amor & Wilson's study found that grouping interior design team members to maximize diversity in Myers Briggs personality indicators sometimes led to weak teams despite the members' diverse personality characteristics.[44]

Guiding Teams Toward Success. Team projects are an example of constructivist learning and have the interesting effect of sidelining the centrality of the educator from the "sage on the stage" to the "guide on the side."[45] This can be at once liberating and terrifying for educators as the apparent loss of control and ability to guide the project from minute to minute is lost. However, several tips can help make the team management process go more smoothly:

1. Providing orientation materials can give learners a sense of security over where they are going. This should include guidance on managing team interactions. For example, learners may be unfamiliar with strategies for taking notes and identifying "action items" during group discussions.
2. Established deadlines can help teams manage their time to meet goals. By identifying the due date, teams can work backwards from this deadline and budget their time.
3. It is necessary to be reasonable about the time teams will take to accomplish tasks. Team projects always take more time than individual projects, and team members may be unfamiliar with this issue.
4. Educators should let teams struggle and resist the temptation to rush in to heal team dynamics disagreements. Often the best and most long-lasting lessons are learned as team members sort issues out themselves. Learners benefit from knowing that disagreements are common and to be expected.
5. Simultaneously, educators should reassure teams that they are there for them as needed. Staying abreast of team progress is critical so that a tip, idea, or nudge toward action can be offered at the right time.

Evaluating team outcomes. The nature of collaborative projects can make the "untangling" of who did what difficult for educators when evaluation time arrives. There are typically three necessary assessment components to ensure fairness and motivation.

1. An individual performance grade ensures individual accountability. This might be through individual tests or independently graded parts of projects.
2. A group performance grade issued by the educator provides incentives to support the group activity components.
3. A confidential peer evaluation keeps learners from feeling they have to either receive a low grade on group assignments through no fault of their own or must do most of the group work themselves.[46] See Figure 4.1 for an example.

The relative weight of these three components must be set in advance so learners understand the emphasis placed on each. It is also possible to place this weighting decision in the hands of learners by having a representative from each team negotiate with the educator to reach an agreement.[47] Additionally, some educators urge learners to establish agreements with each other in writing, indicating the responsibilities of each team member so as to avoid later misunderstandings.

It can be a positive experience for learners if the educator sets incremental deadlines to allow for "formative" team assessment, placing percentages of the project grade earlier than the end so teams have the opportunity to learn and grow from their successes and their mistakes.

Educators should expect that a small percentage of teams will not have a smooth group experience. It is helpful to have an appeals process in place that permits team members to inform their team colleagues during the

INT123 Commercial Studio

Your name: ______________________________

Team Self-Evaluation

Please complete the following regarding your opinion of the team's ability to share work on this phase of the project. Your answers will be held in my confidence and may influence up to 10% of an individual's project grade.

	1	2	3	4	5
Rate your own performance on the project from 1 (poor) to 5 (outstanding) regarding your follow-through and attendance to high quality in your project responsibilities.	☐	☐	☐	☐	☐

Explain/justify your rating here:

Your Project Partners

Reflect on your partners' contributions to the project. Rate their performance from 1 (poor) to 5 (outstanding)

		1	2	3	4	5
Partner 1 name: ______________________	Rating:	☐	☐	☐	☐	☐

Explain/justify your rating here:

Rate your partners' performance from 1 (poor) to 5 (outstanding)

		1	2	3	4	5
Partner 2 name: ______________________	Rating:	☐	☐	☐	☐	☐

Explain/justify your rating here:

Figure 4.1 The peer evaluation form provides learners the opportunity to reflect on the efforts of themselves and their colleagues.

project's progress that the burden is not being equally shared. See Figure 4.2 for an example of an appeals process.

Peer evaluations are a reflection of these sometimes rocky relationships and offer educators the opportunity to discount certain learners' grades if they have failed to hold up their end of the team bargain. Care should be taken, however, in penalizing one learner due to only one other student's say-so. It may be easier to have teams composed of odd numbers (for example, three or five) so that a majority of team members' comments can influence an individual's grade. As personality conflicts are sometimes an unavoidable part of team projects, it is also prudent to keep that percentage of an individual's grade dependent on peer evaluation to a reasonable proportion of the total, such as a maximum of 10 to 15%. This is especially helpful in that learners can at times be judgmental in their evaluations of their team colleagues, which can cause scores

TEAMWORK AND ARBITRATION POLICY

Most commercial design projects are executed by teams of professionals. Because of this reality, you are currently engaged in a team project to provide experience in working with others toward a joint solution.

It is the responsibility of all team members to

- be committed to project activities;
- contribute to project requirements consistently;
- approach the team environment with an attitude of support and an open mind; and,
- support one's partner by setting schedules, upholding commitments, and providing follow-through of tasks.

As in all relationships, effective team interaction must be established, built and maintained. This means

- approach your partner with an attitude of working together to solve challenges;
- avoid an attitude of 'that's not my job'. While each partner has responsibilities that they are held to, most project details need to emerge through collaborative thinking to be cohesive;
- if you agree to do something, follow through and do it on time and to the best of your ability; and,
- exceed your partner's expectations.

It is the responsibility of team members to solve problems, including those arising from your working relationship. It should be rare that issues are brought before instructors. With this in mind, and if all else fails, the following explains the team arbitration process.

Arbitration Procedure

Miscommunication or lack of follow-through can lead to a dysfunctional team and a poor project outcome. Seek to talk things through first. If this fails to resolve the problem, then the following documentation process may be used. The process allows members to air their complaints and keeps all team members appraised of these occurrences. *Note that the arbitration process itself is time intensive and will lessen the time and energy that you have to complete the project requirements.*

Stage 1

Document the issue in writing on the attached sheet.

a. Provide a copy of this sheet to your partner, who then fills out their point of view (rebuttal) on the same sheet and in turn provides you a copy.
b. The initiating partner makes a copy of this completed document and provides it to the instructor.
c. At this point, the instructor does not intervene.

Stage 2

Document the issue in writing on the attached sheet for the second time.

a. Provide a copy of this sheet to your partner, who then fills out their point of view (rebuttal) on the same sheet and in turn provides you a copy.
b. The initiating partner makes a copy of this completed document and provides it to the instructor.
c. Again, at this point, the instructor does not intervene.

Figure 4.2 The appeals process ensures that team members are communicating their disagreements to each other prior to involving the educator. The process is also sufficiently time consuming to dissuade frivolous disagreements from reaching the educator's attention.

Stage 3

a. On the third incident/team relationship issue, the sheet is filled out by both partners for the last time and both team members initiate and arrange an in-person meeting with the instructor(s), bringing the completed report with them. This meeting will result in one of the following options:
   a. The instructor facilitates arbitration to resolve the issues and the team completes the project.
   b. The team is dissolved and each partner completes project requirements that may be modified at the instructor's discretion. *Note that this option will likely require more work and time than the original project format for both partners.*

Working well in a team environment is a main objective of this project and a central skill you should take into your career. Instructors are prepared to assess the situation and, if appropriate, document non-performance by one or both partners which may in turn affect the project grade outcome.

Team Incident Report

Team member initiating this report: ______________________________

Other team member name: ______________________________

Team Incident Report #   1   2   3

Describe the event(s) that led to the completion of this report. Be specific, as appropriate, with dates and other details.

Efforts put forth to date to resolve this issue:

Signature of initiating team member: ______________________________

Date: ______________________________

Other team member rebuttal to this issue:

Signature of team member providing rebuttal: ______________________________

Date: ______________________________

Figure 4.2 (*Continued*)

to differ from what an instructor would render for the same individual.[48]

Seminars

Like team learning, seminars engage learners in group discovery. Originally used exclusively for graduate students, the seminar is increasingly becoming a staple of undergraduate learning as well.[49] Seminars excel in supporting the "intentional learner": a student who is "purposeful and self-directed, an integrative thinker who makes connections between and beyond fields of study . . . and ways of knowing."[50] In other words, seminars work particularly well with self-motivated, focused learners. It also suits the sometimes comprehensive nature of interior design issues and procedures.

The seminar learning format is usually defined by a class size between five and twenty learners and a room configured so all participants can sit in a circle. Some sort of shared focus or task unites a seminar group with the educator who typically assumes a facilitator role. For example, an interior design theory class might together discuss and critique a recently published book.

Much like other classroom learning strategies, seminars are most effective when the educator is prepared both in the target content and to listen and react to learners' comments. Maintaining flexibility with the direction of discussion can help enhance the relevance of a seminar discussion and help learners scaffold new ideas into their current understanding. Educator skill in guiding discussions back to the topic at hand may also be necessary.

Seminars are particularly helpful in giving learners friendly criticism as they work through new ideas or solutions. A sense of participation and responsibility are necessary in seminars, and these qualities can lead to ownership, promoting a group sense of progress toward a shared understanding.[51]

Case Studies

Most would agree that effective interior design decision making is an intricate undertaking wrapped up in the complexities of human dynamics. It is therefore sometimes difficult to untangle distinct pieces of content from the entire canvas of an interior design project. For this reason, case study analysis can bring contextual understanding of complicated issues to learners. By definition, a case study "investigates a phenomenon or setting in relation to the complex dynamics with which it intersects."[52] Case studies are a popular learning method in many fields, including law, business, and medicine. Case studies are also a popular interior design research method, as a yield of 143 hits on the term *case study* at the InformeDesign interior design research website reveals.[53] However, there are key differences between case study research and case studies used for teaching purposes. Case studies in educational contexts are chiefly meant to stimulate focused discussion amongst learners and typically examine only one case, rather than many, at any given time.[54]

The case study learning method holds multiple promises for learner motivation and immersion in new ideas that only discovery can produce. One educator likens the strategy to a journey:

> The explorer . . . does not know what terrain and adventures his journey holds in store for him. He has yet to discover mountains, deserts, and water holes and to suffer fever, starvation, and other hardships. Finally, when the explorer returns from his journey, he will have the hard-won knowledge of the country he has traversed.[55]

Ideally, then, the case study presents situational knowledge to the learner in a personal and psychological way, driving home the importance and context of targeted concepts. The true case study intimately involves the learner in a questioning process designed to prompt logical reasoning.

There are various ways to use case studies for learning in the visual arts. The traditional method used by many fields such as law immerses learners in the primary lineal nature of human interaction, such as verbal or legal procedures. Used in this fashion, case studies can promote introspection and present quality opportunities for making moral and ethical choices. Grounded in the "dirtiness" of life experiences, they can spawn unexpected outcomes that keep learning fresh.[56]

Interior design professional practices topics that explore business procedures, interactions with clients and colleagues, and ethical dilemmas immediately come to mind with procedural-style case studies. University of Manitoba educator Akemi Miyahara found that the case study instructional method lent a "real world" aspect to a graduate-level interior design professional practice course. The integrated involvement of practitioners with the learners underlined the relevancy of case studies presented in the class's issued-based format.[57]

Case studies can be equally useful in the hands of a creative educator to explore how the design process was used to reach a particular finished design solution or how a concept was generated. For example, professional periodicals such as *Interior Design* and *Contract* regularly feature articles that examine a finished interior design project in some depth.[58] A resourceful educator might contact the firm to explore a targeted aspect of the project (such as development of concept, for example) via phone interview. The educator could then fashion a case study around the example and lead learners on a discovery through the "eyes" of the designers. A member of the project's team might even be tempted by the enterprising educator to lead the class discussion him or herself with the help of classroom technology equipment.

Qualities of Good Case Studies

Effectiveness in case study learning lies in the potential to immerse learners in a seemingly real situation. Therefore, sufficient description of the situation, involved persons, and surrounding context are important inclusions. Whether in written or other form, case study material should be well written and expressed in a conversational, narrative style that is clear to learners. The case should also be sufficiently complex to allow the educator to get at complex meanings such as ethics, procedures, or high cognitive-level design thinking such as concept expression. The journey of case study exploration makes this method compelling; thus, a case with alternative paths to success can maintain a pleasing sense of mystery and discovery. Similarly, case studies should not necessarily offer an immediate solution so that opportunities arise for debate and even doubt.

There are many tips for successfully using case study method within instruction:

- It is critical to use a case study strategically, with identified content objectives in mind. The educator must be prepared to guide learners toward key points.
- The educator must be prepared to respond quickly to questions that arise about the case.
- Learners should be held accountable for discovering points and reaching their own conclusions about the case.
- It is tempting for educators to offer their own opinion about the case too early. They should instead allow learners to sufficiently analyze the case before jumping in. At all points, it is important for both

learners and educator to respect others' positions during discussion.[59]

- Careful educator guidance can help learners avoid emphasis on non-relevant information or minute details.
- Case studies can overwhelm beginning or insecure learners with their breadth and complexity. Care is needed to limit the topic or otherwise provide a comfortably sized home base from which discussion can spring.

Further Suggestions for Interior Design Case Study Learning

- Explore a finished commercial project that was completed by a design team composed of various specialty fields such as interior design, architecture, and engineering. How did the team work through its group decision-making process? Did consequences of this interaction affect the project outcome?
- Lead learners on an in-depth discovery of the interior materials specifications for a disastrous project, such as Pruitt-Igoe public housing in St. Louis. What role did the specified materials play (if any) in the project's demolition only a few years later? What alternatives might have been better solutions?
- Take learners on a post-occupancy evaluation tour of a real project in a nearby locale. If possible, have the designer of the project lead the field trip experience, sharing successes and failures of the project solution with learners. Work with the designer in advance of the trip, having him or her fashion a series of questions, prompting the learners to make "decisions" for the project. The designer can then discuss learners' choices while on location.
- Ask learners if they personally like a project. In the context of a discussion of aesthetics, prompt learners to phrase their replies using elements and principles of design terminology (i.e., form, line, proportion, emphasis, scale) to justify their opinions.

Role Playing and Simulations

Like case studies, role playing provides the opportunity to immerse learners in the richness of a specific experience. The goal is to "force [learners] to 'pass through' the actual event within the safety of a classroom."[60] There is a key difference between case studies and role playing exercises. Role playing provides the learner an actual identity within a situation instead of keeping the learner in the observer mode of the case study method. Simulations are similar to role playing except they last longer. This "first person" stance can be an exciting way to instill confidence in learners and prepare them emotionally to deal with future situations. Applied correctly, role playing can be an impactful and enjoyable way to not only learn but also integrate material into a learner's mental framework in a long-lasting way.

A role playing exercise typically involves reenacting a lifelike situation through a short skit. The players are typically two or more learner volunteers. However, it is also possible to give half of the class one role and the other half a second role, charging each team with working their way toward a solution. Like case studies, role playing exercises are best used to explore concepts identified in advance by the educator. Situations that involve two or more persons with potentially conflicting points of view are familiar role playing topics. Role playing exercises can be particularly effective if the educator stops the action at key points and discusses the emotions, decisions, or attitudes of the evolving dilemma.

Role playing is best used when class members are somewhat familiar and comfortable with each other to avoid embarrassment or emotional exposure. The role playing learning strategy offers several positive features to learning:

- Situations make it easy for learners to see the application of learned content.
- Scenarios can help sensitize learners to other points of view. This is particularly true if learners must assume a point of view that is counter to their own beliefs or personality.
- Role playing can help learners emotionally prepare for confrontational situations or issues of ethics and morality and help learners develop the skill to make quick, confident decisions.[61]

The effectiveness of role playing exercises can be maximized with a group debriefing at the conclusion. It is here that a recap of the logical progression through the problem can be analyzed step by step for its appropriateness.

Business relationship issues are potentially strong topics for interior design role playing exercises. For example, Jill Pable created a series of role playing exercises that allow learners to assume a series of paired client-interior designer identities to rehearse relationship dilemmas. Learners read a short story that helped them take on their persona and mood and placed them in a potentially unpleasant encounter with their partner. Learners were asked to play out their part, then work toward a mutually amicable resolution. See Figure 4.3 for an excerpt from these role playing challenges.

Narrative Learning

Case studies, role playing, and simulations explore representations of life experiences.

Client-Interior Designer Role Playing Challenge Exercise

You will play the role of the client. You are the president of the First American Bank and you have hired an interior designer to propose an interior solution for the new downtown branch bank in your city. The First American Bank's corporate identity must exude its long-term stability and reliability to its investors. All of the other nearby branches express this by using early traditional American furnishings and finishes. You are interested in maintaining solidarity with these other branches and wish the interior designer to conform to this style. There are other branches of the bank in nearby cities which break with this mold, but you are less familiar with these more modern styles of finishes, and they strike you as 'cold' and 'sterile'. The interior designer will now meet with you to express his/her early stylistic direction for the branch office.

You will play the role of the designer. You have been hired to propose a new design for the interior of the First American Bank by the president of the downtown branch. In your preliminary meeting with him/her, you have been introduced to the bank's corporate identity and know that stability and long-term reliability are important qualities to reflect in the interior. A review of nearby branch banks shows that most of them use fairly predictable early American furnishings and finishes. However, other branches in a nearby city embrace a more contemporary approach. Having just completed a walk-through of the new branch's building for your project, you note the building's strong modernist character, and sense that inserting traditional early American furnishings into this context will be jarring and inappropriate. You feel strongly that the building should be respected in decision-making for the new branch. You will now speak with the president who would like to know your early stylistic direction for the new branch.

Figure 4.3 A short description of a learner's role sets the scene for a business negotiation. By Jill Pable (April, 1995), Putting Students on the Firing Line: Interactive Multimedia Client-Interior Designer Computer Challenges. International Interior Design Educator's Council Conference sponsored by the Interior Design Educator's Council, Nashville, TN (international). Proceedings pages 114–116.

In this way they are similar to narrative teaching techniques. Simply stated, narrative uses storytelling to impart deep meaning to learners, and can be "deeply appealing and richly satisfying to the human soul, with an allure that transcends cultures, centuries, ideologies, and academic disciplines."[62] Part of the appeal of narrative storytelling lies in its connection to human perceptions of a situation. Theorist Jerome Bruner is an advocate of narrative learning, and he describes the two modes of human thinking. The first is **paradigmatic thought**, or scientific reasoning that relies on explanation and verification. The second is **narrative thought,** which pairs action with consciousness and the willing, feeling, and thinking of a person. "To focus entirely on paradigmatic modes of thought is to pull away from attending to consciousness, and therefore, to the human act of sense-making."[63] Thus, stories demand active meaning-making and serve as "a stimulus to imagination, as well as to greater self- and social-awareness. Story stirs imagination, and it also points to realities that are not easily communicated in conceptual forms."[64]

By its nature, storytelling bears some resemblance to the interior design process, as

BOX 4-1 SPATIAL EXPERIENCE NARRATIVES

Having learners imagine another person's experience of the space they are designing can help them cognitively sort through issues of emphasis, scale, and other key decisions. Written narratives are wonderful tools for describing qualitative aspects of a project. They paint a vivid picture of what if feels like to *experience* the space in such ways as

- Sense of enclosure
- What activities occur in a space
- The emotional quality of an area
- Light
- Materiality

Narratives cannot describe *all* aspects of a space, but they help the designer work through the decision making from the emotional point of view of the client. They are written in the present tense. Although narratives may not accurately represent what is eventually built, they help the designer and client agree on key concepts early on. For example:

The project consists of a series of two aligned chambers; the first one (the foyer) is circular in shape with a tall sculpted ceiling. The foyer provides a cross-axis with left and right access leading to the dining room and bedroom, respectively. The foyer is visually different from these corridors' light level and ceiling height. The chambers progress from compressed and expectant to expansive and wide beyond the foyer as the visitor moves toward the main living area, where exterior window walls are located. During the day this area is bathed with natural light that reflects off the walls and polished stainless steel trim, adding a sense of sparkle and vibrancy to the entertaining that occurs there. A long wall provides a strong, linear and unified backdrop to any activity. The kitchen is to the left within the living area and is visually distinguished from the larger space by its more vibrant color and dramatic stovetop hood, which divides the two spaces. The suite celebrates focal points, creating esthetic scenes at the conclusion of sight-line corridors via art and dramatic spotlighting.

both are engaged in "selecting and organizing chaotic events" and "enable [learners] to discern how diverse elements come together to form meaningful experiences."[65] Learning through stories can be a potent way to instill empathy within design learners for the users of their interior environments. (See Box 4.1 for an example of a "spatial experience narrative" teaching exercise.)

Interior design educators Danko, Meneely, and Portillo successfully used narratives within a corporate studio project. Before the programming phase began, learners read a first person account of a user's perceptions of the workplace to sensitize them to underlying meanings of the space. Prior to drawing in the schematic phase, learners wrote their own narrative in the person of someone visiting the office space they were to design. Narratives were again employed in the final presentation of the project, and learners explained their solution using narrative presented through graphic means and in walk-throughs. The educators reported success with their use of narratives within the design process, noting that they "nurtured empathy, encouraged multi-sensory conceptualization and visualization and facilitated holistic designing."[66]

Drama

Interior design education's emphasis on the personal, human scale of space makes the use of drama, or reenactment, an exciting prospect. The increasing simplicity of sound and image recording software is making design projects using this media more feasible. Studies suggest the use of drama in general can play a key part in arousing and sustaining adult student motivation.[67]

There are many possible ways to incorporate recorded pieces as a vehicle for student learning in interior design. For example, learners might develop a two-minute video that prompts them to test the validity of factual lecture content in a real situation. One possibility is photo-documenting code violations in a public restroom. Another is videotaping the physical challenges of a wheelchair-based person entering a building, capturing their verbal comments and emotions along the way, thus lending a human face to the sterility of codes. Graduate-level study opens up further possibilities. Future educator learners might be charged with developing a new interior design course, then presenting the course to their colleagues through a one-minute "promotional" video. Early learner exposure to video communication methods may also pay off in learners' job-seeking skills, as digital multimedia is playing an increasingly frequent part in graduating portfolios.[68]

Other Learning Techniques

Learning activities by no means must conform exclusively to the techniques described above. Combinations or derivatives of these strategies or entirely different ideas can be successful as well. A list of starter ideas follows, none of which strictly conform to the categories of techniques already discussed.

- Assign a quick open-ended writing exercise to confirm learners' digestion of a topic. For example, have learners write about their experiences about a particular interior design solution from the point of view of a child or someone who suffers from autism.
- Arrange an informal panel discussion. Bring in a faculty colleague to discuss varying points of view on the use of the term *interior architecture.* Or gather several learner volunteers to form a panel of their own.
- Engage learners in interviews, polls, focus groups, or surveys. Parents, friends, or persons on the street can be interviewed about an issue. Have learners write and

administer an opinion poll or focus group on an issue. (Be sure to check your institution's policy on human subjects when involving other persons in activities.) For example, learners could interview friends about their motivations for choosing their home furnishings styles, inquiring about the relative importance of function, cost, and aesthetics.

- Have learners put on a public exhibit or arrange an afternoon symposium to discuss their research with members of the institution or community. This technique works particularly well with design issues that intersect in an impactful, understandable way with the public. Learners might display the results of a sustainability audit for a campus building to the building's users, for example.
- Go on a treasure hunt. For example, have learners identify color palettes in a walk through various campus buildings.
- Consider an idea from a different point of view. What will life be like in residential interiors in 2060? In 2160?
- Let fantasy play a role. Challenge learners to design a desk for a person from another planet who has ten arms.
- Reverse roles. Decide in advance who will be the educators that day, and have those learners analyze a reading or a chapter. (This one is best left to classes with the emotional maturity to make the learning experience positive.)
- Go on a field trip. Seeing the reality of an interior environment often trumps talking abstractly about it in a classroom.
- Consider co-teaching a class with another faculty member or outside expert. This technique can both lighten the teaching load and bring fresh perspective to course content.
- Do something meaningful and interesting with learner results of a class study or project. (Again, be sure to check university policy on human subjects for gathering human data.) Create a presentation for the student union; let the display go on tour throughout the state; or have learners present their information to local professionals.
- Bring in an expert for a specific topic. Educators are not expected to know everything, and detailed or timely information coming from outside sources enhances a course's relevance and credibility.[69]
- Reinforce the meaning behind design decisions. Have learners make something for a close friend or family member, emphasizing the giving aspect of design.[70]

Choosing the Right Strategy for the Learning Objective

Given the many variables of a course, including the learners, the variety of course content within interior design curricula, and the different types of physical classroom facilities, choosing the type of learning strategy can be intimidating, especially for new educators. Table 4.2 provides examples of learning strategies appropriately paired with typical interior design curricular goals.

Tips for Developing a Successful New Class Exercise or Project

One of the most creative activities educators engage in is constructing new learning experiences to meet identified goals. Well-conceived and executed exercises can result in learner motivation and enhanced understanding that help learners comprehend new ideas. Conversely, the experience can be demoralizing, stress-filled, or boring. Some (but not all) of learners' perceptions are the result of educator design and planning of the activity.

Not coincidentally, designing a learning exercise bears a certain resemblance to the design of an interior project, which likely

TABLE 4.2: LEARNING STRATEGIES WITH INTERIOR DESIGN CONTENT

Intention	Interior design example	Teaching technique
Introduce a new topic (involving technical data) that will largely be new to students (freshman students don't know each other that well yet)	Learning the Munsell color system	Lecture
Explore the complexities of an ambiguous topic that involves human choices	Learning about the ethics of "finder's fee" payments in professional practice	Narrative or case study
Explore the ramifications of a decision	Learning about the pros and cons of open office systems	Debate
Examine multiple perspectives on a subject that students have some previous knowledge of	Learning about the advantages and disadvantages of media coverage of the interior design profession	Discussion
Undertake a large task with multiple deliverables	Designing a digital presentation, handout, and hands-on display that explains current building codes to practitioners	Team project
Understand a dynamic, complex process with a start, middle, and end or other identifiable boundary	Becoming familiar with the collaboration strategies within LEED (Leadership in Energy Efficiency and Design) teams, understanding successful and unsuccessful approaches	Case study
Build empathy for different points of view	Learning about body language signals between interior designers and clients as they negotiate a contract	Role playing
Acquaint learners with a procedure or coping mechanisms	Enacting discussion and dialogue in a job interview, exploring potential pitfalls	Simulation

gives interiors educators an edge over instructors in other fields as they create class experiences. Here are behind-the-scenes guidelines that will help ensure that new learning activities go smoothly:

1. *Brush up on skills and knowledge.* Familiarize yourself with new aspects of the learning, task including content, software, or procedures, before committing to its use for learners.
2. *Analyze the time commitment the project will take.* Build in learning curve time if much of the content is new. Also be aware of how much time the project's development will take you, which can be substantial. It is a good idea to visit field trip destinations and interview real clients in advance, for example.
3. *Deal with fear and uncertainty.* Learner evaluations can make educators feel paralyzed. The best way to overcome this is to be organized. It is best to take situations that arise in stride, even seeing their humorous side where you can.

4. *Stay on target with the core skills the project will impart to learners.* Double check that they have the preexisting skills and knowledge to tackle it. Check with their content from other courses. Identify and write the project's objectives early to establish a roadmap of what the experience will accomplish. Double back to this statement often to do a reality check.
5. *Make a game of "making all the mistakes."* Deliberately set out to think of all of the things that could go wrong with the project. Will time run out? Maybe the computers crash and nobody can print. Is the project due on the same day as the learners' giant history test? Ask yourself "What's the worst thing that can happen?" It might be that learners don't grasp an idea as quickly or thoroughly as you would want, but the idea still might be worth pursuing for their later benefit.
6. *Don't be overconfident.* Recognize that it's possible that you "don't know that you don't know" everything. Build in recap and regroup time to a project, and be prepared to make adjustments along the way.
7. *Be conscious of the ebb and flow of learner energy and attention.* Semesters/quarters have the habit of sapping everyone's energy and creative drive. If a project is particularly heavy in thinking analysis or otherwise taxing, consider placing the project in the first half of the semester.
8. *Ask for help.* You can't be expected to know everything. If learners must have in-depth knowledge about radiant floors, call in an expert or point the learners in the direction of outside help.[71]

Strategizing the successful learning experience is the challenge and thrill of teaching. Handled well, classroom experiences can yield positive guidance for learners that nudge them toward eventual career success. The best activities attain the ultimate prize of education: they inspire learners to continue to discover and grow well beyond the limits of their college experience.

B. GIVING TESTS AND ASSIGNING GRADES

Liza Jones has been an interior design educator for fifteen years and is a veteran of writing and giving tests in her history classes. A problem arose this year, however, that had never occurred to her might come up. The midterm exam in the History II course is an important grading component for learners. Liza noticed that one learner was absent as the testing session began. After forty-five minutes, several of the fastest test takers completed the exam, turned it in, and exited the room as instructed. Shortly thereafter, the missing learner entered the room and came to the front of the room to obtain the test materials. Liza was forced to tell the learner that she could not take the exam because others that had already left could have provided insights to her that would negate a fair testing situation. The learner became hostile and explained that car trouble had prevented her on-time arrival. The learner further insisted she had arrived before the end of the exam period and it would be unfair for her to take the exam later, requiring her to study twice. Liza prevailed and had the learner take a second version of the exam the following day at the university's testing center.

The learner reported her complaint to the department chairperson, who fortunately backed up Liza's decision to deny her the exam that day. However, the incident made Liza realize that a syllabus statement was necessary that describes that exams start fifteen minutes into the class session and that only learners' presence at that time permits them to take the exam.

GRADES AND TESTS: STRESS AGENTS FOR LEARNERS

Giving and grading exams and tests are often the major evidence and indicator of a learner's internalization of content. Despite their necessary presence, educators and learners alike often deplore the need for tests. As the preceding scenario shows, even seasoned instructors can have difficulty anticipating all possible dilemmas when giving tests.

Grades, and time-limited tests in particular, tend to incite anxious and emotional behavior in learners. This is understandable given the keen emphasis modern society invests in the letter grade. Grades and testing are often the least enjoyed aspect of teaching. Because stakes can be high for learners' grades and educators' reputations, it is important that testing and grading procedures are clear, fair, and known to learners well in advance of exam or project due day.

This portion of the chapter will discuss tips and procedures for administering traditional tests and assigning grades. Information on assessing studio projects can be found in Chapter 5.

CONSTRUCTING A TEST

Tests help educators determine the extent that learners are successfully internalizing new information. Providing a valid test to learners means more than selecting content, however. The timing of a test, its length, and its format can also influence success.

Matching Tests to Course Objectives

As discussed in Chapter 3, it is important that a course have a series of goals that course content reflects. To ensure that tests reflect these goals evenly, a grid can be created to count the number of test questions per objective. This can prevent overloading or neglecting a particular category of material. Table 4.3 provides an example of a test question count.

How Often to Test

The frequency of testing should be governed by the course content and course level. Some educators test more often in lower-level courses in keeping with rudimentary levels of learning that include memorization of terms and procedures. Others give weekly quizzes that lead up to an exam. It is helpful to keep in mind that tests should be helpful to both the educator and the learners as a means to do a "reality check" of retained content. For this reason, some educators like to give a test three or four weeks into the semester that is weighted less than other tests and course requirements. This gives learners the opportunity to get to know an educator's testing style and prompts good study habits.

Final exams usually occur all at the same time across the many courses a learner takes during a semester or quarter. Since learning (not a test grade per se) is the ultimate goal in a course, some educators require a final cumulative project that requires learners to apply their learning in lieu of a stressful, time-constrained test. Others concentrate "heavy-lifting" content in the first three-quarters of the semester, understanding that learners are often tired and less able to concentrate when beset with multiple exams at the end.

Writing Tests

Information varies widely in its cognitive requirements on learners, and it is important that test question types are both based on the learning objectives and target the desired cognitive level of learning. Figure 4.4 shows that Bloom's taxonomy of learning describes six levels that ascend in difficulty.[72] Each level is associated with words that usually accompany test questions within that division. For

TABLE 4.3: TEST QUESTION COUNT

Course Objectives	Course Content Categories						
	Building Types	Interior wall construction	Plumbing	Electrical	Lighting	Acoustics	Millwork
1. Understand the basic physical principles of non-structural partitions and substructures influencing the interior environment	6	9					
2. Understand selection criteria and installation of architectural envelope elements of walls, ceilings, floors, and related components (including mechanical systems)			6	4	5	2	1
3. Gain awareness of hallmarks of quality construction in furnishings, casework, and other components of interiors					2		11
Total number of test questions	6	9	6	4	7	2	12

A quick tabulation of course goals can help keep testing material proportionate to the original course content.

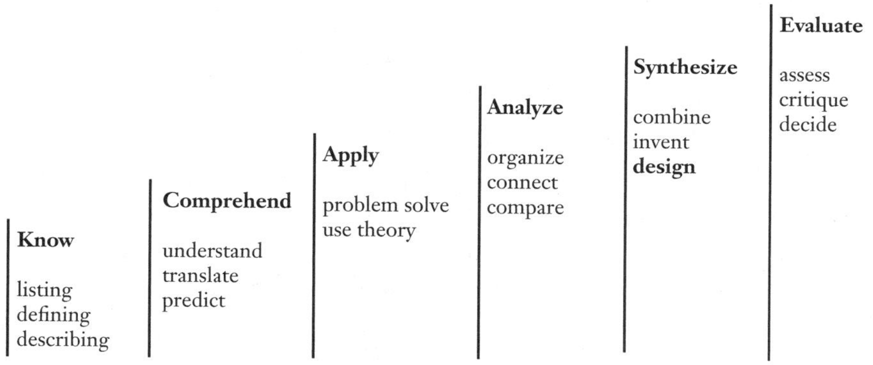

Know	Comprehend	Apply	Analyze	Synthesize	Evaluate
listing defining describing	understand translate predict	problem solve use theory	organize connect compare	combine invent **design**	assess critique decide

Figure 4.4 The six levels of Benjamin Bloom's levels of cognition are associated with active verbs that can be used to construct test questions. It is interesting to note the high level cognitive placement of design along this continuum. Adapted from B. S. Bloom, ed. (1956), *Taxonomy of Educational Objectives: The Classification of Educational Goals.* Susan Fauer Company, Inc., 201–207.

example, a test question that asks a learner to predict the behavior of cotton fiber when it is subject to flame would be a relatively low-level comprehension question. In contrast, an essay question that requires a learner to design a conference center would require high-level learning skills usually associated with more advanced coursework.

It is often far easier for educators to construct a test by writing several questions after each class meeting while content is fresh on the mind rather than waiting until just before a test.

Types of Test Questions and Their Characteristics

While tests can take many forms, a useful discussion here examines the most common types of test questions. Unfortunately, there often appears to be an inverse relationship between the time and effort it takes to construct a test and to grade it. Table 4.4 provides a rule of thumb on this issue.

The choice of test question format is an important one for educators. Certain types of test questions bring issues of logical thinking, spelling, and grammar into play and question format drives the level of cognitive processing learners are undertaking. Therefore, this issue should be carefully matched to the class's information and course goals. It is helpful to understand the implications of test question formats before writing a test. McKeachie offers helpful characteristics of the most common question types as summarized next.[73]

True/false. Many educators do not use true/false questions for several reasons.

- A learner has a 50% chance of getting a true/false question correct without studying.
- Learners can often deconstruct nearly any true/false question and challenge the correctness of the answer by citing unlikely circumstances.

Matching. This question type can be appropriate for low-level terminology defini-

TABLE 4.4: TEST QUESTION COMPARISON

Question type	Time required to construct	Time required to grade	Level of learning
True/False	Fast	Fast	Low
Multiple choice	Slow to moderate	Fast	Low to high
Short answer	Moderate to fast	Moderate to slow	Low to high
Essay	Moderate to fast	Slow	High

SOURCE: W. McKeachie (1986), *Teaching Tips,* 8th ed. Lexington, MA: D. C. Health & Co. Used with permission of Houghton Mifflin Company.

tions but is usually not appropriate for higher levels of learning.

Multiple choice. Constructed correctly, multiple choice questions can measure both low-level and mid-level knowledge. Learners with low verbal ability typically fare better with multiple choice questions than with other types. There are several guidelines to keep in mind when constructing multiple choice questions.[74]

- Three answer options are often as effective as four options.
- The question should be stated in a positive, not a negative form. For instance, stating "All of the following are true *except* . . ." is better than "Which of the following is *not* . . . ."
- Keep all answers as brief and succinct as possible.
- Avoid using "all of the above" and "none of the above." These answers are typically thrown in when no other worthy distracters can be devised.
- Scatter the positions of the right answers. Contrary to popular belief, placing the correct answer in position A or D does not appear overly obvious. Educators should take pains to be sure the old adage "When in doubt, pick C" does not ring true overly often.

Short answer. Short answer questions typically ask for low-level recall of information.

- Short answer questions deny learners the space to get into unnecessary details.
- It is usually easy to assess whether a supplied short answer is correct or not, although alternate forms of the answer may have to be considered.
- Short answer questions can also be used for higher-level learning situations: "How do cotton and wool fiber shapes account for the itchiness of some wool upholstery fabrics while cotton fabrics do not have this problem? Provide a one sentence answer."

Essay. Essay questions are often the closest to the real and complex demands of the interior design profession, promote critical thinking, and provide valuable feedback on what learners are and are not learning. While they take the longest to grade, some educators feel essay questions are the most indicative of learner understanding, especially in moderate- or high-level learning situations such as the following.

- Creating meaningful connections between theory and practice
- Comparing various approaches to an issue
- Explaining the causes that lead to a situation or condition
- Creating a defensible solution to a problem
- Evaluating the quality or appropriateness of a product or procedure

In grading essay questions, educators should avoid assigning points for various details. Instead, the response as a whole should be examined, and some educators include grammar and spelling in this evaluation. When returned with comments, essay questions give learners valuable feedback about the logic and organization of their thinking. Essay questions may not be the most effective measure of learning for a non-verbal learner, however. When constructing essay questions, an educator might include requirements for diagrams and thumbnail sketches to supplement the text answer to a question.

How Lengthy Should a Test Be?

This will depend on the class length and the subject matter, but tests should be planned so that the slowest member of the class has

TABLE 4.5: TEST QUESTION COMPLETION TIMES

Question type	Typical time needed to answer one question
Multiple choice	One minute
Short answer	Two minutes
Short essay	Ten to fifteen minutes
Long essay	Thirty to sixty minutes

McKeachie suggests that test question types are completed by learners in varying amounts of time. This table can help educators estimate the amount of time a learner will require for a test composed of various question types.
SOURCE: W. McKeachie (1986), *Teaching Tips*, 8th ed. Lexington, MA: D. C. Health & Co. Used with permission of Houghton Mifflin Company.

adequate time to consider all the questions. Table 4.5 offers a helpful rule of thumb.

ADMINISTERING A TEST

It is not only the construction of a test that affects performance. While some learners experience test anxiety or inability to perform well on tests under any circumstances, the details surrounding a test's administration can figure heavily into other learners' success or failure.

Preparing Learners for a Test

Educators find that learners are often curious and even anxious about their testing methods. It is worthwhile to approach the testing event with some preparation, forethought, and calm discussion of expectations with learners in advance of the test. The following topics are both worthy discussion items and wise information to include in the course syllabus.

- *Supplies:* What are learners allowed to have with them while taking the test? Blue books? Calculators?
- *Seating arrangements:* To discourage cheating, it is helpful to have learners sit with one seat empty between them as space allows. Reserving a block of seats next to the door for latecomers can ease disruptions.
- *Schedule and time limits:* Telling learners the start and end time of tests can help them mentally prepare themselves for the test's pace.
- *Penalties for not taking the exam:* Some educators permit makeup exams only in the case of illness or death in the family. If makeup exams are permitted, many institutions offer a testing center that will proctor the test on an educator's behalf. Required fees for this service should be described up front.
- *Penalties for cheating:* Honest learners are often encouraged by such a discussion. It is important that penalties are actually carried out when verified cheating occurs. A later section in this chapter offers options that can discourage cheating.
- *Latecomer deadline:* The latest time learners can arrive and be permitted to take the test is important, as the scenario at the beginning of this chapter describes. Some educators indicate a time. Others mandate that no other class member can have completed the exam and left the room before a late-arriving learner starts the exam.
- *Inadvertent information sharing:* Before the test begins, explain the procedures for leaving the room and discussing the exam. Many times, learners are relieved to have finished a test and immediately talk in loud tones once leaving the room. This can both disrupt class members finishing their tests and provide information that influences answers.
- *Preparation for Test Content:*
  - An abbreviated list of test topics is often appreciated by learners, as well as a brief discussion on the types of questions they can expect. Educators should

resist extended attempts by some learners to elicit precise descriptions of the test content. After all, knowledge of the content is the goal, not the specific means to test it.

- To reduce test anxiety, some educators will break learners up into small groups and have them complete a small selection of sample test questions. This tactic has the side benefit of encouraging the formation of study groups.

On the Day of the Test

Educator preparation of the testing environment and test procedure can help learners relax and ensure a fair assessment event. A series of suggestions follow that can help ensure the occurrence of a smooth in-class test.

- Arrive early to arrange chairs or other items as necessary.
- Make sure there are sufficient copies of the test for all learners.
- Proofread the final copy of the test, noting any last-minute changes that must be announced.
- Deflate learner anxieties by saying hello and being pleasant. Avoid any jokes or flippant remarks that might be misconstrued.
- If a test will take only part of a class session, it is often best to have the test first because learners will be anxious and distracted.
- Once class time has arrived, ask if there are any last-minute questions or concerns.
- Reiterate the cheating policy and list all allowed materials learners may use to complete the test.
- Explain any needed changes to the test.
- Have all learners count the number of pages in the test to ensure that nobody is missing a page. If the test is printed front and back on the sheets, be sure to note this to avoid problems with learners explaining they did not realize this fact.
- Remind learners of the amount of time they have to complete the test and announce the actual time on the clock this will occur.
- Explain how learners turn in the test. For example, can they remain in the room? When will class reconvene?
- Minimize interruptions by telling learners that any further comments will be written on the board.[75]

Dealing with Cheating

Unfortunately, cheating can be a common occurrence in college classrooms. While it is difficult to determine how often cheating is really occurring, two recent university studies found that between 70 and 85% of college students have engaged in cheating at least once.[76] Most institutions have an official policy that guides educators' responses to this problem. While no technique is foolproof, there are actions that can reduce the tendency to cheat on a test.

- *Reduce the pressure of the test.* Offering more tests and dropping the lowest test grade is one tactic. Another is to require both test and project assessments that provide learners various ways to demonstrate understanding.
- *Write a reasonable test.* Avoid test questions that inquire about unnecessary details and make sure that the tested material is adequately covered in class.
- *Give two different tests.* Distribute the two tests alternating seats or rows within the classroom. Scramble the order of multiple choice responses as well as the questions themselves and provide different essay questions.

- *Be careful with test drafts.* It is not unheard of for unethical learners to rifle through educators' trash or pay an office assistant for early access to test questions.
- *Change test content often.* Learners in a campus organization or otherwise affiliated outside of class can easily discuss content, and there is little that can be done to avoid this. Many educators do not permit learners to keep written copies of the test to avoid a complete overhaul of the test each semester. Usually an in-class discussion of the test can help learners feel they learned from their mistakes without their retaining the actual test itself.
- *Be aware of current technology concerns.* Learners have been known to store prohibited "help" materials on calculators, personal digital assistants, cellular phones, and even digital wristwatches. It may be necessary to ban these devices from the classroom during test time. If a calculator is necessary, designating acceptable and non-acceptable calculator functions may be necessary.
- *Be mindful of tempting classroom seating sightlines.* It is often worth it to examine the classroom to see if learners can easily see each other's exams while they are taking them. Stadium seating classrooms can be difficult to deal with concerning this issue. One solution is to stagger learners' seating positions or require learners to sit one or more seats apart.

Cheating on papers and projects. An interesting by-product of technological advances is learners' enhanced capacity to cheat on papers and projects in addition to tests. The prevalence of Internet resources and communication has particularly influenced integrity in paper writing. Those intent on submitting plagiarized papers often obtain them from friends at other schools or cut and paste Internet passages verbatim. Other learners may access "online paper mills" that provide access to similar papers or charge $18 to $35 per page to write a new paper for the learner.

There are tactics educators can use to head off the temptation to cheat on a paper.

- *Provide illustrative examples of what cheating looks like.* Despite over twelve years of prior education, college learners may not know what constitutes plagiarism, especially with citation forms and direct quotations versus paraphrased content. Many institutions have references that describe plagiarism for learners. Purdue University offers one such resource plus a learner plagiarism comprehension exercise at http://www.owl.english.purdue.edu/owl/resource/589/01/.
- *Explain institution academic honesty policies to learners.* A reminder of the consequences of documented cheating is a worthwhile discussion. Some states have statutes against the sale of papers and other documents to learners.
- *Do not assign papers with only general requirements.* Instead of requiring learners to "write a five-page paper on anything related to the course," limit the topics or challenge learners to higher-level cognitive thinking by having them analyze multiple specific topics.
- *Require learners to engage the material.* Verbal presentations tend to discourage plagiarism because it is difficult to bluff one's way through content.
- *Have learners submit papers electronically.* This gives educators the chance to scan text for passages lifted from other sources. Some institutions have subscriptions to Internet services that make these scans possible, such as TurnItIn.com.[77]

Cheating on studio projects can also be a problem. Sometimes these transgressions are both egregious and ironic—one interior design educator noticed that a learner had submitted a hand perspective rendering project that was based on a scene that he himself had created several years ago. One solution to discourage cheating in studio projects is to change project types regularly. Another is to include a statement in the syllabus such as: "It is expected that a substantial amount of progress on assigned work will be completed during studio time. The instructor is not required to accept for credit or evaluation any assignment that has not been previously seen in progress during class." Specific program requirements will make plagiarism difficult to carry through convincingly.

Dealing with Missed Tests

Despite class policies and warnings, it is inevitable that one or more learners will miss an important class test. Institution policy varies regarding the best response to this problem and some educators allow test makeups only in the case of verified illness or death in the family. It is important that missed test procedures are detailed clearly in the syllabus. Chapter 3 provides an example of a test policy within a syllabus. There are various tactics that may encourage learners to take tests at regularly scheduled times.

- *Give a shortened version of the original test as a makeup.* While this lessens preparation, some educators feel it is difficult to justify its equality with the regularly scheduled test.
- *Give an essay-only makeup test.* While essay questions take longer to grade, they have a deterrent effect on learners pursuing a makeup test option and make it difficult to copy from learners who took the regularly scheduled test.
- *Do not give a test but provide credit as if it were taken.* Some educators do not give makeup tests with the exception of the final test. In the case of a missed midterm test, the final test grade is counted twice.

Many institutions have testing centers that provide test proctoring services. If use of this service will be required for the class, it is best to state this policy in the course syllabus, especially if there is a fee involved.

GRADING TESTS AND OTHER ASSIGNMENTS

Learners will nearly always expect and institution policy will require that educators render a grade for class activities and the course as a whole. Grading in general falls into the two categories called the absolute and relative systems.

Absolute grading holds learner performance up to an unchanging objective "yardstick." This often means awarding points for performance on course requirements. **Relative grading** is adjusted based on the learners' performance as a group and is often called *grading on a curve.*

There is contention among educators regarding which system is best and many swear by one while condemning the other. The two systems have implications that make them most useful in different learning situations. The University of Washington suggests the following guidelines for use of the two systems.

The Absolute Grading System

The following situations are best suited to the use of absolute grading:

- The course serves as a prerequisite that teaches incremental skills needed for later courses.

TABLE 4.6

Midterm exam score:	64 out of 100
Weighted 30%:	19.2 toward final grade

The actual numerical score and the weighted score for an exam. The 19.2 was calculated by multiplying the 64 by 30%. If a project or exam is worth a number of points different from 100 (e.g., 200 points), then the weighted grade is calculated by taking the exam score, dividing by 200, and multiplying by 30%. This formula can be used in a spreadsheet-style grading form.

- The course's skills ultimately lead to a non-competitive professional situation.
- There is a need to keep the class collaborative and non-competitive.

Using Absolute Grading

Projects are assigned a maximum number of points each; then all projects and exams are assigned a weight that they contribute toward the course grade. Table 4.6 shows an excerpt from a grade book with the actual and weighted grades and their calculation.

The Relative Grading System

The following situations lend themselves to the use of relative grading:

- The course is competitive in nature and learners would benefit from knowing where they stand in comparison to others.
- The course's content is advanced and it is desirable to simulate the competitiveness of the design market, such as being awarded a bid for a project.
- The course content is such that it must be adjusted to learner ability level, such as special electives that lead an educator to group or classify learners by their particular strengths.[78]

Using Relative Grading (Grade Curves)

Projects are assigned a grade based on learner's performance as it compares to others in the class. Ideally, several semesters' worth of learner results are used as a reality check. When plotted out, scores from a reasonably constructed test will typically fall along a bell curve as shown in Figure 4.5.

A set of grades can be "curved" as follows.

1. Find the mean score. Add up all the scores and divide by the number of learners.
2. If the curve has many scores at one end distorting the curve, the educator can alternately locate the median score. This

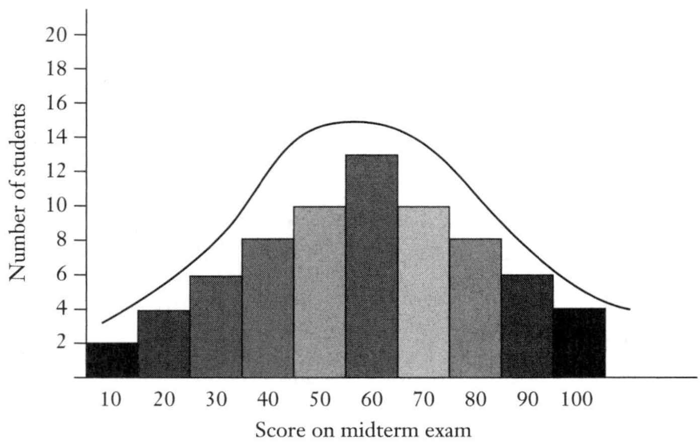

Figure 4.5 Test and project scores usually plot out with most scores in the middle average area and a few in the lower and upper areas.

is the score that is halfway between the highest score and the lowest score.

3. Decide on a grade that this mean score or median score will receive. This typically varies from a C to a C+ or a B–. Historical information on how previous semester's learners performed on this same test can help with this decision.
4. Subdivide the curve into zones assigned to grades A, B, C, D, and F.
5. If an unacceptable number of learners are receiving a low or high grade due to curve distortion, the educator can elect to adjust the width of the letter grade zones. Some educators opt to curve a grade more favorably to a learner, but not lower their score from the typical A = 90%, B = 80%, and so forth.

Some instructors are finding relief in the tedium of calculating and curving grades by using online teaching systems' grading options (such as WebCT and Blackboard). These systems have the benefit of both calculating and making grades available to learners.[79]

HANDING TESTS BACK

Much as with the administration of the test, learners may be stressed when test results are returned to them. Educators should be prepared to rationally discuss the test with the learners and seek to build common ground. It is helpful to recall that everyone is pursuing the same goal of knowledge and understanding of course content.

- Do not return tests in order of low to high or vice versa. This can make learners uncomfortable as others perceive their grades.
- Take pains to not permit other learners to see a specific learner's grade. This includes passing tests along long stadium seating rows.
- In the case of large classes that use computer-scan sheets, place tests in an expanded folder for learners to pick up as they enter the class. Folding and stapling tests will ensure privacy.
- If one or more learners have not yet taken the test, do not allow them to be present in the classroom.
- It is usually best to discuss test results at the end of a class session so that learners will not be distracted from class activities as they think about their test grade. Alternately, schedule a class break to allow a mental breather for everyone. This can sometimes help to dispel elevated emotions.
- In the case of test grades that are less than wonderful, it can be advantageous to break learners into groups of four and have them discuss the test questions by themselves first. Any remaining questions can then be brought before the entire class.
- Avoid protracted debates regarding the correctness of a question. Instead, suggest that learners write down their reasons in paragraph form and place it in your campus mailbox for later consideration.
- It is helpful to invite learners to schedule a one-on-one meeting to discuss test results. This will nullify the increased pressure that a crowd places on this potentially contentious issue.
- Take care not to let learners perceive you are willing to "make deals" regarding which questions count and which do not. This will only complicate the grading process and make you appear inconsistent and unsure. However, if the correct answer to a question is clearly wrong, admit it and explain you will take a look at test grades within several days.
- To ensure that all tests remain in the classroom, place a number on all tests and record the test number that each learner uses. If one goes missing, this simplifies the process of determining the culprit.

Posting Grades

Many educators like to make letter or numerical grades for individual tests or the course grade available to learners by posting it in a hallway or classroom. This helps learners to both see their grade and compare their performance to the class in general. Most university policies are quite clear that anonymity is important in this matter. Several tactics can help instructors ensure privacy.

- Randomize the order of grades so that the listing is not alphabetical. An easy way to do this is to sort the spread sheet grade list by the fourth from the last digit of learners' social security numbers. Avoid posting a learner's entire social security number for theft reasons, and note that some institutions forbid even the partial posting of social security numbers. An alternative to the social security number is to assign a confidential code number to each learner at the beginning of the class.
- If possible, post grades in a protected location, such as a locked glass cabinet.
- Online course programs such as Blackboard permit educators to post grades for learners' private review. While this eliminates the need for hallway postings altogether and ensures privacy, it can hamper learners' understanding of how their grade compares to others unless efforts are taken to provide this information.
- Note that many institutions forbid the discussion of grades with anyone except the learner. This includes curious parents who may call to discuss their child's performance.

Grading Rubrics

Tests and other assessments offer learners a way to gauge their progress against established university and educator expectations. A rubric is a helpful reference tool that provides a comparative benchmark for learners, equating test and project performance to a letter grade and grade point average. The four-point grading scale (where A equals four points, B three, C two, D one, and F zero) is widely accepted in higher education. Some institutions break down the grade point average divisions further to plusses and minuses as shown in Table 4.7.

TABLE 4.7

Grade	1971-2001	2001-Current
A+	4.00	4.00
A	4.00	4.00
A–	–	3.67
B+	3.50	3.33
B	3.00	3.00
B–	–	2.67
C+	2.50	2.33
C	2.00	2.00
C–	–	1.67
D+	1.50	1.33
D	1.00	1.00
D–	–	0.67
F	0.00	0.00

The University of Nebraska, Lincoln, recently changed its grading scale to accommodate plus and minus letter grades.

The University of Washington offers a helpful explanation, or **rubric**, of performance level for each grade in Table 4.8. Educators should consult their institution for specific rubrics and grading scales.

Rubrics like that shown in Table 4.8 are helpful but usually quite general. Some educators also opt to include a rubric specific to interior design in their syllabus so that learners can gauge the probable assessment of their work prior to its submittal. See Chapter 5 Figure 5.5 for an example of a grading rubric specifically for an interior design studio course.

THE UPSIDE OF TESTING

While test assessments and grading can be among the more unpleasant aspects of teach-

TABLE 4.8: TYPICAL GRADING RUBRIC

Range	Quality of performance
3.9–4.0 (A)	Superior performance in all aspects of the course with work exemplifying the highest quality. Unquestionably prepared for subsequent courses in field.
3.5–3.8 (A–)	Superior performance in most aspects of the course; high quality work in the remainder. Unquestionably prepared for subsequent courses in field.
3.2–3.4 (B+)	High quality performance in all or most aspects of the course. Very good chance of success in subsequent courses in field.
2.9–3.1 (B)	High quality performance in some of the course; satisfactory performance in the remainder. Good chance of success in subsequent courses in field.
2.5–2.8 (B–)	Satisfactory performance in the course. Evidence of sufficient learning to succeed in subsequent courses in field.
2.2–2.4 (C+)	Satisfactory performance in most of the course, with the remainder being somewhat substandard. Evidence of sufficient learning to succeed (with effort) in subsequent courses in field.
1.9–2.1 (C)	Evidence of some learning but generally marginal performance. Marginal chance of success in subsequent courses in field.
1.5–1.8 (C–)	Minimal learning and substandard performance throughout the course. Doubtful chance of success in subsequent courses.
1.2–1.4 (D+)	Minimal learning and low quality performance throughout the course. Doubtful chance of success in subsequent courses.
0.9–1.1 (D)	Very minimal learning and very low quality performance in all aspects of the course. Highly doubtful chance of success in subsequent courses in field.
0.7–0.8 (D–)	Little evidence of learning. Poor performance in all aspects of the course. Almost totally unprepared for subsequent courses in field.
0.0 (E)	Complete absence of evidence of learning. Totally unprepared for subsequent courses in field.

Institutions sometimes have general grading rubrics to help learners understand expectations for their performance. Often these rubrics can be accessed through an institution's teaching center.
SOURCE: University of Washington (n.d.). Faculty Resource on Grading. Retrieved 3/3/07 from http://depts.washington.edu/grading/practices/guidelines.html. Reproduced by permission of the University of Washington Office of Educational Assessment.

ing, they are a necessary yardstick of achievement that demonstrate effective learning. When learners perceive that an educator offers a fair testing situation, credibility and educator-learner relationship building can result. It is easy to forget the joy and sense of accomplishment that an honestly earned grade rightfully instills in a diligent learner. Well-constructed assessments can maintain motivation and promote a sense of progress, both important underpinnings of an effective learning environment.

C. CLASSROOM MANAGEMENT

Adjunct instructor Jonna Adams' senior capstone course was the final class learners had to take prior to graduating. Its six-hour credit made it the largest hurdle of the semester, and its requirements always demanded learners' significant concentration to meet expectations.

Senior student Alex Bonavich's success in the interior design curriculum had been consistent and positive during his first three and a half years of work. His B+ average placed him solidly on track for graduation as planned.

However, Jonna began noticing that Alex would come unprepared for announced desk critiques of his work in the senior capstone class, and he offered increasingly unconvincing excuses for his lack of preparation. "I've been really distracted and unable to concentrate," said Alex, responding to Jonna's repeated questions for explanation. "I'll have more for you to see next week." Despite the promises, Alex continued to slide farther behind his colleagues in his progress. One week prior to the project's final presentation, Alex finally came to Jonna's office and emotionally fell apart. It was only then that Alex confided to Jonna the abuse his mother's new boyfriend was inflicting on him and his siblings, making Alex his family's primary defender against physical injury. Recognizing the seriousness of the situation, Jonna gave Alex the phone number for university counseling. Stemming from the advice of his counselor, Alex took a semester off to resolve the crisis in his personal life before returning to complete his degree.

THE RARELY ACKNOWLEDGED EMOTIONAL SIDE OF LEARNING

Besides responsibilities in teaching appropriate information, educators also experience the challenges of managing and reacting to the issues, emotions, and habits of their learners. The emotional (or affective) development of learners is often a large, but frequently unacknowledged, factor in education. Adding further complexity to the situation is the educator's own emotional approach to teaching and learning.

Expectations of personal privacy in Western culture often compel learners to conceal potentially embarrassing situations that can stem from a variety of sources including family, work, substance dependencies, or romantic relationships. Oftentimes repercussions of such events can manifest themselves in a learner's classroom habits or progress on assignments. It is the unspoken responsibility of educators to help learners find a way to meet their academic challenges, often in the face of such obstacles.

Educator Classroom Management Styles

An educator's learning management style emerges as a natural companion to his or her own personality, and the style often develops by trial and error as teaching experience grows.

Parenting Style as a Potential Influence on Teaching Style

The Center for Adolescent and Family Studies sees parallels in educator management styles and parenting styles, identifying four educator classroom management profiles:

- *The authoritarian style:* This style is characterized by firm limits and defined boundaries between learner and educator.
- *The authoritative style:* The educator places limits and controls on learners but simultaneously encourages independence and flexibility.
- *The laissez-faire style:* Few demands or controls are given to influence learners' activities. The educator accepts learners' impulses and actions as necessary and places high emphasis on learner well-being.
- *The indifferent style:* The educator appears aloof from learners and places much responsibility for education on the learners themselves. There is little flexibility or updating of classroom activities.

These four styles are not independent of each other, and an educator may display aspects of several profiles simultaneously in their behaviors. The Center for Adolescent and Family Studies offers a short online quiz that gives educators the opportunity to examine their own classroom management style. While it is primarily geared toward middle school teaching styles, it also has insights for college-level educators. It is available at http://education.indiana.edu/cas/tt/v1i2/what.html and offers a full description of the four classroom management profiles.[80]

Other studies similarly explore relationships between one's parenting style and classroom management style. One study suggests that educators who are parents themselves tend to vary in their classroom management style from educators without children, tentatively suggesting that older educators who are likely to have children exhibit a more controlling classroom management style than younger educators. However, further research is needed to confirm if this is due to teaching experience or family life experience.[81] Other factors such as gender may also have bearing on an educator's classroom management style, and one study determined that male educators were more likely to employ dominance tactics than female educators.[82]

Sensitivity in Dealing with Learner Issues

It is important to remember that students' lives are as full as educators' outside of the classroom, and a learner's inappropriate behavior may stem from occurrences wholly outside educator control, such as family upsets, work issues, or illness. Thus, it is often best to accept that "life" at times will influence students' attention to class activities and performance on projects and tests. An understanding attitude, at least at first, is conducive to building a positive teacher-student relationship, and multiple grading opportunities within a course can mitigate isolated slipups. However, this does not mean that performance standards should be put aside.

More than anything else, a positive and open educator attitude can help to put learners at ease and contribute to an attitude of a learner-educator partnership in which both are working toward a common goal. Many learners are sensitive to perceptions of a combative, punitive environment and may respond negatively to these influences. Fairness coupled with professional friendliness can promote an accessible, productive environment. Behaviorally challenged students can learn much from positive educator examples.

Common Classroom Management Issues

Several negative learner behavioral issues are particularly common in college classrooms. These can include

- Poor attendance
- Arriving late and leaving early
- Not completing class readings or assignments
- Inappropriate verbal or other behaviors

While each behavioral situation and circumstance will vary, there are time-tested techniques that can help mitigate these classroom complications, are addressed in the following sections.

Poor Attendance

- Arrive to class in advance and begin class precisely on time every time. This rewards punctual students and sends a message that the class and its content is important. Students learn by educator example.
- Make attendance mandatory. Record absences by seating chart, calling names, or passing around a sign-in sheet. Explain in the syllabus that one or more absences are allowed "for free" and no explanation or note is necessary. However, after those absences are taken, every other absence is a course grade reduction (e.g., from a B to a B-). A mid-semester reminder of this policy is a good idea.
- Some educators do not require attendance per se. However, frequent announced

or unannounced quizzes that influence the course grade can assure learners' presence.

Arriving Late and Leaving Early

- A sign-in sheet that records attendance can easily reveal those who arrive late. A policy that equates lateness with absenteeism after an identified number of excused misses tends to reduce learners' need to inform the educator of excuses. (Time focused on listening to excuses is time away from focus on learning activities.)
- If a break is necessary, write on the board when class will resume. To discourage students from leaving during break, announce that you will sometimes take attendance again after the break, should the need arise.

Not Completing Class Readings and Assignments

- First, examine why students may not be completing these requirements. It is possible that readings are too long or students know that you will not ultimately test their knowledge of this information. Quizzes that count or merely provide rehearsal for the midterm test can serve as motivators to complete assignments. While it means work for the educator, requiring "minute papers" that ask students to summarize what they learned from readings serve as proof of their participation and can help them organize their thoughts and questions for class time.
- Engage learners in the reading's content. Regular discussion or quick in-class assignment demonstrates to learners that reading content is relevant and important to their progress. For example, a learner's application of programming research in studio courses can be determined by requiring a short programming summary as a part of the project's deliverables.
- Learners respond well to ongoing formative evaluation. For example, incremental studio critiques that contribute to project grades along the way tend to keep motivation higher than waiting until the project's end to issue a grade.

Inappropriate Verbal or Other Behaviors

Some learners may tend to monopolize discussion, are prone to emotional outbursts of frustration while working on a project, or challenge educator authority outright in the classroom. DeBruyn has identified 117 misbehaviors that can affect learners and educators at his Master Teacher website at http://www.disciplinehelp.com/teacher/list.cfm?cause=All. While this online reference is primarily developed for K-12 educators, the list includes behaviors such as habitual absenteeism, crying, and blame displacement, all of which can equally afflict higher education learners.[83]

DeBruyn also describes that most misbehaviors can be traced to one or more of four root causes:

1. *Need for attention.* This is the typical reason for monopolizing conversations, correcting an educator's facts in the middle of lecture, and overly frequent visits to the educator's office for consultation.
2. *Need for power.* While all people have a reasonable innate need to feel empowered, some learners may exhibit behaviors that go beyond the typical. Open dissent, being notably and unnecessarily controversial, and being tyrannical in team project situations may be indicators of a need for power. It may also manifest itself in racist, sexual, or gender bias.
3. *Need for revenge.* This need, while likely more rare than the others, can be responsible for inappropriately hostile critiques or the sabotage of others'

work. Threats of lawsuit or violence against others are more dramatic examples of the need for revenge. This root cause can be traced to feelings of anger or fear of other learners or the educator.

4. *Lack of self-confidence.* Students exhibiting this characteristic may honestly have the ability to do well in class, but they or others have convinced them that failure will result. Blame displacement is one of many examples of lack of self-confidence. This behavior is frustrating to both the learner and the educator.[84]

Strategies for Dealing with Inappropriate Behaviors

Inappropriate classroom behaviors vary widely and therefore it is difficult to discuss a one-size-fits-all remedy. In general, the following tactics can help:

- Create a mutually respectful atmosphere within the classroom, where each learner's input is valued. Other students often follow the educator's example and quickly apply these verbal and nonverbal cues towards each other.
- Attempt to diffuse a tense situation by reiterating an outspoken learner's stated problem, and seek to direct the disruptive learner to a private meeting at a later time. Differences in opinion are easier to resolve in a one-on-one situation rather than in front of the class.
- It is sometimes helpful to require learners to submit their complaints to you in writing. This will help them compose their thoughts and allows a "cooling off" period from the heat of the moment.
- In the case of severe or reoccurring misbehaviors, further private guidance may be best for the learner. In some reoccurring or severe situations, it may be advisable to have an additional faculty member present for the private discussion. Recognize that some situations are best placed in the hands of qualified counselors.[85] It is important that educators are familiar with policies concerning on-campus counseling, as an educator is not always permitted to refer a troubled learner.[86]
- In one-on-one office counseling sessions, it is a good idea to keep the office door open. This small issue can become important if accusations concerning sexual harassment are brought up by a learner.
- Be familiar with appropriate phone numbers and the location of the nearest phone for unforeseen classroom emergencies. This is especially important when teaching at night or on weekends when few staff and faculty colleagues are nearby.

Setting the Right Emotional Tone

Unfortunately, there is no magic bullet for establishing the right emotional backdrop for effective learning. Variables including learner state of mind, educator personality, nature of the content, and class meeting day all serve to complicate the situation, making each class unique. Educators even note differences in emotional tone and learner behavior between two class sections of identical content that meet at different times of day.

Managing learner behaviors and actions are often challenging for new and seasoned educators alike. Clarity in written course materials and policies can establish solid ground for expectations. Calm consistency in educator actions and reactions can help mitigate challenges and help the educator respond quickly and appropriately to classroom challenges that inevitably arise. In the realm of the emotional/affective, perhaps the only constant is change, and gaining comfort with this fact is a good first step.

ENDNOTES

1. Adapted from Magnan, R., ed. (1990). *147 Practical Tips for Teaching Professors.* Madison, WI: Atwood Publishing.
2. As paraphrased by Carroll, S. (January 18, 2007). Teaching Excellence Series: Enhancing Interaction. Seminar, Florida State University, Tallahassee, FL.
3. Ibid.
4. Ibid.
5. Ralph, E. (1998). *Motivation Teaching in Higher Education: A Manual for Faculty Development.* Stillwater, OK: New Forums Press, p. 13.
6. Ibid., p. 16.
7. Filene, P. (2005). *The Joy of Teaching.* Chapel Hill, NC: University of North Carolina Press, p. 82.
8. As assembled by Ralph, E. (1998) quoting Creed, T. (1993). The Seven Principles . . . Not! *American Association for Higher Education Bulletin 45*(7): 78–80; Davis, J. (1993). *Better Teaching, More Learning.* Phoenix, AZ: Oryx; McCown, R., et al. (1996). *Educational Psychology: A Learning-centered Approach to Classroom Practice*, Canadian ed.. Scarborough, Ontario: Allyn and Bacon.
9. Ralph (1998), p. 15.
10. Davidson, C. & Ambrose, S. (1995). Leading Discussions Effectively. *The Teaching Professor 9*(6): 8.
11. See Kolb, D. A. (1981). Learning Styles and Disciplinary Differences. In A. W. Chickering, ed. *The Modern American College.* San Francisco: Jossey-Bass. Also Gardner, H. (1993). *Frames of Mind: The Theory of Multiple Intelligences*, 10th anniversary ed.. New York: Basic Books.
12. Ralph (1998), p. 123.
13. Ekeler, W. (1994). The Lecture Method. In *Handbook of College Teaching: Theory and Applications.* K. Pritchard & R. Sawyer, eds. Westport, CN: Greenwood Press, p. 85.
14. Ralph (1998), p. 117.
15. Ralph (1998), p. 117–118. Also McKeachie, W. (1986). *Teaching Tips: A Guidebook for the Beginning College Teacher.* Lexington, MA: Heath, p. 71.
16. Ekeler, W. (1994), p. 91.
17. Ralph (1998), p. 117; McKeachie (1986), p. 72.
18. Ralph (1998), p. 118.
19. Ekeler (1994), pp. 93–94.
20. Adapted from McKeachie (1986), p. 80.
21. Ekeler (1994), p. 97; Ralph (1998), pp. 123–124.
22. Adapted from Ralph (1998), pp. 123–124.
23. Bowman, D., Hodges, L., Allison, D. & Wineman, J. (1999). The Educational Value of an Information-Rich Virtual Environment. *Presence 8*(3): 317–331.
24. Frederick, P. (1994). Classroom Discussions. In *Handbook of College Teaching: Theory and Applications.* K. Pritchard & R. Sawyer, eds. Westport, CN: Greenwood Press, p. 99.
25. Dunkin, M. & Barnes, J. (1986). Research on Teaching in Higher Education. In M. Wittrock, ed., *Handbook on Research on Teaching*, 3rd ed., pp. 754–777. New York: Macmillan.
26. Ralph, E. (1998), p. 130.
27. Ibid., p. 130.
28. Adapted from Frederick. (1994), pp. 103–108.
29. Woolcock, M. (2007). Constructing a Syllabus. The Harriet W. Sheraton Center for Teaching and Learning. Brown University. Accessed 3/2/2007 from http://www.brown.edu/Administration/Sheridan_Center/publications/syllabus.html.
30. Waxman, L. (2007). Getting Them to Talk. A presentation of the Teaching Tidbits: Successful Teaching Strategies Workshop facilitated by Denise Guerin at the International Interior Design Educators Council Conference, Austin, TX.
31. Pable, J. (March 2007). 3D Graphics in Design: A Comparison of Educator and Practitioner Attitude, Use and Perceptions of Student Preparedness. *Proceedings of the International Interior Design Educators Council Conference.* Austin, TX, pp. 273–283.
32. Council for Interior Design Accreditation (2006). Standards 1f and 1g. *Professional Standards.* Grand Rapids, MI: Council for Interior Design Accreditation.
33. Denton, H. (1997). Multidisciplinary Team-based Project Work: Planning Factors. *Design Studies 18*(2): 158.
34. Michaelsen, L. (1994). Team Learning. In K. Pritchard & R. Sawyer, eds., *Handbook of College Teaching: Theory and Applications.* Westport, CN: Greenwood Press, pp. 150–152.
35. Park-Gates, S., et al. (April 2002). Effects of Group Interactive Brainstorming on Creativity. *Proceedings of the 2002 International Interior Design Educators Council Conference.* Santa Fe, NM, pp. 46–47.
36. Ibid., p. 147.
37. Ibid., p. 148.
38. Pable, J. (April, 2002). Giving Back: Student-Generated Product Research for Practitioner Benefit. *Proceedings of the 2002 International*

Interior Design Educators Conference, Santa Fe, NM. pp. 99–100.

39. Anderson, B., Honey, P., Kaup, M., and Zuo, J. (March, 2004). Strategies for Implementing Group Work and Teaming in Interior Design Education. *Proceedings of the 2004 International Interior Design Educators Conference*. Pittsburgh, PA.
40. Denton (1997), p. 159, citing Hackman, J. (1983). A Normative Model of Work Team Effectiveness. *Technical Report Number 2, Research Project on Group Effectiveness.* Office of Naval Research Code 442, Yale School of Organizational Management.
41. Fiechtner, S. & Davis, E. (1985). Why Groups Fail: A Survey of Student Experiences with Learning Groups. *The Organizational Behavior Teaching Review 9*(4): 58–73.
42. Tuckman, B. (1965). Developmental Sequence in Small Groups. *Psychological Bulletin 63*(8): 384–399.
43. Denton (1997), p. 159.
44. Amor, C. & Wilson, J. (March, 2004). Collaboration Studio: Correlation between Design Outcome and Personality Types. *Proceedings of the 2004 International Interior Design Educators Conference.* Pittsburgh, PA.
45. King, A. (1993). From Sage on the Stage to Guide on the Side. *College Teaching, (41)*1: 30–35.
46. Michaelsen, L. (1994), pp. 143–144.
47. Ibid., p. 144.
48. Miller, N. & Webb, J. (March, 2004). Firewalking: Threading Your Way through Team Assessment. *Proceedings of the 2004 International Interior Design Educators Conference.* Pittsburgh, PA.
49. Gale, R. (2006). The "Magic" of Learning from Each Other. *The Carnegie Foundation for the Advancement of Teaching.* Retrieved 7/22/07 from http://www.carnetgi foundation.org/perspectives/.
50. Ibid., p. 1.
51. Ibid., p. 2.
52. Groat, L. & Wang, D. (2002). *Architectural Research Methods.* New York: Wiley, p. 347.
53. InformeDesign (2007). Available at http://www.informedesign.umn.edu. University of Minnesota. Inquiry conducted April 17, 2007.
54. Yin, R. (2003). *Case Study Research.* New York: Sage, p. 2.
55. Christensen, C. (1987). *Teaching and the Case Method.* Boston: Harvard Business School, p. 24.
56. Weaver, R., Kowalski, T. & Pfaller, J. (1994). Case-Method Teaching. In K. Pritchard & R. Sawyer, eds., *Handbook of College Teaching: Theory and Applications.* Westport, CN: Greenwood Press, pp. 174, 178.
57. Miyahara, A. (March 2003). Theory and Practice: The Need for a Discourse in Design Education. *Proceedings of the 2003 International Interior Design Educators Council Conference.* San Diego, CA, p. 44.
58. Many design books also reference case studies such as *How Designers Think* by B. Lawson (1997, Architectural Press) and *The Culture of Design* by G. Julier (2000, Sage Publications).
59. Lawson (1997), p. 173.
60. Ralph (1998), p. 153.
61. Ibid., p. 155.
62. Rossiter, M. (2003). Narrative and Stories in Adult Teaching and Learning. Ericdigests.org. Retrieved 4/15/07 from http://www.ericdigests.org/2003-4/adult-teaching.html.
63. In Moore, M. (Winter 1988). Narrative Teaching: An Organic Methodology. *Process Studies 17*(4): 248–261. Retrieved 4/15/07 from http://www.religion-online.org/showarticle.asp?title=2765. See also Bruner, J. (1985). Narrative and Paradigmatic Modes of Thought. In Elliot Eisner, ed., *Learning and Teaching the Ways of Knowing.* Chicago: University of Chicago Press.
64. Ibid.
65. Danko, S., Meneely, J. & Portillo, M. (2006). Humanizing Design through Narrative Inquiry. *Journal of Interior Design (31)*2: 10–28. Retrieved 3/28/07 from http://www.idec.org/publication/JID31.2.pdf.
66. Ibid., p. 10.
67. Ralph, E. (1997). The Power of Using Drama in the Teaching of Second Languages: Some Recollections. *The McGill Journal of Education 32*(3): 273–288.
68. According to a research study by Margo Hutcheson, career coordinator for the College of Design at Iowas State University. As referenced in Linton, H. (2003). *Portfolio Design*, 3rd ed. New York: Norton, p. 165.
69. Adapted from Magnan. (1990).
70. Cooke, S. (2007). The Care of Making—Towards a Theory of Design Benevolence. *Proceedings of the 2007 Hawaii International Conference on the Arts & Humanities.* Honolulu, HI, p. 44.
71. Adapted from Mann, T. (2004). *Time Management for Architects and Designers.* New York: Norton, p. 29.
72. American Psychological Association. Using the New Bloom's Taxonomy to Design

Meaningful Learning Assessments. In *APA Online Applying Assessment Strategies in Psychology.* Retrieved 7/9/07 from http://www.apa.org/ed/new_blooms.html.

73. Ibid.
74. For a full treatment of multiple choice guidelines, see McKeachie (1986).
75. Adapted from Lyons, R, Kysilka, M, and Pawlas, G. (1999). *The Adjunct Professor's Guide to Success.* Boston: Allyn and Bacon.
76. Lupton, R., Chapman, K. & Weiss, J. A. Cross-National Exploration of Business Students' Attitudes, Perceptions, and Tendencies Toward Academic Dishonesty. *Journal of Education for Business,* 75(4): 231–235. Also Kleiner, C. & Lord, M. (Novem-ber 2, 1999). The Cheating Game: "Everyone's Doing It," From Grade School to Graduate School. *U.S. News & World Report,* 55–66.
77. Adapted from McMurtry, K. (November 2001). E-cheating: Combating a 21st Century Challenge. *THE Journal.* Retrieved 3/3/2007 from http://thejournal.com/articles/15675_5.
78. University of Washington. (n.d.). Faculty Resource on Grading. Retrieved 3/3/07 from http://depts.washington.edu/grading/practices/guidelines.html.
79. This author has encountered one pitfall of posting learner grades using online class systems. If the system informs learners of their grades prior to in-class discussion of the test, learners can be upset and stew about their grade without having access to knowing the content they got wrong. This can be remedied by careful instructor attention to settings in the online system that delay postings.
80. Bosworth, K., et al. (n.d.) What Is Your Classroom Management Profile? From *Teacher Talk.* Retrieved 7/9/07 from http://education.indiana.edu/cas/tt/v1i2/what.html. Adapted from Santrock, J. (2005). *Adolescence.* New York: McGraw-Hill.
81. Martin, N. & Shoho, A. (2000). Teacher Experience, Training and Age: The Influence of Teacher Characteristics on Classroom Management Style. Paper presented at the Annual Meeting of the Southwest Educational Research Association. Dallas TX.
82. Martin, N. & Yin, Z. (1997). Attitudes and Beliefs Regarding Classroom Management Style: Differences between Male and Female Teachers. Paper presented at the Annual Meeting of the Southwest Educational Research Association. Austin, TX.
83. The Master Teacher. You Can Handle Them All: A Reference for Handling over 117 Misbehaviors at School and Work. Retrieved 7/9/07 from http://www.disciplinehelp.com/teacher/list.cfm?cause=All.
84. Ibid.
85. One memorable example of this occurred when a learner called the author in her office and declared that if she hung up on her, she would commit suicide. Thankfully, an extended conversation with the learner coupled with a simultaneous concealed conversation between the author and her chairperson talked the learner down from her ledge. She withdrew from the course shortly thereafter and sought counseling.
86. This policy may change in the aftermath of the 2007 tragedy at an eastern university where a troubled student killed instructors and students in a Columbine High School–like assault.

CHAPTER 5

Studio Learning

Tom set his book bag down at his desk and looked around at the empty stations surrounding him. Thinking back to the project design development critique during yesterday's class, he thought about the hours of investment and energy he put into his project, the multiple lenses he viewed the problem through, and how Ms. Anders, the studio professor, had encouraged him to go way beyond his normal approach. Granted, his normal approach had earned him passing grades, but yesterday's critique was something to write home about! While comments were direct and constructive, he came away filled with an excitement of possibilities to finalize his design.

His wife marveled at how he could leave so early this morning, yet he couldn't wait to try some of those suggestions. This had to be his best project yet. Why hadn't he pushed himself before? Soon, the work stations around him would fill with his colleagues, each still reflecting on yesterday's critique. Many in the class truly examined both the project and possible solutions and now saw the difference in how critique played such a critical role in the development process. For now, Tom put on his music and looked forward to his day, and engaged in conversations with his studio colleagues about their projects.

Increasingly, business and other disciplines are looking to the effectiveness of the design studio model in education and practice. Commonly termed the D-school (design school) approach, this contrasts with the B-school (business school) way by emphasizing and valuing the resourcefulness and creative problem-solving process critical to continued success in today's global economy and workplace.

Design disciplines are familiar with the benefits of studio instruction as a formative experience in addition to forming bonds within a culture of exploration and learning. This chapter explores the phenomenon of studio design education by first defining and examining the role of studio within an overall curriculum, then exploring the framework for teaching and learning and discovering those activities and processes that encourage a quality studio educational experience. Establishing an atmosphere of respect and collaboration is addressed in the etiquette and critique sections of this chapter and then relative merits and forms of assessment are discussed. Lastly, ideas that others have effectively incorporated into a variety of levels and types of studio courses conclude the chapter.

STUDIO IN GENERAL

Studio, a term used in design education, is richly embedded with a tradition of creative problem solving, process, making, place, culture, and community. Design studio offers learners an opportunity to explore problems without known results.[1] Students learn to express and explore design ideas through graphic, physical, verbal, and written means. At its best, the studio environment supports a creative energy that permeates throughout the curriculum. In a *Journal of Architectural Education* article, Jeffrey Ochsner, FAIA, professor and chair of the Department of Architecture at the University of Washington, suggests that while design studio teaching addresses many aspects of education, including analytical thinking, technical abilities, and both graphic and verbal presentation skills, these are rarely the primary goal. He suggests that development of a personal process of discovery leading towards a design solution is the primary focus.[2]

Studio provides the epitome of project-based learning exercises, with activities that include research, inquiry and analysis, synthesis, criticism, collaboration, and communication. Through the linked acts of drawing, looking, and inferring, designers propose alternatives and interpret and explore their consequences—activities representing the highest levels of Bloom's cognitive taxonomy. (For a review of Bloom's taxonomy of learning, see Chapter 2.) This may be why it is so difficult to teach and learn studio techniques! Studio provides a safe environment for exploration and, in fact, multiple variants are an expectation.

Studio classes engage learners in many possible skills and knowledge areas:

- Programming
- Concept generation
- The design process from initial concept to design development stages or beyond
- Graphic communication and model building
- Presentation
- Building codes and accessibility standards
- Lighting and building systems
- Methods of construction
- Materials specification

Studio procedures are closely linked to the needs of learners. For example, beginning learners prompt unique challenges in studio and other learning environments, a fact recognized by the enduring nature of the *Conference of the Beginning Design Student*, a yearly event that brings educators together to discuss pedagogical advances for beginning designers.

Keeping the Purpose in Mind

Many in design education see studio as the opportunity to integrate knowledge and process gained into a higher learning experience that results in a product of one sort or another. Business educator Clark Kellogg relates the aspects of the current design model important to business schools, stating: "Studio as a learning environment has characteristics that are well-suited to the demands of complex, multi-variant and dynamic problems that define the nature of design challenges in the built environment and increasingly, in business social sciences, education, and politics. Interestingly, if the vocabulary of the design culture is replaced with more widely understood synonyms, it is possible to describe studio a little differently. In this light, the studio model has immense value as a creatively driven teaching and learning environment: one-to-one communication, rich peer-to-peer learning, Socratic discourse, iterative progression, learning by doing, and enhanced visual literacy."[3]

In Learning from Studio, a *DesignIntelligence* Knowledge Report, Kellogg proposes twelve characteristics common to all design studios:

- *A Think/Do Methodology:* A process of creating things twice, once in the mind or imagination, next in the real world.
- *Visual and Spatial Literacy:* In studio, learners learn to evaluate, think, and communicate in visual terms. They are able to understand, organize, and create space and place. He suggests that for the spatially literate, movement, light, sound, objects, and people can be components of problems and solutions.
- *Sketching, Drawing, and Thinking in Visual Terms:* Those who can draw and communicate with sketches, symbols, and images have access to different ways of thinking, seeing, and understanding. In studio, learners learn to see objects and draw them with computers and by hand. Those who can capture an idea with a few lines on a piece of paper have a powerful advantage in both conceptualizing ideas and communicating them.
- *Understanding and Synthesizing Information:* Studio teaches one how to value and make judgments about different types of information. Designers understand filtering, that is, valuing, synthesizing, and ignoring information as appropriate.
- *Modeling/Prototyping/Changing Scales:* As problem-solving tools, the problem may be understood in more ways. These procedures help learners understand both the problem and the solution in ways that more typical linear and analytical processes cannot.
- *Creating Multiple Solutions:* Studio teaches learners to create multiple solutions to problems, explore alternative approaches and different views, simulate solutions, and investigate and evaluate the effectiveness of each.
- *Comfort with Ambiguity:* A tolerance for uncertainty or multiple meanings is a key component of virtually all creative work. Comfort with ambiguity creates a situation where new insights and solutions are more accessible.
- *Creativity:* Studio builds competence in domain-specific knowledge, creative thinking skills, and passion for work.
- *Cultural History:* The historical basis within projects delves into material and social culture with the architectural surroundings as a backdrop.
- *Working Collaboratively:* Many problems are too complex for just one body of knowledge or skill set to solve. In studio, learners learn to work together in different ways across boundaries of discipline, space, time, and culture.
- *Meeting Deadlines:* Deadlines bring a tremendous creative focus.
- *Communicating Ideas, Concepts, and Solutions:* Effective, persuasive, and powerful presentation of an idea is how every project is communicated, every idea is sold, and every studio project is explained.[4]

Studio in the Curriculum

Within design curricula, the studio typically plays a significant role in accomplishing educational objectives. Interior design educator authors Diane Bender and Jon Vredevoogd recount the rich, historic tradition of the studio experience that began with the French Royal Academy and continued with the methodologies of the École des Beaux-Arts. United States schools similarly patterned their instruction in Beaux-Arts format, which placed the studio in the center of the curriculum's focus.[5] Bender and Vredevoogd further observe that studio instruction, for one reason or another, has essentially remained unchanged in the United States since the early twentieth century.

They go on to describe how the studio procedure has both advantages and drawbacks: "Learners then and now attend a studio where instruction is delivered from master to apprentice within a small group setting. Faculty to learner ratio can range from twelve to twenty-four learners per instructor, with an average of seventeen to one. Studio classes may range from four to twelve hours per week, during which the instructor works with each learner independently for short periods of time. It may be common for a learner to wait almost three hours for a few minutes of insight and direction. While waiting, a learner may not have the opportunity to view and hear the critique addressing the work of classmates."[6] On the other hand, tremendous potential is embedded in that few minutes of feedback, given that the nature of studio is a setting where learners are struggling with similar problems and intentionally overhear educator's comments to individual learners. While learners may indeed be awaiting their individual time with an open ear, they benefit from multiple approaches and discussion at adjacent desks.

In interior design, studio often comprises a quarter to a third of the number of hours of the entire curriculum. This studio educational experience typically begins at the freshman level and continues each term through graduation.

A FRAMEWORK OF STUDIO TEACHING AND LEARNING

While the studio model for teaching and learning has its root in design and architectural practice, momentum is building for the studio model's inclusion in many fields of study. Often, the term "inquiry-based learning" is used, rather than "studio." The commonalities in approach that frame a successful teaching and learning studio environment communicate inspirational and well-crafted objectives and project descriptions that demonstrate the value of resourcefulness, creativity, multiple perspectives, and inquiry.

Defining Objectives

Strong objectives within a studio class help both faculty and learners stay focused. When making a determination of objectives for a studio course or an individual project, it is helpful to keep the overall picture in mind. Each studio course contributes to the overall curriculum, and therefore expectations for the unique contribution of the course must be folded into course objectives. Goals for a studio course typically include particular knowledge areas learners should master as well as a responsibility to introduce, build, or reinforce particular skills. Further information about developing objectives for the overall course can be found in Chapter 3, under Matching Course Goals to Measurable Outcomes.

Within the framework of the studio course objectives, it is helpful to establish where the individual objectives are best met. Some objectives will be met through the instructor presenting and then learners incorporating information. Other objectives may be met through individual research components, while others may be most effectively met within an individual project process. When defining objectives for individual projects, a similar process ensues.

Writing a Project Description

A description for a studio project may be as brief as a few sentences, or may comprise

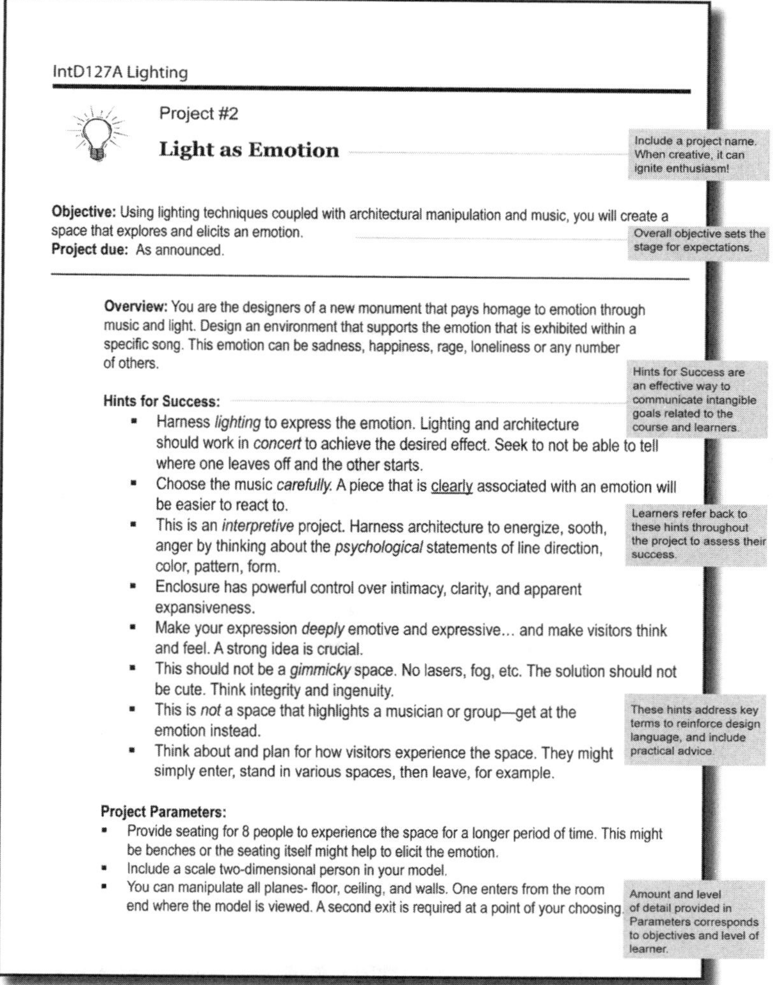

IntD127A Lighting

Project #2

Light as Emotion

Include a project name. When creative, it can ignite enthusiasm!

Objective: Using lighting techniques coupled with architectural manipulation and music, you will create a space that explores and elicits an emotion.
Project due: As announced.

Overall objective sets the stage for expectations.

Overview: You are the designers of a new monument that pays homage to emotion through music and light. Design an environment that supports the emotion that is exhibited within a specific song. This emotion can be sadness, happiness, rage, loneliness or any number of others.

Hints for Success:

Hints for Success are an effective way to communicate intangible goals related to the course and learners.

- Harness *lighting* to express the emotion. Lighting and architecture should work in *concert* to achieve the desired effect. Seek to not be able to tell where one leaves off and the other starts.
- Choose the music *carefully*. A piece that is clearly associated with an emotion will be easier to react to.
- This is an *interpretive* project. Harness architecture to energize, sooth, anger by thinking about the *psychological* statements of line direction, color, pattern, form.
- Enclosure has powerful control over intimacy, clarity, and apparent expansiveness.
- Make your expression *deeply* emotive and expressive… and make visitors think and feel. A strong idea is crucial.
- This should not be a *gimmicky* space. No lasers, fog, etc. The solution should not be cute. Think integrity and ingenuity.
- This is *not* a space that highlights a musician or group—get at the emotion instead.
- Think about and plan for how visitors experience the space. They might simply enter, stand in various spaces, then leave, for example.

Learners refer back to these hints throughout the project to assess their success.

These hints address key terms to reinforce design language, and include practical advice.

Project Parameters:

- Provide seating for 8 people to experience the space for a longer period of time. This might be benches or the seating itself might help to elicit the emotion.
- Include a scale two-dimensional person in your model.
- You can manipulate all planes- floor, ceiling, and walls. One enters from the room end where the model is viewed. A second exit is required at a point of your choosing.

Amount and level of detail provided in Parameters corresponds to objectives and level of learner.

Figure 5.1

several pages, depending upon the level of studio course, the learning objectives associated with the project, and the common understanding desired as learners enter the project. Project descriptions may come in many forms. Figures 5.1 and 5.2 illustrate two approaches, each addressing a different phase of a similar project.

At a minimum, a project description should include the following elements.

Name of the Project

This can be as generic or creative as desired. When determining the project's name, keep in mind that the name of the project can often ignite enthusiasm in learners!

Spirit of the Project

While a line item in the description may not be present with this heading, the intent is to describe the non-tangible aspects of the project. Some educators insert a poem or words to a song here; others use narrative to describe an experience a user may encounter in the finished design, while others may approach it through the eyes of a well-known designer or architect.

Functional Parameters of the Project

As with all aspects of the project description, the detail provided here will correspond to the level and educational objectives of the studio. Functional parameters can be as brief

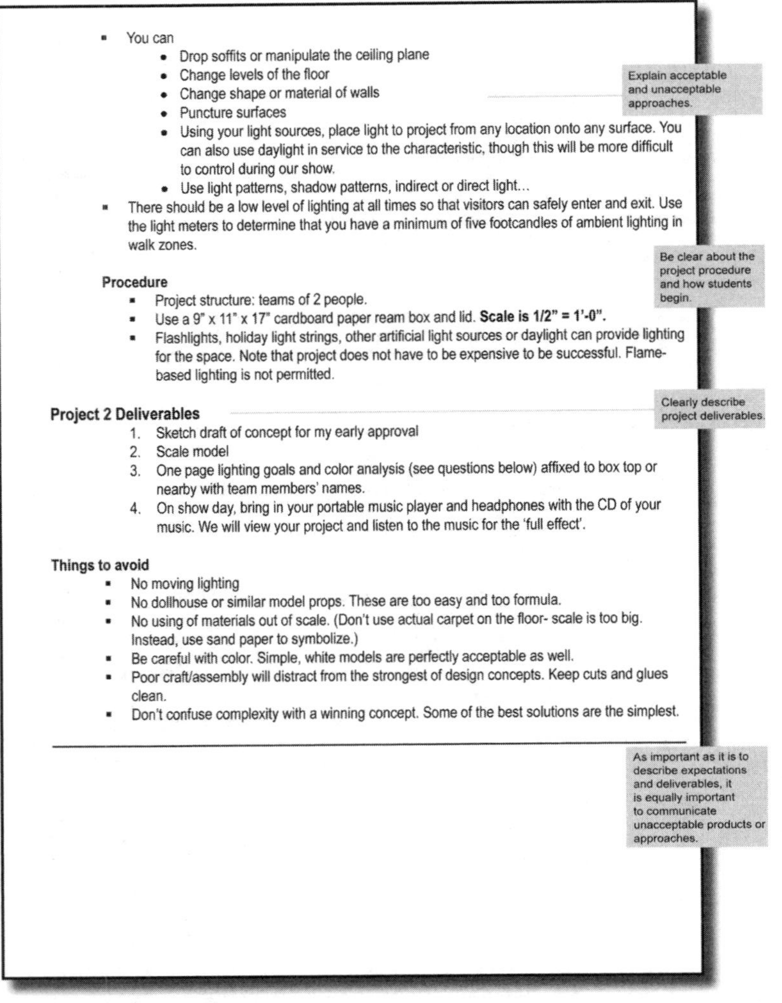

- You can
  - Drop soffits or manipulate the ceiling plane
  - Change levels of the floor
  - Change shape or material of walls
  - Puncture surfaces
  - Using your light sources, place light to project from any location onto any surface. You can also use daylight in service to the characteristic, though this will be more difficult to control during our show.
  - Use light patterns, shadow patterns, indirect or direct light...
- There should be a low level of lighting at all times so that visitors can safely enter and exit. Use the light meters to determine that you have a minimum of five footcandles of ambient lighting in walk zones.

Explain acceptable and unacceptable approaches.

Procedure

- Project structure: teams of 2 people.
- Use a 9" x 11" x 17" cardboard paper ream box and lid. **Scale is 1/2" = 1'-0".**
- Flashlights, holiday light strings, other artificial light sources or daylight can provide lighting for the space. Note that project does not have to be expensive to be successful. Flame-based lighting is not permitted.

Be clear about the project procedure and how students begin.

Project 2 Deliverables

1. Sketch draft of concept for my early approval
2. Scale model
3. One page lighting goals and color analysis (see questions below) affixed to box top or nearby with team members' names.
4. On show day, bring in your portable music player and headphones with the CD of your music. We will view your project and listen to the music for the 'full effect'.

Clearly describe project deliverables.

Things to avoid

- No moving lighting
- No dollhouse or similar model props. These are too easy and too formula.
- No using of materials out of scale. (Don't use actual carpet on the floor- scale is too big. Instead, use sand paper to symbolize.)
- Be careful with color. Simple, white models are perfectly acceptable as well.
- Poor craft/assembly will distract from the strongest of design concepts. Keep cuts and glues clean.
- Don't confuse complexity with a winning concept. Some of the best solutions are the simplest.

As important as it is to describe expectations and deliverables, it is equally important to communicate unacceptable products or approaches.

Figure 5.1 *(Continued)*

as describing a "restaurant for 60 patrons," where the learners are then responsible for gathering remaining information regarding the functional aspects of a restaurant that allows 60 patrons to be served. At the other end of the spectrum, the functional parameters can describe the number and size of tables and booths, size of waiting area, amount of storage in receiving areas, floor space for the kitchen, and the like.

Client and End Users of the Project

Learners need to understand the concept of a defined client (whether real or fictitious) and who the end users are. If learners are to determine one or both of these as a part of research for the project, state so here in the project description.

Physical Location and Description

At a minimum, this should include the city or general locale of the project, along with the building shell. A reduced scale plan and any other views of the existing space (if there is one) may be included here. Information about where a floor plan and other descriptive building information may be accessed (via CD-ROM, physical drawing location, site visit with associated field measurements, etc.) by the learners should be placed in this section. Discussion of context, existing materiality, particular code considerations, major

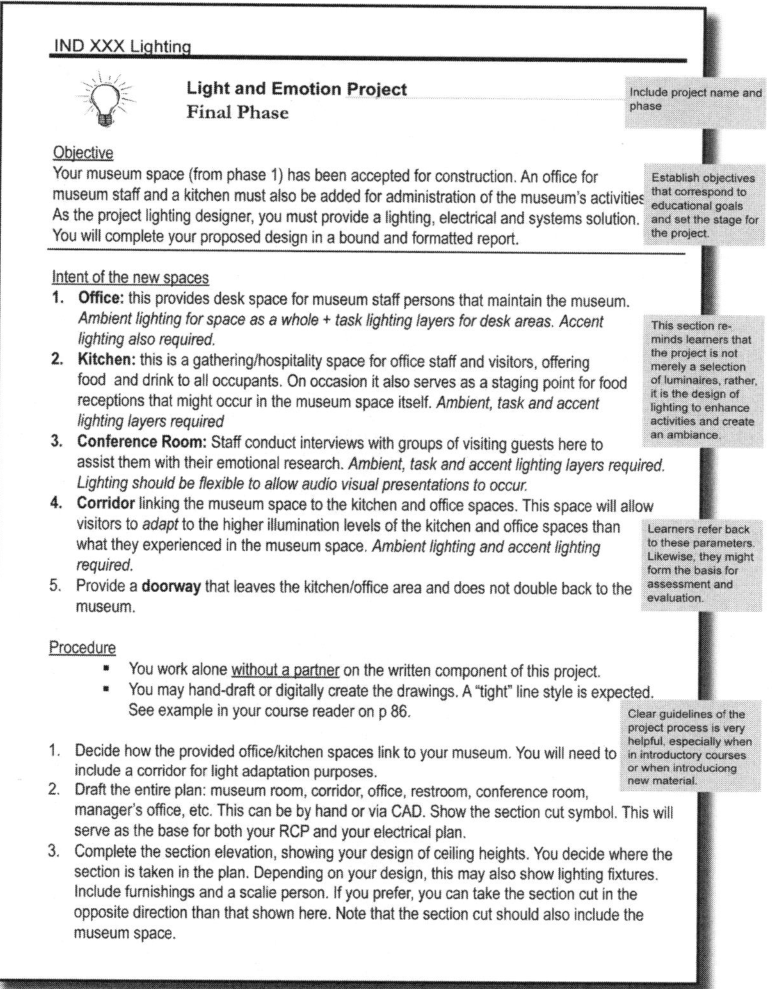

IND XXX Lighting

Light and Emotion Project
Final Phase

Include project name and phase

Objective

Your museum space (from phase 1) has been accepted for construction. An office for museum staff and a kitchen must also be added for administration of the museum's activities. As the project lighting designer, you must provide a lighting, electrical and systems solution. You will complete your proposed design in a bound and formatted report.

Establish objectives that correspond to educational goals and set the stage for the project.

Intent of the new spaces

1. **Office:** this provides desk space for museum staff persons that maintain the museum. *Ambient lighting for space as a whole + task lighting layers for desk areas. Accent lighting also required.*
2. **Kitchen:** this is a gathering/hospitality space for office staff and visitors, offering food and drink to all occupants. On occasion it also serves as a staging point for food receptions that might occur in the museum space itself. *Ambient, task and accent lighting layers required*
3. **Conference Room:** Staff conduct interviews with groups of visiting guests here to assist them with their emotional research. *Ambient, task and accent lighting layers required. Lighting should be flexible to allow audio visual presentations to occur.*
4. **Corridor** linking the museum space to the kitchen and office spaces. This space will allow visitors to *adapt* to the higher illumination levels of the kitchen and office spaces than what they experienced in the museum space. *Ambient lighting and accent lighting required.*
5. Provide a **doorway** that leaves the kitchen/office area and does not double back to the museum.

This section reminds learners that the project is not merely a selection of luminaires, rather, it is the design of lighting to enhance activities and create an ambiance.

Learners refer back to these parameters. Likewise, they might form the basis for assessment and evaluation.

Procedure

- You work alone without a partner on the written component of this project.
- You may hand-draft or digitally create the drawings. A "tight" line style is expected. See example in your course reader on p 86.

1. Decide how the provided office/kitchen spaces link to your museum. You will need to include a corridor for light adaptation purposes.
2. Draft the entire plan: museum room, corridor, office, restroom, conference room, manager's office, etc. This can be by hand or via CAD. Show the section cut symbol. This will serve as the base for both your RCP and your electrical plan.
3. Complete the section elevation, showing your design of ceiling heights. You decide where the section is taken in the plan. Depending on your design, this may also show lighting fixtures. Include furnishings and a scalie person. If you prefer, you can take the section cut in the opposite direction than that shown here. Note that the section cut should also include the museum space.

Clear guidelines of the project process is very helpful, especially when in introductory courses or when introduciong new material.

Figure 5.2

circulation paths, and other physical information are included here as well.

Design Phases

Use this section to communicate where the learners' participation in the project begins and ends. For instance if the programming is given, perhaps this project begins with concept development. Within the overall course, perhaps this project will stop at a schematic design level. Or perhaps this project is intended to serve as a capstone experience and progress through each of the phases, including programming and construction documents. In any case, it is important to lay the ground work of expectations between educator intent and the learners' performance at the project's beginning.

Grading Criteria

Educational objectives and project emphasis are communicated here without lengthy description. This section is often viewed first by learners! For example, a project might be worth a total of 100 points: 5 points allocated to programming, 50 points to schematic design, 30 points to design development, with remaining points distributed equally among other project phases. Learners recognize the emphasis on schematic design and will subsequently focus more on that phase than programming because they see that it car-

You will create the following components of the design:

Item	Scope	Details
Museum concept statement	Museum	Revise (if necessary) your previous concept statement so that it, at a minimum, answers the following questions within its narrative: • Music you chose and qualities in the music piece that express the target emotion. • How does the physicality of the architecture support the target emotion? (i.e. form, scale, texture, circulation, etc.) • How does the lighting solution support the target emotion? (i.e. placement, color, level of illumination, etc.) You should reference at least two lighting fixtures selected.
Museum Color Analysis	Museum	Include your previously completed color analysis. Revise and polish this from your previous submission. Also include paint chips as before.
Photos of your museum model solution	Museum	One or more *high-resolution* photos of your model solution. Describe the song and artist chosen and restate the emotion.

Reflected Ceiling Plan/Lighting Plan	▪ Kitchen
	▪ Office & associated spaces
	▪ Corridor
	▪ Museum
		Shows
		• HVAC (1 24" x 24" supply per 300 sf or less; 1 24" x return per 400 sf. or less) (use symbols)
		• Ceiling height changes (lines, notes and arrows with "__'-__" A.F.F.")
		• Emergency exit lighting fixture locations (at each exit). These are not switched.
		• Smoke detector locations (1 per 200 sf and at least 1 per room)
		• Sprinkler head locations (1 per 100 sf; locate at least 4' from walls in an *orderly* pattern)
		• Ceiling-based lighting fixtures (use symbols)
		• Wall-based lighting fixtures (if any) located 48" or higher on the walls (use symbols)
		• Lighting fixtures located 48" or lower on walls or the floor. (note these with labels/arrows in plan to avoid confusion*) (use symbols) This includes portable lighting fixtures.
		• Switches showing control of all permanent non-emergency lighting in the space. Note:
		  ○ Heights of switches (<u>only</u> if not 42" AFF)
		  ○ Presence of any control, such as dimming, photosensor, motion detector (via symbol)
		  ○ Your option: either show dotted lines OR show a numerical symbol next to both the switch and the fixtures it controls.
		• See example on p. 86 of your class reader.

Tie current activities to previous phases of the project when possible.

Project descriptions also serve to educate learners. Wherever possible, take advantage of this opportunity.

Figure 5.2 *(Continued)*

ries more relative "worth." Sometimes this is a subtle reminder of the educator's attitude toward the relative importance of particular phases of a project. Be sure that the manner in which points or percentages are distributed reflects the educational emphasis of the project.

Some educators also include a detailed description of the grading criteria associated with particular grades in this section of the project description. Grading criteria may communicate the nuances of relative merit or focus for a particular project phase. For some projects, this information might best be communicated within the project description. For other projects, where the instructor wishes to keep learners focused on the phase at hand, the criteria may be distributed as that phase begins. More information on developing and communicating evaluation information is available in Chapter 4, Grading Tests and Other Assignments.

ACTIVITIES WITHIN STUDIO

Given that studio projects often involve incorporating many different skills that learners covered in past classes, instructors must be prepared to provide a small review of certain skills so that learners are comfortable with project requirements.

Information Gathering

Learners must learn to gather information of a variety of sorts and from multiple sources to inform their design processes and projects. These skills may range in scope from basic to more advanced research techniques. Time collectively spent in class discussing potential information gained with the most likely exploration techniques and potential sources for that information will pay dividends. In facilitating class discussion, this approach helps avoid repeating the same information to many learners individually, and the depth and breadth of information gathered will be higher (resulting in better informed design results).

Sometimes it is instructive for learners if they brainstorm possible information sources together. Typical sources available to learners for information gathering include

- Past courses
- Library
- Client interviews
- User interviews
- Site visits
- Guest speakers
- Internet sources
- Academic and trade journals

Information Sharing

Depending upon the information, there are several modes of sharing background findings amongst learners. Lecture or presentation mode allows a single information "source" to share their topic with the class. The lecturer or presenter may be the instructor, a guest invited to class, or a learner sharing their research topic. Groups of learners may be assigned particular research topics and then asked to present their findings to the class. When planning for face-to-face sharing of information, it is important to allow time for and encourage questions. Remember, a valuable skill to learn in design is the ability to ask pertinent questions. More information regarding discussion techniques may be found in the Learning Strategies: Definitions and Examples section of Chapter 4.

Regardless of who gathers or prepares the information for sharing, it may be made available through additional means. If groups of learners are assigned particular topics (a team approach to information gathering and sharing), printed "books" including each team's findings can be compiled by the learners. Likewise, the research may be presented with PowerPoint or another program, and the files placed in locations accessible to all necessary parties. This can be accomplished with Blackboard or WebCT, by placing a CD-ROM with the files on reserve in the library, or through circulating a CD-ROM or flash drive among learners in studio.

When embarking on team research that will be compiled into one presentation or document for the class, it is helpful to assign one team or person the responsibility for establishing the graphic identity and layout of the presentation format to ensure consistency and clarity.

Studio Class Formats

Program philosophy, physical and human resource availability, and academic structure each play a role in determining the type of studio structure embedded in the curriculum. The two most common types of studio structure are described here.

Horizontal Studios

Most design curricula include studios that are taken by learners at a particular level in their educational process. Terms vary when discussing particular studio identities, and "Junior Studio" or "Fourth Year Studio" are common descriptors. These are each examples of **horizontal studios**. Within the overall curriculum, studios at each educational level incorporate projects at an increasing level of complexity and, often, size. Horizontal studios may also contain a single or series of topical bases. For instance, the third year studio may also be where learners are introduced to retail design. Multiple emphases are included each term, and each creates a scaffolding process for future endeavors.

Vertical Studios

Some design programs have arranged their curriculum to include **vertical studios**. Vertical studios are typically topic-based. For example, the focus of a vertical studio may rest on the project type or particular emphasis (for instance there may be a Retail Studio and a Residential Studio). In vertical studios, learners are at differing levels of their educational process. Proponents of vertical studios advocate the opportunity this mixed environment affords for learners to grow, learning and teaching each other as they progress.

Regardless of the studio structure, physical resources of the institution coupled with enrollment challenges may cause studio spaces to be used multiple times during a day or week. When this is the case, and learners do not have a specified proprietary work space, the desks are termed **hot desks**. In many programs, the initial studios (often those in the first and second years of study) are hot desks, while the remaining years offer **cold desks**, those that are used by only one learner for the academic term.

PROCESS MANAGEMENT

Regardless of the level or focus of studio, design process plays a role in the educational experience. Ochsner describes this creative process as the "experience that allows us to see the external world as we rationally know it to be, but also allows us simultaneously to imagine the world as it might otherwise be."[7]

Design Processes

During beginning design studios, a process or multiple processes are introduced to learners and applied to limited-scope projects. Multiple opportunities for repetition of process help solidify an approach to problem solving for learners during their education. Most learners do not enter design programs with previous experience in design "process" to guide their investigation and procedure; therefore design process will often receive a strong emphasis. This emphasis is typically coupled with an introduction to appropriate skills for exploration (sketching, introductory diagramming, physical and computer modeling) as well as sources for inspiration. Interior design educators Stephanie Clemons and Lisa Waxman used this studio procedure to integrate Oldenburg's *Third Place Theory* into a design studio setting. Within this project, learners conducted field observations using a described procedure, took digital photographs, and developed an analysis booklet with specified software.[8]

Visual and oral presentation as well as pinup and critique also find a foothold in most beginning design studios. Design educators often introduce good practices in visual and oral presentation during early, informal critiques. This also provides opportunities to initiate design discussion and constructive feedback loops. Educators may find it helpful to videotape student presentations at various points in the learner's academic career to self-assess verbal presentation skills for idiosyncrasies.

As learners progress through the design studio sequence, other design processes may be introduced and integrated to suit particular project parameters. Project processes may include narrative; be driven by concept; or use spatial organizers, phenomena, events, or other initiators as means to inspire ideation, iteration, and project development. Design decision making is therefore given a research and process framework. For example, educator Rula Awwad-Rafferty implemented a community-based project into a senior-level design studio, to provide a "canvas for innovation, integration, and immersion into the worldview of another culture; thus empowering the shift in design thinking between the designer's worldview and that of the community and client served."[9]

The project's first site visit began the process of new thinking: "Look at the mountain out there and tell me what you see. Don't look with your eyes, look with your imagination and memories," said Mr. Appeney, a Shoshone veteran and tribal elder, embarking the viewers on a personal and professional journey. The tribes afforded the students entrance not only into the project site but also into their sacred spaces and lives.[10] The studio design process was a hybrid of established interior design problem solving and Shoban traditional decision-making and storytelling approaches.

Studio organization, formal feedback, as well as grading opportunities are often structured to resemble contractual phases of practice (program, schematic design, design development, construction documentation) with additional phases included (concept, final presentation). Suggestions regarding evaluation are found in the Studio Assessment section of this chapter.

Studios typically include crafted opportunities for peer feedback, reflective activities, and increased communication skills (graphic, oral, written) on the part of designer and learner reviewer. Similar to learning a design process, students must learn and practice the art of effective critique. Suggestions regarding critique are found in the Critique section of this chapter.

Time Management Skills for Learners

A part of teaching in design studios is helping learners understand their own initial approach to a given problem and how to improve that approach for the most effective and insightful explorations. Time management often plays a role in how learners approach design problems. Pressures from other courses (preparing for exams, writing papers, preparing presentations) may distract learners from focusing on the design studio and the design problems presented.

Through the project schedule, educators communicate expected relative emphasis on project phases. Setting incremental due dates establishes a process learners can emulate in the future. Learners at sufficiently advanced stages in the curriculum might also be engaged in setting group incremental deadlines for large studio projects. This often can provide a sense of ownership and collaboration that exerts a positive influence on class attitude. Some educators find it helpful to establish guidelines for expectations of progress for each studio meeting time, others on a weekly basis. Regardless, there should be an expectation that some progress will occur outside of official studio class time.

Often, a lack of time management prioritization becomes an issue for particular learners. Educators can help learners understand the value of working on studio activities during studio hours so that the creep or intrusion of outside demands or additional courses is avoided. Quick exercises can assist those learners with "analysis paralysis." Some instructors encourage learners to set a timer (cell phone, watch, computer) for thirty minutes and generate as many solutions to a particular problem as possible. It sometimes helps to quantify expectations: "In the next thirty minutes, I want to see nine alternative solutions to that entry experience." Once learners see the amount of progress and thought that can be generated in such a short time, they are intrinsically encouraged to go forward enthusiastically (or at least less reluctantly!).

ETIQUETTE IN THE STUDIO

A subculture may develop within the physical studio environment, and this is especially true when the learners have dedicated studio space. This culture plays an important role in the entire learning process during studio, or it may work against the educator's best intentions. As with any society, a common expectation of behaviors and values is necessary for the effective functioning of studio.

Respect

Learners bring their own personalities and idiosyncrasies to studio (as do educators!). A cornerstone of effective studios is respect—respect of learners for each other, respect of learners for the instructor, and respect of the instructor for each individual learner are all key components of a functioning learning environment. An educator's respect for learners is communicated through his or her verbal and nonverbal communications. It is important to be aware of certain behaviors that can transmit unwanted signals:

- Constantly avoiding particular learners
- Spending more time with particular learners
- Exhibiting a bored or expectant body and facial expression when talking with the group or with particular individuals
- Using different tones of voice when addressing particular learners

Each learner deserves a level of respect from the instructor. An effective means of learning is modeling behaviors and approaches, and learners acutely observe these in the studio setting. Many learner respect issues can be addressed through the establishment of a set of studio rules.

Studio Society Rules

Many problems can be avoided through the establishment of a set of rules during the initial meeting of a studio course. Instructors may engage learners in the rule-setting process through verbal or written suggestions that are subsequently discussed. People in general are more likely to uphold a set of rules that they have helped to generate themselves, and existence of rules can be a relief when issues arise. Some of the common "problem" topics to address with rules are

- Borrowing tools
- Noise (music and other)
- Cell phones
- Constructive criticism (attitude in studio)
- Guests (including their independent access to studio during off hours)

CRITIQUE

In *Designing Criticism: Integrating Written Criticism in Interior Design Education*, Mary Anne Beecher notes the importance of criticism's role in interior design education and explains that criticism is particularly evident in the design studio, where critical judgments are conveyed on a regular and often public basis.[11] Critiques may involve day-to-day or specially timed interactions between instructor and learners, guest designers, learners, or any combination thereof. Critiques may be informal or formal, and it is important for learners to adapt their behaviors and presentation of information to the educator's stated expectation of critique formality.

Unlike the critique of a new restaurant published in the morning newspaper, where the reviewer may be incognito and the review may be read in private, critique in design education is a highly personal event. Readying learners to arrive prepared for the type, length, and formality of a critique paves the path to a highly informative experience. Many have questioned the process of critique, and the dynamics established during particular critique sessions. These will be addressed further in the Formalized Critique section that follows.

Role of Critique

For as long as design studios have existed, critique in one form or another has played a major role in the educational process. Critique, when delivered with respect and as constructive criticism, can be a pivotal experience for a learner. Likewise, when critique turns ugly, it can be a pivotal experience as well. Most designers remember their worst critique session more than their best during school.

Informal Critique

Informal critique implies meaningful and purposeful dialogue regarding a project with its learner-creator present. Opportunities for informal critique occur frequently within class times as well as during off hours.

Desk Critiques

Often referred to in shorthand language as **desk crits**, these provide an almost daily opportunity to gauge a learner's progress and engage them in discussion regarding aspects of their projects. It is sometimes the case that an instructor will go to a learner's desk and hear, "Well, I haven't done anything since I last spoke with you." Rather than moving to the next desk, this sentence might initiate a teaching moment. Perhaps this learner needs assistance in time management or setting goals. The perceptive educator does not leave their desk without establishing goals for the next time (even if it is two hours hence). For many educators, desk crits are the most fulfilling part of teaching, for it is here that they feel most directly the impact of their guidance, probing, and questioning and can encourage learners' independence.

Tips for Desk Critiques

- As time is always limited during studio, provide critique criteria to learners and pair them up to review each others' work before arriving. This makes the most of studio time and also prompts learners to learn from and teach each other.
- Know how much time is available to spend with each learner so that it is distributed equitably with each one. Have learners sign up on a centrally located sheet of paper, chalkboard, or whiteboard for their critique session to insure a level of preparedness and expectation.
- Utilize a variety of means to alter the order of desk critiques. Communicate to learners when a sign-up for desk crit is to be utilized, when you will begin at one end of the room and move to the other, or begin in the middle and work your way around. Be careful not to repeatedly start or end at the same learner's desk.
- Reinforce the learner's creative exploration and individual process.
- When appropriate, encourage surrounding learners to gather around when you are giving a critique that you know is needed by many. This may be impromptu, when a particular issue is seen at multiple times. Small group gatherings at learner desks alleviate the need to repeat similar information time and again and serve to allow the instructor to utilize various examples to illustrate a point.
- Remind learners that they might additionally take advantage of office hours should they need further guidance. Some educators also offer extra opportunities for guidance at critical junctures of a project, or move critique to the privacy of their offices with sign-up times for intensive one-on-one reviews.

Formalized Critique

A hallmark of the studio experience, the "jury" process of formalized critique has perhaps nonetheless garnered the most criticism of any aspect of design education. Boyer and Mitgang, in what is commonly referred to as the "Boyer Report," encourage free-flowing dialogue in design critiques, rather than one-way conversations in which faculty and invited critics talk while students remain silent. The latter, they contend, sets up tension-packed, autocratic experiences. Suggestions follow to assist educators in encouraging positive critique experiences.[12]

Interior design educator Mary Anne Beecher, in a recent JID article, discusses benefits of formalized student-generated written criticism. "Offering students the opportunity to develop their own critical writing abilities also provides them a chance to apply and expand their creativity. The development of a strong written critical argument requires the critic to make a series of creative decisions that are analogous to those used in the architectural design process. When constructing an effective argument, he or she must make decisions regarding context (the argument's site and framework), concept (the critical position), materials (the words chosen to articulate ideas), and details (the supportive evidence). Design students engaged in writing criticism should see the process as a creative act that enables them to express their voice in a range of forms. As with design, their success relies on making good choices about structure and language."[13]

Tips for Formalized Critique

- Determine in advance educational goals and procedures for the formal critique and communicate these to the reviewers.
- Pair guest critics so that they complement each other in approach and experience.
- Structure the physical environment, positioning reviewers, other learners, and the presenting learner in positions where the lighting is supportive and the project will be seen in a non-distracting manner.
- Split up learners to a manageable review group size of around six learners to keep perspectives fresh and comments engaging. Facilitate a comparison of comments in each review group once the entire studio group is reassembled as a basis for discussing relative merits, valuing diverse views, and redirecting learner energies towards the next phase or project.
- Ask critics to make a final summary set of observations or comments when all learners in the group have been reviewed.

Peer Critique

Learners can be thoughtful and insightful critics. They are familiar with the intricacies of the project (having tried to work out their own solutions) and can comment on many areas of their peers' designs. One reason to engage learners in peer critiques is to assist them in forming constructive criticism skills. These critiques may occur at various stages of the project.

Peer groups may be formed with four to five people. These groups may meet periodically, often at times related to the phases of the project's design process. These smaller peer groups may compel learners to get more comfortable in presenting their ideas and progress, and groups can follow and nurture a fellow learner through their individual challenges. These peer groups work well when all learners engage in the discussion and offer suggestions. Instructors can "float" among groups, observing process and progress with an eye to potential problems.

Peer evaluations may be written. At the schematic design phase, for instance, learners may be assigned to write a structured peer evaluation of three other learners' work. Instructors may use this opportunity to

IDES 450

Design Development Peer Review

Name of Designer: ______________________

Your Name: ______________________

Include a space for designer and reviewer for accountability. Learners may converse after the evaluation period to clarify comments.

Answer the following questions thoughtfully and clearly, be as helpful as possible to the designer. Use specific examples to ensure clarity in your observations and advice.

Over-generalization is avoided when specific examples are required.

1. Overall situation: What steps should the designer take to complete the **decision making** on this design? Be both specific and helpful in listing the three most important actions below.

A.

Avoid yes or no questions. In this case, learners must first examine the project carefully, then discern the most important 'next steps.'

B.

C.

2. Do the drawings reinforce each other and give a clear idea of the intentions of the designer? If not, give specific suggestions for improvement.

Draw reviewer's attention to specific aspects of the project at this phase. Always include requirements for constructive observations and resulting statements.

3. Indicate program and functional requirements that are not currently met, along with potential solutions to resolve the situation.

Peers have been working with similar program and functional requirements and are often the quickest to see where these have not been fulfilled in another's project. Asking for potential solutions challenges the reviewer to a higher level of learning.

Figure 5.3 Peer review forms give guidance to learners as they structure feedback and direct their attention to respond within a particular construct. Likewise, students receive constructive comments that direct growth in their project. It is advisable to assign a minimum of three reviewers to each project; in this way, learners both give and receive multiple responses.

heighten the variety of problem-solving approaches, assigning peer evaluations among learners who approach the problem differently or who are weak or strong in identified areas. Peer critique may be structured differently for projects early in a design learner's career as a means of teaching about "effective critique" as well as providing less threatening feedback to the designer. An example of a peer review form utilized in a senior design studio, along with suggestions to engage learners, is shown in Figure 5.3.

In *Re-Thinking Studio Critique: Three New Strategies*, Watson-Zollinger and Salmi suggest three strategies—Prompts; Praise, Question, Polish (PQP); and Six Hats of Critique—for peer critique when an established framework is utilized by the studio educator.[14]

Prompts. Prompts are simple guidelines based on learner readings, class discussion, or a taxonomy of criticism developed by the instructor and they form the foundation of this method of critique. Prompts can also consist of a more formal taxonomy that employs normative, interpretive, and descriptive criticism as types of criticism within which to frame the critique:

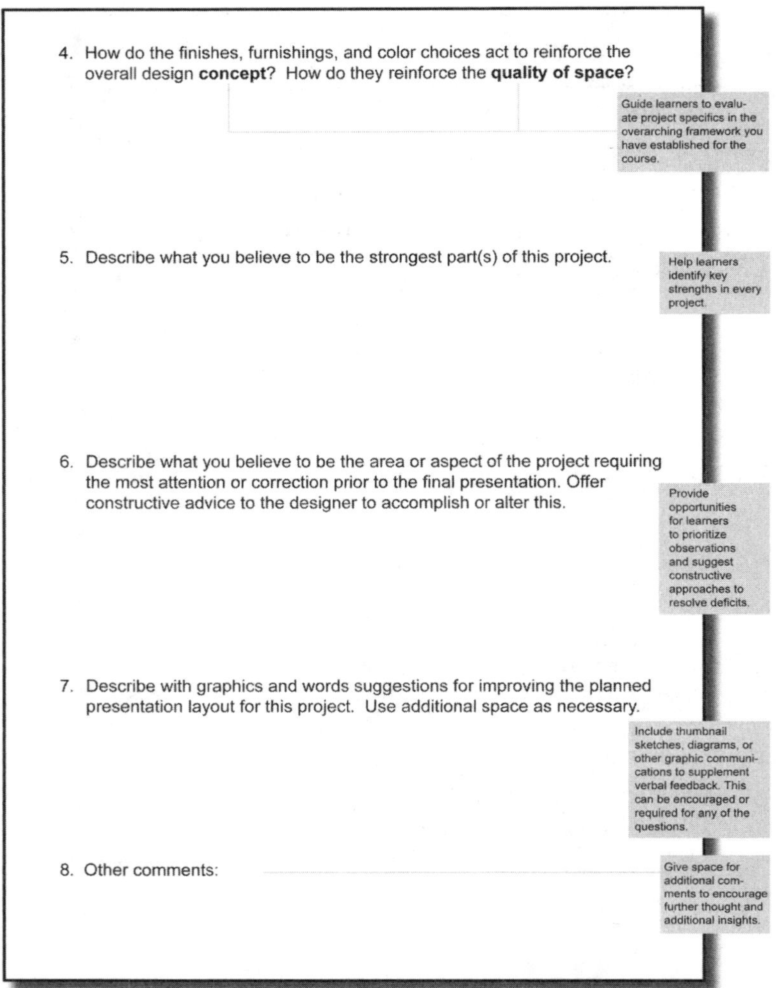

4. How do the finishes, furnishings, and color choices act to reinforce the overall design **concept**? How do they reinforce the **quality of space**?

Guide learners to evaluate project specifics in the overarching framework you have established for the course.

5. Describe what you believe to be the strongest part(s) of this project.

Help learners identify key strengths in every project.

6. Describe what you believe to be the area or aspect of the project requiring the most attention or correction prior to the final presentation. Offer constructive advice to the designer to accomplish or alter this.

Provide opportunities for learners to prioritize observations and suggest constructive approaches to resolve deficits.

7. Describe with graphics and words suggestions for improving the planned presentation layout for this project. Use additional space as necessary.

Include thumbnail sketches, diagrams, or other graphic communications to supplement verbal feedback. This can be encouraged or required for any of the questions.

8. Other comments:

Give space for additional comments to encourage further thought and additional insights.

Figure 5.3 (*Continued*)

- **Normative criticism** depends upon formal aspects of design, with primary observations of style; mass/space; scale and proportion; material and balance; form, texture, rhythm, light, color, pattern, and ornamentation. These observations, as well as organizing principles for analysis, help learners interpret relevance.
- **Interpretive criticism** attempts to make learners see the designed environment in a subjective way by relating to feelings and impressions. Impressions projected onto a space by descriptions such as solemn, inviting, cheerful, soft, or edgy exemplify some of the emotionally descriptive terms representative of interpretive criticism.
- **Descriptive criticism** provides a social, political, and economic context affecting design decisions. It provides a glimpse of how ideas develop based on a broader context than the learners' own experiences.

Praise, Question, Polish (PQP)

- PQP is most effective while work is in progress and when learners work in small groups (three to four people).Using design vocabulary, learners make praise statements about each piece of work.

- Learners ask questions about anything pertaining to the project—technique, content, plans, and the like.
- Discussion finally centers on polish—suggestions for improvement.

Six Hats of Critique. Based on the book *Six Thinking Hats* (1999) by Edward deBono, each hat represents a role the mind plays in the critical thinking process. Learners are forced to look at the project from a variety of perspectives by switching from one hat to another. Each learner writes a minimum of three statements for each of the six hats, assuring the studio educator that the major points in the critical thinking process have been covered. For instance, if a learner is "wearing" the Red Hat, associated with the emotional responses, they would acknowledge their non-rational response to the project, asking such questions as "Does the design have potential?" or "What does this design remind me of?" Likewise, if the learner is "wearing" the Black Hat, their responses would be focused on the weaknesses of the project solution and ask questions such as "What problems will be created if this solution is accepted?" or "What are the weaknesses of this project solution?"

STUDIO ASSESSMENT

Studio educator evaluations may have a formative or summative assessment purpose, or a combination of the two. Evaluations become an additional teaching tool, communicating the educator's perception of how well the learner met stated objectives for the project, class activity, or course.

Benefits of Formative Assessment

Formative assessment is offered to learners while the studio project is in progress. When initiating a project description, the educator has an opportunity to determine when evaluation opportunities present themselves. On many projects, the process of design encourages incremental phases where evaluation occurs. For other projects (usually of limited scope), only a single evaluation may be necessary. Some instructors find that it is most helpful with large studio projects to build in and adhere to incremental deadlines and requirements. These requirements, for instance, might mirror the real-life stages of a design project, such as concept development, schematic development, design development, and so forth. There are benefits to such incremental deadlines:

- Keeps learners motivated and continually advancing.
- Educators can more effectively critique and shape work that is evolving over a period of time.
- Learners have an ongoing understanding of their progress and learning and can target weaknesses along the way.
- Learners feel less pressure at project's end because they are aware of their ongoing successes and challenges.

Multiple Feedback

As students each learn in their own fashion, they similarly internalize feedback in different ways. Multiple modes of feedback insure that each learner is able to process information appropriately. Next are tips for providing various methods of feedback.

Written evaluation ideas

- Provide grade sheet to learners in advance so they are familiar with grading criteria.
- Photograph in-progress or completed work and insert the image on the grade sheet. Learners enjoy seeing their work in this fashion, and this can ease the

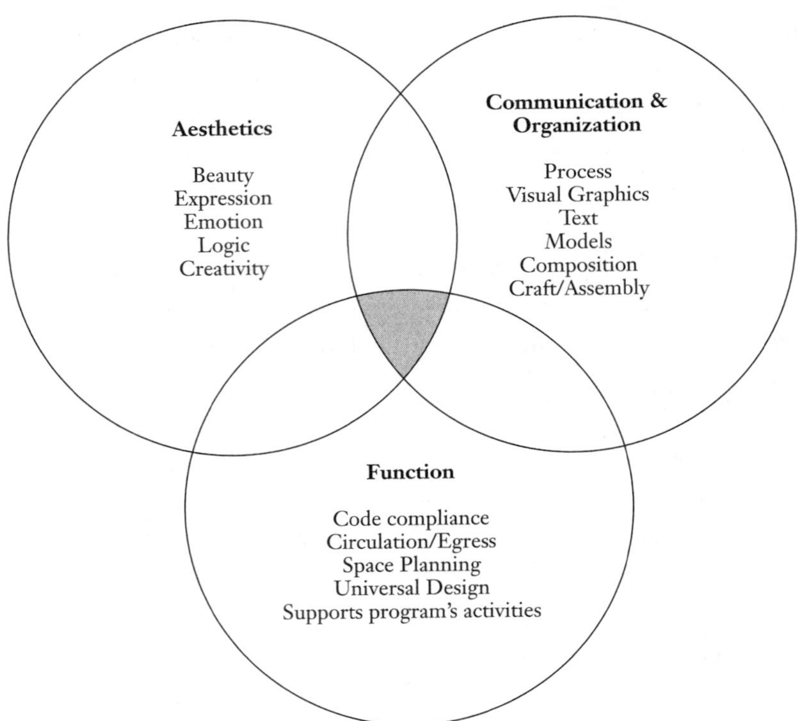

Figure 5.4 An excellent studio project involves thoughtful attention to three different aspects of design. The gray area shows that the best projects find balance in all three, achieving a harmony where no element is over- or underemphasized.

honest comments that must accompany grades.

Verbal evaluation ideas

- Videotape learners' verbal presentations to allow their later review of body language, verbal habits, and speaking qualities.
- Provide learners with guidance on their verbal delivery. Most learners are tempted to painfully walk observers through minute details while never fully offering a glimpse of the projects' main concept. Reviewing past semesters' videotaped presentations can be very enlightening. Be sure to verify with your institution any privacy requirements or permissions required from previous students prior to showing the examples.
- Require learners to provide a preview of their verbal presentation in written outline form.

Studio grading rubrics. Studio projects can be among the most difficult to grade, especially when projects are advanced in nature and incorporate many different types of competencies. It is helpful to share with learners at the beginning of the semester the types of skills they will be asked to develop and express, and a generalized studio grading rubric such as that illustrated in Figure 5.4 can assist with this.

This generalized rubric can then be expanded as appropriate for assessment of the specific semester projects. A rubric that describes a theoretical project earning a letter grade of A, B, and so on is also helpful in describing expectations to learners. An example of this rubric type can be found in the Grading Rubrics section of Chapter 3.

Summative Assessment

While formative assessments are designed as a part of the ongoing process of design studio, typically providing learners with guid-

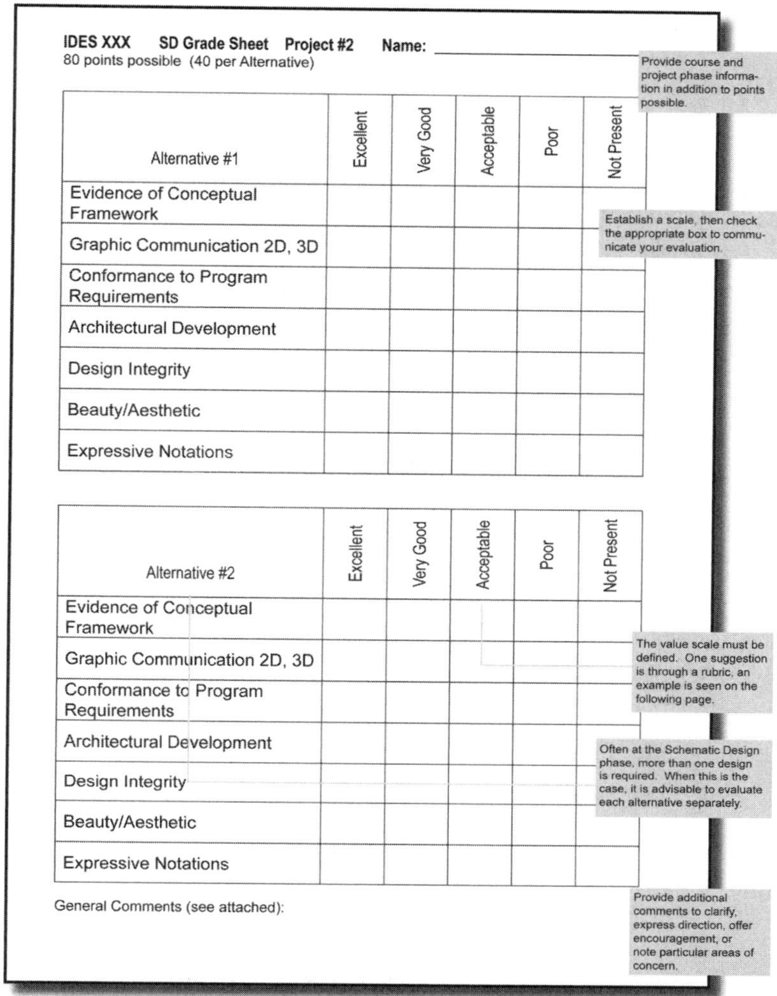

IDES XXX SD Grade Sheet Project #2 **Name:** ____________________

80 points possible (40 per Alternative)

Alternative #1	Excellent	Very Good	Acceptable	Poor	Not Present
Evidence of Conceptual Framework					
Graphic Communication 2D, 3D					
Conformance to Program Requirements					
Architectural Development					
Design Integrity					
Beauty/Aesthetic					
Expressive Notations					

Alternative #2	Excellent	Very Good	Acceptable	Poor	Not Present
Evidence of Conceptual Framework					
Graphic Communication 2D, 3D					
Conformance to Program Requirements					
Architectural Development					
Design Integrity					
Beauty/Aesthetic					
Expressive Notations					

General Comments (see attached):

Figure 5.5 Rubrics associated with grade sheets communicate assessment criteria as well as expectations for excellence.

ance and direction, **summative assessments** are designed to determine if and how well the learner succeeded at particular activities. Summative assessments answer the question "Did the learner achieve desired learning outcomes to the desired level of mastery?" Figure 5.5 provides an example of a summative assessment. Notice the large amount of information and expectation communicated in the associated rubric.

FURTHER IDEAS

The studio provides a rich environment for collaboration and exploration. Additional ideas to consider when planning a studio course:

- Collaborate with learners in other majors such as psychology, graphics, or anthropology. Learners come to understand the value and context of design within larger society through collaboration between fields of knowledge and expertise.
- Use digital technology to partner with other institutions' learners or practitioners. Multiple voices from various perspectives enrich the learning environment. Create times for a synchronous critique using digital technology, or create asynchronous posts to the Web where

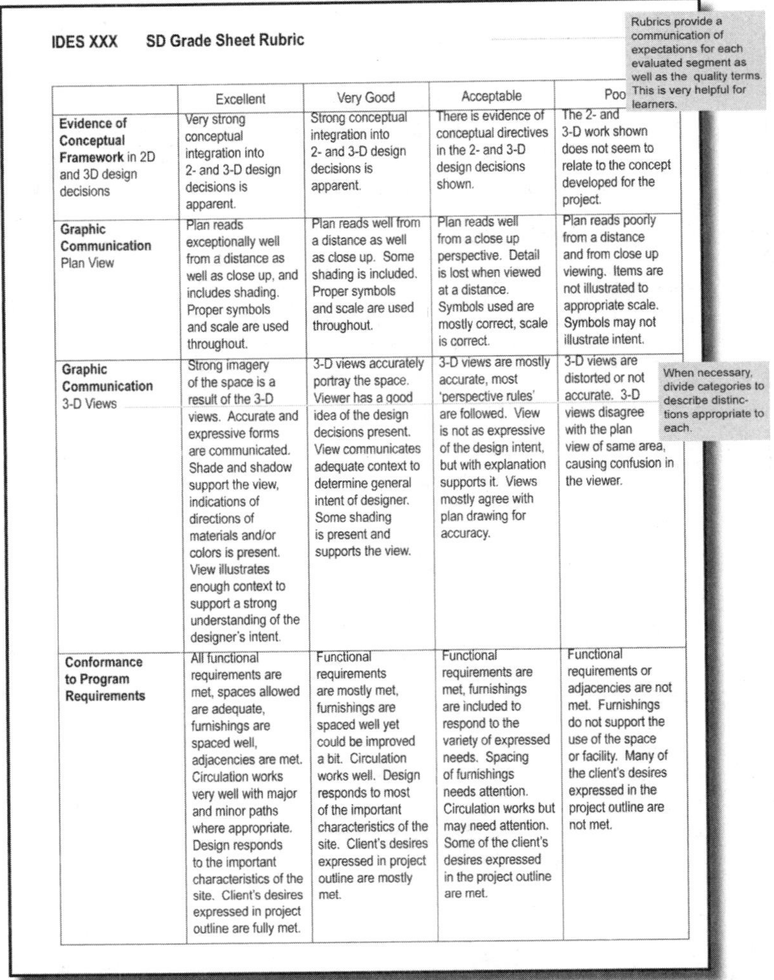

IDES XXX SD Grade Sheet Rubric

	Excellent	Very Good	Acceptable	Poo
Evidence of Conceptual Framework in 2D and 3D design decisions	Very strong conceptual integration into 2- and 3-D design decisions is apparent.	Strong conceptual integration into 2- and 3-D design decisions is apparent.	There is evidence of conceptual directives in the 2- and 3-D design decisions shown.	The 2- and 3-D work shown does not seem to relate to the concept developed for the project.
Graphic Communication Plan View	Plan reads exceptionally well from a distance as well as close up, and includes shading. Proper symbols and scale are used throughout.	Plan reads well from a distance as well as close up. Some shading is included. Proper symbols and scale are used throughout.	Plan reads well from a close up perspective. Detail is lost when viewed at a distance. Symbols used are mostly correct, scale is correct.	Plan reads poorly from a distance and from close up viewing. Items are not illustrated to appropriate scale. Symbols may not illustrate intent.
Graphic Communication 3-D Views	Strong imagery of the space is a result of the 3-D views. Accurate and expressive forms are communicated. Shade and shadow support the view, indications of directions of materials and/or colors is present. View illustrates enough context to support a strong understanding of the designer's intent.	3-D views accurately portray the space. Viewer has a good idea of the design decisions present. View communicates adequate context to determine general intent of designer. Some shading is present and supports the view.	3-D views are mostly accurate, most 'perspective rules' are followed. View is not as expressive of the design intent, but with explanation supports it. Views mostly agree with plan drawing for accuracy.	3-D views are distorted or not accurate. 3-D views disagree with the plan view of same area, causing confusion in the viewer.
Conformance to Program Requirements	All functional requirements are met, spaces allowed are adequate, furnishings are spaced well, adjacencies are met. Circulation works very well with major and minor paths where appropriate. Design responds to the important characteristics of the site. Client's desires expressed in project outline are fully met.	Functional requirements are mostly met, furnishings are spaced well yet could be improved a bit. Circulation works well. Design responds to most of the important characteristics of the site. Client's desires expressed in project outline are mostly met.	Functional requirements are met, furnishings are included to respond to the variety of expressed needs. Spacing of furnishings needs attention. Circulation works but may need attention. Some of the client's desires expressed in the project outline are met.	Functional requirements or adjacencies are not met. Furnishings do not support the use of the space or facility. Many of the client's desires expressed in the project outline are not met.

Figure 5.5 *(Continued)*

others may view and post comments for various phases.

- Incorporate service learning into a project. For example, provide design services for a non-profit organization or department at the institution. Vischer and Poldma describe an example thusly: "Teachers work in collaborative teams to promote both individual and collaborative learning in each year, depending on the skills and concepts being investigated and the educational goals of the particular studio topic. The first year design studio consists of an exploration of evolving and changing lifestyles and approaches to living in a complex, technologically charged, and socially mutating world. This urban exploration of social issues in design is explored on three levels, including the homeless, socially challenging neighborhoods, and the design of interior spaces for families with 'real scenarios' of living."[15]
- In the case of complex projects, split up the necessary programmatic research and require learners to provide handouts and give verbal synopsis presentations to each other regarding codes, adjacencies, and other issues.
- For interest, require that some projects are taken to the full extent of design development, complete with "tight"

line style, full color rendering, and other refined treatments. For other, perhaps shorter, projects during the academic term, set the standard at a more "loose" design development style that is presented in booklet form. This may mimic that real-life project on a short turnaround and demonstrates to potential employers that learners can react favorably to condensed project schedules.

- It is helpful to keep in mind that not all project components must be taken to a high level of refinement to assess learners' capabilities. Similarly, accreditation standards rarely dictate a full presentation progression for all projects. Be sensitive to the length of time learners will require for the labor-intensive refinement and presentation aspects of studio projects.
- Learners learn a great deal from the work of others. Photograph the best of each semester's projects and provide a presentation of them to the next semesters' learners, explaining positive and could-be-improved aspects of the projects.
- Have learners keep a course or project journal. Educators Miller, Sattar, and Gentry found that journals encourage a connection of past experiences and prior knowledge to current situations, thus increasing the level of critical thinking in the studio. Journals can include a combination of observation through annotated sketches, recording of facts and perceptions of peer and educator feedback, and reflective writing.[16]

Studio is one of the defining attributes of a design education. Through studio, a culture that values creativity, design, and respectful discourse is established and nurtured. Careful attention to the physical and educational aspects of studio can promote the highest level of integrative and evaluative learning. Crafting of project descriptions, design of assessment strategies, and approach to critique opportunities—each communicate to learners the values and expectations for success.

ENDNOTES

1. Ochsner, Jeffrey Karl. (2000). Behind the Mask: A Psychoanalytic Perspective on Interaction in the Design Studio. *JAE* (May): 195.
2. Ibid., p. 195.
3. Kellogg, Clark. (January 2006). Learning from Studio. A *DesignIntelligence* Knowledge Report, p. 4. *DesignIntelligence* is a product of Greenway Communications International, LLC. Clark's background is in design, business, and education, with over twenty-five years experience in architecture, product design, graphic design, communications, exhibits, and film/video.
4. Ibid., adapted from pp. 5–12. While this publication has a distinctly architectural bent, the discussion of studio is no less relevant to interior design.
5. Bender, Diane & Vredevoogd, Jon. (2006). Using Online Education Technologies to Support Studio Instruction. *Educational Technology & Society, 9*(4): 115.
6. Ibid.
7. Ochsner. (2000), p. 196.
8. Adapted from Clemons, Stephanie, et al. (2007). Infusing Third Place Theory into a Studio Environment: A Qualitative Inquiry. *Proceedings of the 2007 International Interior Design Educators Council Conference.* Austin, TX, pp. 138–147.
9. Awwad-Rafferty, Rula. (2006). Designing in Two Worlds: Shoshone Bannock Tribes Inspire an Alternative Worldview for Interior Design Studio. *Proceedings of the 2006 International Interior Design Educators Council Conference.* Scottsdale, AZ, pp. 113–117.
10. Ibid.
11. Beecher, Mary Anne. (2006). Designing Criticism: Integrating Written Criticism in Interior Design Education. *Journal of Interior Design 31*(3): 54–61.
12. Boyer, Ernest L. &. Mitgang, Lee D. (1996). *Building Community: A New Future for Architecture Education and Practice.* Princeton, NJ: Carnegie Foundation.

13. Beecher. (2006)., p. 54.
14. Watson-Zollinger, S. & Salmi, P. (2006). Re-Thinking Studio Critique: Three New Strategies. *Proceedings of the 2006 International Interior Design Educators Council Conference.* Scottsdale, AZ, pp. 75–79.
15. Vischer, J. & Poldma, T. (2003). *Growing a Discipline: Evolving Learning Practices in Interior Design.* Retrieved 9/30/07 from Interior Design/Interior Architecture Educators Association at http://www.idea-edu.com/alt_content/pdf/2003/Dr_Jacqueline_Vischer_and_Dr_Tiiu_Poldma.pdf.
16. Adapted from Miller, Nancy, Sattar, H. & Gentry, M. (2006). A Shifting Paradigm: Integrating Critical Thinking with the New Learning Styles of the Millennium Generation. *Proceedings of the 2006 International Interior Design Educators Council Conference,* Scottsdale, AZ, pp. 149–154.

CHAPTER 6

Teaching and Learning at a Distance

Interior design student Martin Jones checks his watch. He does not want to be late for the scheduled online session as he eagerly awaits the guest speaker. Persons other than the instructor have formed an important part of this seminar course. Martin thinks back to his parents' tales of college life. They were required to be physically on campus every day. Bringing in a speaker often meant air travel, a car to the airport 140 miles away to pick up the speaker and bring them to campus. The changes from then to now have been dramatic, and technology has made communication easier–almost literally a keyboard click away.

Martin checks his watch again, anticipating the discussion session scheduled to follow the presentation. He goes online to flip through his classmates' web posts, marveling at the variety of experiences and locations of each. He reviews the speaker's biography and recent projects. Almost time, he types in the URL and joins the real-time class session pre-arranged for this speaker. The past speakers from London, Chicago, and San Francisco have been inspiring and true leaders in their individual specialty practice areas. Martin enjoys the ability to ask questions and have a record of both the presentation as well as the following discussion. He wonders what the concluding questions will be this week and how his classmates in India and France will frame their responses.

Imagine a community, composed of learners and educators from around the globe, interacting and learning from one another. Such is the potential of distance education and the potential reality with online education opportunities. Regardless of location, distance education provides opportunities for students and faculty to engage in a wide variety of activities, some real-time and some asynchronous. With increasing bandwidth and information transfer speeds, many of the earlier technical concerns and perceptions of online distance education are diminished. However, technical issues are but one facet of distance education, just as the classroom is but one part of the learning equation for traditionally delivered education.

Distance education has been present at many universities for many years. What differentiates current distance learning from its historic form is largely technological advances. Because interactive online education is a relatively new endeavor, educators have questions and concerns covering a wide variety of issues, including how students learn online, potential benefits and detriments to increasing online education, how to develop a new or translate an existing course to an online format to the greatest advantage, and what lessons have been learned from other interior design educators in developing and delivering online courses (or online components of traditional, face-to-face courses). This chapter addresses each of these topics and also provides an overview of how distance education in interior design has evolved.

STUDENTS AND ONLINE LEARNING

Increasingly, the Internet provides a social context unique in several attributes and possessing an evolving set of social constructs. Rather than looking at learning as the acquisition of certain forms of knowledge, researchers Jean Lave and Etienne Wenger place it in social relationships, or "situations of co-participation." Conceptually, this learning theory maximizes opportunities for students to negotiate meanings in social contexts—to communicate and test understanding with and against that of others in an environment that is familiar and safe for the learner. This can be within their social environment, the course environment, and web-based communities as "Communities of Practice" develop around things that matter to people.[1]

Educational psychologist William Glasser's research on learning modes demonstrated that people typically retain 80% of what they learn when actually experiencing the content. When learning experiences are designed and delivered that actively involve students in the creation of their own knowledge, it follows that learning is enhanced. This constructivist approach to learning supports the scaffolding of new knowledge, and while Internet and web-based learning does not exclusively imply that this approach is inherent, it provides opportunities for new experiences and a new kind of social interaction.

Evolution of Distance Learning in Interior Design Education

While the concept and practice of distance learning has been present in higher education for decades, the widespread application to various facets of interior design education is relatively new. The earliest days of distance education took the form of correspondence courses in a wide array of disciplines including interior design. Examples of these correspondence courses date back to the first half of the twentieth century and span to present times. Utilizing the traditional postal system to distribute and collect materials, courses were restricted in deliverable content and necessarily involved a passage of time. Course deliverables in this venue were and are typically geared towards the individual learner.

A new wave of distance teaching followed, often accomplished through one- or two-way closed-circuit television typically oriented toward particular branch campus locations. An early example of this closed-circuit television system was the Washington Higher Education Telecommunication System (WHETS), founded in 1983 to serve as the principal distance learning delivery tool for the developing Washington State University branch campuses in Tri-Cities Vancouver and Spokane.[2] This system made it viable to provide interior design lecture courses such as professional practices to groups of learners simultaneously at two geographically remote campuses.

Multiple technical personnel, such as camera operators and technical assistance for the instructor, are needed to make closed-circuit television possible. Use of a closed-circuit interactive television system allows a (more or less) traditional community–a class–of learners, requires of faculty a similar approach to teaching as a traditional classroom (albeit with slight differences in issues of inclusion and delivery style), and at a minimum allows direct audio contact among students (and at a maximum, allows video and audio contact). However, cost of personnel and the need for specific facilities can cause similar scheduling and space issues as traditional campus classrooms.

Changes in perception of the value of distance learning along with technological advances have encouraged creative thinking toward the potential impact of this learning approach. Whether a truly asynchronous course, a synchronous, or hybrid approach to the distance component, increased Internet bandwidth and speed of information processing has encouraged a more seamless flow of information. Early experiments with distance education using the Internet in the 1990s met resistance in large part due to early limited bandwidth and the limitations of personal computers. While the concept of universal reach and availability provided hope, the reality of dial-up modems in student homes provided frustrations and, in some cases, inability to access course components. In many ways, these attempts modeled the earlier correspondence course attitudes and approaches, merely using new technology to accomplish the same ends.

Current practice and research regarding distance learning within interior design education typically focuses on the two course types of lecture/seminar and studio. However, a trend has developed to incorporate principles of distance learning in additional course types, such as discussion-based seminar courses.

General educational literature supports and describes effective strategies of teaching and learning in the online environment for lecture and seminar courses, and studies can be found that explore both its advantages and challenges. As the number of instructors who have taught an online course increases, educators have increased support among peers, and administrators have a wider range of examples to base time estimates on.

While studio courses have often been seen as inapplicable to online education, with the exception of critique, the potential of teaching studio in an online environment is becoming a more realistic possibility. The online environment for studio is currently finding success in guest critique and participation or collaboration among universities on a shared project. In part, this may stem from the success of project-based learning approaches in other disciplines and subsequent publication on successful strategies. Increasingly interactive software that can provide a digital environment to support studio activities may play an even larger part.

Students and expectations of education are also evolving. Research presented in a recent Pew Internet & American Life Project suggests a culturally different college experience is dawning, at least as far as the Internet is concerned. Nearly half the students surveyed indicate that email is a communication tool that "allows them to more freely express their ideas to professors"[3] and "allows social connections already forged to continue to be cultivated in addition to allowing new relationships to be formed."[4] The study further describes that virtual study groups are commonplace. Consequently, the Internet "is allowing students who live off campus to maintain a relationship with their academic environment from a distance. Three-fourths of college students reported using the Internet to communicate with classmates about group projects."[5] As students and faculty alike become more digitally versed and the Internet continues to provide the means of gaining information and facilitating communication, course delivery may experience similar changes. Case studies at the end of this chapter describe individual experiences in distance education for interior design courses.

Potentials and Pitfalls of the Remote Teaching/Learning Environment

The potential for reflection, rich discussion, freedom of participation at any time (usually during an established calendar time frame), and removal of geographic barriers are some of the most compelling potentials of distance learning. The impact of distance education through online methods lies in providing opportunities to those place-bound for whatever reason and to allow exposure to a more enhanced and diverse tapestry and depth of knowledge than is often possible in the physical classroom.

In *Designing Courses and Teaching on the Web*, noted educational technology expert Dr. Mercedes Fisher describes the potentials of distance education: "The rapid pace of technological change and its requirements for life-long learning, the complexity of our society and its escalating challenges and finite resources, and the need to prepare an increasingly diverse student population to live productively and harmoniously requires academia to discover new ways of addressing the discovery, dissemination, and implementation of knowledge. Education can no longer be defined by static guidelines but rather by growing, changing, and evolving new sets of opportunities, projects, technology, and people. Education is the soul of the new information-systems society. It serves as an enabler for students to synthesize knowledge and to create, perform, and encourage their passion for learning."[6]

This potential does not come without cost, however. For many instructors, online instruction requires a shift in paradigm, learning to thrive in a new culture of teaching and learning, and adapting to new technologies (where often the only constant is change).

While many educators have embraced, or at least acknowledged, the potentials of distance education opportunities in interior design education, some express an underlying trepidation about the challenge of learning new technologies in addition to remaining current in their area of expertise. However, technology is becoming more user-friendly to the educator-user. This, coupled with increased accessibility of interior design-specific examples, will likely decrease the fear factor while increasing objective evaluation. In many cases, the complex and changing software does not need to be mastered by the educator; rather, understanding the limitations and potentials of the digital terrain in which to work is key.

According to Fisher: "The most challenging obstacle instructors will experience is their own fear of delving into the unknown. That is not to say that instructors are afraid of technology but of the consequences of technology. The Web presents a call to shift major paradigms about the ways in which learning takes place."[7] Those who currently teach an online course might sum up challenges as increased time in initial preparation, answering emails, and the administrative attitudes concerning workload.

Basic challenges of online education in any field can be summed up in these issues:

1. Engaging the students attention in the absence of direct eye contact.
2. Facilitating interaction not only between student and instructor but between student and student.
3. Creating a sense of community among

students who are separated in space and time.[8]

This may prove an extra challenge in interior design education, where much of the educational process is typically centered on a direct relationship and proximity of educator and learner.

Students and Learning in the Virtual World

The new generation of traditional college students has grown up with the Internet and computer use for communication, entertainment, and information. The most recent high school graduates have not known a time without the Internet and computer technology, and most were creating PowerPoint presentations in elementary or secondary school. From their experience, communicating through the Internet is as seamless and natural as picking up a phone. Retrieving information from online sources is the first inclination of most students, as are obtaining news and current events. Movie and game entertainment is also prevalent through the Internet. A growing percentage of learners come to physical class with extensive experience using multiple technologies for social, educational, and recreational purposes, which in essence makes them more facile with technology than many educators. "In practical terms, the most compelling questions represent two sides of the same coin: How will teachers who know how to teach but are not fluent in new technologies teach students who are fluent with new technologies but don't know how to use them critically?"[9] With the increasing availability of distance learning technologies, learners are altering when they sleep, when they work, and when and how they take classes. And, unlike the early forms of distance education where isolation and separateness prevailed, learners are now able to benefit from an educational experience that may be even more engaging and fulfilling than that of face-to-face learning.

Comfort in the Virtual World

The pervasive quality of technology in society is, not surprisingly, affecting students' affinity for how they learn. Exposure to entertainment, the tools they use to communicate, their mobility, and the Internet are all factors in the desire for increased project-based learning. Learners want education that better serves their needs and interests. They learn best when the topic is of immediate value. Educators can tap into this diversity of experience and idea sharing to enhance courses and learning for all.[10]

Tapping into the potential of the Internet to deliver and facilitate learning holds significant potential. The ability of the Internet to provide active learning opportunities (interactive, discussion, and project-based activities) provides richness in the new paradigm of education. In order to be successful, however, online learners must possess a healthy amount of self discipline, responsibility, and organization.

Motivation to Take an Online Course

There are several reasons students may elect to engage in online learning:

- Online learning offers the opportunity for students to learn at their own pace, focusing on learning new content while skipping through material they already know.
- Flexibility in timing allows students to learn when it is most convenient for them.
- Multiple content delivery styles allow students to choose and use their best personal learning styles.
- Learners are able to formulate thoughtful dialogue, respond, or initiate discussion without the direct pressure of a classroom of people.

- Flexibility in learning allows students to access information where it is most convenient for them.
- Online learning provides opportunities to connect with the larger professional community, to collaborate with a wide range of peers and faculty, and to reflect on experiences.

APPROACH TO TEACHING

The digital classroom presents a different dynamic than the one for which most instructors have been trained, if they have received training at all. Many instructors model the educational strategies of their own teachers. The tools and pedagogy that are available through the new medium of online learning are changing and improving at a remarkably rapid pace and make the whole education enterprise more innovative and exciting for those who partake. With distance learning technologies, educators can develop and embrace new teaching methodologies rather than merely adapting old pedagogy to their online courses.

Course Design and Development

Whether developing a new course, or translating an existing course to an online offering, the same basic premises of creating a quality learning environment are often used (though perhaps envisioned differently). For more information on the learning styles or theories discussed here, see Chapter 2. Much can be gained from several published sources with solid advice and approaches to online education across disciplinary fields.[11] In addition, examples of online uses in interior design education are presented in the Interior Design Educators Council (IDEC) International Conference Proceedings, as well as the *Journal of Interior Design* (JID). The listserv available through membership in the IDEC organization provides a rich source of colleagues across the continents who are willing to share their experiences in this venue. Specific conferences are available that address online education, notably the Annual Conference on Distance Teaching and Learning at Madison, Wisconsin. This conference provides an exchange of current resources, research, and best practices from around the world relevant to the design and delivery of distance education and training in all educational fields.

When considering design of the virtual classroom and the learning activities that will occur within it, a parallel analogy to the traditional classroom can serve as a valid starting point. Regardless of whether the course is offered online or face to face, effective classrooms have the following characteristics:

- They provide the tools learners need when they need them. If it is not possible to have all the tools in the classroom, an effective educator explains where the tools can easily be located.
- They create an expectation for and an environment conducive to learning.
- They bring together educators and learners to share information and exchange ideas.
- They allow learners the freedom to experiment, test their knowledge, practice completing tasks, and apply what they have discussed or read.
- They provide mechanisms for evaluating performance.
- They provide a safe haven in which learning can occur.[12]

Just as with face-to-face education, the educator must develop course content that sets high expectations for learners and makes tools for learning easily and readily available. Most face-to-face college class activities fit into

- Instructor presentations
- Discussions
- Group-oriented work
- Learner presentations
- Research
- Assessment

As with most valued face-to-face educational practices, taking the time to plan quality, interactive lessons is critical to successful online courses.[13] Iverson, a noted e-learning researcher and author, believes that for online education to be successful, learning must be

1. Engaging and active (get learners actively involved)
2. Positive and supportive (a caring, positive atmosphere)
3. Collaborative (cooperative and group learning)
4. Contextual (relevant with real-life applications)[14]

Many steps are involved in the effective design and development of an online course, whether beginning a new course or adapting an existing course. In the case of the latter, it is often beneficial to re-conceptualize the existing course with the same approach one would take with a new course, with a fresh outlook. One such process for creating an online course is outlined here.

1. Identify learning objectives for the course. Refer to Chapter 2 for an in-depth discussion of writing objectives.
2. Determine the content that is critical to teach and that which is beneficial but not essential to accomplish the objectives.
3. Identify available resources. Think of resources in terms of reading materials, useful websites, guests, students, delivery systems, and time.
4. Write and post the syllabus. Ideally, the syllabus contains links to course content areas, such as "grading criteria," "course description," and the like.
5. Identify measurable learning outcomes that will demonstrate whether course objectives have been met. Chapter 2 discusses the development of effective student learning outcomes.
6. Determine the delivery system (for instance, a particular course management system such as Blackboard that the institution subscribes to).
7. Determine the assessment strategies for the learning outcomes. In many cases, established online assessments templates are available that ease educators' need to develop their own documents. In addition, rubrics and other tools to assess items such as discussion board participation are readily available. Guidelines and rules for online discussion should be developed that encourage learners to share experiences and refine ideas.
8. Create lessons, units, or modules (sometimes chapters in books can be module topics). Each unit focuses on a different topic and/or competency. Create five to ten units based on the length of the course and content. (Each unit does not need to be the same length.) Envision the content delivery and activities that will encourage learning. Visualize both content delivery and activities in a broad way, and be open to new ideas for interaction and discovery. Remember that in many cases, the delivery and activities may be prepared in advance and made accessible during particular time frames during the course. In other instances, a synchronous approach may serve best. Both can be accommodated within the same course. Consider the contribution of

- Collaborative work
- Balance of instructor-led versus learner-centered learning activities
- The value of discussion (Provide forums for interaction and create discussion questions.)
- Existing course materials (lecture notes, PowerPoint presentations, slides, images, and the like)
- The desirability and availability of audio

9. Develop a storyboard or flowchart diagram that can be used to sequence learning activities and can also serve as an overall reminder or teaching guide for the educator.
10. Finally, gather materials and web resources, scan materials, and assemble the course. (Refer to Chapter 3 for guidelines on Fair Use of materials for online teaching.) Even within established course management software, a certain amount of flexibility is available to design the "look" of the course and to determine which areas are accessible by students. Maintain a consistent visual identity to the course.

Some programs of interior design (or their institutional home) make available instructional design support to assist educators as they venture into the world of developing online courses. When this is the case, most of the steps outlined still apply; however, instructional designers bring a vast experience with teaching methodologies and are valuable counterparts to bounce ideas off of and collaborate with.

A useful springboard for correlating the instructional strategy, learning requirement, and instructional method for distance learning is provided in Table 6.1. While the table presents instructional strategies based on the learning requirement, it does not specifically address interactive activities between learners. Many sources are available that provide a plethora of suggested activities to engage online students in the course and with each other. Representative examples of these strategies are listed here, and the reader is encouraged to pursue the additional readings for a full complement of ideas.

- *Online Scavenger Hunt:* Send students on an online scavenger hunt to acclimate them to using web technologies. Include a variety of items to recover, including those found in academic journals (requiring online research and library skills), verifiable facts about a famous designer (requires more than one source), phone number or property address of a given firm, or other content. Be sure to require the online source URL.
- *Online Gallery Tour:* Engage in a virtual tour of a museum of art and ask learners to discuss perceptions of navigational ease, design of the "museum," and ease of locating works of art within.
- *Round Robin Activities:* Pose a topic or question, have learners start an answer, and then forward to another learner to add on, until a required number of learners have participated. Share the results by posting where the group or class can access the results.

With each of the strategies, it is important to remember that the educator must be explicit and up-front regarding expectations of learner participation and assignment quality. Additionally, with the advent and increasing use of online education, new (or changed and enhanced) theories of learning impact course design and delivery.

Chapter 2 discussed Gardner's theory that learners possess multiple intelligences, or ways of knowing. Similarly, in their work *Multiple Literacies: New Skills for a New Millennium*, Andrea Oseas and Julie M. Wood pro-

TABLE 6.1: MATRIX FOR SELECTING ONLINE DELIVERY METHODS BASED ON LEARNING REQUIREMENTS

Learning requirement	Instructional strategy/tactics	Instructional method (simplest possible)	Online delivery method
Fact	Rehearsal Mnemonic storage	Lecture/presentation, independent study	Web text pages, Web slide presentations
Concept classification	Show examples List critical attributes	Tutorial	Web text pages, online tutorial
Understanding (ideas)	Show relationships	Lecture/presentation, independent study	Web slide presentation, Web text pages, interstudent conferencing
Understanding (causal)	Build mental model through elaboration process	Laboratory	Website with database
Principle (recall)	Rule/example	Lecture/presentation, independent study	Web text pages, online tutorial
Principle (apply)	Rule/example plus elaboration	Tutorial	Online tutorial, inter-student conferencing
Procedural skill (recall)	Demo/modeling Rehearsal, mnemonics	Demonstration, lecture/presentation	Multimedia CD-ROM
Procedural skill (apply)	Practice & feedback	Drill & practice, laboratory	Multimedia tutorial
Generic thinking skill	Simple-to-complex sequencing, elaboration	Tutorial, laboratory	Online tutorial, website with database
Interpersonal skill	Provide a model Practice & feedback	Demonstration, simulation	Videoconferencing, interstudent conferencing
Attitude	Provide a model Practice & feedback	Demonstration, simulation	Videoconferencing, interstudent conferencing
Motor skill	Demo/modeling Practice & feedback	Demonstration, simulation, laboratory	Streaming video, videoconferencing

pose that learners will require more literacies or intellectual skills to function in the current transformational society of face-to-face and online situations. Multiple literacies can be conceived as learners' ability to identify and analyze messages embedded in a variety of different modalities, as well as the capacities to use these media to create and express their own messages.[15] In today's digital classroom, media literacy, visual literacy, and information literacy are of greatest consequence.[16]

In the design of learning environments associated with technologies, the attention to multiple literacies, especially media literacy, visual literacy, and information literacy is critical for learners to succeed in the present and future world. What are these new literacies?

In the current media-saturated culture, learners must learn to "read" as well as produce images with accuracy and effectiveness. *Media literacy* is the process of accessing, analyzing, evaluating, and creating messages in a wide variety of forms. It uses an inquiry-based instructional model that encourages people to ask questions about what they watch, see, and read.[17] *Visual literacy* is the ability to interpret, use, appreciate, and create images and video using both conventional and twenty-first-century media in ways that advance thinking, decision making, communication, and learning. *Information literacy* is the ability to know when there is a need for information, to be able to identify, locate, evaluate, and effectively use that information to address the issue or problem at hand.[18]

Arguably, information literacy is perhaps the most unwieldy of the new literacies; as the Internet serves up a smorgasbord of reliable and unreliable information, the need to discern the validity of the information is critical. Students must learn to locate information that is accurate and appropriate and then use it competently. Once they locate it, they must divine their own path as they are enticed to follow a series of promising links. They must also be able to recognize information that is tainted or fabricated and understand how it is used to sell, manipulate, and/or exploit.[19]

Recognizing these and other learning strategies, courseware platforms and software for course design contain several features that offer opportunities for multiple activities for learners and ease for educators. Examples of these (depending upon the originator) include

- Real-time chat tools that create a personal and immediate time/space connection
- Threaded discussion board that allows students and educators to respond over a period of time to multiple discussions
- Visually integrated notes and advanced hyperlinking
- Simplified web template development
- Electronic library resources and reference sources such as InformeDesign
- Private rooms for synchronous and/or asynchronous group work
- Interactive digital whiteboards that may create an online environment similar to a traditional desk critique
- Streaming video/audio and slide shows with audio capabilities to reinforce multiple learning styles
- Animations or other forms of multimedia illustrating sequencing or processes
- Tools for providing feedback and tracking performance that are private or designed for multiple viewers
- Test software that randomizes questions from a created test bank
- Archive features to reduce redundant activities for the educator each term

Course design and development, therefore, becomes much more that scanning notes and posting them, or videotaping lectures and making them available. Online education provides an opportunity to weave together a vast array of activities that engage and encourage learners.

Time Expectations

Although there are generally accepted ranges of time commitment involved in lecture, seminar, and studio courses delivered in traditional forms, online education presents a challenge to educators and administrators alike. (For traditional time requirement rules of thumb, see Chapter 3.) For educators, the initial time invested in developing the course to an online form is significant. However, time well spent in these initial phases pays dividends in the subsequent course offering.

To think that distance education is a means of reducing instructional load is a mistake. In their paper "Teaching Time: Distance Education Versus Face-To-Face Instruction," interior design educators Bender, Wood, and Vredevoogd evaluated a 75% asynchronous communication course (distance education) with a 75% synchronous course (face-to-face) with identical content but dissimilar instructional models. They found a significantly higher time input for faculty and teaching assistants in the distance course.[20]

From a teaching standpoint, instructors must re-evaluate their time commitment and frame of reference. To maximize course success, the instructor's presence should be felt by learners within the learning environment. While this may not necessarily be signified by a constant "hovering" presence, it must be consistent enough to engage the learners meaningfully. Consequently, much of the educator's time during the course is often involved in email and postings on a discussion board.

In *An Administrator's Guide to Online Education,* Shelton and Saltsman address faculty issues related to online education. They cite that course load consideration is the most common form of compensation to faculty involved in offering online courses. They report a 2004 study by Hislop and Ellis that found "instructors worked an average of six more minutes per student in an online course than in a classroom. In a course with 30 students, that's about three more hours per semester."[21] Other studies have reflected that the perception of workload is higher for online courses because the distribution of time is chunked differently than for face-to-face courses. Clearly, as online education increases, examples and studies of actual educator time involvement and support will become more readily available.

Operating the Course

Once the course is designed or adapted as an online course, the educator becomes involved in course delivery. Educators need to be organized, provide clear direction, and set clear guidelines, expectations, and policies for the course. They must also employ many similar techniques as in face-to-face courses to engage learners and encourage learning.

Some suggestions include

- Get to know the learners.

    - It is sometimes possible to arrange a face-to-face meeting for the initial class meeting. Interior design educator David Matthews, in a 2006 IDEC presentation, Design Instruction through Distance Education: Is it Possible?[22] indicated that in the online learning experiences he has facilitated, effective initial face-to-face meeting of the class has led to successful subsequent online interactions.
    - Require a short autobiographical paragraph for the first assignment.
    - Require an autobiographical web page (many course management software systems include a template that is simple to drag and drop information into) with a photo of the person or their favorite

project or dog, for example, along with some relevant information that distinguishes them. When posted, these lessen perceived "distance" and bring a personalized touch so that students understand who their fellow learners are.
- If a learner has not been participating, contact them immediately. They may be struggling with the class, or a simple computer glitch, but timely contact can prevent their frustration.
- Include smaller group discussions so that learners respond frequently to a "known" set of peers.

- Let the learners know you.
    - Establish regular "office hours" for learners who have questions. This means being available online for real-time chat, or quick turnaround on email, or phone availability.
    - Share relevant personal information with your learners, much as would happen during a traditional class.
    - Post an abbreviated website for yourself, with similar information that you request from students. Include your picture.
- Participate regularly.
    - Developing initial prompts and discussion questions typically happens as a part of course development and is supplemented during the course.
    - Find a balance in online discussion. Let the learners know of your presence, but do not command the discussion. As a rule of thumb, input when the discussion appears to be going astray of the objective or when particularly thoughtful comments provoke new thoughts.
    - Use email to send messages to all learners in the class regularly (at least once a week). These might be reminders of upcoming events, or invitations to participate in a guest lecture or other activity.
- Maintain the announcements or welcome page.
    - Include announcements, upcoming activities, timely bulletins about changes and updates to the course, and instructions and notes for each section. Announcements may be written prior to the course beginning, with projected dates.
- Educator space and activity
    - Establish a physical setting where you can teach online without distraction or interruption.
    - Log into the course once a day or every other day.
    - Post a technical hotline (or help desk) phone number and email address.

If the course has been well designed and the development work completed prior to beginning the term, operating the online course can be a rewarding and invigorating experience. Budgeting time for individual correspondence and reading posts on the discussion boards often provides the most challenge for educators.

Maintaining the Course

Courseware and other platforms offer extended educational opportunities for instructors to explore, build, and teach their courses and to maintain course content over time. Fisher offers the following suggestions for maintaining the online course for future offerings:

- Update readings so they contribute a variety of outside resources in the hopes of building a knowledge base for the learner that is well rounded and up to date.

- Incorporate guest speakers and content experts as they become available.
- Align course goals with new local and national standards or proficiencies as they emerge in your workplace.
- Re-sequence activities if needed so the structure of online activity remains organized, purposeful, and on task.
- Continue to frame questions in terms of the concepts you want to remain focused on.
- Update logistics: dates, times, and deadlines, as well as a list of class membership for arranging class group activities.
- Check functionality of all links and web-based resources, and update rubrics and checklists.
- Add new services as they evolve.
- Be willing to introduce new learner tools and capabilities as they emerge.[23]

LEARNING MODULES

As online learning continues to develop, the opportunity to create a library of "learning modules" of varying sizes and complexities becomes an increasing reality for interior design education. No longer is the access to a particular set of information or renowned educator limited to the few who might be in the same space and time as the educator. Online education offers the potential to create modules that might successfully be incorporated into a variety of design education curricula. These modules might be small, incremental learning objects that could be inserted into traditional face-to-face courses as a technological enhancement, or combined into larger segments within a hybrid course, or woven into a rich tapestry of an online course.

Many situations make learning modules a good idea:

- Increasing resource restrictions placed on interior design programs
- Decreasing availability of new teaching faculty
- The exciting potential to strengthen learning experiences and build the knowledge base of interior designers

If one thinks in a general manner about a traditional course, it is created from a number of experiences, opportunities for discovered knowledge, application of knowledge, and assessment of knowledge. One might consider a learning module as a replacement for a small portion of a traditional course. For instance, imagine the scenario of a studio course focused on healthcare design. The course's learners have already successfully completed a basic lighting course prior to the particular studio. Not all programs of interior design have immediate access to experts who might share knowledge and experience with lighting in healthcare situations. A learning module dealing with just this topic, however, might be included with the course through a web-based application, whether as an asynchronous active online experience or a module the instructor could include with course management software such as Blackboard. This learning module might include video of the "expert" discussing the lighting, specific background readings, identification of the specific needs in healthcare practice that require specialized lighting, enviro-social aspects of healthcare and how lighting contributes to comfort, examples of effective lighting solutions with associated rationale, or animated scenarios illustrating varying combinations with commentary. In short, learning modules can be a rich experience for learners, making the best use of experts in the field and excellence in teaching.

The possibilities to enhance existing curricula in both topic and scope is exciting. The MERLOT Project (Multimedia Educational Resource for Learning and Online Teaching, http://www.merlot.org) is one example of a large repository of peer-reviewed learning objects applicable for use in a wide array of academic fields. Specific interior design examples are not present on the site at this writing, however examples of fine arts, art movements, cinema, and the like are.

Learning modules are also referred to as learning objects. A learning object allows for the learner to chunk pieces of information together to build a network of knowledge.[24] Chunking course content into meaningful groups means that working memory capacity is utilized efficiently and students learn more. This is important as learners scaffold knowledge and build schema that help integrate new knowledge with prior knowledge. Chunking permits individuals of different ability levels to succeed at the same complex tasks.[25] Chapter 2 offers further discussion on chunking and cognition.

EXAMPLES IN INTERIOR DESIGN ONLINE LEARNING

Increasing numbers of books and articles are available that discuss aspects of online education. In general, many of these sources provide useful information for the novice and experienced online educator alike. Several papers and presentations presented at Interior Design Educators Council conferences have focused on some aspect of online education or a blend of online with traditional education in courses. Examples are provided here that illustrate effective uses of specific online strategies by interior design educators involved in online education.

Utilizing Free Web Technologies

Many educators perceive that operating effectively in an online environment requires expensive software or extensive technical knowledge. Douglas R. Seidler, an Assistant Professor of Interior Design at Suffolk University and a lead faculty member for Foundation Design at the Boston Architectural College, shares his experience using free web technologies in studio courses.[26]

> Balancing limited weekly contact time with the need to provide clear, direct, and regular feedback to guide students in understanding the fundamental concepts required for success in design school is a challenge facing foundation design instructors. Foundation design students at the Boston Architectural College (BAC) meet in studio with their instructor for three consecutive hours per week. This limited contact time makes it difficult for instructors to provide feedback to students more than once a week. This case study will detail how I incorporated free web software to increase the amount and quality of feedback foundation design students receive in their first semester at the BAC.
>
> I teach a section of the Masters A Foundation Design Studio, which is the entrance studio for all Master of Architecture and Master of Interior Design students at the BAC. Using free web technologies by Google, I redefined the typical BAC studio environment by creating a virtual class meeting each week. In June of 2006, Google launched Picasa Web Albums, a photo-sharing web application. Picasa Web Albums is available free and allows users to store and share 1GB of photos. At the beginning of the semester, I informed the students

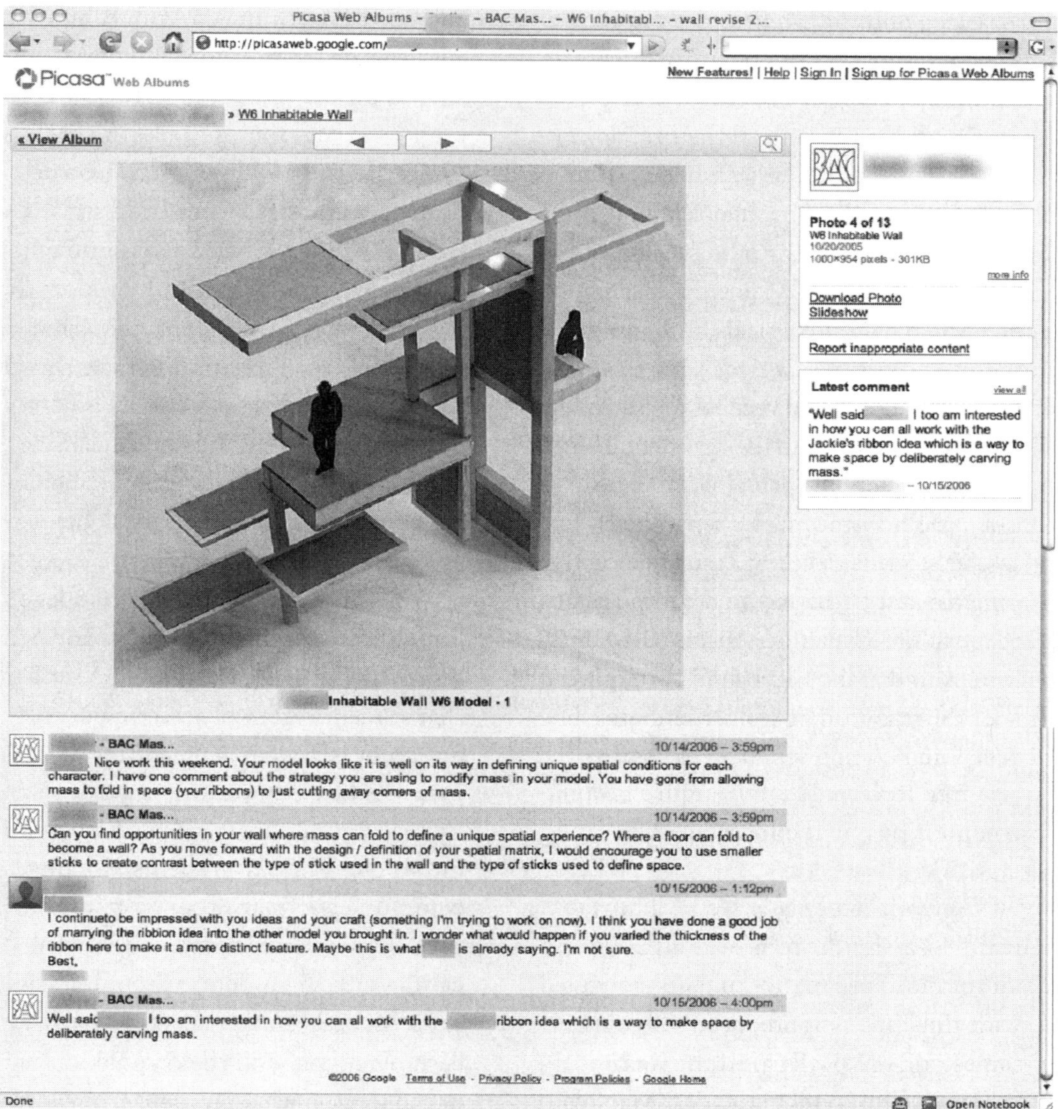

Figure 6.1 Mid-week student submission with instructor and peer feedback.

that our studio would use Picasa Web Albums to supplement in-class studio time through mid-week deadlines. These interim deadlines provide an opportunity for me to give pointed feedback to each student at the half-point of each assignment.

At the mid-week deadline, each student sends the required images to me via e-mail. I then upload these images to a new Web Album and provide a written critique for each student. The combined critiques are distributed via e-mail to each student and posted under each image in the Web Album. Students are encouraged to visit the web album (see Figure 6.1 for an example) and provide additional discourse on any or all images. I found over the last year that the amount of time needed to conduct this virtual class meeting, including image organization, written critique, and upload time does not exceed two hours per virtual meeting.

Case Study: 85 Students and Picasa Web Albums. The BAC has open enrollment for the Masters A Foundation Design Studio that extends until the first day of class. In order to evenly distribute the incoming students by quantity, ability, and number, official studio sections are not announced until the second class meeting. In the first week, students are required to meet as a large group for an opening lecture and receive the same first assignment. This assignment explores basic design principles and notions of Phenomenal Transparency[27] by asking students to create multiple two-dimensional figure-ground compositions that explore visual oscillation between foreground and background through the manipulation of scale, hierarchy, order, and composition. Students are required to complete four figure ground compositions by the following week's class.

I introduced Picasa Web Albums to this first assignment in the Fall 2006 semester. Because many students struggled with this first assignment in previous semesters, I hypothesized that in incorporating web technologies we could provide students critical visual feedback on their progress before the completion of the first assignment. The assignment was modified to incorporate a mid-week submission of the students' first figure ground composition. Student's photographed their project and submitted it to me in jpeg format[28] via e-mail.

I assembled and uploaded 85 images to a Picasa Web Album using Google's free upload software.[29] In collaboration with the other studio faculty we nominated the projects that best demonstrate understanding of project objectives and highlighted these strong projects in an additional web album. Students were able to visit both Picasa Web Albums (all projects album and strong projects album) Sunday morning to review both their work and their peer's work.

In the Fall 2006 semester, instructors reported that 84 out of 85 students completed the first week's assignment. In previous semesters faculty report that only 60 out of 85 students completed the first week's assignment. I believe that the increase in completed projects is connected to both the mid-week deadline[30] and the visual understanding gained by reviewing peer submitted work before an assignment deadline.[31]

The Boston Architectural College's limited contact time in Foundation Studio created a unique challenge for me in that students often procrastinate and/or do not get adequate feedback on their progress between major assignments. By integrating Picasa Web Albums into my studio, I helped students visually communicate their progress to me and their studio community. In communicating with 85 students through Picasa Web Albums, faculty identified a discernible increase in the completion rate of the week-one assignment from 76% to 99% completion. In communicating with a single studio section of eight students the Author identified a higher rate of project completion and a stronger overall understanding of each project's goals. Regardless of studio size, the mid-week assignments helped students both manage their time and visually connect to their peers outside of the traditional studio space.

Studio and Critique

Studio embodies the hallmark of design education, and is the last place educators typically think that distance education is viable. While conducting the entire studio class online may not be looming in the immediate future for many programs, certainly aspects of studio may be conducted online with great benefit.

Critique opportunities online can encourage a multitude and diversity in feedback. Practitioners, students, and faculty from other universities can be invited to post comments in an asynchronous manner, or in a synchronous session that might utilize software such as Breeze. With this application, images can be "projected" on the "whiteboard" that is the computer screen. With a mouse and a simple palette of drawing tools provided in the program, the image may be drawn over (almost as though a transparent layer is present for the drawing) and the resulting "minutes" of the critique session saved for future reference by the student as they proceed with their work.

In a 2006 article published in Educational Technology & Society, Bender and Vredevoogd describe a blended (face-to-face and online) learning model for studio that enhances the impact of critique sessions for all students.

> The argument proposed in this study is that blended learning will enhance studio courses. Studios are unique learning environments embedded in an historical context. This article presents a process of infusing a traditional studio with online technologies. The result is a more streamlined course that enhances student learning, provides targeted instruction to individual students, serves a larger group of students than a traditional studio, and does not increase faculty workload.[32]

They describe a unique approach to online studio critique, incorporating recorded audio comments in the online course that are available to students for review.

> This study demonstrates that blended learning can revolutionize instruction in the design studio. Student learning can be enhanced by having pertinent course material available online whenever students wish to access it. Project critiques can be delivered in both audio and text format. They can be reviewed at any time and as many times as needed. All students can view and hear projects and comments of the entire class, which is something that is often missing in studio.[33]

Another approach is framed by Sally Levine and Warren Wake of the Boston Architectural College (BAC).[34] This approach is aptly termed "hybrid" teaching because it combines online aspects with traditional education. BAC in its first two years of offering the hybrid studio had students develop websites embodying their design presentations, with electronic bulletin boards provided for exchanging peer and instructor comments.

> The discussion and feedback normally forgotten in the course of a traditional studio is inherently captured and becomes a valuable resource to students throughout the semester, recorded on the class bulletin board.
>
> Guest critics can then attend the virtual studio meeting and review student work at their leisure, from the comfort of their office or home. Students can begin to incorporate valuable feedback throughout the design process instead of hearing "formal" feedback only at the mid-point and end of the term.
>
> Just as the design of the physical space is a representation of the idea and not bricks and mortar, the design of the virtual space is presented through drawings and images, rather than by constructing interactive environments. We introduce students to many web-based

> software programs the way we introduce students to construction details and materials, but our major focus is the design exploration.[35]

Discussion Boards and Group Discussion

For synchronous online discussions, many opportunities are available. Several years ago, a major determining factor in considering online group discussion was the bandwidth available (the speed of the Internet connection). This is still a concern for students with dial-up connections, but for the most part a combination of software development, increased speed of computer equipment, and increased available Internet speed has decreased this concern and allows combinations of text, audio, and video feeds to be utilized. Issues are currently more centered on the pedagogical issues combined with technical issues, rather than on technical issues alone. Depending upon whether the desire for group discussion is to be written (real-time chat) or supplemented with audio or video feeds of each participant, the technology is readily available to accommodate learners.

When using chat features with a group of learners, it is important to keep the discussion moving in the correct direction. This author's experience with several learners involved in one chat leads me to recommend keeping chat groups for synchronous chat small (perhaps fewer than five learners). Confusion arises with larger groups in that a statement may lead to a different train of thought (a valuable event in real-time, in-person discussion but one that can lead to a frustrating discussion experience online) when learners respond to a comment made a few minutes previously and others go on with a new line of thinking.

It is possible and effective to use audio connections, either phone land lines (if budget allows) or through the Internet, especially when groups of learners can be at various terminals. Speaker phones combined with computer screens make valuable use of images and audio. Where Internet bandwidth is not sufficient, however, audio feed can be delayed, causing some frustration among users.

Threaded discussion boards are particularly effective in online courses. Most online courses have threaded discussion of some sort, where the educator poses an insightful observation or provocative question about a reading (or assignment) and requests reaction. Threaded discussion effectively engages thoughtful dialogue, especially among those learners who are less than eager to speak up in a face-to-face class setting. When learners from varying geographic regions and professional levels are present in the course, the level of student-to-student learning is quite high. During these discussion posts, I have kept my presence noticeable but not overbearing. I want learners to understand that I am involved, and directing the focus of the discussion (or redirecting the focus), but not autocratic. At some points, assigning a student to be the moderator of the discussion board for a week is effective. In this scenario, the moderator posts a critical review of a required reading and other learners are graded on a required number of substantive postings for the week's discussion.

Collaborative Work/Group Projects

Interior design academic Diane Bender describes an effective process of collaboration in her 2005 IDEC presentation:

> The course took advantage of faculty with complementary skills to provide a unique learning experience to a larger group of diverse students. Students and faculty met weekly for 12 weeks to discuss issues through onsite videoconferencing and online discussions. Students

in this course learned how the various disciplines from the built environment interrelate in terms of their professional responsibilities, values, tools, theories, and processes. Discussions included ethical, social, and legal topics for both timeliness and controversy. By purposely including controversial topics, multiple perspectives were shared and students became more actively engaged in debate. Students and faculty gained an awareness of the various design disciplines and how they are interrelated, in addition to seeing how computer and Internet technologies can better facilitate communication. Participating faculty gained knowledge and experience with advanced online technology and learned how to collaboratively develop and teach an online course.[36]

Student-Created Websites

Whether integrated within a studio course or as a stand-alone activity, student-created websites offer many opportunities as an online educational tool. The strategy and design of the website offers a venue for reinforcing communication and the "message" communicated. Opportunities to discuss navigation within the website (which may be thought of as wayfinding in the virtual world) may spark additional discussion on wayfinding in the designed physical world. Any number of commercially available html programs, most of which are drag and drop, can be used to create the website. Skill in this endeavor, as with other skills in design communication, adds to the overall skill set of the graduating student.

During the final semester at the University of Nebraska-Lincoln, interior design students create and maintain individual websites containing progress on their terminal project as well as other projects they wish to feature. (In this case, not only is the website used as an integral and graded portion of the studio course, students may, and often do, choose to feature their portfolio of work on the site and list the web address on their resume or cover letter to potential employers.) After a short initial program training session and site design discussion, students propose their designs. Feedback from the instructors takes the form of screen captures and comments submitted through email. Benefits of the websites are many:

- Students are forced into a weekly or biweekly evaluative mode on their progress to post the most relevant decisions and process work.
- Remote critics can be effectively utilized.
- Students become conversant in a new technology.
- The studio professor can maintain vigilance of student progress outside the confines of regular studio hours and physical location.
- Peers access each other's websites, and comment to each other, reinforcing a learning community experience.

University of Missouri professor Ruth Tofle describes an assignment in a professional practices course:

> *Exceeding the Limits with Web Site*
>
> One project assignment requires students to develop a web site using Dreamweaver featuring a minimum of a resume, electronic portfolio and links to the department. Using Cuff's[37] notion that excellence comes when the designer goes beyond the minimum requirements, the web site project allows students to pour unlimited creativity and energy into their homepage. It begins with an in-class exercise of student teams critiquing web sites from some of the

largest architectural firms in the U.S. Evaluations are made on graphics, ease of access, and related criteria. Students voice opinions and develop a personal vision for their own web site. Following this introduction, personnel from the campus information technology division are invited to teach Dreamweaver software during in-class sessions. Students that fall behind in class tutorials are encouraged to attend open labs the campus has twice a week.

Students complete their web site and a class critique is conducted for evaluation. Going the next step beyond a class assignment, students sign a Family Educational Rights and Privacy Act (FERPA) agreement to release their web site with personal information and their names are listed as graduating students on the department web site. With this easy retrieval of information, potential employers review student portfolios and resumes online to increase employment opportunities in the near future. The duration of web sites is unfortunately a limitation at this time since the campus keeps student web sites alive for 6 months past graduation. As a result, students are encouraged to develop their own personal web site so it can be viewed on a continuous basis in the alumni section of the department home page.

Online Student Presentations

Student presentations often take the form of a combination of verbal and graphic modes. In the face-to-face classroom, students may create a PowerPoint presentation with examples that illustrate their research or incorporate images of a student project. Online opportunities avail themselves to similar experiences and interior design educator Lori Kinley describes how student presentations are incorporated into an online course.

With the onset of online learning and the influx of interior design students, traditional colleges and universities have begun offering courses via the online format. Some online courses are in conjunction with on-ground courses, however, there are a few programs that are offered entirely online. A majority of time course information can be relayed without personal interaction, however, student presentations can prove challenging. Being able to communicate effectively is a skill all interior design students must perfect. Yet, how can this be accomplished in an online format?

In the course I currently facilitate, Basics of Interior Design, the students' final project consists of space planning and selection of furniture and materials & finishes. Each student is given a client profile with space requirements in which their design must meet, as well as the shell for the loft space. Over the three-week period, the students post their progress and at the end, each student presents the final floor plan, furniture, and materials & finishes selected for the space. As of now, each student provides a written statement with scanned versions of the presentation boards. It is requested that the students follow a standard format of introduction, body and conclusion as well as include the design concept statement and reasoning for their selections. With the client in mind, the students provide a room description for all designated spaces within the floor plan. Classmates and the professor comment within the discussion thread just as a critique would be completed in an on-ground environment. Unlike on-ground courses, the final project is not a complete surprise to other students as all have viewed and commented upon the progress with weekly checkpoints.

However, as online courses become more mainstream, it may be beneficial to investigate other ways for students to enhance their presentation skills. Although preparation for a formal presentation is important (and addressed in the current project), avenues that focus on the verbal portion could prove beneficial.

For example, students could self-record videos and have available to classmates and the professor via a Podcast, a personal website or a wireless phone that has Wi-Max technology. This would be one step in the next direction if the student should be required to provide a verbal presentation for grading purposes. Others could access at a most desired time, which is one of the reasons why many complete degrees on-line.

It could also be possible to test verbal skills by posting their design boards to the course thread, then use a conference call to present the information. Using WebEx (online web meeting service) or video conferencing would also allow complete interaction. The student could practice speaking in front of a group and field questions regarding their project. However, these options would need to be planned and do not allow unscheduled access. All of these options would need to be analyzed, as some technologies may not be immediately available to all students based on their geographical location.

In any course, whether on-ground or online, there are sections that can be improved, tweaked or shifted. A successful course is definitely fluid. In this case of student presentations, it may be beneficial to investigate further applications that allow the student to present their final projects either recorded or real time. Although presenting design boards face-to-face is the most desired, the other options could be a satisfactory substitute.

Observations from an Online Student

Each of the sections of this chapter has thus far approached online education from an educator-based view. Education, of course, also involves learners who experience technological delivery in various ways. (For other learner observations on teaching, see Chapter 9.) Trisha Otto, a University of Nebraska-Lincoln graduate student, shares observations of online education from her student viewpoint.

> I received my master's degree in interior design through distance education. Nearly all of my credits were obtained from on-line courses. As a full-time professional interior designer, the distance education option provided me with the opportunity to pursue an advanced degree.
>
> Based on my experience, I feel that on-line classes can be a viable alternative for design education in some, but not all, areas of study. While there are on-line courses that make a good effort to incorporate student interaction, on-line chats or responses are still not an equivalent to being in an actual classroom setting with direct instructor and student interaction. In my opinion, this type of people interaction is most crucial during undergraduate education. Skills learned from working with and learning from classmates in some cases are just as, or even more, valuable than the actual course content. Learning how to professionally interact with others and solve design problems in a team environment are vital skills needed to be a successful interior designer because we work closely with clients and co-workers

on a daily basis. Presentations requiring students to describe design work in front of a group of peers and critics would also be difficult to replicate through on-line education. For these reasons, I feel that certain courses, such as studio, could never be replaced or offered as an on-line option.

Other classes are feasible to take on-line, but this may not be the best type of education for certain areas of study. For example, statistics was the most difficult on-line course I completed. With a math class it is not easy to learn the material on your own by primarily reading a text book. The statistics class I took had taped actual classes from a previous semester, which was taught by a different instructor than the one conducting the on-line class. We were to watch the recordings in addition to reading the chapters. The videos were critical in understanding how to solve problems, but even with the ability to rewind at times it was still frustrating to not be able to directly ask questions. While my instructor did make some effort to arrange study groups on-line, they were not successful, and actually somewhat of a waste of time because it was just too difficult to verbally explain mathematical problems and equations with a group of people using a computer. Even trying to explain a question and figure out the answer over the phone with an instructor was sometimes a challenge.

Based on my experience, courses most suited for an on-line option include those covering specific topics learned primarily through research, reading, and writing. In order for these types of classes to be most effective it is crucial to make interaction with other students a mandatory part of the class through responses or types of chat sessions. Just as in studio, much is learned from reading about different views, interpretations, and applications of other students. In terms of reviewing and making suggestions on how to improve written assignments, the instructor for my research methods course had some interesting approaches and methods for on-line teaching. He held live chat sessions with the class. For those students with microphones, we could actually hear each other talk and were able to have a conversation back and forth. The students without microphones were able to type responses and questions in more of a typical chat format. The other interesting part of these sessions was the instructor's ability to display his computer screen to everyone logged in. We would mail him our papers, and then he would review them live as we watched the movements from his computer on our screens. This created the ability for "live" office hours. Based on my experience, these types of sessions could be very applicable and useful for a variety of on-line courses.

On-line education seems most appropriate for earning a majority of credits at the graduate level. For those of us who decide to go back to school while still working full time, on-line classes are a great and sometimes the only alternative. Since graduate education tends to be more research, rather than studio, based there is a great opportunity to expand the number of potential students interested in obtaining a masters degree by offering on-line courses. One of the greatest benefits of these types of classes is their flexibility to work with the busy schedules of full time professionals living in remote locations.

Many people have the preconceived notion that on-line classes are "easier" and take less time. Based on my experience and six years of education, I would make the argument that this is not the case. Due to the added flexibility, on-line classes demand the student be self-disciplined and dedicated to individual tasks and assignments. The fact you are not part of a class that meets weekly can also add to the time required to understand course content and assignments.

I would make the following suggestions to distance education instructors. It is important to prepare assignments and provide due dates for all assignments well in advance. For a distance student who may have other work and family commitments in addition to school, the worst thing an instructor can do is have last minute assignments. It is important for students to be able to plan their schedules in advance around family and work. Another suggestion for instructors is to incorporate distance students in some way with the entire class, especially when the class meets on a regular basis with only a few distance students. One way to bridge the gap between these two types are students is to have both distance and in-class students post assignments and responses on-line. By doing this the distance students can stay better connected with others and the course content. Finally, as students are corresponding with others on-line, I found it very helpful to have each person make a web site with their pictures and background information. These personal web pages made it easier to understand the posted work and responses of other students.

Online education presents opportunities to re-strategize programs of interior design and to create courses that are not bound by a physical place (or necessarily, time). These opportunities present unique challenges to educators who may imagine a rich tapestry of course participants and learners. Technology is available to encourage offering online courses. However, to be most effective, the opportunities and challenges should be based in sound teaching and learning theory and educational practices.

ENDNOTES

1. Wenger, Etienne. (June 1998). Communities of Practice: Learning as a Social System. *Systems Thinker;* Wenger, Etienne. (1998). *Communities of Practice: Learning, Meaning, and Identity.* Cambridge, MA: Cambridge University Press. Communities of Practice is a construct introduced by Jean Lave (a social anthropologist with a strong interest in social theory; her work has focused on the "reconceiving" of learning, learners, and educational institutions in terms of social practice) and Etienne Wenger (a teacher who joined the Institute for Research on Learning, Palo Alto, CA, having gained a Ph.D. in artificial intelligence from the University of California at Irvine).
2. Academic Media Services, Washington State University, http://whets.wsu.edu.
3. Jones, Steve. (2002). *The Internet Goes to College.* Washington, D.C.: Pew Internet & American Life Project. p. 9.
4. Ibid., p. 8.
5. Ibid., p. 13.
6. Fisher, M. (2003). *Designing Courses and Teaching on the Web: A "How-to" Guide to Proven, Innovative Strategies.* Latham, MD: Rowman & Littlefield Education. p. 13.
7. Ibid., p. 167.
8. Ko, S. & Rossen, S. (2001). *Teaching Online: A Practical Guide.* Boston, MA: Houghton Mifflin. p. 56.
9. Ko & Rossen. (2004). p. 11
10. Fisher, Mercedes. (2003).
11. Examples include Shank, Patti, ed. (2007). *The Online Learning Idea Book.* Wiley.; Shank, Patti & Sitze, Amy. (2004). *Making Sense of Online Learning: A Guide for Beginners and the Truly Skeptical.* New York: Pfeiffer/ Wiley; Salmon, Gilly. (2004). *eModerating: The Key to Teaching & Learning Online, 2nd*

ed. London: Taylor & Francis Books. (2004); Conrad, R. & Donaldson, J. A. (October 1996). *Engaging the Online Learner: Activities and Resources for Creative Instruction.* San Francisco: Jossey-Bass; Chickering, A. & Ehrmann, S. C. (October 1996). "Implementing the Seven Principles: Technology as a Lever." *AAHE Bulletin, 49*(2): 3–6.

12. Porter, L. R. (2002). *Virtual Classroom Distance Learning with the Internet.* Canada: Wiley.
13. Bacon, Pamela S. & Bagwell, David Jr. (2005). *Creating Online Courses and Orientations: A Survival Guide.* Bridgeport, CT: Libraries Unlimited. p. 34.
14. Adapted from Iverson, K. (2005). *E-Learning Games: Interactive Learning Strategies for Digital Delivery.* Upper Saddle River, NJ: Pearson Education. p. 1.
15. Oseas, A. & Wood, J. (2003). Multiple Literacies: New Skills for a New Millennium. In David T. Gordon, ed., Better Teaching and Learning in the Digital Classroom. Cambridge, MA: Harvard Education Press. p. 12.
16. Ibid.
17. See http://www.medialiteracy.net/research/definition.shtml.
18. National Forum on Information Literacy, http://www.infolit.org.
19. Ibid.
20. Bender, D. M. & Vredevoogd, J. D. (2006). Using Online Education Technologies to Support Studio Instruction. *Educational Technology & Society 9*(4): 114–122.
21. Shelton, K. & Saltsman, G. (2005). *An Administrator's Guide to Online Education.* Greenwich, CT: Information Age. Hislop & Ellis. (2006). Issues in Measuring Time to Teach Information Systems Online. *Information Systems Education Journal 4*(57). See http://isedj.org/4/57/.
22. Gabb, B, Case, D, Ankerson, K, Matthews, D. (2006). Design Instruction through Distance Education: Is it Possible? *Proceedings of the 2006 International Interior Design Educators Council Conference.* Scottsdale, AZ, pp. 55–60 and presentation.
23. Fisher, M. (2003). pp. 165–166.
24. Ibid., p. 30.
25. Brooks, David. (2007). Paper available at http://dwb4.unl.edu/dwb/Research/TheoryPaper/CompTh.html.
26. Portions of this research were initially presented by Professor Douglas R Seidler at the 2007 International Conference on the Beginning Design Student in Savannah, Georgia.
27. Students are introduced to concepts of Phenomenal Transparency through Colin Rowe and Robert Slutsky's 1963 essay Transparency: Literal and Phenomenal. *Perspecta 8:* 45–54.
28. Students were asked to use a common filename convention (lastname-firstname.jpg) to help the author organize the 85 images.
29. Software is available for the Mac at http://picasa.google.com/web/mac_tools.html and for the PC at http://picasa.google.com.
30. Students report they are less likely to procrastinate on starting assignments with the additional mid-week deadlines.
31. Students who traditionally struggle with theoretical foundation design assignments say that seeing peer work helps them better understand assignment objectives.
32. Bender, D. M., & Vredevoogd, J. D. (2006).
33. Ibid., p. 121.
34. Levine, Sally L. & Wake, Warren K. (2000). Education of Artists. Hybrid Teaching: Design Studios in Virtual Space. Presentation at the National Conference on Liberal Arts and the Education of Artists. New York: SVA. Access at http://research.the-bac.edu/sva/index.htm
35. Ibid.
36. Bender, D. M. (2005). Developing a Collaborative Multidisciplinary Online Course. *Proceedings of the 2005 International Interior Design Educators Council Conference.* Savannah, GA, pp. 16–17.
37. The course content is parallel to many of the ideas described by Dana Cuff, who is known for her work in demystifying the profession of architecture. Cuff articulates "dynamic forces and principles for uncertainty" that characterize excellence in architectural practice in her 1992 text *Architecture : The Story of Practice.* Cambridge, MA: MIT Press.

CHAPTER 7

Trends in Interior Design Teaching and Learning

In his 2005 book *Design for Life*, architect Sim van der Ryn takes on the broad question of design's future direction in relation to the dynamic changes currently occurring in human culture. He theorizes that the present age is a critical turning point that is moving away from concentrated control toward an epoch characterized by decentralization, collaboration, and a growing realization of interconnectedness.[1] In some ways, the interior design profession is ahead of the game with regard to these qualities, which characterize its mission to accommodate the personal and uniquely human within interior environments.

A review of trends in interior design education, as evidenced by recent conference presentations and scholarly works, mirrors these broad cultural movements of connection and outreach. They chronicle the growing maturity of the interior design profession that is reaching a place of peace with its own identity and lending its influence to broader culture in numerous ways:

- Seeking new collaborations with other fields and groups, reflecting the cross-discipline imperatives of modern society
- Striving to include real-world applications, engaging learners in hands-on, applied learning activities that mirror learners' future career responsibilities
- Continuing its dialogue with technology, using these tools in new ways that exploit their advantages while retaining traditions that remain meaningful
- Expanding conversations beyond once-traditional geographical borders, establishing connections with overseas groups to mutual advantage
- Thinking beyond previously conventional expectations of interior design service to assist those of differing ability levels and socio-economic means, and embrace the natural environment as well

This chapter seeks to define some of these trends through a collection of essays, recognizing that the dynamic changes in interior design education are best told in the voices of those deeply engaged in pushing the ordinary boundaries of traditional education who are challenging instructors to new levels of application, connection, and technique.

EVOLVING EDUCATIONAL TECHNIQUES AND APPROACHES

Interior design educators are rethinking the methods by which they communicate knowledge to learners and the nature of learners' active involvement in the educational process. These changes reflect the acceptance of a growing number of points of view that now embrace actual clients, other disciplines, other learner groups, and a growing diversity of world cultures as these essays describe.

Collaborations

In their 2006 predictions for the future of the interior design profession for the Council of Interior Design Accreditation, Coleman and Sosnowchik were "struck by the blurring of boundaries, not just those that distinguish market segments but those that define who we are and what we want and need. It is obvious that the world can no longer be observed through a solitary set of lenses. . . . What we discovered was a multitude of intrinsic links."[2] For some interior design educators, collaborations between their students and other groups explore these links, providing fulfilling and exciting methods of learning interior design procedures and honing teaming skills. For example, John Weigand, professor and chair of Miami University's Department of Architecture and Interior Design, has long explored collaborations of many kinds in his instruction and offers key insights and advice on their use:

Corporate America and the design professions are quick to tout the virtue of "collaboration." Management hierarchies have flattened to support an agile exchange of ideas, projects are tackled by teams of specialists, assembled and reassembled as the projects change, and clients are now active participants on the project team. All of this collaboration is supported by new communication technologies that permit a fast and fluid exchange of information between team members.

In an effort to keep pace—and sometimes to set the pace—design education has also supported collaborative efforts in the classroom. This is really not new. The occasional team project has long been offered up as a counter to the predominant one project-one designer teaching model. Students struggle to negotiate their ideas with one or two of their peers and often complain, in the end, that these ideas have been compromised.

But things are changing. Students' ability to collaborate is now an essential skill rather than a luxury. It is demanded by the profession and increasingly stressed by academic accreditors. One's ability to be an effective team player requires a mix of interpersonal communication skills, an understanding of team dynamics and leadership dynamics, and, increasingly, an ability to make decisions from ethical perspectives. While the design graduate must continue to understand problems holistically so as to be able to communicate effectively in the team setting, increasing value is placed on the designer's ability to provide specialist knowledge—to become an "expert" in something. All of this requires that students work easily with the digital and communication tools needed to support collaboration.

Today's student is also different. These students have grown up with the computer and the internet. They very likely possess a greater knowledge of these technologies than their teachers. And they are possibly the first generation that is not only comfortable working in teams but expects to work in teams both in the academic and professional settings.

At my home institution, we have attempted to stay ahead of this curve by building collaborative learning experiences into the curriculum. These experiences are constructed not only within the confines of the classroom, but are increasingly interdisciplinary, pairing design students with students from other majors across campus. This is not only reflective of how teams are assembled in practice, but it forces students to identify where their own interests and abilities lie and how they can best contribute to a team effort.

A recent project asked students to rethink how walls are constructed in commercial interior environments, and challenged them to pursue sustainable materials and technologies. The chosen solution used recycled paper, compressed into modular wall panels and supported by a ceiling system that permitted the panels to be easily moved. This required a thorough understanding of existing wall and interior construction systems, paper technologies, and business models. An interdisciplinary team was assembled that included majors in interior designer, architecture, paper science, manufacturing engineering, and marketing. Again, an obvious benefit of the project was that our interiors students were forced to assess their own contribution to the team effort. Given the size of the team, and the fact that it was spread across campus, digital communication was a given. A project website was critical to students' ability to access and update information, and students needed to possess, or quickly learn, how to bring content to and from the shared site.

Another series of projects in our department is not only interdisciplinary but inter-university. These "internet studios" pair students with counterparts at other universities and—since face-to-face communication is difficult—place internet communication technologies at the core of the learning experience. Students quickly gain a facility with web design, film editing, 3D modeling, and a host of communication tools including video-conferencing and file sharing in order to collaborate from a distance. These projects have implications for how work is accomplished in the professional setting by allowing clients and consultants to be active participants in the design process from remote locations.

Across the curriculum, internet communication can be used to involve practicing design professionals in the learning process. Our internet-based studios will typically include professional designers as on-line critics, or they will function in an instructor role by framing the design problem and participating in student assessment. More conventional studios will often require students to seek out professional "partners," who can dialogue with students about their design solutions using websites, email, or on-line chat. This ability to involve practicing designers in the learning process is nothing short of a paradigm shift. Because the practitioner can work from a distance, and because their interaction with students can be asynchronous (at a time convenient to their work schedule), they are able to play a role in design education that has not previously been possible.

In the same way, partnerships are possible with industry. On the wall project described above, various corporate manufacturers participated by helping to evaluate (and validate) student solutions. Corporate partners can also contribute financially to projects, and more importantly help to ground student learning in the real world.

These diverse collaborative experiences support student learning on several levels. Students not only hone interpersonal communication skills and gain a fluency with cutting-edge communication tools, they are forced to define their own unique expertise and contributions to the team. These collaborative experiences also democratize the learning process. Instructors and participants from practice and industry can partner with students as equals, thereby better modeling the learning process. As more equal participants, students can take a proactive role in defining projects and in constructing their own learning. This fundamentally challenges the more typical passive, top-down learning model and promotes the need for designers to take leadership roles. At some level, there is no greater achievement as an educator than to nurture the student's innate passion for the subject and to then teach the student how to take control of their own learning.

These new types of collaborative experiences also pose challenges. They can be difficult logistically, since universities are not set up to support this type of ad hoc collaboration outside the classroom. Course times and locations need to be coordinated, requiring extra effort and lead-time on the part of faculty. As always, student assessment is difficult on group projects since universities ultimately require that individuals, rather than teams, be evaluated. By de-emphasizing individual assessment, however, students are allowed to tap into more of an intrinsic motivation, altogether not a bad thing. Finally, program accreditation may need to adapt to a greater emphasis on collaborative learning. Current accreditation guidelines emphasize content-based outcomes more so than process. This leads to prescriptive curricula, which can leave little time to develop more ad hoc and flexible types of collaborative learning experiences.

In the end, however, collaborative learning is a demonstrable trend in design practice and in education. While it presents challenges in the academic setting, it also promises to enrich the educational experience and to produce a cohort of graduates better able to tackle design problems for the 21st century.

Learner Collaborations with Actual Clients

Interior design learners possess a freshness of perspective, enthusiasm, and energy that some instructors access for actual design projects. Interior design educator Jean Edwards at the University of Louisiana at Lafayette has found success in engaging her interior design students in local community design issues within interdisciplinary teams, providing benefits to both learners and residents:

As an Associate Professor teaching interior design in the School of Architecture and Design at the University of Louisiana at Lafayette, I have had regular opportunities to be involved with my students in a variety of community projects that have made real and positive contributions both to the quality of our students' education, and to the improved quality of the designed environment. Involvement in real community projects contributes in significant ways to the enhancement and relevance of interior design education. This overview will focus on these contributions as they impact both the students and the involved communities.

The 1996 Boyer Report entitled Building Community: A New Future for Architecture Education and Practice called for "an Enriched Mission" recommending that

> *schools of architecture should embrace, as their primary objectives, the education of future practitioners trained and dedicated to promoting the value of beauty in our society; the rebirth and preservation of our cities; the need to build for human needs and happiness; and the creation of a healthier, more environmentally sustainable architecture that respects precious resources.*

This call stresses the socially responsible role of architects (and, I would add, interior designers) in the development of livable and sustainable communities. Our School of Architecture and Design, which includes programs in interior and industrial design as well as architecture, has strived to meet this challenge through the encouragement of faculty and student involvement in community service projects. One of the venues for this engagement that has evolved within the School is the Community Design Workshop (CDW), an entity hired by municipalities to help identify and define community design problems and then develop strategies to address these problems. The Workshop, in turn, hires faculty and students over the summer to work directly with community groups, the public and with city governance officials in the development of these strategies. The CDW has provided opportunities for collaboration between faculty and students from the diverse design disciplines with various community representatives and organizations in a number of community projects of differing scopes and complexities.

Throughout seven years of involvement with the CDW, I have overseen several different projects in various communities. These projects have provided a number of interior design students the opportunity to work directly with architecture students, urban planners, government officials, and members of the various communities dealing with both the urban scale and the more intimate interior scale. This working environment has encouraged mutual respect between the architecture and the interior design students, a respect that is often not apparent when the studios are kept separate.

The primary and most obvious benefits to students of their involvement in real community projects can be summarized as follows. Students are provided the opportunity to

1. *Interact with real clients in the context of real problems;*
2. *Collaborate with other designers, professionals and community members in the development of design solutions;*
3. *Appreciate the complexity of addressing design problems in the context of real material, financial, political and social constraint; and,*
4. *In some cases, see the realization of their design ideas in a finished project.*

Communities and their constituents also benefit through the opportunity to

1. *Come together to expose and express not only problems, but also dreams for change;*
2. *Collaborate directly in the design process;*
3. *Increase awareness of the contribution that design can make to the improved quality of life; and,*
4. *Become empowered to make desired changes.*

The result can be characterized as a win-win situation for the students and for the communities involved. Communities are able to use the strategic plans that the CDW develops to go after grants and funding opportunities to meet the needs of their projects. Students have gained the experience of working with clients to solve real world problems. An added benefit we have discovered is that many students who have struggled with hypothetical studio problems have adapted and excelled in the context of the collaborative CDW working environment.

In addition to my experience with the CDW, I have also directed a number of other community projects with my students in the more traditional studio setting. These have been conducted variously as team projects (for example, my second-year studio teaming with the third-year studio), as individual studio assignments (each student developing her own design solution), and as independent studies involving a limited number of students. The most important first step is to make the commitment to integrating these projects into the studio curriculum. It is also important to match the project to the particular pedagogical goals of the overall educational experience. I think that flexibility of approach is the key to success.

Interdisciplinary Collaborations

Interior design educators are introducing projects that immerse learners in broader approaches to programming and design by virtue of partnerships with other disciplines both inside and outside the design fields. For example, Louisiana State University interior design educator T. L. Ritchie partnered with Anne M. Spafford, Assistant Professor of Horticultural Science, and Renee Major, Instructor, Department of English in the design of an urban nature facility:

In many design professions, interdisciplinary teams are often formed to encourage creative problem solving. At the university level, an introduction to collaboration offers students the communication, leadership, and problem-solving skills that will be required of them later on in their careers. The LSU Bluebonnet Swamp Learning Community was a collaborative project that brought together the four disciplines of English (American nature writing), Graphic Design, Interior Design and Landscape Architecture. The subject of the semester work was an urban nature facility. This client offered the students a unique opportunity to study the relationships between human beings and their ecological, cultural and built environment from a variety of disciplinary perspectives.

The discussion here focuses on the design of the learning community, concentrating on the landscape and interior design disciplines, and the opportunities seized for enhanced educational exploration. The planning of this project had a two-fold purpose. The first, as expected, was to encourage the skills of collaboration, shared experience and broadened perspective while investigating a potential interpretive center and site. The second concern, especially for the design studio disciplines, was to explore an expanded methodology in terms of the design process. The course plan encouraged creative or metaphorical thinking as a stimulator of the normal design process.

First, the learning community project reinforced values identified as essential to learning and particularly critical for design professionals. These values include the ability to integrate input from various sources, recognition and use of cross-disciplinary resources, and sensitivity and facility in teamwork strategies. In addition to the hands-on aspects of this cooperative effort, students learned the benefits of community outreach and public service.

We focused on addressing issues of team and multidisciplinary collaboration. Our approach encouraged teaming skills, shared experience and broadened perspective working with other disciplines. The vehicle of this involvement commenced during the research and discovery phase of the project. Interior design and landscape architecture jointly focused on the techniques of the traditional design process. Students conducted exercises in systematic observation, analysis and investigation of the experiential qualities of a site and building. In a joint studio, interdisciplinary teams investigated these aspects of the project forming opinions and benefiting from the perspective and techniques of the other discipline. Experts and professionals interacted with the discovery process before, during and after decision making. An atmosphere was engendered that was open to new investigation and viewpoints and helped to disintegrate the grip of preconceived notions.

The phenomena of viewing not only the subject area, interior or landscape; but also the methodology, (such as site inventory as a landscape architect and building analysis as a designer) blurred the differences and encouraged common ground between the disciplines. In a liberal and exploratory atmosphere, the students were engaged in a variety of creative and design exercises to realize their own ideas about an actual client that involved nature and the development of a sense of place. Their consciousness was opened to not only alternate points of view, but an expanded awareness of their ability to affect the real people and subject environment of the project.

The second concern for the semester's collaboration was the expanded methodology of Exploration, Discovery, Assimilation, Application, and Reflection. The landscape architecture and interior design studios worked together in both classroom and studio settings as well as at on-site locations on field trips. The first phase of the semester encouraged the unprimed and creative experience through exercises to nurture metaphoric thinking and to awaken or expand the students' sense of curiosity. The second half of the semester was devoted to interdisciplinary teamwork on projects.

The slightly uncomfortable juxtaposition of unlikely teammates, topics and assignments gave a distinctly foreign cast to the studio and classroom. At first awkward, and then liberating, a fresh aura of exploration emerged. Using the deeply sensitive but highly stimulating milieu of the collision of nature and the built environment, the creators of the project fearlessly plunged the students into collaborative interaction and the design process with a refreshing tonic of visionary metaphoric thinking. The project resolutions reflected sensitivity to the interface of nature and the urban context, and a sense of place instead of an abstract imposition upon the landscape.

Exercises in reflection and evaluation of this learning community were included at the end of the semester. The benefits of reflection became clear during the semester through journal exercises, discussions, and critiques. At the final exhi-

bition, written evaluations were solicited from a panel of involved students, peer students, peer educators and professionals from the four disciplines. These indicators and focus group interviews have allowed each faculty to return to their respective disciplines with informative evaluations that challenge standard practice and refresh teaching approaches.

In bringing these groups of students together, we fostered exploration and discovery that would have been unavailable to single disciplines in an isolated classroom setting. Negotiating goals and sharing tasks in team projects encouraged students to become more aware of the strengths and limitations of their own particular disciplinary approaches to their subject. This collaborative work enabled them to broaden their understanding and appreciation of other approaches. These are skills necessary for graduates in today's and tomorrow's marketplace. Students who participated in the Bluebonnet Swamp Learning Community became prepared to enter the "knowledge economy," which depends on problem-solving innovation generated by diverse views and creative talents.

Collaborations with Industry

By its very nature, design implies a close connection with industry, which fabricates products interior designers specify, creates software designers use, and often employs recent graduates. When handled deftly with regard to potential conflicts of interest, industry can provide significant assistance to educational programs. Mt. Royal College's Program of Interior Design has established a long-term successful relationship with the design industry in Calgary to the significant benefit of students, faculty, and the local design community as a whole, as interior design educator Jacqualine McFarland describes:

As I tour prospective students through our interior design program, I do all the usual stuff: show them our design studios, discuss the CIDA accredited curriculum, talk about our learning-centered approach to teaching, and all those other things that these increasingly sophisticated applicants have heard before. But if there is one thing turns their somewhat indifferent gaze to one of interest, it's when I mention that each year we award over 52 interior design scholarships to our student body of 120. The total amount of money awarded each year is close to $43,000.00—much of this amount coming from endowed funds.

This really is an embarrassment of riches. Our institution, Mount Royal College, offers 437 scholarships to its entire student body of 12,700. Our modest department, consisting of seven full-time instructors, accounts for 12% of these scholarships. It is something of an anomaly to be sure, and even the Foundation Office in our institution looks to our fundraising efforts to see how they can bolster their own. What makes us even more sheepish is when we say that all it comes down to is one thing: Throwing one heck of a great party.

This all started in the spring of 1991, when our Interior Design Program Advisory Committee ruminated over how to embellish our six existing scholarships and to raise the profile of our program. Although it was mentioned rather irreverently, the idea of hosting an industry-wide party began to take root. The idea was simple: invite as many guests related to the design industry as possible to a venue that was jazzy and served wonderful food. If all we gained from this event was enhanced exposure, and a few profits from ticket sales, we felt that the effort would be worth it.

The first party was an unintended and overwhelming success. The venue was filled to capacity and the atmosphere was electric. It could have been the time of year (March, when the thaw of winter was finally taking hold and Calgarians were desperate to see the light of day), or the fact that ticket prices were only $10.00 to cover party costs—which, in 1991 was entirely possible. But what made it most special was that this was the first event in Calgary's design industry history whereby competitors such as Steelcase and Herman Miller hoisted a drink together in the *same room. Since it was hosted by the local design school, all industry felt comfortable, if not compelled, to attend. We had no real goal for how much money we wanted to raise, but we did come away with a moderate $3500.00 that went toward boosting existing scholarships.*

What we did come away with was an unexpected and unprecedented "ask" from all facets of the design industry to participate in the party in some way the following year. Designers saw this event as simply great fun and a place to share war stories. Industry leaders such as Shaw Contract and Contemporary Office Interiors declared this the event in which they could see most of Calgary's design community in one room, whereby business could be conducted surreptitiously in a lively, jovial, social setting. As for us, it was a way that we could introduce our students to their future colleagues, and show the industry what dynamic and talented individuals they were.

Sixteen years later, we still host the party. It has grown from a modest 250 attendees to over 800. Tickets are now $60.00 to cover the costs of excellent food, live jazz music, and graphics and party decor. We earn a modest amount of money ($8,000.00) from beverage sales, silent auctions and feature door prizes. This goes toward scholarship activity in the department such as our annual field trip. It is an expected event by designers, manufacturers, developers, contractors and sales representatives. We no longer ask for sponsors to financially embellish the event, rather we use the event to say "thank-you" to our industry partners for providing such wonderful support to our students in the way of work-experience opportunities, field trips, guest lecturers, and of course, scholarships. Curiously, by seeing their name in lights, or on banners as the case may be, we typically end up with at least four more companies wanting to establish scholarships in their name.

This event benefits far more than our students. It is the one event of the year in which our design community strengthens their bond with one another, celebrates their interconnectedness, and establishes new and valuable relationships. This event is seen as playing a key role in ensuring our design community remains strong, vibrant, and collaborative. The party will never end.

Experiential Learning

Hands-on "learning by doing" lies at the heart of the design studio experience. Yet, learners' studio classroom designs often remain on paper (or computer screen) due to time and monetary restrictions. Some instructors seek to transcend these limitations by immersing students in real-world activities that show them the challenges of problem seeking and the larger real-world context of design. Dr. Ronald G. Phillips of the Department of Architectural Studies at the University of Missouri-Columbia has engaged interior design students well beyond both the classroom and, provocatively, the sight of any land whatsoever:

Transformational teaching principles are based on creating educational opportunities that elicit individual growth and development in students by promoting participation in experiences that are physically and mentally active and often outside their comfort zone. As a transformational learner, students take responsibility for acquiring knowledge, for developing a system of organization, and for placing it in context. Students build a personal way of knowing through participation in real-life experiences, helping them to retain information and offering a background for further development of those skills. The transformation lies in the value instructors place on students' personal experiences and acknowledging students' personal learning styles and their own skills and confidence.

A strategy was needed that immersed students in an unfamiliar context and forced them to come to terms with the nature of that context—a process that forces them to "look" at their environment simultaneously from the users' and the designers' perspectives. After years of searching for a learning approach that could accelerate students' understanding of clients' needs, I devel-

oped an understanding of what was lacking—the empowerment and knowledge derived from living life. Transformational learning experiences appeared to provide this opportunity. Transformational teaching experiences share common procedures:

1. *To create educational opportunities for individual growth and development;*
2. *To emphasize small group participation and student responsibility for managing the group;*
3. *To facilitate communication among learners rather than between students and instructor;*
4. *To select experiential settings that maximize a process through which the student constructs knowledge, skill, and value from direct experiences;*
5. *To provide ample feedback encouraging risk-taking thinking and venturing "outside of the box";*
6. *To evaluate successes based on fulfillment of student needs as opposed to externally defined criteria.*

Because I had recently become a certified sailing vessel captain, I set out to expose my landlocked students to this unique, but quite learnable, environmental context. Students have spent from three days to three weeks crewing sailboats, learning to share and design confined spaces with me, their studio professor AND captain. Classes have been held onboard from the Greek Islands to the Florida Keys, Lake Michigan to the British Virgin Islands.

While sailing competencies grow exponentially throughout the passages, it is the students' self-awareness in this new context that is strikingly enhanced. The six, seven, or eight student crews are responsible for provisioning the vessel (planning meals, purchasing water and food sufficient for the passage), creating a sail plan and navigating while underway and getting to a safe overnight anchorage while learning how to sail a large sailing vessel. Everything onboard the vessel is unfamiliar—even on land geographic and cultural differences are challenges.

The evening crew meetings onboard focus on the existing yacht design improvements. Relevant issues include sleeping, eating, and living layouts; storage, hand-holds; cooking and eating underway; comfort; hygiene; and safety—topics now part of their experience, not merely "design considerations." Crew members learn the importance of personal space and the need to maintain some degree of privacy in a space no larger than a semi-tractor trailer—they learn to work together to achieve group goals and they are transformed into a crew. The yacht is now their responsibility and they take command. The group synergy is palpable—they have the helm.

The outcomes of these experiences continue to transcend my imagination. Students return to the studio more responsible and with a greater insight into the nature of the design problem. Students apply these experiential lessons across all of their design work. Transformational learning works because it is about the students and their learning experiences. The students are empowered; they have learned to see in very new ways.

The design studio professor must provide sufficient encouragement to ensure that students continue to confront the challenges of the activity and ample feedback so that students visualize the steps to the outcome and understand their own progress through the activities.

Conventional interior architecture and architectural design studio instruction rarely provide opportunities to transcend the professor's imagination. The need for instructor-control over educational objectives and the quality of design outcomes is paramount in typical studio pedagogy. There are alternatives to this control-based approach that are learner-centered, not professor-centered. Educational opportunities can be created that foster individual growth and development. Experiential learning—learning by doing—offers an approach that has the potential to let student work surpass the professor's imagination, and give the student competencies that carry over into the real world of work. Experience, in this case, is the best teacher!

Global-Scope Learning

The volatility of recent world events prompts a natural reaction of ethnocentrism and isolation both in general society and education. This tendency runs counter, however, to other forces compelling new international connection, including the global economy and new cost-efficient technological capabilities that make intercontinental associations feasible. Many academic institutions have maintained alliances across national boundaries for years. However, in their recent review of interior design issues, what Coleman and Sosnowchik describe is "a growing imperative" for higher education to "integrate an international intercultural dimension into teaching, research and community service in order to enhance their academic excellence and relevance of their contributions to societies."[3]

Many interior design programs have overseas study curricula that broaden the perspective of their learners. Some institutions such as Texas Christian University are taking the next step of participating in consortiums of institutions that cross national borders, as Figure 7.1 shows. Interior design associate professor and TCU Director of International Studies Jane Kucko describes her involvement in international education and the North American–based Consortium on Design Education (CODE) program:

I first became involved in international education in 1993 while taking students to Oxford England. Observing students' exposure to another country was extraordinary and the critical nature of international education became apparent. In 1994, my colleagues and I developed an interdisciplinary program in Edinburgh, Scotland. During the summers, TCU students and faculty of interior design, psychology, and geology come together to study the Enlightenment.

While there are several wonderful study abroad stories, one of my favorites demonstrates the critical need for American students to be exposed to the world. While walking to the refectory in Edinburgh, I met a student with her U.S. stamped postcards in hand ready to mail. After explaining that the United Kingdom has Royal Mail, the student was quite embarrassed. The smart and talented individual had not reflected upon the fact that she was in a different country and her usual mode of operation was no longer relevant. Perhaps this was the most valuable lesson as a result of the study abroad experience.

Figure 7.1 Consortium on Design Education (CODE) students in the interior design class room at the Universidad de Autonomous, Guadalajara, Mexico. Photo courtesy of Jane Kucko.

The turning point for my passion for international education was participation in the Consortium on Design Education (CODE)—a United States Department of Education project between six North American institutions. Physical exchanges and virtual dialogue between Canadian, Mexican, and United States interior design programs provided rich international opportunities.

International education has evolved into formal exchange programs, virtual universities, and dual degrees between global institutions. Interdisciplinary approaches as well as integrating community leaders and service learning into study abroad opportunities is necessary to address the complexity of global issues. While studying abroad provides meaningful experiences, technology plays an integral role in embedding international activities into the classroom particularly for students who cannot go abroad.

Higher education's emphasis upon developing world citizens mandates interior design programs integrate internationalism into their curriculums. Lock-step programs, inherent in design curriculums, are not excused from offering study abroad and international opportunities for interior design majors. Given the key role interior designers play in global issues such as sustainability and social justice, our future designers must be internationally culturally literate.

World emphasis upon globalism has transformed international education from an evolutionary to revolutionary movement. The rapid pace of change and development of extraordinary experiences has increased international opportunities for students and faculty. Several interior design programs across the globe are models for internationalism. My advice for faculty new to international education is to converse with as many different colleagues as possible. Organizations such as NAFSA, the Forum on Education Abroad, and IES are other valuable resources. Other suggestions include:

- Funding. *Grants through the U.S. Department of Education, Fulbright, and corporate foundations are available to support developing study abroad and/or international opportunities.*
- Technology. *Integrating global perspectives into the classroom can be achieved through technology such as Internet 2, Blackboard, Ecollege, and other mechanisms. Technology can be utilized for charettes, class discussions, and on-line conversations from different parts of the world.*
- Start Small. *Building international collaboration requires time. Perhaps begin by sharing a common reading between students from two different countries and hold class discussions through technological methods. Faculty should visit other institutions to build camaraderie necessary to develop more in depth and long term programs.*
- Collaborate. *The long standing model of U.S. faculty taking students abroad only to stay in U.S. owned housing and take coursework among themselves is old-fashioned. Study abroad programs must integrate other cultures, faculty, students, community leaders in interdisciplinary learning in order to prepare for global issues. Coalitions or interior design programs coming together to create shared international opportunities is another way to develop experiences that effectively utilize resources.*
- The World is Our Classroom. *Embrace the fluid nature of global education where structured teaching (9 to 11:00 MWF for example) is broken and adaptability is required. The world is our classroom and teaching is sinuous. Release exclusive focus upon course requirements and embrace the extraordinary opportunities that international education offers.*
- BRIC. *Brazil, Russia, India, and China (BRIC) are the new global leaders. International education must be integrated with these parts of the world in order to prepare our students. Western Europe and other world locations offer extraordinary opportunities;*

however, interior design programs must not ignore the new players in the world.

It is the responsibility of faculty to educate individuals who can cross borders with knowledge and poise. International opportunities that embrace interactive learning, critical thinking, and opens minds to the rest of the world are paramount in preparing our future interior designers. The contributions interior design makes to the world's built environment requires a global perspective of our graduates.

Interior Design as a Lifelong Learning Pursuit

Technological advances and communication availability have exploded limitations that once constrained the educational workday to 8 A.M. to 5 P.M. Similarly, Western culture is also rethinking the proper place of specialized education within the overall human life cycle, and interior design education is similarly reconsidering the traditional paradigm of the exclusively higher education timeframe, both from the pre-college and post-college points of view.

K-12 Interior Design Education

There may be considerable advantages to the early, accurate introduction of interior design concepts to K-12 learners, both for future interior designers and their clients. Dr. Stephanie Clemons, professor in the Department of Design & Merchandising at Colorado State University, is a long-term advocate of accurate and professional interior design content for this age group. Figure 7.2 documents her students' involvement with K-12 students. Clemons' research describes the advantages and challenges of expanding interior design instruction to a point prior to the college classroom:

Youth in elementary and secondary grade levels are often exposed to numerous careers during their formal education. As early as first grade, children learn about teaching, law enforcement

Figure 7.2 Colorado State University interior design students introduce K-12 students to designing a house on another planet. Photo courtesy of Stephanie Clemons, Ph.D., FIDEC, ASID, and professor in the Department of Design and Merchandising, Colorado State University.

and fire fighting. In some curriculums, third grade students are urged to begin the development of personal career portfolios. How should our youth be exposed to the career of interior design?

Interior design is a natural topic to intertwine into the learning environment. Youth move in and out of commercial and residential spaces from birth. Similar to the childhood story "The Three Bears," a small child constantly evaluates the design of furniture and interior spaces. "This chair is too high. This chair is too low. This chair is just right." Youth are surrounded by human behavior, interior spaces, and design in general, yet they are rarely exposed to the field of interior design in elementary or secondary grade levels (K-12).

In the early 1990s, interior design educators were urged to get involved in elementary and secondary levels in answer to the national education reform movement.[4] *Studies were conducted to determine the place of interior design in the built environment.*[5] *Results indicated that the field of interior design was not accurately portrayed.*

About the same time, I began to teach week-long, summer computer animation workshops to K-12 youth (third grade through high school levels) at Colorado State University.[6] *I was intrigued with the students' interest in design and composition.*[7] *My interest rubbed off on our American Society of Interior Designers student chapter. We took junior and senior college students to visit elementary schools—specifically third grade students—and engage them in building models that exposed the youth to the design process of interior spaces, yet support the general education academic standard they were studying at the time. I was thrilled to see how building a "model of their home on a planet of their choice" could assist students understanding their living environment and how it could be shaped and impacted by a lack of gravity or surrounding fields of asteroids.*

During 2000 to 2002, the International Interior Design Association Foundation (IIDA) offered me two research grants to 1) determine what materials were available to K-12 teachers and students about interior design, and 2) determine what interior design educators and practitioners perceived to be the most important interior design content areas to infuse in K-12 levels as well as the types of materials that would be helpful to K-12 teachers. The results of the focus groups indicated that educators and practitioners alike felt it very important to become involved in infusing interior design into K-12. Lesson plans were developed with a model suggested for dissemination.

Issue: K-12 teachers have minimal formal education and/or practice to teach their high school interior design classes. *Today, the need to accurately infuse interior design content into K-12 grades is even more critical. Many states (e.g., Utah, Colorado, and Connecticut) are currently offering interior design courses at the high school level and developing examinations that result in college credit for those who successfully pass. However, the high school teachers typically have little interior design education and/or experience. Many times, they feel inadequate and undertrained to accurately teach the course. Our involvement in working with the high school teachers and/or developing accurate curriculum materials is pivotal to their increasing success.*

Issue: Family and Consumer Science (FCS) standards are used to guide the content of interior design high school courses. *The national Family and Consumer Science standards are uniformly utilized to guide the development of interior design high school courses. The standards are currently related to housing, interiors and furnishings. Therefore, high school curriculum (including assignments and lesson plans) is strongly skewed toward residential design. The standards are currently being evaluated and revised, but we are unclear of the result. The national FCS standards need to more accurately reflect the interior design profession.*

Issue: More teens are attracted to the interior design career based on HGTV design-reality shows. *In 2000, our interior design programs have doubled in student size due to HGTV design-reality shows such as Trading Spaces and Design on a Dime. Their popularity is somewhat due to teens' desire for creative personal spaces. Just as youth use tattoos on their bodies to express their personality, the personal spaces of teens relate to their development of self-identity.*

HGTV shows have caused design conversations to take place that may not have otherwise occurred. However, the portrayal of the career of interior design has again not been completely accurate. Many incoming freshmen select the interior design major based on design reality shows rather than on accurate knowledge about the career. How do we educate our students better so they can more quickly determine if interior design is truly the major they desire?

Secondly, institutions are struggling to locate enough qualified interior design educators to teach incoming students. At a time when many educators are retiring, we have an influx of students—particularly at the freshmen/sophomore levels. How can we more creatively and effectively manage the number of students coming into our interior design programs? One answer may lie in the education of high school teachers. If high school teachers could accurately educate their students in their interior design classes, we may have fewer students that are more qualified and highly motivated coming into our programs.

Issue: Textbooks for high school teachers are renewed every 10-12 years. *Interior design textbooks that are used by high school teachers are sometimes rotated every ten to twelve years. The teachers are frustrated that they do not have more up-to-date material about the interior design profession that is so fast-paced and trend-oriented (e.g., color). State curriculum specialists are requesting more assistance in locating up-to-date materials that would supplement their texts concerning interior design.*

Issue: Need for interior design curriculum materials to support national academic standards. *Like any interior design educator, the elementary and secondary education teachers are inundated with high expectations, limited resources, and little time. Any interior design materials or resources we offer need to support the national academic standards by which they are annually assessed. Asking the high school teachers to "add on" additional interior design curriculum materials rather than integrate them would be unsuccessful.*

What can we do as interior design educators? If you are interested in helping your K-12 community concerning the interior design profession, there are many opportunities that may reflect your personal or professional interests. Below are a few ideas.

- *Teach a workshop related to interior design—either to students or teachers.*
- *Expose teachers and students to the annual career day.*
- *Write a high school interior design text book.*
- *Share PowerPoint lectures concerning interior design with the high school teachers.*
- *Offer interior material samples from your resource library and other visuals to the high school teachers.*
- *Ask college students to get involved in teaching a design project to youth as a service project.*
- *Work with your national interior design professional organizations to get them more involved.*
- *Invite high school teachers and students to campus to: 1) tour your program facilities, 2) attend a Senior Show or a design critique, or 3) participate in a joint charette.*
- *Offer a phone call to your nearby high school teachers to ask them to identify their needs. Then see if your faculty can assist.*
- *Help your state in revising standards and developing new interior design curriculum.*

- *Welcome college students majoring in Family and Consumer Science to visit your classes to become more educated about the interior design profession.*

In the last two years, we've seen more movement toward infusion of interior design curriculum into K-12. The interior design professional organizations—ASID, IIDA, NCIDQ, CIDA, and IDEC—developed a joint website for those students investigating the profession: www.careersininteriordesign.org. ASID is disseminating a DVD concerning the career of interior design: A Career in Interior Design. A new edition of Christine Piotrowski's book concerning the career of interior design is to be published shortly. These are all great strides to more accurately educate our youth.

The impact of our involvement in K-12 can have lasting dividends. Teaching the youth results in teaching adults. Children teach parents. Children and teens appreciate learning "why they are learning, what they are learning." Interior spaces offer an ever present learning laboratory to relate academic standards to real life. The appreciation of good design is a lasting legacy to leave this generation and the next. Our youth today are our future consumers, clients, educators, and designers.

Interior Design Education After the College Experience

The knowledge that interior designers must grasp to design safely and effectively is far from static, and the exponentially increasing magnitude of content is forcing careful choices in curricular content and degree of depth. The burgeoning scope of information is also compelling interior designers to consider the conclusion of the college degree to be only the beginning of a lifelong learning odyssey in order to remain relevant and competitive. Near constant revisions in technology, codes, and trends is a reality recognized by many professional associations' and states' mandates of continuing education (CE) requirements as a condition of interior design professional membership or licensure.

Some interior design educators are realizing the need for quality educational content for CE practitioner and educator learners and have built a part of their careers and financial futures on their consistent offering of learning experiences beyond the college classroom.

The Interior Design Continuing Education Council (IDCEC) is a consortium of IDEC, ASID, IIDA, IDC, and NCIDQ that develops standards and administrates the approval processes for CE educators.[8] The increasing number of states, jurisdictions, and professional organizations that require continuing education are adhering to the IDCEC-approved system to assure quality in continuing education courses. More information on IDCEC is available at the website http://www.idcec.org.

Interior design educator Holly Cline serves as the chairperson of the IDCEC and is an enthusiastic champion of lifelong learning for educators, students, and practitioners:

Teachers know that education does not end with a diploma or certificate of completion. You are reading this book because you are hoping to learn something new—you love to learn. As teachers, we must find ways to help our students become lifelong learners too who are passionate about furthering their knowledge. And our personal desire for continuing education is a tremendous way to "lead by example." Continuing education emphasizes attitudes, competencies, knowledge and skills in a specific subject that enhances an individual's performance. As an educator, you get to "model" this behavior to your students, involving them in life long learning opportunities before they graduate.

Continuing education should not be a mandatory requirement but an intrinsic component of our designers' toolbox.

Interior Design Education that Transcends Traditional Systems

It remains to be seen if the model of the traditional single-institution degree will withstand the pressures of an increasingly attractive à la carte system of pick-and-choose content. Such flexibility is increasingly desirable to business model consumers looking to increase their competitive edge with a degree customized to their aspirations. Many institution's articulation agreements are already significantly blurring the boundaries of the single-institution diploma system.

It is not entirely fantasy that higher education instructors will become freelance experts that offer online education to learners across the globe regardless of institution. Such educational systems currently exist, and some cater to adult learners who are not concerned with course credit. For example, the private corporation The Teaching Company offers a collection of pre-recorded lecture learning experiences geared for adult learners taught by carefully selected professors from institutions including Notre Dame, Yale, Emory, and the University of California at Berkeley. The content is sold to learners as audio-visual digital files on DVD disk and is marketed as "homework-free, tuition-free, risk-free, and guaranteed."[9] Some universities such as Florida State University are similarly developing on-campus institutes that offer courses specifically for those over 50 who simply wish to stay engaged in knowledge beyond the traditional college degree without the fuss of enrolling in an entire degree program.[10] Given the expanding number of affluent retirees, many of which may be keenly interested in a deeper understanding of their personal interior environments, it is not unreasonable to envision that interior design content could follow in a similar vein, engaging learners beyond the bounds of traditional higher education.

EMBRACING EMERGING PARADIGMS

Interior design educators are rethinking not only the place of interior design education within the human life span, but also responding to emerging attitudes in cultural thinking, changes in human values, and calibrating its responses to technological innovation. The following essays lend clarity and definition to the influences of several of these cultural catalyst topics.

Technology

The far and pervasive reach of technology permeates most aspects of the teaching and learning environment in some manner. Technology holds much potential to not only make existing tasks easier but also allow designers to now consider previously unattainable questions. For example, virtual design and lighting simulation technologies permit the exploration of the interactive experiential relationship between user and environment. Technology permits the examination and capture of an elusive element—the passage of time and influence of motion. As Ohio University interior design educator David Matthews explains, "the merit of virtual reality may be in its ability to present complex ideas of time that other media cannot express."[11]

While many educators and researchers explore many of the fascinating implications of technology as design tools, University of Nebraska-Lincoln Professor Katherine Ankerson has explored the potential of animations, simulations, and technologically interactive strategies to create tools that actively engage the learner. Ankerson describes her view on the evolution and potential of specific technologies in design:

At a time in the not-to-distant past, a discussion about technology in interior design education would typically center on whether AutoCad was taught as a stand alone course or integrated as a tool into course content, or how computer assisted technology was used to create dynamite presentations. In the last few years, we have seen that discussion evolve to using technology with broader intention:

- *Collaboration between a growing diversity of design stakeholders;*
- *Cohesive interface between concept, schematic explorations, experimentation with form and space, and the accurate representation for fabrication and construction;*
- *Effectively modeling interiors for creative and diagnostic purposes;*
- *Teaching and learning in a virtual world, and understanding the implications this virtual world has for the real one;*
- *Creating virtual mock-ups of designs that one may 'walk-through'; and,*
- *Seamlessly bonding the acts of design, fabrication, and management into one activity through database use.*

We see technologies depicted in movies ("Minority Report" as a recent example) with features based upon current research conducted at the M.I.T. technology laboratories, and understand that much lies in our near future. This challenges our thinking about concept of self and privacy, and about the inherent benefits of technology as it supports human habitation and health.

What does this mean for interior design education? We are preparing students to enter a world much different from that many of us entered upon graduation. As I began my professional work, much of construction documentation was accomplished in pencil lead on vellum. The next step included a vacuum frame, where multiple layers of mylar could be placed over one another, aligned with a series of metal pins through punched holes at the top. In this way, information could easily be thought of as layers, or components that combined with other disciplines or sheets to give a particular view of a project. It was a systems approach to construction documents, and a prelude to the concept of layering in CADD programs. Fast forward to the present. Our graduating students go into a professional world where they may create construction documents by slicing through a three-dimensional virtual model of the project, zooming in on intersections for details, being alerted to potential conflicts spatially in ceiling and other plenums, where work on a project is in an online database, developed simultaneously by colleagues in offices around the globe.

Continuing the expansion of integrating technology into the educational realm, teaching and learning occurs with colleagues and students in varying ways. In my work at the University of Nebraska-Lincoln, I encourage students to view technology as an imaginative tool, providing new ways of exploring and investigating, and of capturing aspects or influences in projects that would otherwise go unnoticed or perhaps be unintentionally obscure.

Teaching and learning tools integrating animations and simulations in interactive settings are designed to enhance student understanding and ultimately, learning. I have designed these tools for a number of subjects and course integrations, including Construction Documents, Codes, Interior Systems, Introduction to Design, and overviews of history. Strengths of the interactive digital work are that learners may access them as often and repetitively as needed to accommodate their individual learning, process and sequence of events may be illustrated effectively, and relationships may be drawn amongst seemingly disparate chunks of information. In some cases, the interactive tools are available online, in others through CD-Rom. In addition to students' use in learning, I also employ the tools in a teaching capacity during lecture courses. These efforts have not gone unnoticed by the students, as course evaluation comments demonstrate. Researchers have noted the positive effect on learning of these tools as well.

Students enter a world where now, more than ever before, they are part of a global design com-

munity. They must be facile with technology for collaborative design, for effective presentation of ideas at all stages of the process (whether through rapid prototyping, animated walk-throughs, immersion in a virtual world), and for communication and documentation. They must have an open mind to the critical use of technologies (rather than technology for technology's sake), the confidence to embrace it, and the wisdom to recognize the circumstances of its appropriateness.

I encourage you to look at the possibilities technology offers, not with a view to its limitations, rather with a view to enabling possibilities. Not with an eye to technology as a 'stand alone' or merely as a presentation tool, but rather as seamlessly integrated into a process, whether for learning or practice. Envision creating learning environments (and I use that term to mean physical as well as virtual) that embrace the ideals of design education, creating an interactive, engaging, and provocative experience, with an open mind to the possibilities technology might create or enhance.

Inclusive Design

The Americans with Disabilities Act recently experienced its seventeenth anniversary. At the time of its passage, a reported 43 million Americans had a physical or mental disability. According to the Census Bureau, in 2002, the number had escalated to 50 million persons, in part due to the aging Baby Boomer phenomenon. While the newness of universal design and its sibling concepts of trans-generational and inclusive design have largely worn off, the need for learner empathy and application of these ideas remains solidly valid and necessary for interior designers. The professional interior design experiences of University of Idaho educator Dr. Shauna Corry showed her the continuing relevancy of inclusive design, and this issue has become Corry's primary research topic:

From the time I completed a Housing in Society course as an undergraduate, I have been an advocate for the importance of inclusive design, design that improves life quality for all users regardless of their abilities. I remember touring an accessible home and being struck by the homeowner's desire and passion for independence. She wanted a home that functioned perfectly for her and looked just like everyone else's right down to a large, multi-paned picture window in the living room—a window that her sister-in-law warned her against installing by stating, "I'm not going to come over and clean those crappy little windows!" After graduation, I was frustrated when the builder and subcontractor changed the design for one of my first clients with a disability, "forgetting" to widen one of the halls and install the electrical outlets at 36" above finished floor. As I progressed in my career, I was often dumbfounded when a designer, contractor, or architect would be dismissive of making small changes to a plan that would have positive impacts for people with disabilities.

In my first teaching position I stressed the need for incorporating accessible design in all phases of the design process, and with the advent of the Americans with Disabilities Act (ADA) I started learning more about accessible design in an effort to be a better designer and educator. However, it was not until I became an associate faculty with the first Universal Design Education Project (UDEPI) that I began to understand the concept of "Universal Design," or truly inclusive design. My participation in that germinal project fueled my life-long passion for teaching, researching and practicing Universal Design principles.

For the next fifteen years I incorporated the principles of universal design in all my courses, from a graduate course in the built environment, to interior design history and beginning studio. However, last year at a conference the critical need to continue to advocate for Universal Design and accessibility issues as an integral component of the design process was again raised. While talking to a colleague about our research interests she made the comment that Universal Design was a past trend. I was taken back. A past trend? Although I understood what she meant, that in all disciplines certain issues come to the forefront based on societal concerns, my hope is that design educators never treat Universal Design as a has-been. I believe and teach that designers have a powerful social responsibility to create functional, supportive, and meaningful environments for all users, and as design educators we play a pivotal role in the transformation of society through teaching the principles of Universal Design as an integral part of the design process. We can truly change the world through design.

I suggest the following tips to encourage transformative thinking in your students on this issue:

1. *Incorporate disability consultants and advocates in your courses and projects. Actually having disability consultants participate in the design process is invaluable.*
2. *Incorporate service learning. Having students work with users with mobility disabilities is important. Have them spend a few hours every week for the course of a semester volunteering.*
3. *Empathetic experiences work. Some of my most memorable experiences as an educator are the transformational reactions students have when encountering barriers in the built environment.*
4. *Increase understanding of the issues. Have the students read books by people with a disability and watch movies about people with disabilities. Moving Violations: War Zones, Wheelchairs and Declarations of Independence by John Hockenberry and Waist High in the World: A Life Among the Nondisabled by Nancy Mairs are two good books; and Waterdance and My Left Foot are movies that realistically highlight some of the problems caused by the built environment.*
5. *Observation analysis is effective. Have the students complete observation analyses of area stores, theaters, recreational facilities, offices, etc.*
6. *Conduct building evaluations. Have the students conduct building evaluations using the ADA Checklist (available at http://www.access-board.gov/adaag/checklist/a16.html).*

Green Design

Since the 1970s, volatility in world energy markets has occasionally elicited a surge in interest in the West for conservation. After 2000, this sometime trend evolved into what may be a movement capable of transcending the cyclical rise and fall of energy prices. Beyond implications of economic costs, however, loom the very real implications of global warming only recently identified by a compelling consensus of the world scientific community. Even these very real reasons for sustainable practices, however, may not eclipse the fact that to conserve resources is to simply do the right thing for fellow humans and the only planet at this time known to be habitable. Virginia Polytechnic Institute and State University interior design educator Lisa Tucker explains her personal entry into this critical issue and the attitude shift that will be necessary to effect enduring change:

During the past decade, sustainable design has become increasingly important to interior design, industrial design and architecture as an awareness of the impact of design on the world's resources has come to the forefront. As early as the 1970s, Victor Papanek called for an end of wasteful design practices in the industrial design arena, claiming that design for obsolescence was unethical.[12] *While his book was widely read, it had little overall impact on the processes of design or design education in the U.S. As designers it is important that we ask ourselves "Why is sustainable design important?" To answer this question, we must first turn to the state of the world in which we are designing today.*

In the 21st century, human beings live separate from the natural world. At some point during our evolution we (in the West, at least) have chosen to separate ourselves from the nature that surrounds us. We construct buildings in which we live and work that are totally insulated from the outside world. In our effort to expand our lifestyles, we have left a significant mark on the environment.

At this moment in time, global warming is a common topic on the evening news. Species continue to disappear from the planet earth at an alarming rate. Gas prices continue to rise as the demand exceeds the supply. In the global community in which we live, we now understand that all we do has an impact somewhere in the world.

So why is sustainable design important? Because our very survival as a species depends on it.

Designers have a tremendous role to play in the future of the planet. According to the Energy Information Administration, the U.S. consumed 99.89 quadrillion BTUs of energy in 2005. This averaged out at 337 million BTUs per person in the U.S.[13] *In the same report, the U.S. consumed 10,126,000 barrels of oil per day resulting in a net dependence on import sources for 59.8% of this oil. In 2005, commercial buildings were responsible for the use of 5,820 trillion BTUs of energy and residential buildings for 27.5 trillion BTUs.*[14] *As the population continues to explode around the world and as other nations become more developed, the energy use in the world will be staggering. It is our job as designers to do our best to make efficient and healthy buildings.*

My own entry into the arena of sustainable design came through my professional practice in historic preservation in the early 1990s. When first introduced to the notion of "sustainability" in the late 1990s I immediately saw the connection between it and preservation sensibilities. (I was also reminded of those ugly solar houses of the 1970s and the need for energy conservation which was the issue of the day.) Reusing an existing building, by its very nature, removes the need for new materials, massive demolition, and new land use. The connection between historic preservation and sustainability is an area that has received a great deal of attention in recent years.[15] *As a result, the Association for Preservation Technology created a task force to examine Sustainable Preservation in 2002. Since this time, papers about sustainability and historic preservation have been presented at each annual international conference. A few members of the Interior Design Educators Council have also explored this connection.*

The definition of an interior designer is one who protects the life, safety and welfare of the public. In this capacity, designers must take responsibility for their design decisions at every level from education through practice. Each material selection, design proposal, and specification has an impact on the state of the world's resources and our future as humans on this planet. Unlike what some have proposed, sustainability is not a trend. It is a required attitude for any person practicing design in the 21st century. It is not something to learn about; it is a place to come from which necessitates respect for the earth and all life on it. Our livelihood and continued prosperity are directly tied to our ability to alter the direction of design practice to meet today's needs and those of the future.

Diversity

Many pre-Renaissance interior design history courses begin their discussion by recounting that interior design's cultural imperative has existed since the first drawing was created on a cave dwelling wall. Given the ubiquity of humans' need for interior enrichment worldwide, it is curious that modern interior design and its education in the West is guilty of concentrating its attention almost entirely on Europe and the United States. The bountiful cultural legacy other global cultures offer have much that can enrich interior design education in both aesthetic and functional ways. University of Oklahoma interior design associate professor Abimbola O. Asojo is a strong advocate of increasing diversity not only within interior design curricular content but also within the population of interior design learners as both the following essay and Figure 7.3 describe:

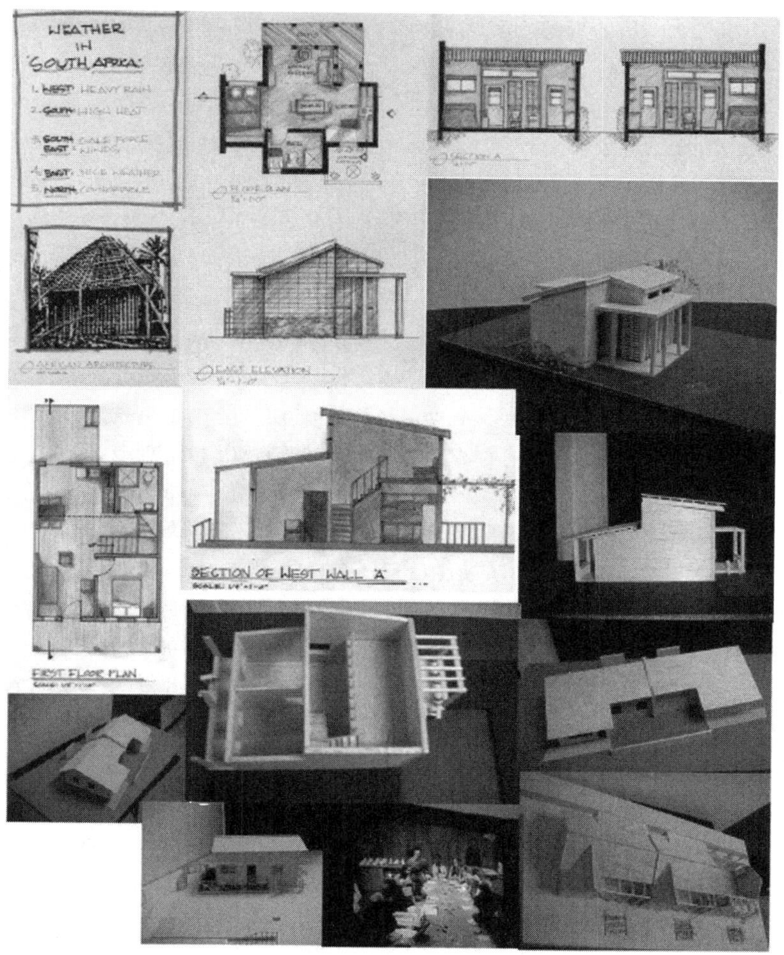

Figure 7.3 Affordable housing prototypes for South African citizens designed by University of Oklahoma Interior design sophomores. Photo courtesy of Abimbola O. Asojo.

I strongly believe that interior design scholarship ought to reflect our very diverse societies, as well as our global communities. The advocacy of diversity issues within interior design education is very important. Through the integration of diversity issues in design education, educators can help students gain both disciplinary and civic benefits which will allow them view the world from multiple perspectives and equip them with skills to be actively engaged in society. As educators, we need to actively promote an inclusive environment that acknowledges the contributions of all to the global design discourse, and especially the often neglected and forgotten minority cultures through our teaching and research.

As educators, we cannot deny or ignore the importance of diversity in design education. In 2005, the U.S. Census Bureau estimated that ethnic minorities make up 25% of the U.S. population. One in four Americans is a minority, and this indicates that we live in a very multicultural society and that our future design clients will be very diverse. Pluralistic multicultural design curricula will be important to ensure future designers success both in the classroom and public service. Our students now more than ever need to understand multiple cultures. We as educators need to promote and value the creative expressions of other cultures and teach our students about them. I believe a more inclusive design curriculum will promote an increase in minority representation in design related fields. Further, I feel valuing the contributions of minority cultures will encourage more young minorities to pursue design related fields, particularly because the often invisible minority cultures will likely now become more visible in design scholarship.

My interest in diverse issues stems from the under-representation of minorities in design related fields, the lack of documentation of contributions of minority cultures in the U.S., and the lack of documentation of the contributions of non-Western cultures to design discourse. Through my research and teaching, I have been involved in disseminating and expanding knowledge on African and African-American cultures as well as developing pedagogical models for integrating diverse theories in design creative thinking and problem-solving. My most recent upcoming article in the Journal of Interior Design in Fall 2007 entitled "Technology as a Tool for Globalization: Cross-cultural Collaborative Design Studio Projects" argues that the knowledge of cross-cultural and global issues are important for design students and illustrates how technology can be utilized to facilitate that process. The article illustrates through two projects (an affordable housing project in Nigeria and South Africa and a lighting design project in Nigeria) how design educators can provide students with practical and intellectual skills to be actively engaged in an increasingly global society.

My previous research similarly advocates for studies that introduce diverse perspectives in design education. Professor Vibhavari Jani and I conducted a survey of interior design educators in the U.S. to determine the level of integration of non-Western perspectives in interior design education. Our findings indicated not much progress has been achieved in this realm, and these educators indicate the need for materials and resources on diversity issues. Some publications do exist on this critical topic, as this selection demonstrates:

- *"Preserving the Past and Designing the Future: A Tale of Two Communities" by Abimbola O. Asojo and Vibhavari Jani presented at the 2004 Diversity in Beginning Design Conference in Hampton Virginia.*
- *"Design and Social Justice: An Investigation of Non-Western Perspectives in Interior Design Curriculum" by Vibhavari Jani and Abimbola O. Asojo presented at the 2007 Interior Design Educators Council Conference in Austin, Texas.*
- *"Hybrid Forms in the Built Environment: A Case Study of African Cities" by Abimbola O. Asojo in Migrations and Creativity in Africa.*
- *The African Diaspora edited by Toyin Falola, Niyi Afolabi, and Aderonke Adesanya, ch. 7.*
- *"A Spiritual Celebration of Cultural Heritage," Abimbola O. Asojo and Professor Katharine Leigh in the Traditional Dwellings and Settlements Review published by the International Association for the Study of Traditional Environments (IASTE), University of California at Berkeley.*
- *"Pattern and Artwork Design: Generative Theories in Yoruba African Forms" by Abimbola O. Asojo published by International Association of The Study of Traditional Environments (IASTE) Traditional Dwellings and Settlements Working Paper Series.*

There are also opportunities to become involved in advising minority students to increase their involvement in interior design. For example, I am the faculty mentor of the University of Oklahoma Organization of Black Designers, a student association of minority students from architecture, interior design, construction science, landscape architecture and regional and city planning within the college of architecture at the University of Oklahoma.

I want to challenge us as design educators to tackle the problems of under-representation of minority cultures in design and lack of documentation of contributions of minority cultures to the design discourse in several ways. Firstly, I encourage the active exploration of diversity issues in de-

sign curricula through the study of design precedents from diverse perspectives and design studio projects which address diversity issues. Secondly, I encourage educators to publish work and share their experiences on diversity issues to help other educators integrate this important element in design curricula. Thirdly, interior design as a profession needs to promote the recruitment and retention of minority students and faculty through mentoring programs. I strongly believe that advocacy of more studies on diversity issues is a starting point to address these challenges.

Social Justice

Humans have enriched their own interior environments for millennia. As societies progressed to embracing the division of labor, some persons became the designers and builders of spaces for others, thereby reducing the personal do-it-yourself aspect of interior design. It is only recently that interior design came to be identified in popular culture as the exclusive purview of the wealthy. Florida State University educator Jill Pable suggests that this attitude about interior design now may be changing based on the collusion of several societal forces. She traces the history of social justice at the broad cultural level, then suggests how interior design might contribute to an enhanced awareness of social justice issues. Figure 7.4 provides a project example that engaged interior design students in social justice concerns.

As alien as it may seem today, the foundation moral code for how humans should treat each other has been a moving target throughout history. Prior to the mid twentieth century, for example, the idea of "utilitarianism" dominated political thought, declaring that the morality of one's actions is judged entirely by its contribution to overall benefit. In his 1971 book A Theory of Justice, political philosopher John Rawls put forth a new vision of cultural behavior with these words:

"Each person possesses an inviolability founded on justice that even the welfare of society as a whole cannot override. For this reason justice denies that the loss of freedom for some is made right by a greater good shared by others."[16]

In so stating, Rawls declared an alternative to utilitarianism, substituting in its place the concept of 'justice as fairness', and embraced equality of basic human rights for those who are less fortunate economically, educationally or otherwise.

Inequities of wealth, gender, orientation, age, ethnicity and other barriers too often play a regrettable part in war, environmental degradation and other societal ills. Undoubtedly one challenge to solving the problems of social justice issues lies in the issues' connectivity to public good will, funding availability, and the public's varying awareness of the extent of these problems.

Issues of social justice stand forefront in the winds of political change in the United States, and periods of interest and apathy in these issues mark the nation's history. The early 21st century seems a particularly appropriate time to advance the causes of social justice, given that issues such as poverty, living wage disparities, and homelessness are gathering strength within the United States. Ironically, social justice is a starkly salient topic despite the United States' seldom disputed reputation as the most powerful nation in the world. Social statistics in a variety of issues including poverty, homelessness, and discrimination remain persistent or are increasing in scope and impact:

- *One out of five children lives below the official poverty line in the United States. The population of America's working poor has grown because the wage floor has failed to keep pace with the cost of living over the last three decades.*[17]
- *Reflecting the decrease in public service funding, lack of affordable housing is the leading cause of homelessness, not substance abuse or criminality. 32% of requests for shelter by families were unmet in 2005.*[18]

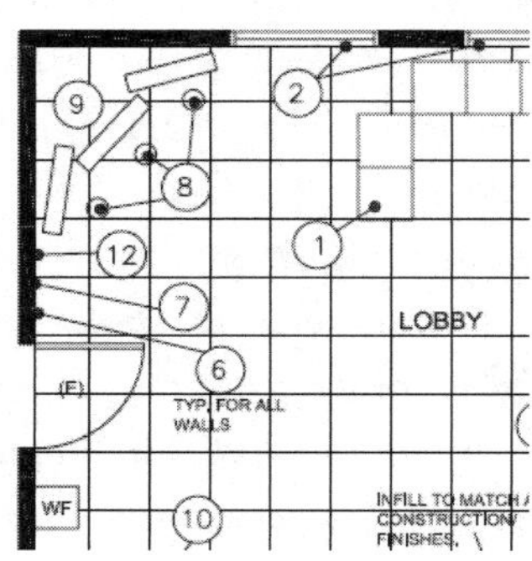

Figure 7.4 The homeless are often suspicious of institutional help. Because success stories of others' escape from the streets can inspire new shelter users to do the same, an interior design and graphic design student partnered to create the Wall of Hope, a collection of homeless persons' photographs, stories, and talismans in the waiting room of the local homeless shelter. Design by Kerri Ann Uchida, interior designer, and Christine Lee, graphic designer.

- *Hate crimes continue within the United States with approximately 7,500 incidents reported each year. Additionally, hate crimes escalate following tragic events such as the September 11, 2001 attacks.*
- *Recent controversy concerning inequities in governmental aid in the wake of Hurricane Katrina has helped bring racial issues back to public attention.*

The persistence of these inequities is now contemporary with a gradual public awakening about the importance and societal consequences of both good and bad design. The most recent decade has witnessed the rising ubiquity of "democratic" design and its potential to enhance the comfort, convenience and aesthetics of persons of all means. Fueled by the lengthy and prosperous period of the 1990's, this current serendipitous crossroad of technology, wealth, and cultural awareness has led in part to the new "golden age" of design.[19] *From Michael Graves' toilet brushes available at Target Stores to the innovative and effective kitchen utensils by OXO, design has discovered the masses, and the masses have returned the favor.*

In terms of general public and interior designer awareness, environmentalism is several steps ahead of social justice in its ability to shape action. However, it is likely that social justice will follow green design's initiative in establishing methods and procedures to act responsibly with regard to sourcing, issues of human labor, and fair treatment. In a recent panel discussion at the Neocon 2006 contract interiors conference, Ken Wilson of Envision and the recipient of Contract magazine's 2006 Designer of the Year Award noted a "shift in the value equation toward a social responsibility that is fully integrated with design." While his comments were offered in the context of a design competition chiefly concerned with ecologically sustainable design case studies, the breadth of his statement also speaks to a rising of collective consciousness amongst the design profession concerning issues of social justice in general. His comments echo the wider observations of other societal observers such as Paul Ray and Sherry Anderson, whose recent book The Cultural Creatives describes a 50-million and growing United States population segment, fully 25% of the country, as "tempered radicals" bent, among other things, on progressive social improvement.

What can design educators do? Design students may be uniquely positioned to explore the application of democratic design because their learning experiences allow time for necessary re-

search and their energy and youthful idealism fuel their intentions to make a difference.

- *Engage learners in projects that immerse them in interacting with disadvantaged populations. Design educators have reaped much success from projects that explore the issues of Native American populations, migrant workers, the homeless, and the socio-economically challenged.*
- *Explore field trips, guest speakers, and audiovisual opportunities to broaden learners' perspectives of other cultural groups. College learners are sometimes crippled by their predetermined stereotypes about cultural groups that differ from their own.*
- *Explore service learning as an option. Many institutions have an office of service learning that can assist instructors in building relationships with local charities and non-profit organizations. These alliances can lead to hands-on learning for interior design students that transcend classroom case studies and lead to long-lasting attitude change and civic commitment.*

Interior design higher education can be a vivid opportunity for learners to design for disadvantaged human cultures that differ radically from themselves. It is here that cultural and social justice sensitivity can be germinated, potentially leading to a lifetime punctuated by civic engagement and giving back to others.

Trends in interior design education reflect the excitement and uncertainty of the coming age. The challenges to existing structures and assumptions in higher education are startling and will test the adaptation ability of many. Yet, interior design's historic flexibility and attendance to the intimate human environment may serve it well. If van der Ryn's prediction of the dawning "Integral Age" filled with collaboration and decentralization proves true, design—and interior design specifically—may be well positioned to make a positive contribution to human environments that exceeds even its current achievements.

ENDNOTES

1. Van der Ryn, S. (2005). *Design for Life.* Salt Lake City, UT: Gibbs Smith.
2. Coleman, C. & Sosnowchik, K. (September 2006). *Interior Design Trends and Implications.* Grand Rapids, MI: Council for Interior Design Accreditation, p. 5.
3. Ibid., p. 45.
4. Dohr, J. (October 1992). Six predictions: The Future of Interior Design. *Interior Design 63*(14): 131.
5. Portillo, M. & Rey-Barreau, J. (1995). The Place of Interior Design in K-12 Education and the Built Environment Education Movement. *Journal of Interior Design 21*(1): 39–43.
6. Clemons, S. (1994). "Pat's Place": A Child's Animated Storybook. *IDEC Southwest Regional Meeting Proceedings.* El Paso, TX, pp. 17–19; Clemons, S. (1998). Computer Animation: A Tool for Teaching Design Fundamentals to Elementary School Students. *Journal of Interior Design, 24*(1): 40–47.
7. Clemons, S. (1999). Development of Interior Design Career Information for Dissemination to Students in Grades Six through Eight. *Journal of Interior Design 25*(2): 45–51.
8. These organizations are IDEC, the Interior Design Educators Council at http://www.idec.org; ASID, the American Society of Interior Designers at http://www.asid.org; IIDA, the International Interior Design Association at http://www.iida.org; IDC, the Interior Designers of Canada at http://www.interiordesigncanada.org; and NCIDQ, the National Council of Interior Design Qualification at http://www.ncidq.org. CE educators can submit their applications to any of these organizations, which will forward it on for IDCEC review and approval.
9. For more information, see The Learning Company website at http://www.thegreatcourses.com.
10. For more information, see The Academy at FSU website at http://www.pepperinstitute.org/Academy/.
11. Matthews, David. (2001). Making Connections Between Virtual Reality and the Design Process: A Media and Language for

Presenting Interiors in Four Dimensions. *Interior Design Educators Council International Conference Proceedings*, p. 54.
12. Papanek, V. (1982). *Design for the Real World: Human Ecology and Social Change*, 2nd ed. Chicago: Academy Chicago Publishers.
13. *EIA, Annual Review 2005.* (2005). Department of Energy. Retrieved 3/23/07 from http://www.eia.doe.gov/basics/energy basics101.html.
14. Ibid.
15. Hyllegard, K., Ogle, J., Dunbar, D. (2003). Sustainability and Historic Preservation in Retail Design: Integrating Design into a Model of the REI Denver Decision-making Process. *Journal of Interior Design 29*(1, 2): 32–49; Tucker, L. M. (2002). *The Void between Sustainability and Historic Preservation.* Paper presented at the Interior Design Educators International Conference, Santa Fe, NM.
16. Rawls, J. (2005). *A Theory of Justice.* New York: Belknap Press/New Edition. pp. 3–4.
17. Responsible Wealth.org. (n.d.). Why We Take Action. Retrieved 4/25/06 from http://www.responsiblewealth.org/aboutrw/whywe act.html.
18. United States Conference of Mayors, Inc. (December 2005). *Hunger and Homelessness Survey: A Status Report on Hunger and Homelessness in America's Cities.* Retrieved 12/5/05 from http://www.us mayors.org/uscm/hungersurvey/2005/ HH2005FINAL.pdf.
19. Gibney, F. & Luscombe, B. (March 2000). The Rebirth of Design. *Time 155.* Retrieved 6/30/07 from http://www.time.com/time/ archive/preview/0,10987,996372,00.html.

CHAPTER 8

Improving Teaching and Learning

Year after year Professor Glade dreads handing out the student evaluations. Just finding the perfect day to do so is a challenge. The uncomfortable waiting while the students fill out the forms, wondering if they will comment on his lack of preparation that one day, or the quality of the speaker on another (even though the delivery was admittedly a bit dry). And then, the third test seemed a disaster from the student's viewpoint. That was hardly Professor Glade's fault, he thought. Their studio project date was moved up and created a direct conflict with his course exam! No wonder they performed so poorly. He just wished they would actually read the materials assigned. College students these days! Last year, his merit raise suffered because of those darned student evaluations. How can anyone possibly think students are the best judge of his course! Colleagues always seem to have ratings above his in teaching, even though they are relatively new without the repository of information and handouts. Probably just because they are young and energetic. How could that be his fault? And now the chair wants to discuss his teaching performance.

It is often helpful to remember that teaching evaluations are not intended to be punitive instruments[1] but rather a gauge of effective teaching and classroom techniques. Whether used in formative or assessment manners, it is also not the intent of evaluations to place blame but to identify strengths and opportunities for instructional improvement.

DEVELOPMENT OPPORTUNITIES

Teaching is far from an exact science, and as presented in earlier chapters, learning is a process influenced by many factors, not the least of which is a student's prior knowledge, experience, and particular learning style. Often, the improvement of teaching is also an individualized process, although several common themes and suggestions will improve many aspects of almost everyone's teaching. Whether motivated by a desire to pursue excellence in teaching and subsequent student learning, or to strengthen particular elements of teaching performance, suggestions contained in this chapter will be of benefit.

Given that a desire to improve is present, the opportunities for development fall into two categories:

1. Defining where to improve
2. Determining how to implement improvements

Defining Where to Improve

A variety of factors influence an instructor's success in fostering students' learning. Engaging in teaching rarely involves only the presentation of material. While the overall curriculum structure may determine both general topics and specific information to be gained from a particular course, it is the structure within the course of information, the design and flow of learning experiences, selection of materials to reinforce lecture, expectations of the instructor (both stated and inferred), quality of guest speakers, attitude and approachability of instructor, and level and quality of student preparedness, among other items, that affect the quantity and quality of learning that will occur.

Researchers suggest four major roles instructors have in teaching:

- Instructional delivery
- Instructional design
- Content expertise
- Record keeping/management

Each of the roles is best and most accurately evaluated by particular constituencies. For example, a student is not the best judge of content expertise. Constituencies can be divided into

- Students
- Peers
- Self
- Department/program chair

Raoul Arreola, author of "Developing a Comprehensive Faculty Evaluation System" offers the following suggestions for the entity best suited to offer evaluation of each of the roles.

- Instructional delivery skills: students and self
- Instructional design skills: students, peers, and self
- Content expertise: peers, self, and department/program chair
- Record keeping/management: self and department/program chair.[2]

Gathering the information from appropriate sources may take varying forms. When obtained from students, the most common information form is a questionnaire, typically in the format of a course evaluation. Students may also be engaged in discussion by experts in teaching and learning and not associated with the course to gain insights for the instructor. Peers often give feedback based on videotapes of lectures, evaluation of course materials, and observation of course conduct. Careful evaluation of course materials, feedback from students and colleagues, journaling, self-evaluation of videotaped lectures, and reflection will lead to identification of areas for improvement by the instructor. Department and/or program chairs may offer suggestions for improvement based on student comments and evaluation, course materials and delivery, peer comments, and their own insights and experience in education.[3]

Determining How to Implement Improvements

Several sources are available to assist instructors wishing to implement improvements within their teaching. Discussion of student evaluation and subsequent interpretation and implementation of improvements is discussed in detail later in this chapter. Opportunities to improve based upon peer evaluation and mentoring are additional means. The Peer Review of Teaching Project is one such formalized structure for peer review. Begun in 1994, this initiative has engaged hundreds of faculty members from numerous universities. Their website, http://www.courseportfolio.org, contains a searchable repository of course portfolios, as well as examples of course portfolios from a variety of fields. The process of peer review of teaching involves compiling information from a course or courses, writing reflectively about that material, and then gaining peer insight into it. When working with a peer to improve teaching, the process often involves written materials but can also include experiencing a peer's teaching firsthand. Documentation of improvement assists both the instructor and the community of teaching and learning at large.

Workshops are available on many campuses through teaching and learning centers, through academic affairs offices, or through a group honored for teaching effectiveness, which may possess a title of Academy of Distinguished Teachers or the like. These same groups often suggest peers across campus who have a desire to engage in positive and constructive discourse towards improvement. The common thread running amongst all of these groups and individuals is a desire to improve teaching in higher education. Perhaps surprisingly, peers need not be in the same field of study, as insights from effective teachers often cross disciplinary boundaries.

Instructors themselves may take steps to implement improvements. Reading tips from other teachers, research regarding the improvement of teaching, and case studies are often first steps in the strategy. Engaging colleagues in conversation about effective strategies employed in their courses is another excellent step. Another critical component is self-reflection. Reflecting upon courses taught includes examining the course objectives established and how effectively they were accomplished, along with considering ideas for improvement. Instructors are encouraged to think about timing and length of assignments as well as their format, with an eye to educational objectives. It is often helpful to keep a course journal, noting throughout the sequence of the course particularly effective (or ineffective) guest speakers, visual aids, or where more (or less) time would be advantageous for particular concepts.

Instructors also find it helpful to write a personal teaching philosophy. Many candidates for teaching positions are caught unaware if they have not at least considered their personal teaching philosophy, as it is often a required submission in the search process. This is not a static or historical document; rather, it is a document (whether a paragraph or pages long) that captures an attitude towards teaching and learning and the role of the instructor in it.

Department and program chairs are excellent sources for suggestions to implement improvements. While their interests may be vested toward particular aspects of an instructor's teaching performance, they have typically encountered additional knowledge that can lead to improvement. Chairs may team up particular instructors in mentor relationships, or may see trends within the department that warrant a guest speaker or specific workshop. Alternatively, they may elect to send individuals or groups to targeted conferences, or have suggestions of collegial relationships between universities.

Improving instruction is an ongoing process for all persons engaged in delivering education. Identifying a need for improvement and specific areas to improve and then identifying and taking steps toward improvement is seldom an entirely individual process. Information gathered in varied ways from a variety of sources provides a rich and fruitful experience. Improving instruction enlivens the classroom experience not only for students but for instructors as well.

EVALUATIONS

As mentioned, an evaluation of courses and instruction within them is a typical part of higher education. In part, this documents teaching performance and effectiveness for merit, tenure, or promotion purposes. In a large way, it is also done for formative reasons to engage instructors in conversation and activities that will improve teaching.

Student Evaluations of Teaching

Many institutions require that students complete a series of questions at or near semester's end to assess teaching success. Student questionnaires of this sort are highly contentious amongst faculty and educational researchers, and some feel that ratings are biased toward inherently interesting course material, "fun" teachers, or teachers that are easy graders. Other research suggests that student assessments are a valid and balanced indicator of teaching quality regardless of course content, personality, or other issues.[4] Most researchers agree that student evaluations of faculty should be only one of many sources of information on teaching performance that personnel decision makers reference.

Each university has a defined procedure instructors must follow when administering course evaluations. It is possible that instructors will be given the choice of day that students will complete their evaluations of the course. If this is the case, avoid administering the evaluations at an emotionally contentious time, such as when a test or project is administered or returned.

In general, the educator instructs students to return completed evaluation forms to a manila envelope (or something similar), assigning a student to deliver the forms to the appropriate administrative assistant. The instructor should be absent from the room during the time learners complete the evaluations and should instruct that learners complete the forms individually. When all have completed the evaluation forms, the instructor is notified to reenter the room. The instructor will not see the evaluation form results until after the time grades are turned in at the completion of the course.

Common Teaching Evaluation Questions

It is helpful to review teaching characteristics that are commonly represented on student evaluation questionnaires conducted at or near the end of the term. Here is a selection of typical student evaluation questions answered on a scale of Strongly agree to Strongly disagree or Not applicable.

- Lecture Class Questions
  - The instructor clearly explained the course objectives.
  - The instructor effectively organized the course.
  - The instructor was well prepared for the lecture.
  - The instructor clearly presented the course material.
  - The instructor helped me understand the importance of the subject matter.
  - The instructor encouraged questions and discussion in class.
  - The instructor was available during office hours and by appointment.
  - The examinations and/or assignments were relevant to the subject matter.
  - The instructor clearly explained the grading criteria.
  - The instructor returned the graded assignments in a reasonable amount of time.

  - The instructor had a considerate attitude toward students.
  - Overall, the instructor was an effective teacher.

- Studio Class Questions

  - The instructor clearly explained lab/activity techniques and the use of equipment.
  - The instructor explained and emphasized safety procedures when applicable.
  - The instructor was available and helpful during laboratory/activity.
  - The instructor effectively coordinated the lecture and laboratory/activity.

Each of these questions represents factors of effective teaching directly related to the instructor. Other questions may be included that address issues pertaining to the course that are sometimes beyond the instructor's control, such as room and equipment.

Engaging students in evaluations and course feedback earlier in the semester may prove helpful in gaining insights that can improve the course midstream (and thus the end of term evaluations). Early evaluations may be conducted after the first five to six weeks of a semester-long course or two to three weeks of a quarter-long course. This allows enough time for students to have a reasonable sample of teaching to make substantive comments.

When conducting midterm course evaluations, some tips are provided here that will ensure the most useful results.

- Use open-ended questions that elicit comments and suggestions.
- Conduct the evaluation during the first ten to fifteen minutes of class.
- Discuss early evaluation results with the class, thanking them for their effort and input. It is important to frame the discussion to maintain a positive tone, where the instructor does not come across as defensive, angry, overly apologetic, or hurt.
- Online course instruction packages such as WebCT and Blackboard offer instructors the opportunity to administer anonymous surveys to learners. This technique has the added advantage of providing learners the ability to speak freely because their identities are not known by the instructor.
- Implement appropriate alterations in the course in a timely manner. For instance, if student comments consistently mention the readability of onscreen writing or images, the instructor may immediately implement a change to a larger font, larger image, or fewer talking points per screen.

Regardless of whether you can alleviate their particular problems, students appreciate the simple gesture of an instructor asking how they are doing. Here is an example of a written in-class survey:

How are you doing/feeling/faring? Please complete this anonymous questionnaire. Its purpose is for me to determine what issues are on your mind at this point in the semester so that I can best help you. Do not sign this sheet so that you can speak freely.

1. *How many credit hours of classes are you taking this semester?*
2. *How many studio classes are you taking this semester?*
3. *List the studio classes you are currently taking.*
4. *If you are working, how many hours per week?*
5. *List two adjectives (such as* happy, sad*) that best describe your current state of mind about how your semester is going in general.*
6. *Briefly explain why you chose these words.*
7. *If appropriate, describe how I can best assist you more fully this semester. If there is some-*

thing that I am successfully helping you with, please describe that also.

This example shows that a survey can also gently remind learners that their learning experience, to a degree, is up to their commitment and ability to balance their life activities in relation to course requirements. It also shows the learners that the instructor is aware that they are taking other courses simultaneously and is sensitive to the learners' overall success.

It is important when conducting course evaluations to remember that the instructor is not engaged in a popularity contest. Rather, the goal is to provide the best learning situation possible for all students to gain the most knowledge from the course. As discussed in earlier chapters, each student learns a bit differently and has a personal style that best accommodates their learning process. It is not unusual, then, that comments may be contradictory.

Actions to Improve Teaching Based on Evaluations

Student evaluations of a course (and of teaching) are read with trepidation by the seasoned educator as well as newcomers to the classroom. When viewed objectively, feedback may inform and improve one's teaching and potentially point to areas of behavior, teaching style, or listening skills that could realistically use some improvement.

Open-ended questions typically yield diverse responses, which at times may seem contradictory and a bit overwhelming until analyzed. Here are some suggestions for gaining clarity and making the evaluation most useful from an instructional point of view.

- Break apart comments into phrases, which can be organized and rearranged into common topical areas, then sort the phrases by topic.
- Tally the number of responses for each topic or general area the phrases address. Areas of consensus often form the instructor's highest priorities in considering directions for improvement.
- Keep focused on potentially constructive changes. When evaluating the comments, cluster them into groups such as Strengths, Ideas for change, and Issues beyond my control.
- If the evaluation is done midterm, determine those changes that can be accommodated immediately (usually addressing teaching behaviors, such as speaking too softly or not facing the students when presenting materials) as well as those that must be addressed at a larger scale or for the next time the course is taught (organizational flow of material, for instance).[5]

In the Newsletter of the Teaching Resource Center for Faculty and Teaching Assistants at the University of Virginia "Teaching Concerns", Robert Bruner gives this advice for constructive steps to take when evaluating student evaluations:

- Write your own evaluation of the course.[6] Examine the course syllabus; reflect upon course design, materials, and experiences. Engage in this exercise while the course is still fresh in your mind. This assessment will help frame the student feedback of the course so that rather than a dichotomy of Good versus Bad comments, the degree of alignment between instructor and student about the course may be seen.

When reading the student evaluations:

- Look for cross-sectional patterns. There may be clusters of comments that point to a common behavior. Try to separate comments by focus of criticism: teaching versus materials, versus course design. Note

what seems to be going well and should be continued. Note patterns in the comments that might lead to improvement.
- Look for command and connection. Effective instructors have a command of the subject and project confidence. Connection refers to the perceived as well as actual availability (both in listening and in physical presence) of the instructor. Both of these areas can be remedied.
- Look at the details of the evaluations. While it may be tempting to look at the overall rating of the course or teaching, it is the details that will facilitate improvement. The written comments, when combined with numerical ratings, point to particular aspects that can be improved on when necessary.
- Examine trends over time. Comparisons of teaching evaluations over time will lend additional insights, especially if the evaluations examine the same course. Comparing self-reflective course notes with these evaluations can attribute improvements to changes made and can illustrate areas for further development.[7]

When determining the steps to take for improvement, Bruner suggests the following.

- Crystallize your priorities. Think critically about what the students want changed, keeping in mind that not all requests must be granted. The underlying consideration must be whether the change will promote better learning.
- Manage the course evaluation process. Consider administering less formal mid-course evaluations in addition to those at the end of the course. Engage in peer observations and feedback of teaching.
- Be student-centered and trust that decent evaluations will follow. In general, students value instructors from whom they have learned well. That suggests that the straightest path to positive evaluations is to focus on learning and the delivery of an intellectually valuable experience.
- Accept variance. Uncomplimentary feedback is the occasional companion of any instructor who takes risks with new material, tries new teaching styles, gets a poor draw of students, or believes that challenging students is good.
- Be action-oriented. Focus on what you can do differently next time rather than what happened in the past. Distill what you have learned from the evaluations into a few prioritized "to do's" rather than a detailed inventory of all possible improvements. Include action steps such as reading on teaching techniques, attending teaching and learning workshops on your campus, asking to observe a successful colleague's class, asking a colleague to observe you at a few points during your course, or searching for more suitable course materials.[8]

Actions to Improve Teaching Based on Self- and Peer Review

Administrators are often positively influenced when instructors voluntarily undertake self-evaluation of their teaching. Here are some techniques to consider addressing:

1. Ask a teacher colleague in your department to observe your teaching style and then offer a review of their impressions to you.
2. Self-assess your teaching. Lyons, Kysilka, and Pawlas offer this questionnaire that can prompt your introspection:

   - How do I typically begin the class? Briefly review key points of the previous class? Use "advance organizers"? Share current news events or real-life examples?

- Where/how do I position myself in class? Stand behind a podium or table? Regularly move throughout the classroom? Sit on a table to speak less formally?
- How do I move in the classroom? Back and forth across the front, or toward students and back to the front creating a sense of active interchange?
- Where are my eyes usually focused? On lecture notes? On the rear wall of the classroom? Scanning eyes of the students?
- Do I facilitate students' visual processing of course material? Do I use a chalkboard or overhead projector to reinforce key points? Do I overwhelm with too many words at once, or are items displayed at their processing speed?
- Do I change the speed, volume, energy, and tone of my voice? Can students perceive which points are more critical?
- How do I ask questions of students? Do I allow enough time for consideration of a question? Do I answer too many of my own questions?
- How often, and when, do I smile or laugh in class? Do students smile or laugh with me?
- How do I react when students are inattentive? Ignore it and continue to "plow through the material"? Nonjudgmentally state what I see and offer a solution?
- How do I react when students disagree or challenge what I say? React as if threatened? Acknowledge the viewpoint and objectively explain its weaknesses?
- How do I typically end a class? With planned material unaddressed? Smoothly, predictably?[9]

3. Observe the style of others in your department who teach similar classes to yours. Pretend you are a student and observe how visible notes are on the board, how easy or difficult it is to hear, and when the class tends to drag down or become boring. This often inspires different ideas you have not previously considered.
4. Seek out resources on your campus for teaching and learning. Quite often there are qualified persons ready to help.
5. Videotape one of your class sessions. Review the tape either alone or with another instructor and discuss your shared impressions.
6. Take a trusted student out for a soda and ask their impressions of your teaching style. If you approach them with a sincere desire to understand students' point of view, you may be surprised about what you learn.
7. Query your students yourself, apart from the end-of-semester student evaluations institutions often require. This is an especially good idea if you perceive students are not doing well or are otherwise having difficulties.

RELATIONSHIPS WITH YOUR INSTITUTION

Many instructors are accomplished professionals, quite possibly with current or past design firm experience of their own. They are undoubtedly familiar with the fast pace of work life and hold high expectations for those they work with. These are qualities that probably contributed to their hiring as a faculty member by the institution. However, it bears remembering that many professionals are sometimes surprised by the differences in office procedures and management between the private sector and the large public or private institution.

Suggestions for Action

Here are some suggestions that can help the instructor relationship with his or her institution remain smooth and positive.

- Institution administrators and office personnel are often overworked and do not have sufficient time to properly orient new faculty. Ask for information, forms, or assistance with humility and sensitivity to others' time needs.
- Procedures often take longer than in the private sector. Anticipate this and submit needed forms well in advance of when you will need a reply. This includes scheduling of audio-visual equipment, paper copying, working with the library, and ordering textbooks.
- Touch base with the departmental person who hired you at least once a semester, even if this meeting is not invited. Keep the meeting upbeat and, if appropriate, inform this person of the interesting and positive learning activities occurring in your classroom.
- Be sensitive to the condition in which you leave classrooms. This is particularly true of studio classrooms and sample resource rooms, which can become quickly disorganized. Have students pick up after themselves at the end of each class. If something is broken, immediately report this to the department office.
- Recall that the department office is likely a busy place. Familiarize yourself with their policies concerning students turning in late assignments there and other impacts.
- Keep other instructors and the department chairperson aware of the content of your course. This is very important if your course content directly impacts the next course in the studio sequence, for example. You might proactively create a course outline and distribute it to others affected by its content.
- If you are an adjunct faculty member, do not feel offended or snubbed if you are not invited to faculty meetings or other department activities. (Full-time faculty often dislike these meetings anyway!) Policy on this varies, but typically such meetings are only attended by full-time faculty. Be attentive to changes in policy enacted by others.

Recall that one of the strongest assets that most design professionals bring to their institution is a current and thorough knowledge of the design industry and its practices. Whether a full-time or adjunct faculty member, there is much to offer that the department might not think to consider. This includes real-life venues for senior studio projects, industry contacts for guest speakers, professional organization activities, and relationships built with architects, contractors, and specialty trades. A sure way to build rapport with colleagues is to approach them with a helpful and willing attitude. By being a consistent influence for good, friendships will be engendered and a collegial environment promoted.

ENDNOTES

1. According to Aleamoni, research shows that typical faculty concerns about student evaluations of instruction are largely unfounded. In "Typical Faculty Concerns About Student Evaluation of Teaching," he offers discussion on eight of the most common concerns. Aleamoni, Lawrence. (Fall 1987). In L. M. Aleamoni, ed., *Techniques for Evaluating and Improving Instruction. New Directions for Teaching and Learning*, no. 31. San Francisco: Jossey-Bass, pp 25–31.
2. Arreola, Raoul. (2000). *Developing a Comprehensive Faculty Evaluation System: A Handbook for College Faculty and Administrators on Designing and Operating a Comprehensive Faculty Evaluation System*, 2nd ed. Boulton, MA: Anker Publishing.

3. Ibid. Arreola makes a strong case for linking faculty evaluation with faculty development opportunities.
4. Kulik, J. A. (Spring 2001). Student Ratings: Validity, Utility, and Controversy. In M. Theall, P. C. Abrami & L. A. Mets, eds., *New Directions for Institutional Research*, no. 109. San Francisco: Jossey-Bass. This article provides a discussion of research supporting and disputing various factors affecting student evaluations.
5. Adapted from Distributing and Responding to Early Course Evaluations. (2002). *Enhancing Education @ Carnegie Mellon*. Accessed 8/23/07 from http://www.cmu.edu/teaching/assessment/feedback_students.html.
6. This suggestion is also inherent in the Peer Review of Teaching Project. Faculty prepare course portfolios and work in concert with a colleague for mentoring and improvement strategies. View the Peer Review of Teaching Project at http://www.courseportfolio.org.
7. Adapted from Bruner, Robert F. (Fall 2002). Taking Stock: Evaluations from Students. In *Teaching Concerns. Newsletter of the Teaching Resource Center for Faculty and Teaching Assistants at the University of Virginia*. Accessed 8/23/07 from http://trc.virginia.edu/Publications/Teaching_Concerns/Fall_2002/TC_Fall_2002_Bruner.html. Bruner is a Distinguished Professor of Business Administration and Executive Director of the Batten Institute, Darden Graduate Business School.
8. Ibid.
9. Adapted from Lyons, Kysilka, Pawlas. (1999). *The Adjunct Professor's Guide to Success: Surviving and Thriving in the College Classroom*. Boston: Allyn & Bacon.

SECTION THREE

The Teaching Experience

CHAPTER 9

Essays and Inspirations

The spectrum of human experience that an academic life in interior design education offers is broad and varied. For this reason, it is somewhat difficult to characterize its qualities by discussing it in only a general fashion. Perhaps the true nature of the teaching experience is best expressed by examining it from a variety of individual points of view, bringing the dialogue to the personal, intimate level where human learning, of course, really occurs.

For example, an understanding of teaching will be quite different for a new instructor seeking tenure versus an experienced interior design administrator. Instructors' priorities will similarly vary depending on their individual circumstances. For some, finding and maintaining life balance while nurturing a teaching career will be quite important, and for others, it can be a time of reflection on a long career that offers the opportunity to pass on advice to others traveling a similar academic road. This chapter seeks to tell the stories of numerous interior design educators whose comments demonstrate this variety of experience.

Lastly, the story of interior design education is one authored not only by instructors but also by their learners. It is all too often that the conversation ceases with a discussion of top-down teaching strategies, with little notice of the message for learners that is actually getting through the noise. Therefore, the chapter concludes with a revealing look at instructor quirks and habits that affect learning for better or worse through the eyes of their students. It is here that the value of the instructor's small gesture of outreach is recognized for the power it holds for learners.

REFLECTIONS OF SEASONED EDUCATORS

It would be an interesting endeavor to count the collective number of years of teaching experience that all educator members of the Interior Design Educators Council possess (IDEC, in the opinion of these authors, is the primary organization for interior design education). Those educators with lengthy teaching careers have particularly valuable advice gained through years of testing, adjusting, and adapting. This section acknowledges that those who possess an enduring career in interior design education offer distinctly valuable insights about learners, values, priorities, and procedures.

A Voice of Experience

Professor Pat Hilderbrand served as an interior design faculty member for thirty-two years, receiving recognitions for her excellence in teaching and advising. She has been an IDEC member for over twenty-five years. In recognition of her numerous awards and leadership positions in this organization including Membership chair, Computer Network chair, and Corresponding Secretary, she was inducted into the IDEC Fellows, an honorary IDEC membership category accorded to those with enduring exemplary service. Professor Hilderbrand has also served the Council for Interior Design Accreditation (formerly FIDER) for fifteen years as a site visitor, chair of visiting teams, chair of the Accreditation Committee, and chair of the Accreditation Commission.

Hilderbrand's extensive experience in teaching and accreditation assessment made her keenly aware of beginning students' struggles with three dimensional concepts. Here she isolates the details of this curricular requirement, exploring the "street level" experience of a learning concept, a project strategy, and her reflections on meeting its challenges.

My experience both as an instructor for the beginning interior design studio and as a leader in accreditation reviews repeatedly made clear one of the challenges of beginning students: difficulty bridging the transition from basic two-dimensional and three-dimensional design to successful application for interiors.

To help students learn to visualize interior space and utilize basic design skills in manipulating that space, I developed the following 3D project for the beginning interior design studio. An efficiency apartment, with given dimensions, was used so that in addition to considering design elements and principles, students needed to apply many "minimum clearance" guides and experiment with visual definition of activity areas. A client with specific needs/requests was assigned. Ceilings taller than 8' opened three-dimensional learning to different floor and ceiling levels. A large window area on one wall allowed the space to be viewed through the windows.

Before beginning the project, students were asked to bring in photos of interiors that demonstrated ways to visually define several activity areas without use of solid walls. These were grouped by technique, discussed, and posted in the studio. Two class sessions were allotted to start designing with 2-D drawings, usually bubble diagrams and floor plans.

To assure that students used 3D construction for visualization and design development for the project, only two class sessions were allotted to start designing with 2D drawings, usually bubble diagrams and floor plans. To facilitate quick 3D construction, a pair of scissors and cardstock with printed 1/4" grid were used to demonstrate how ½" scale 3D shapes of interior components (including furnishings) could be made in just minutes. About one week was allotted for initial experimenting in 3D. To keep the focus on 3D development, the project did not include selection of actual furnishings or materials, and models were usually restricted to all white.

After this initial 3D experimentation, a complete draft model (illustration or foam board perimeter with cardstock interior components) was required for critique. It took several semesters for me to realize that just asking for a complete draft was not enough. Students often came in with partial constructions that were insufficient for good critique. To get past this, a set number of points toward the final project grade were available for having this stage complete on time. Points were not assigned on design quality as it was expected that further development would be needed.

Improvements based on the first model critique were due at the next class session. To help me remember the models so I would know if further development occurred, sometimes the first drafts were digitally photographed and printouts made for this critique. If there were only a few students, this would not be necessary. However, with two studios and at least 40 students, I needed the extra help. Having the photos, along with the designation of additional points for this stage, encouraged students to participate. About a week was allowed for further refinement and final construction.

Use of modeling and timeline requirements were frustrating for some students, but when the project was finished, most felt they learned a lot. Many "lightbulb" moments were rewarding for both the students and me. Success with the process was evident when many students coming in with the first draft model said that seeing the space in 3D had already caused them to change aspects of the design.

What would I do differently if I knew then what I know now?

- *Give more positive feedback. We all usually react more positively, feel good, and work harder to improve when we know what we are doing well. I included some positive feedback for projects, but often wished I had done more in this area. In addition, I would try to make time to write notes to students at the end of each semester to address their overall strengths and weaknesses.*
- *Use interior design television shows as a basis for discussion with students. These were just getting started when I retired and I heard faculty and designers speak negatively about the image they portray. I think there are better programs out there today and new ones will come along. Students watch them and they can provide good material for discussion.*
- *Emphasize verbal skills coupled with positive aspects of personality for effective communication in interior design. While many programs require a speech class to help with verbal presentations, I don't think enough is done in this area in many educational programs.*

One last recommendation: Think of yourself as a learning facilitator. Instead of thinking you are giving students knowledge or "teaching" them, think about what you want students to discover or learn. When provided guidance as this project describes, students are more likely to remember better than through lectures, readings or merely seeing examples. Thinking this way may lead to preparing assignments a little differently.

Reflections on Studio Learning

Professor Paul Eshelman was educated in the field of Industrial Design at Kent State University and the University of Illinois, Champaign-Urbana, earning an MFA degree in 1972. Following a period of professional design experience as Senior Designer for Amtrak and Designer and Research Associate for Herman Miller Research Corporation, he joined the faculty in the Department of Design and Environmental Analysis at Cornell University in 1978. He teaches interior design and furniture design studios and applies his design expertise to his research focus—design for special populations including people with Alzheimer's disease. From 1990 to 1994, he served as the editor of the *Journal of Interior Design (JID)* and proposed changes in title, format, structure, support, and overall design that raised the quality and visibility of *JID*, the only research journal dedicated to the discipline of interior design. He continues to serve on the *JID* Editorial Review Board.

Eshelman's other leadership roles in the IDEC organization have included vice president, corresponding secretary, board member, *IDEC Record* editor, and chair of the Research Committee. Cited for his leadership and service to the organization and discipline, Professor Eshelman was inducted as a Fellow of the IDEC organization.

Consistently respected in the profession as well as the academic world, Eshelman was recently one of only three educators from design schools interviewed for an IIDA Perspectives article titled "Design: The Next Generation." Eshelman summarizes his path to teaching and offers sage advice to novice educators regarding the value of professional organizations, the studio component of design education, and the aspect of risk taking.

My path to teaching interior design at the college level began with an undergraduate minor in art education. During graduate school I was fortunate to have a teaching assistantship in interior design as a lab section instructor in a survey course taught by University of Illinois Professor Harold Alexander. After six years of experience in professional practice, first as a train car designer for Amtrak and then as a furniture designer/researcher for Herman Miller Research Corporation, I returned to the thought of teaching. The ensuing search led me to Cornell University, now nearly three decades ago.

I began teaching at Cornell when the design major included both interior design and product design. Shortly thereafter the design faculty collectively made the decision motivated by student preferences to focus on the interior design portion of the major and eliminate the product design offering. Because I was enjoying teaching at Cornell and wanted to continue, I found myself in the position of needing to learn about design at a different scale than I was familiar with given my educational and professional background in product design. This is where the Interior Design Educators Council (IDEC) played a formative role for me. Through the interaction IDEC afforded me with other interior design educators and representatives from the practitioner organizations allied with IDEC, I was able to gain valuable understanding of issues central to the education of entry level practitioners of interior design.

At Cornell, my primary responsibility is teaching studios, a course type that is a marvel in higher education. What sets the studio apart from other course types is the opportunity it provides for students to immediately apply what they are learning, a pedagogical approach that fosters intrinsic motivation to learn and, thereby, elevates learning. I have come to realize that my goal as a studio instructor is to capitalize on this inherent strength of the studio approach by doing all I can to reinforce intrinsic motivation for each student. Time, experience, and interaction with colleagues at Cornell and in IDEC have provided me insights about how I can pursue this goal.

One particularly valuable insight involves the issue of risks. For students to grow in their appreciation of true creativity in design, they must be willing to step outside their comfort zone—take risks with their ideas. Fear of failure reduces willingness to take design risks and lulls students toward safe and even stereotypic ideas. When students do take risks and fail, they need to be able to learn from those failures, not be made to feel discouraged by them. Putting this insight into operation, I work hard to structure assignments that allow students the freedom to try again. In studios organized around multiple assignments, I do introduce new material with each new assignment but hold constant fundamental aspects to enable students to revisit issue they previously addressed. In studios where I engage students in a semester-long assignment, I deliberately frame a process that allows them to work iteratively, cycling through their ideas at progressively higher levels of discrimination and refinement.

ACHIEVING TENURE AND MAINTAINING LIFE BALANCE

For many full-time educators, the early period of establishing a teaching, research, and service record of achievement during the tenure process is among the most busy and stress-filled of their careers. As higher institutions come under increasing pressure to economically justify long-term salary costs, administrators look for assurance that investments in their faculty are solid and reflect the mission of the institution well. The following essays provide insights into managing not only the pressure cooker tenure period, but also finding long-term happiness and peace in an academic career within the larger spectrum of life.

Advice on Achieving Tenure

Dr. Stephanie Watson Zollinger is an Associate Professor and Program Director within the Department of Design, Housing, and Apparel at the University of Minnesota. A veteran with twenty years of interior design education experience, Watson Zollinger began her teaching career at the University of Southern Mississippi, then taught at the University of Arkansas before moving to Minnesota. Her successful path to tenured status provides her the means to offer practical advice to others engaged in a similar career quest.

Over the years, one of the biggest challenges for me has been maintaining balance. The demands on faculty involving teaching, research, and service are considerable, and at times appear overwhelming. I have learned that smart choices *are the key in maintaining the necessary equilibrium. I offer the following advice for making wise decisions that can lead to tenure.*

Mentoring. *Mentoring is a process through which a new, untenured faculty member receives guidance and support from senior faculty for successful career enhancement and professional advancement. I recommend setting up a mentoring committee. The benefits of mentoring are many:*

1. *assistance in understanding the structure and culture of the department/unit and developing a professional network;*
2. *individual recognition and encouragement;*
3. *honest criticism and feedback;*
4. *advice on responsibilities and professional priorities;*
5. *knowledge of the "system" as well as informal rules;*
6. *long-range career planning;*
7. *support and advocacy from colleagues; and,*
8. *opportunities for collaborative projects.*

Teaching. *Don't put too much pressure on yourself to be a "perfect" instructor. There is no such thing. Every instructor has his or her strengths and weaknesses, and you will be no exception. Instead, focus on what you can reasonably expect to teach your students within 15 weeks, then decide what you think will be the most effective way of getting this knowledge across. Knowing your objectives at the beginning of the course helps you to determine the pace and organization as the semester progresses, and it also helps you to keep your goals for the class in sight.*

Be prepared. *For me personally, my propensity to organize and compartmentalize systematically has proven invaluable. Planning ahead can increase your pedagogical effectiveness and reduce your stress as a teacher.*

Having a well-thought-out plan for each class meeting helps your students to take you more seriously and shows them that you are putting as much work into the course as you expect of them. It also reduces student anxiety by letting them know what your expectations are. Solid preparation can help reduce the stress of trying to prepare a lesson at the last minute or squeeze too much work into the last few weeks of the semester. Finally, by creating a teaching plan for the semester, you may be able to avoid having to grade exams or papers at the points in the semester when you are most busy with your own work.

Pay attention to evaluations. *When you receive student evaluations at the end of each semester, be alert to what they have to say. While you will need to take them with a grain of salt, the majority of evaluations can provide useful information about your strengths and weaknesses as an instructor. Evaluations provide an objective view of your strengths and weaknesses as an instructor, and they are often reassuring in that they remind you that overall, you're doing a good job.*

Publishing. *Faculty in virtually all the nation's leading colleges and universities are expected to conduct research and to publish their findings. I have learned that research is the main criteria for advancement, not quality teaching. While we may not like these priorities, know the game and play it well. Here are smart strategies for publishing that I have learned.*

- *Select the publication outlets (journals or academic publishers) that will enhance your reputation.*
- *Target journals. Identify the journals that would be most interested in your manuscript. Look at the recent articles each journal publishes to develop a sense of the work they publish.*
- *Keep your academic work focused, and avoid too many uncorrelated research pursuits. Become thematic.*
- *Research the turn-around time for manuscript review. Some manuscripts have a longer turn-around time than others. Be strategic in your planning.*
- *Schedule time for research and writing. Learning to reserve time for writing is not easy, but it is essential. A realistic strategy is to set aside time for daily writing sessions ranging in duration from less than half an hour to no more than two hours maximum.*
- *Collaborate. Identify individuals who have expertise and interests complementary to your own. Consider working with a senior faculty member who can serve as a mentor. An alternative strategy is to partner with a third or fourth-year faculty member—someone who, like you, is fairly new, shares your enthusiasm, and has been around long enough to have learned a few things and developed some good work habits.*

Institutional Service. *Service to the academic institution in the form of committee assignments is also often included in tenure criteria. These committee assignments are an important part of shared governance. Examples are faculty committees that deal with issues such as curriculum development, the approval of new courses, student discipline, the quality of student life, student success, and even academic freedom and tenure.*

Serving on committees is important and I do recommend it. It is probably the best way, aside from mentoring activities, to meet colleagues from a wide variety of disciplines from across campus. Do know that not all committees are created equally. Stave off the impulse to join important, political and time-consuming committees.

- *Avoid excessive committee and administrative work early in your career. It will interfere with your chances for tenure.*
- *Choose your service carefully. Pick one area where you can make a positive difference in your department. Something that will average no more than 2 hours per week during the course of the semester and that can be dropped cold in the summer is best.*
- *Try to not waste your time serving on committees that are not valued. Be sure to seek advice from senior faculty members about what committees to serve on, and then volunteer for those committees. Do try, however, to avoid being talked into becoming a committee chair.*

In my case, I have to admit that other factors in addition to those above have proven helpful in enabling me to complete my tasks as a University of Minnesota faculty member. A comfortable place to read and write certainly is beneficial, but so too are adequate exercise, humor, and an attitude that declares things to be half full, not half empty. Supportive family members can be most significant of all.

Finding One's Passion in Academic Life

Professor Lynn M. Jones is an interior design educator, practitioner, author, former Chair of Art & Design and current Graduate Coordinator of Interior Design at Brenau University. Throughout her numerous career pursuits and accomplishments, Jones has observed that the natural environment provides a thread of continuity, and this passion has helped her maintain her focus and continual drive for achievement. Her career story provides insights and inspiration for others seeking balance and meaning in their career and life.

My earliest childhood memories shaped my career choices. My mom, aunt and godmother all taught; my other aunt worked in the school system. My sister decided she would be a teacher. After years of hearing their stories, most of them horror stories, I swore off teaching at an early age. I was the artist in the family. I painted, sketched, sewed, and played in my father's workshop. And like many young aspiring designers, I laid out floor plans on graph paper, raked leaves into room shapes, created labyrinths in the snow (although I wouldn't have a clue what that word meant for another 15 years), and of course moved the furniture around my room. I decided architecture was the career path I would travel.

My childhood memories additionally focused on family travel. Yes, picture the station wagon towing the trailer cross-country with the kids and dog in the backseat. Each summer we had three to four glorious weeks visiting historic sites, national parks, and camping along the way. What stuck was the love for the environment, historic structures, the Wild West, and what is now termed biophilia: the connections I seek, consciously and unconsciously, with the natural environment.

Laying the foundation: Secondary education. *Alas, the universities I visited as a prospective student pursuing architecture left me cold. However, the Environmental Design Program at Purdue University fit the bill. As the professor said, "You could repeatedly redesign the interior of the building; the structure was built only once." Sounded like job security to me! What I found that really interested me about the program were its ties, not only to interior design, but also to engineering and, in particular, landscape architecture . . . the environment. There it was; I could walk the fence between design and nature. To this day, my favorite college course blended site analysis with the design of a building. Graduation arrived quickly as I crammed the four years into two.*

Design experience. *What could be better than to be a recent graduate moving to the warm South to pursue a design position? I landed a job with Davis-Kloss, a small firm in Atlanta, working on large scale hospitality projects. The experience was outstanding and I was blessed with excellent employers. Pursuing NCIDQ certification was the next educational step. I excelled in the design portion; the written portion required a second sitting. I soon wanted to experience other design specialties and sought employment with Godwin and Associates. Here I gained practical knowledge in healthcare design and large scale commercial office design. Contacts made during this phase of my career have sustained me for decades.*

Breakthroughs happen on the edge: Academic experience. *During my early years of practice, I noticed an announcement from a local school searching for evening instructors for their Continuing Education Program. Upon approval from my full-time employer, I began teaching in the evening. One thing quickly led to another, and soon the school offered me a full-time position as their Director. There are points in your life when you change directions, and this was one of those. While I had sworn off teaching as a kid, it never occurred to me that teaching adult students in a college setting would be so rewarding, and the horrible discipline problems I heard about were not part of the job. And, frankly, the two weeks of built-in summer vacation were calling. And so I directed, managed, became actively involved in the professional design organizations, freelanced some design work, and taught. And, I traveled in the summer with my husband to the Wild West. There I was again, walking the fence, work and travel.*

It took another two years for me to embrace education in its full glory and pursue a professorial position at Brenau University. They hired me without a lick of graduate education. To this day, I'm told I was hired because of my quality portfolio, but I sometimes wonder if they were just desperate for an energetic (read naïve) instructor. Nevertheless, they did require me to complete a terminal degree—pronto! The next few years of my life were chaotic.

Chaos cultivates creativity and critical thinking. *Post-Secondary Education. I enrolled in a local MFA program in Interior Design, only to find the courses repeated what I already knew through prior education or experience. I moved to a Master of Historic Preservation degree. The MHP is a terminal degree in a related field of interior design; the knowledge base was refreshing and that tie to the environment created a strong pull. The culmination of most terminal degrees requires an in-depth study of a topic and a significant publication to advance the knowledge base in the chosen field. I recognized immediately that this project would consume my life, so I better enjoy the topic. Therefore, I selected the study of structures and their relationship to the environment. My thesis, "The Design of National Park Visitor Centers: The Relationships Between Buildings and Their Sites," was the culmination of that effort. Over the next few years, my husband and I, in a Volkswagen van, visited over 100 national parks. Fence walking, . . ., higher education, nature, travel.*

Practice what you teach: The professor. *Those early years of professional practice, my continued involvement in my own practice, and the professional design organizations enhanced my teaching. Students tell me it's my stories that make the courses come alive. Those stories would not exist without my professional practice. The connections I made as a young designer also tie me to the practitioners. These connections draw in guest lecturers, jurors, and adjunct faculty. My former employers serve on the program's advisory board. In my students' eyes, the practice validates the teaching. How can we preach the importance of the NCIDQ exam, unless we too have passed the exam?*

Balance: Work and self. *Once a bit more settled into my teaching routine, I received a call for proposals to update a classic introductory textbook. I took this opportunity, wrote a new chapter, and developed a revised outline for the text. It was through my securing of this contract that I found more balance in my life. Writing requires significant quiet time involving in-depth research. For me, this is best accomplished far from the university setting in a cabin in the wilds of Montana. It is also the perfect biophilia.*

Teaching can be emotionally and physically challenging. There is a reason that professors have an extended summer leave. It is for rejuvenation. Use those three months to your advantage. Take time for yourself and avoid the temptation of summer employment. There is also a purpose for sabbaticals. Request and take them to pursue your professional development. Yes, you will have to relinquish your favorite class and yes, it will not be taught the way you want it taught. Your students will survive and you never know, they may flourish despite your absence!

Fence walking has defined my lifestyle and created opportunities that embrace my life. It requires balance in the dichotomy of practice versus teaching and in professional versus personal life. Fence walking is chaotic, but that disturbance cultivates creativity and critical thinking. Breakthroughs happen as you are falling off that fence edge, but you will flourish because you laid a strong foundation. Fence walking has ultimately enabled me to enjoy life.

Maintaining Life Balance

Interior design educator Hannah Mendoza is a professor at Savannah College of Art and Design. Previous to her current appointment, she served as an adjunct instructor at the Art Institute Online, Valdosta State University and Florida State University and was an assistant professor at West Virginia University.

Mendoza approaches her academic career with a sense of efficient strategy that assists her in finding balance between family, career, and her continuing academic preparation.

For the last two years I have been among the huddled masses of faculty yearning to achieve tenure at a research-intensive state institution. During my day, I must divide my time among my husband, my three year old, and the courses and research required to finish my PhD. In addition, this fall, my husband and I are expecting our second child. I don't say this to impress you with how much busier my life is than others, but rather to reassure you that you are not alone in your list of responsibilities, whatever form they may take.

Tenure has been described to me alternately as a hurdle or a goal, and I must admit that I swing back and forth between the two conceptualizations quite often. There are three pieces of advice that I would offer to those just beginning an academic career.

First, it is important to make everything you do "count" in as many ways as possible towards tenure. This hasn't meant abandoning those things that I see as important, but rather integrating them into my research and teaching agendas. I was asked to be part of a curriculum development team for a design-based study abroad experience in Italy. Generally, serving on this committee would count as service which is beneficial. However, with other members of the committee, I additionally wrote an article which is soon to be published and have created a survey to continue to mine data for future publications. In this way, what would have been simply a time consuming, although wonderful, experience counting only towards the 10 to 15 percent of my year's activities helped to advance my research goals as well.

Second, I think you have to love what you do. If you don't have passion for all of the parts of the job, the burden can begin to weigh too heavily. I don't think you have to love them all equally, or love them all the time, but there must be a personal interest and desire to complete all of the activities. For me, this is conceptualized as a love of knowledge, sharing it through teaching, creating it through research, and providing it through service. This is the only way that the sacrifices I have made have seemed worthwhile, in terms of time spent with my family. As a benefit to being on the curriculum development committee for the Design in Italy study abroad experience, I had the opportunity to travel to Italy for 10 days, leaving my then two year old son and my poor, overworked husband behind in the States. Obviously, this was a wonderful and exciting experience, but I felt pangs of guilt and loneliness for my family the entire time. Having passionate feelings about what I was doing helped me to overcome the negative aspect of being separated from my family.

Third, I think you absolutely have to know when to say "no," politely but firmly. The passion I feel for my work is balanced by the passion that I have for my family, and while I do make sacrifices of my personal time to participate in activities that are either incredible opportunities or truly beneficial, I also have to make sacrifices of my professional time to participate in the incredible opportunities available at home. As a woman, I found myself truly struggling between an idealized image of who I should be as a mother and an idealized image of who I should be as a working woman. Unfortunately, the two seemed rarely compatible. It took me a year of struggle—feeling guilty about not being home when I was working, and feeling guilty about not being at work when I was spending time with my family. I haven't completely overcome every internal struggle and certainly continue to err in both directions. My husband, with his infinite patience, allows me the luxury of discovering the balance that works best for me. Being able to say "no" helps me make my work minutes count and frees me to leave my work when time would be better spent with my family.

Everyone has a different set of personal and professional responsibilities which they must learn to balance if they are to not just survive the pre-tenure years, but to allow themselves to enjoy them. Some will care for an aging parent while others need to take time to devote to an art form. Whatever the complex set of responsibilities and pleasures that make up daily living for you as an individual, I hope that what I have learned can help you make sense of how to achieve balance.

OBSERVATIONS FROM ADJUNCT EDUCATORS

The academic experience of adjunct educators differs in key ways from that of full-time instructors. In addition to navigating the educational waters of the large institution and its many policies, adjunct educators are often simultaneously managing their own firms or otherwise engaging in a primary full-time career. When travel time, student out-of-class communications, and grading are added to this mix, it is clear that the adjunct instructor experience is daunting, yet filled with potential to enrich students' futures. These essays from successful interior design adjunct educators demonstrate the unique, fulfilling experience that this position holds for those that take up its challenges and opportunities.

Harnessing the Lessons of Practice

Ann Camp, ASID, has been a successful interior design practitioner and business owner for thirty-five years and for nine years has served as an adjunct interior design educator with the Florida State University's Department of Interior Design. Her considerable practice and entrepreneurial experience has helped to shape and ensure her success in teaching. She describes that teaching is a way of giving to others that differs from practice, yet offers its own unique rewards:

In the early 1970s while I was working toward a master's degree in interior design and simultaneously starting a business, little did I know that 40 years later I would be teaching a course in a highly regarded school of interior design.

"Fools rush in where angels fear to tread" describes my blind enthusiasm that led to the ownership of a firm that began with me and a designer who became my friend in graduate school. It grew to include a staff of seven licensed interior designers, all professional members of ASID, and a support staff of six.

After I received my graduate degree in interior design and began building my business, I was asked to teach a course in residential design as an adjunct instructor, and did so for several years until the demands of my growing business no longer allowed me to teach. Fast forward through 36 years of successful interior design business management. After the resignation of another practitioner who could no longer teach at the university, I was asked to teach a course entitled Business and Professional Practices for Interior Designers. At that time I was suffering burnout in my role of owning and managing a large, successful firm and realized that my creativity was being depleted. I had become responsible for marketing, finances, hiring and firing, employee satisfaction, client/designer relationships, incorrect shipment of merchandise ordered, delayed shipments, plumbers, painters and wallpaper hangers who didn't show up as scheduled, and many other issues over which I had no control. My only outlet for creativity was the selection of resources for my staff and furnishings for a large showroom. My usual good nature was gradually being replaced by frustration, anger and fatigue.

The opportunity to teach, which I believed would come naturally to me, provided a new challenge to share my years of experience in professional practice with a new generation of promising, well-prepared students completing their final semester in school, assisting in their transition to the real world of interior design practice beyond the university experience.

Utilizing a textbook and augmenting it with varied, actual experiences has allowed me to enhance the course I teach. Recollections from years of practice allow me to literally put a "face" and a "place" on textbook material, and often to address issues not covered.

Most often my teaching experiences have been positive, but I am compelled to share a negative outcome that proved helpful. After my first semester of teaching many years ago, I read the objective comments on the back of the student evaluations and discovered that several students commented that it appeared that I had not been happy in the practice of interior design. What an eye-opener that was, and I was fortunate to get that feedback early on. I realized that the students had not been made aware of the inherent negative things that can go wrong; that the practice is fraught with chances of making mistakes that can result in costly, unsatisfactory, and even unsafe projects. They were graduating with a naïve perception that projects would always be successful and easy!

Fortunately, I created different approaches from a positive perspective and have not had those comments since then. In fact, they are the opposite. I am now affirmed by feedback from students that they are learning the hard, cold facts of business for the first time in the program and are better prepared to enter their chosen profession. The student evaluation example has helped me to be a better instructor, and I continue to benefit from this tool.

My years of experience have provided skills and perceptions to me that I did not previously possess which enhance my teaching. For example, I found that I had not been personally academically prepared to apply skillful interviewing techniques which are the key to successful, satisfying projects. I was forced to pick this ability up by trial and error. To my knowledge, none of the available professional practice textbooks address this issue to the degree needed by new practitioners. Here was an opportunity to pass along my hard-won skills that can only have been acquired by experience! As a result, I developed fictitious client scenarios that prompt students to ask appropriate questions. This exercise now provides them the skills to obtain pertinent information early in the designer/client relationship.

My practice and management experience heightens my awareness of knowledge necessary to a beginning interior design practitioner. In my first class session each semester, I ask the students to make a short list of topics they need to learn about that have not been covered in the curriculum that they feel insecure in as they finish their last semester in the program. As the semester progresses and nears an end, I review their comments and make certain that I have addressed them all. In my opinion, it would not be possible to successfully, sensitively and enthusiastically do this without years of practice and insight into the profession.

Reflecting on my career journey to date, I recognize I had no plans to teach as I proceeded through the various stages of my business, but now realize that each stage helped to prepare me for this pursuit. Had I missed out on even one phase of business development, I would be less prepared to teach a course concerning business and professional practices. I can honestly say that every facet of my past career has given me self-confidence in knowing that I can effectively bring to the classroom the "real world" from which I come. No textbook or degree alone could have prepared me for my latent teaching career. Having been in the "trenches" has eventually served me and my students as well!

Necessary qualities for successful adjunct instruction. *What makes a practitioner an effective adjunct instructor? First and foremost is experience; the longer and the more varied, the better. Equally important is an awareness and respect for the educational requirements and standards for professional licensure, as well as personally having met those standards. A graduate degree in the field should be a prerequisite.*

Continuing to maintain membership in a professional organization, licensure in the state of practice, and investment in continuing education are necessary to be an effective instructor. Equally important is a personal awareness of advances in the field and a curiosity of current trends.

Not all successful practitioners can become good instructors! First of all, how is success defined? Our profession hasn't been around long enough for that to be determined beyond minimum standards, and all states do not have those in place. We have a long way to go. Unfortunately, a few designers satisfy their ego rather than meet client needs and often are considered successful, but would have little to offer in accredited interior design programs. Some don't meet the educational standards to be a part of a university faculty, and don't share or are unaware of the goals that must be reached to insure progress in our pursuit of recognition as a profession.

Finally, anyone interested in being an adjunct instructor should be motivated and passionate to provide a practical dimension to the education of future practitioners, and to augment the instruction of full-time faculty as a part of a team.

For practitioners who reach a stage in their careers when a change may be an option, teaching can be a way to share insight and experience with students launching their careers. Simultaneously, teaching allows us to feel that we have much to offer in a way different from practice.

Although I still maintain a small client base, I am most fulfilled by my role as an educator, affirming my lifelong goal to affect quality of life in places where we live and work, and to passionately continue to do so through my relationships with students. I am a link between the educational experience and the practice of interior design, both a challenge and an honor!

An Entrepreneurial Spirit

Tom Allisma is an energetic force in practice, and a designer with numerous awards and both national and international project publications to his credit. An avid force for design, he is also an accomplished business owner and students recognize his enthusiasm, quality of design, and varied knowledge and experiences. Allisma regularly travels abroad to gain first hand knowledge of a culture to inform his culinary venues and design inspirations.

My background is extremely complex and diverse which requires me to do some explaining. I graduated with my Masters in Architecture seven years ago from the University of Nebraska at Lincoln (UNL). During my two final years of graduate school, I was a second year design studio teaching assistant. Once I graduated in 2000 I went on to work for five years at a firm in Omaha, Avant Architects. During that time I acquired a business partner and the two of us have developed multiple restaurant and bar concepts together in the Omaha area. To date I am a business partner in three restaurants, two bars, and a catering company which in total have 200 plus employees. I also own my own practice, TA Productions Inc., in which I work on numerous commercial and residential interiors each year.

During the 2003–2004 and 2005–2006 academic years I was asked by UNL to be an adjunct Interior Design studio professor. Being "Mr. Workaholic," I couldn't pass up the opportunity and I accepted the offer. During the spring of 2006 I was hired on at UNL as a full-time assistant professor (tenure track). I currently teach fourth year Interior Design studio and third year professional practice.

It took me many years of 90 plus hour work weeks to get where I am, but let me tell you it was all worth it. The last seven years have been a whirlwind for me, but I am finally beginning to see the calm. My life has been put into balance thanks to the experiences that I have gained through teaching.

Practicing and teaching at the same time is a very difficult task and requires some great juggling skills. The real trick is finding a balance between the two. I have been very fortunate with the path that I have taken in attempting both. I have eased my way into teaching over the years as I have simultaneously created my own practice and other personal businesses. I am a very self-motivated individual and this quality has been a huge contributor to my success. Self-motivation is something that I try to instill in all my students because I feel this quality will allow each of them to fully maximize their potential in the real world.

Motivating students has always been the biggest challenge that I have encountered through all my years of educating. I have always found in the courses that I teach there are usually a handful of students that are independently self-motivated and the remaining students are usually dependent on a lot of guidance. Recently I made a breakthrough discovery in a senior design studio when I gave the students a real project with a real budget. This opportunity arose when one of the beverage suppliers for all of my bars and restaurants, Red Bull, approached me and asked if I would be interested in creating a student competition. I of course jumped at the opportunity because I had a feeling that the students would be very excited to participate in such an event. Well my gut instinct was correct and the project was a success in more ways than one.

During the first two weeks of the spring semester of 2007 we presented the students with the challenge and explained to them what the task was; redesign a small back room of an existing bar into a modern lounge with a budget of 10,000 dollars. The students worked in teams of two and generated multiple solutions along with construction budgets. During this process I stopped into studio at random times, day and night, and in most cases all the teams were there working continuously. I had never seen a group of students work so hard and productively. It was obvious that they were all hungry to win.

At the end of the two weeks the student teams presented their designs to the bar owner along with the Red Bull representatives who then picked the winning solution. On top of the winning team getting their project constructed the two teammates were also awarded a weekend in Los Angeles, expensed by Red Bull. Their trip to LA included accommodations at a trendy boutique hotel along with a tour, by the designers, of the new Red Bull North American headquarters in Santa Monica.

Due to the success of this first competition that Red Bull presented my studio, I am now working with them along with some of my other product suppliers to create small, 2 week long design competitions. I am harnessing my business world contacts and allowing my students to reap the benefits. The students had to put a lot of time and energy into the competition, but they were all excited and enjoyed the opportunity.

Now I am not suggesting that you go run out and team up with a bar owner and a beverage company and put together a design challenge. What I am suggesting though, is that if you can come up with your own individual way of increasing the competition level within your design studios, I can almost guarantee you will be impressed with the outcome. Motivation levels will increase and productivity will be outstanding.

Practice and Theory

Lindsey Ellsworth Bahe finds her voice in the delicate intersection of practice and education, weaving a thread of theory through both. Educated as an architect, she provides one segment of a diverse body of knowledge contributing to the professional education of designers. As an adjunct faculty member, Ellsworth Bahe taught primarily in the visual literacy areas (first year course with a combined population of interior design, architecture, fine arts, textiles, and clothing design students) as well as second year design studio (combination of interior design and architecture students) . She is working towards successful passage of both the Architectural Registration Examination and the NCIDQ examination. Wearing dual hats of architecture and interior design, she addresses the role of theory in education and practice.

> The architect should be equipped with knowledge of many branches of study and varied kinds of learning, for it is by his judgment that all work done by the other arts is put to test. This knowledge is the child of practice and theory. *Practice* is the continuous and regular exercise of employment where manual

> work is done with any necessary material according to the design of a drawing. *Theory*, on the other hand, is the ability to demonstrate and explain the productions of dexterity on the principles of proportion.
>
> —*Vitruvius*

> The mother art is architecture. Without an architecture of our own we have no soul of our own civilization.
>
> —*Frank Lloyd Wright*

It was once thought that the architect was responsible for the safety and delight of the public. The skill and craft of creating uniquely inspiring and purposeful spaces for people was something that was once highly regarded. The architecture itself was an event that told a story in space, history, and function; speaking to its user and not just facilitating its use. However, the importance of design and its role in both the public and private realm has faded into a plethora of uneventful, repeated and muted ideas of space and function as the developer has, through time, replaced the role of the once sought after architect. Under this current situation, it seems that we as designers are viewed as the means to an end, a perceived stepping stone in the developer's and construction contractor's quick fix ideas that have been shaping our neighborhoods and commercial districts. Therefore, it is my intent as both a practicing designer and active design educator to find ways in which architecture and design can re-enter our cultural landscape as a thoughtful, resourceful, and inspiring professional service. To create places with "soul" on various scales, from a gesture in the design of something as small as a chair, to the design of a residence, or an entire development.

Long ago, Vitruvius stated that practice and theory were both equally important in the knowledge and success of an architect. It took my own experience practicing in the professional world to be able to realize exactly what Virtruvius may have meant by this and also why our voice in society has seemingly diminished in importance. My personal experience made me realize there needed to be a higher level of integrity and pride in architectural creation. What is needed is the courage to have a voice that does not settle for quick and easy re-creations of historical styles with standard programmatic layouts. After various professional experiences in various roles, I have found that practice [the act of exercising manual work] *in a professional office at times lacks the passion and intention that engaging in the theory* [ideas, intentions, poetics] *of design entails. This lack of theoretical investigation into projects is what may have slowly decreased the appreciation and awareness of architectural and design service. Architecture has somehow lost its presence as a contributing factor to the sociological development of our communities. Mindless post-modern suburban developments and one shopping strip after another have sprawled across our landscape, leaving behind various urban and residential centers to deteriorate. Without innovative investigation or clear intention of the architect/designer, the developer has cleverly elbowed his/her way into the process of making. Most often this process seems to be driven by time, money, and ease of construction. Ideally, these are hardly the components that should be the priority and driving force of our communities.*

Academia on the other hand tends to be the place of intention and dreams. Some argue that academia focuses too much on the poetics of theoretical design and leaves students unprepared for the day to day of the professional practice that awaits them. But it is this very attitude that I believe is keeping the practice of architecture at a standstill, not progressing towards an optimistic future. The importance of academia is not to solely produce architects who can properly draw construction documents or mimic a "style" to face the elevations of a generic plan which often seems to be the expectation and process of a new intern; but to learn to use drawing as a means to communicate beautiful ideas of living and being in public and domestic space. It should be the goal of the educator and the student to establish confidence in speaking and use of architectonic language in order to sound proficient, resourceful, and inspiring to the other "players" involved in the making of our space and place in which we live.

Projects should encourage the students to communicate a thoughtful design idea that is not simply a cultural fad of materiality and form, but a design solution with greater intention for the social, environmental, or cultural good. Beautiful solutions that delight the user through sensory experience are important, but the existence of an optimistic intention that leads to something greater than just form gives the designer the power to become a greater player in the development and growth of our communities. Therefore, it is vital for students to be challenged to obtain the knowledge in how to bring their intentions to fruition through the understanding of craft and construction. In the future, this increased knowledge of craft and construction, when applied with theory, will allow for greater communication lines and means of direction with the contractors and others who are responsible for building the structures we dream of.

Beginning to understand the advantages between the overlap of practice and theory is where successful and beautiful architecture and design will be created. The two trajectories of the profession should be entirely dependent on one another in order to re-introduce the designer's role in not just the monumental structures that are commissioned and gain acclaim through publication, but in the architecture of the everyday that the public engages and gains rewards from on a daily basis. Academia and professional practice should constantly reflect on each other's successes and failures in establishing an overall service to be proud of and to be sought out. This is where I find my strength as an educator, and as a practitioner. Through practicing at a local firm (studio951) I have the opportunity to overlap. I get to be directly engaged with the process of design and can identify where we as designers have the ground to reclaim our importance of the service and craft that we possess and areas where our service is lacking. This identification allows me to use my experience "in the field" to help shape the way I approach design studios; intentionally blurring the boundary between practice and theory.

It is clear that when these two worlds collide, and intention and craft are pursued, the design itself will make a difference. The solution will not just be a functional fix for the user or developer, but a solution for the delight of the user and respect for its place and time, while optimistically representing the future. The public will be delighted and take note, and thus the demand and respect for our services will increase.

THE GRADUATE TEACHING ASSISTANT EXPERIENCE

With one foot in the student world and another in the instructor realm, graduate teaching assistants experience interior design education as few others do. This dual existence requires adjustment to simultaneously achieve a level of comfort that requires the assumption of a new identity and grasp of new policies and procedures. Graduate teaching assistants Marlo Ransdell and Erin Trofholz provide a glimpse into this dynamic, transitional stage of the academic experience.

At the Intersection of Teaching and Learning

Interior design educator Marlo Ransdell obtained her master's degree in interior design at the University of Kentucky and is currently completing her doctoral degree at the University of Florida. She is an instructor in the Florida State University's Department of Interior Design teaching studio, computer-aided design, and introductory courses. She discusses the unique position in the learning-teaching continuum that graduate teaching assistants occupy and offers strategies to manage this dynamic phase of the academic career.

When I returned to school, it was with the intention of obtaining a graduate degree in interior design in order to pursue a career in higher education. Therefore, I jumped at the chance when offered an opportunity to teach an undergraduate class on my own. Not only did this supplement the costs of graduate school, it was a great experience and a chance to work out my own teaching style and philosophy.

I started the semester cruising down the road of the full-time graduate student engaged in my own curriculum and entered new territory as a teaching assistant with one class. I soon realized this would be an experiment in balancing my time and energy between these two paths. It also became clear that people viewed me through very different lenses with regard to these two activities. Teachers saw me as a student, and students saw me as a teacher. So who was I? As I stood at the intersection of teaching and learning, it was sometimes difficult to comprehend the path I should take, and the mantle of identity I should assume.

For me, this question was answered depending on the day of the week in which it was asked. After my first semester as a student/teacher, I was asked to continue teaching. I happily accepted, and fortunately was scheduled to teach two undergraduate classes on different days of the week than my own courses occurred. This was a stroke of luck that saved me. During my first semester, I found it easy to become so involved with the teaching responsibilities to my undergraduate class that the efforts I spent on my own research and coursework began to dwindle. Finding balance in the time and energy I spent on each took some time, but it was a process I had to go through. Clearly defining and separating my two chosen paths during later semesters helped me maintain balance in my educational career and keep it on track. I also found it easier to tackle my varying responsibilities to each. I was able to turn the teacher mode in me off (even if just for a little while) which allowed me to become a focused student in my own interior design education. Through this experience I learned to focus on one direction at a time.

Another valuable lesson learned was that these two paths (and perhaps more paths than two) would continue throughout my career. Teachers in higher education are not only charged with quality instruction of their students, but they are expected to carry out a meaningful research agenda. Now as I stand before the same intersection of teaching and learning, I see these paths stretch out infinitely, but I also am looking to the future and, with my previous training and experience, can see that the two converge at times to inform each other.

A Fulfilling Experience

Erin Trofholz gained her undergraduate degree in interior design from the University of Nebraska-Lincoln. Following years of professional practice, she returned to Nebraska to pursue graduate education. Recently completed studies have led to the Master of Science, with a thesis topic centered on sustainable issues. Trofholz notes the difference in engagement of students at the undergraduate versus graduate levels and relates her experiences as a teaching assistant.

My first experience with the interior design program was a basic design course. This was the first course in college that I truly enjoyed. From that class on my passion blossomed and continued to grow over the next three years.

At the end of my undergraduate experience I took a course, Contemporary Issues in Interior Design, where I first learned about an upcoming graduate program in our college. I gained valuable information in this course regarding the Masters program and its implications to my career and future.

Upon graduation I decided to move to Phoenix, Arizona where I worked at a small architectural firm. While in Phoenix, the graduate program kept returning to my thoughts. I missed home and had some family issues arise, so after much debate I decided to move back home to attend graduate school.

Graduate school was a completely different experience than undergraduate school, and much different than I had anticipated. Although I did have a passion for design in undergraduate classes, my passion was somehow different in graduate school. My courses were now filled with classmates that shared this same passion. It seemed as no one was forced to be there, but that they wanted to be there.

During my first semester of being a teaching assistant my responsibilities included grading student work and updating the interactive class website. The second semester my responsibility expanded to lecturing a couple classes here and there. Lecturing in front of 100+ students gave me confidence to talk in front of any group of people, large or small. This was another valuable experience that helped me out immensely in my professional career.

My first experience as a teaching assistant was for the same basic design course that had started my interior design program. It was eye-opening to be on the other side especially since I had been the student not too long ago. Balancing my life as both a student and a teacher was a struggle as I have always been the type of person to put all of my effort into one major thing. It was very difficult for me to give that up and to balance my time equally among two major things. Looking back on it now as a professional I see how valuable the experience was. On a daily basis I have to balance my time between projects, clients, and co-workers.

THE INTERIOR DESIGN ADMINISTRATOR'S POINT OF VIEW

It is often the fascinating individual instructor or superb student that is remembered long after graduation. Individual moments experienced within a design education coalesce into an entire canvas of recollections. However, at its core, program leadership and administration plays a critical role in the climate of this education. Administrators encourage faculty, staff, and students in their professional development and set the tone for professional conduct within a program. Administrators must retain clarity when viewing the overall educational picture, keep abreast of university requirements and citizenship, act as a conduit of information, maintain positive ties to alumni and potential donors, manage schedules and facilities, and often teach a full or nearly full complement of courses. For some, becoming an administrator is a career goal, while others serve in a rotating or interim period. What are the intrinsic rewards and responsibilities of program leadership? Two effective program chairs share their individual experiences and advice.

The Big Picture: Advancing the Interior Design Profession

Betsy Gabb has been a Professor and Director of the interior design program in the College of Architecture at the University of Nebraska-Lincoln since 1993. She serves on the Boards of the Council for Interior Design Accreditation, *Journal of Interior Design*, and in many capacities within the Interior Design Educators Council organization and has been recognized with Fellow status. Recently, Gabb has served as a Board member for the Coordinating Committee for the Interior Design Coalition of Nebraska, an organization actively working to achieve title registration for the state. Gabb has served as participant in the International Interior Design Congresses and in the Interior Design Research Summit at the Salk Institute. In addition to her service beyond the university setting, Gabb is noted for teaching excellence through numerous awards and citations. She has been instrumental in the development of a post-professional Master of Architecture Program with a Specialization in Interior Design offered both in residence as well as fully online. Further, Gabb has directed the Kruger Miniatures Gallery and served as editor of the scholarly journal *InForm*. Gabb shares insights and advice related to the role of program chair, drawing from her significant breadth of experience.

I would encourage all interior design faculty to play a role in the larger arena of the profession; locally, regionally, nationally. A part of being a professional in any discipline is the importance of interaction with other professionals and the willingness to aid in the development of the profession itself.

Program Chair as a professional career move. *While the role of Program Chair or Coordinator can be fulfilling, it is important for an individual to realize it is also a time consuming commitment. Guiding faculty in the establishment and growth of a design program can be exciting, exhilarating, and challenging at the same time. Before assuming such a role, it's important for the individual to consider where they are in their professional career. With the role of Program Chair comes a larger commitment and responsibility to the larger "good," e.g., students, program, college, and university, and thus often takes away time from individual goals.*

Often because Interior Design Programs tend to be relatively small and combined administratively with other programs, the Program Chair may not be an administrator with much decision-making power other than "please and thank you." When this occurs it's important that all programs in the administrative unit have an equal voice in decisions affecting the unit and a "definitive" voice in decisions affecting the Interior Design Program.

In order to develop the best possible program, the Program Chair serves as a mentor to all faculty in the program, helping them achieve both their own professional goals and those of the program. Often the Program Chair is called on to facilitate communication among several individuals or programs in order to accomplish a desired goal.

A network of peers. *It's always important for the Program Chair to have an opportunity to share and discuss with peers the role and responsibilities of the Chair. This may include sharing strategies for success as well as problem solving. This can happen informally within the institution, but it can also take place at professional conferences such as the Interior Design Educators Council (IDEC). IDEC sponsors a loosely organized gathering of Program Chairs and Coordinators at each International Conference. This provides those interested with a forum for dialogue and discussion.*

Legislative action. *Architecture is a mature field—literally one of the world's oldest professions—and one which is comprehensively served by the American university system. The discipline of interior design is relatively young and has only experienced significant recognition and the development of research and theory related to the interior built environment since the mid-twentieth century with the increased complexity of the interior built environment. Therefore, interior design, as it now exists, is by contrast a new discipline, and one which is predicted to grow exponentially in the coming decades.*

As codes and standards have been established for the interior environment, it is important to recognize individuals qualified to implement not only the design of an interior environment, but to create an environment meeting all codes and standards of a particular project, thus protecting the health, safety, and welfare of the public. "Every decision an interior designer makes in one way or another affects life safety and quality of life." This may mean space planning that provides for egress in case of fire, it may mean specifying furnishings and fabrics that comply with fire codes and toxicity standards, or it may mean designing for individuals with special needs (Interior Design Coalition of Nebraska). With each proj-

ect, interior designers work with other allied professionals to create the optimal solution, not only aesthetically but also functionally. Therefore it is imperative that qualified interior design professionals be recognized as contributing members of the allied design disciplines through appropriate legislative action.

Accreditation and other program evaluations. *As a long time/seasoned design educator, and participant in numerous program accreditations by FIDER/CIDA, it's my belief that preparation for accreditation provides a program an opportunity for reflection. The preparation of the Program Analysis Report and Display of Student Work gives faculty, administration, and supporting professionals an opportunity to 'step back' and examine the program as a whole.*

And while the preparation for the accreditation site visit is important, ongoing program assessment and analysis is critical to positive program development as well. Ongoing assessment, integral to program development, becomes a natural process by which the program can define itself, not only in terms of meeting accreditation standards, but more importantly in determining program direction and emphasis. It helps answer such questions as "Are we doing what we want to do?" and "Are we doing what we say we're doing?" and if not, "How can we change?"

In addition to the "traditional" assessment methods, a particularly beneficial review and evaluation for our program has been the "end of semester review." A day is set aside at the end of each semester for all faculty members (in our case interior design, architecture, and landscape architecture) to pin up samples of student work from all studio courses taught during the semester. As a group, we discuss the merits and weaknesses of all projects. This allows faculty teaching the courses to make changes and adjustments for the next semester in which the course is taught, and it allows the faculty teaching the next course(s) in the sequence to understand the level of accomplishment they might expect for the next semester. The ongoing system of studio reviews provides the mechanism for all faculty members to observe and evaluate student work produced at all levels of the program.

Integral Leadership

As part of her Ph.D. candidacy in Communications and Culture, Lynn Chalmers is researching privacy and identity in the workplace environment. She is using theory to frame a humanistic view of values in workplace environments. She is also interested in the role of theory in design and has lectured in Glasgow at the 2007 Inside the Box Conference, organized by The Interiors Forum Scotland on Inserting Theory into Disciplinary Practice. She also co-presented a workshop with Professor Sam Davis of University of California, Berkeley, at IDEC's International Conference in Austin, Texas. Through her studio teaching, she maintains a focus on socially responsible design projects. Chalmers teaches studio at both the Masters and the undergraduate level and continues to develop, critique, and write about interior design pedagogy. She has presented papers and provided guest lectures to forums on Interior Design education across Canada and the United States, and internationally.

Chalmers has served in a variety of leadership roles, including Course Coordinator of the Interior Design Program and Associate Dean of Teaching and Learning at Louis Laybourne School of Design University of South Australia. She is currently a faculty member and Department Head in the Architecture Department at the University of Manitoba. Chalmers provides her view of the diverse and comprehensive issues that influence leadership in academic settings.

Why would you want to be program leader when everyone knows there are very few rewards for taking on this position? Embroiled in the politics of the Faculty, you will have to manage difficult staffing situations, resolve disputes between staff and students, evaluate peers and be open to criticism for almost every action you take.

In a position of leadership you will have the opportunity to lead the vision and direction of Interior Design education at your institution. You will assist your program team in evolving and innovating curriculum, carrying out quality control and accreditation and engaging with the profession.

The opportunity to participate in and learn the business of running an academic unit is another benefit of taking a leadership role. The experience of working with other Program Leaders and Deans will deepen your understanding of the structure and systems that operate in the academy. My own experience as Program Co-Ordinator and Departmental Head in two different institutions has given me a better understanding of the university as a system, with its own particular culture, political framework and economic structure.

The Program Leader has an important role in adjudicating disputes between students and faculty regarding grades and the assessment of work. It is critical in situations such as these to remember the pressures that both faculty and students are working under, and allow both parties to be heard and to hear each other.

Take advantage of opportunities to learn more about dispute resolution in courses offered to faculty that might develop your skills in this area. In fact, taking some personal development courses offered by your university is very beneficial to determining if a leadership role is something that you might be interested in. I participated in a forum called Women in Leadership early in my academic career. I learned a great deal and, more importantly, I met some senior academics and developed a network that gave me support when I took on my first leadership role. I also took advantage of the opportunity to have a mentor, who gave me the confidence to pursue further studies and to contextualize many of the practices of the academy that seemed strange to the eyes of a recent professional Interior Designer.

The Program Leader is primarily a facilitator of students and teaching faculty, and this often means their own research and teaching agendas will come second, depending on numbers of students and faculty they are responsible for overseeing. However, the time spent building relationships with students and faculty will be some of the most rewarding and satisfying tasks of the Program Leader position.

The health and vitality of the program or unit is significantly affected by the quality of relationships and the energy the Program Leader brings to the position. The position offers the opportunity to nurture new teachers and support research, encouraging faculty to continue to pursue personal development and growth. Sometimes this involves encouraging teaching faculty to take on new subject areas. As curriculum changes, so teachers need to continue to develop skills in new areas such as the environment, new materials, theory, and digital technology.

Program Leaders need to be able to bridge the connection between the profession and the academy. As the person responsible for staffing courses, the Program Leader needs to build good connections to significant practitioner/teachers to bring professional expertise into the program. It was of considerable benefit to me that I had ten years of fulltime practice before entering academia. It influenced my decisions related to curriculum and provided me with the skills for managing processes such as accreditation report writing, the organization of reviews involving the profession, fundraising, and development related to scholarships and special initiatives. However, I would equally assert the significance of the things I have learned as an academic that I may never have come to know as a practitioner. I benefited greatly from my Masters study and my PhD preparation and have moved my view of Interior Design, as training for the profession, to a view of the discipline of Interior Design informing and going beyond the knowledge of the profession.

The Program Leader has to respond to constant demands for fiscal restraint and responsibility and yet be alert to opportunities to support new ideas and initiatives. It is important to stay informed about developments in the profession, within the state or province and across the country, with a greater emphasis being placed on understanding the international environment for Interior Design education. I found it very helpful to read widely in education and allied professions to understand trends and the language used for fund writing and grants within the academy.

The Program Leader needs to understand the significance of research and the state of the academy in recognizing research in the design disciplines. Belonging to a professional organization such as IDEC is a wonderful vehicle for understanding the North American context for interior design education. The annual conferences offer a forum for engaging in discussion about the practice of Interior Design education and developing a sense of the research areas that are being explored in the discipline. They are a source of networks, enduring friendships and good ideas.

Some universities expect interior design professors to maintain a practice—this satisfies their institutional requirement for visibility and continuing intellectual engagement. Other universities require faculty to be writing and publishing at an academic level, in peer reviewed journals, or winning grants and researching in collaboration with other disciplines or industry partners. The problem is that neither scenario allows the sort of focused vision and innovative program development that programs must formulate in response to rapid and continually evolving changes in the profession and in education.

I benefited greatly from pursuing my Masters of Design on the topic of change: looking at the drivers of change to understand their significance to the profession of Interior Design and the education of designers. This knowledge has helped provide me with courage for the difficult decisions that allow a program to move forward—eliminating courses that have become dated, and developing a more critical and research-based approach to design studio.

Leadership determines the path for curriculum review and program development, so it is incumbent upon the leader to have done thorough research and be able to bring ideas to and from the faculty to fruition.

Program Leadership is a great job, if you have the desire for a challenge requiring developing knowledge, good people skills, the capacity to listen, and enormous energy. It is a job where you will have both the opportunity and the necessity to continuously learn.

I suggest that the position is no longer one for life, and that not everyone is cut out for the role. It shouldn't be seen as a career move—in the sense of a replacement for academic achievement. It is increasingly important for the discipline of Interior Design to have credibility in the academy, in terms of qualifications and research and creative practice achievement. However, from my own experience, I can vouch for the personal satisfaction and professional growth that accompanies the challenge of leadership.

THE LEARNER PERSPECTIVE

Education by its nature involves a learner, and it is the learner's outcome which dictates the success or failure of the educational experience. Consequently, one would be ill advised to explore successful methods of teaching and learning without acknowledging learners' perceptions of instructor attitude, classroom, and communication style.

For example, a junior interior design student writes:

As a current second year student of interior design and third year college student, I have had the opportunity to explore many different techniques of learning. One of the most invaluable experiences I have found thus far is individual hands-on guidance from a knowledgeable instructor. In saying this, I would also like to confirm the importance of regular lecture and demonstration, but with extended assistance. The reason being that while lecture and demonstration may be steady curriculum designed for an entire class, I believe each student has distinctive ways of obtaining knowledge. Therefore, I've found that I obtain the most information when an instructor can supplement his/her lecture by offering direction designed specifically for my individual learning needs. This increases my confidence and allows me to advance in a more timely fashion.

As Chapter 2 describes, learner demographics, attitudes, and expectations concerning their education are in constant change. The preceding essay demonstrates a confidence many Millennial-age students have come to embrace and belies their hope for customized instruction and attention that may or may not always be realistically feasible. It is helpful for instructors to understand the expectations of their learners, even if all wishes are not capable of being fulfilled.

Recent higher education surveys suggest that learners generally desire the following attributes and actions from their instructors:

1. Teach well.
2. Keep order.
3. Explain clearly.
4. Be interesting.
5. Treat learners fairly.
6. Act friendly.
7. Create an environment of emotional safety.
8. Have a sense of affiliation with learners.
9. Develop learners' self esteem.
10. Allow learners to make some of their own educational decisions.[1]

Beyond these broad descriptors lies the terrain of daily classroom drama (or in the case of online learning, the virtual classroom), where interpersonal actions play out and learning occurs. What do learners think about their instructor's teaching habits? In 2007, an informal group of interior design learners was asked to provide a specific example of one or more memorable positive *or* negative teaching habits, personality traits, or learning strategies they had witnessed from their instructors that impacted their educational experience. They were also asked to describe how this action made them feel. Table 9.1 shows that their answers often corroborate the broad recommendations listed but also reveal the diversity of their needs and the importance of even small details of instructor personality and outreach.

TABLE 9.1: INTERIOR DESIGN STUDENT REFLECTIONS ON INSTRUCTOR HABITS AND STRATEGIES

Instructor habit or character trait	Detailed example	How this made the learner feel
Personal presentation styles		
The teacher had a tendency to talk very fast in lecture. She was always stuttering and acting like she was extremely nervous.	Every lecture she would stress me out because of the way she was going about speaking.	It made me feel like she was uncomfortable and unprepared. She made me very nervous just listening to her.
Using uncommon and obscure words	It was so difficult to understand what class was about, what was due, what was wanted, and what I was trying to learn because my classmates and I couldn't understand what the teacher was saying without the use of a dictionary. No one ever wanted to talk to him because you could neither get a simple answer out of him nor decipher the answer he gave you.	I felt annoyed, stupid and angry. I also felt that he didn't want to relate to the class on our level.
Saying "um" as a filler word *a lot* during class.	It was so distracting I actually counted how many times she said it for a 1 1/2 hour class—367 times!	It made me feel like the teacher was insecure.
Speaking too quickly about something inherently difficult to understand	I had a statistics class that was hard to understand and it was made worse because the teacher went too quickly.	Confused.
Not speaking my language well	I had a teaching assistant for a graphics class. Although she was knowledgeable, I never understood a word she was saying. Her English was so bad it was a struggle to get any meaning from what she was teaching, and the context and syntax of her grammar made it additionally hard to understand.	Frustrated! And like the department didn't monitor what was happening within.
Reading a PowerPoint presentation directly from the slides	I had a history class where the professor would post the slide show online before class so we could take notes. However, during class he would read directly from the slides, and I didn't have any extra information to add from his lecture.	I would be bored during class because all I would be doing is reading along.

(continued)

TABLE 9.1 *(continued)*

Instructor habit or character trait	Detailed example	How this made the learner feel
PowerPoint slides with only images	I remember a class where the PowerPoint presentations were only images. The teacher never verbally emphasized what was the most important, so we wrote down everything he said. One day, his graduate student presented with slides that had *words next to images*. I remember more from that day than the rest of class. Being visual people, our class responded very well to that material.	Less confident in what I was supposed to learn.
Using multiple synonyms while describing one concept	My art history professor will present a work of art and describe it probably five different ways using synonyms. For example, she might say, "The artist created a sense of tight enclosure in this piece. Like the walls are closing in. A real suffocating feeling. Giving the viewer a claustrophobic feeling." And so on	Sometimes this sort of description really drags on, especially when she does it for every piece of work. It would be fine if it was only every so often to really emphasize certain points.
Talking about his own projects and his successes *all the time*	Sharing personal experience is very helpful, but this professor brought up his projects and awards so often that it sometimes seemed like a class on his portfolio.	I felt inadequate and annoyed. I didn't feel like he was very approachable because of this.
Sharing personal examples of how what we are learning relates to me	I have had a number of teachers share with my classes how they use or don't use this information we are learning in class in the real world and how it impacts them.	It made me feel that I could relate to the teacher and that the teacher was willing to share and be real with us.
Being overly excited	I had a teacher who was so passionate about design that when she would come over to talk about your project she would start re-designing it. If you chose not to change it exactly to what she wanted, your grade would suffer.	Frustrated. You either had to give up ownership of your project or get a bad grade.
Using sarcasm to explain and critique an idea	Getting good information out of a critique or evaluation of your work can be difficult. I have had a teacher that would use sarcasm to explain their thoughts about my project.	It makes the student feel stupid and that the teacher is talking down to them.

(continued)

TABLE 9.1 *(continued)*

Instructor habit or character trait	Detailed example	How this made the learner feel
Making statements about how lazy the class is to the entire class and others	I have had a teacher that would pull all the students together and lecture us about how lazy we were. At that time I was working on studio outside of class time an average of 12 hours a day—not including working on other classes or going to class. I was also there enough to see that many others were also putting in extra hours. Later, I also heard from other students in different years that the teacher had told *them* how lazy we were.	It depressed me. I put in more hours than I could physically handle and was being called lazy. It made it hard to care about what I was doing and I very often wanted to give up all together. It really made being creative impossible.
Varying learning strategies		
Showing students hands-on or gives examples in class	I am able to learn if something is drawn out for me or I am able to go through it with the instructor instead of reading about it in a book.	I feel that the instructor cares and is able to take the time to help a student learn.
Videos really helped me understand.	I remember details from the video that would have gone through my ears in a lecture.	I felt more prepared for exams.
Using other mediums to emphasize a point.	I had an amazing African Art & Esthetics class for my undergraduate degree. Every class period, we would walk into a jazz or blues piece playing over the sound system. The instructor read an excerpt from "Roots" where the Africans had been kidnapped and were chained in the ships on their way to slavery. While he read, the lights were off and there was the sound of the ocean and a rocking boat playing. When he finished there wasn't a dry eye.	I felt that the instructor really cared about what he was teaching. His enthusiasm was infectious.
Showing visual examples or diagrams to help explain an assignment	I was introduced to architectural diagramming and if it weren't for the visual examples I think I would have struggled to grasp the idea completely.	My own thoughts were either changed or confirmed about how to best use diagrams to explain design.
Offering outside resources for inspiration, like local and/or famous architects	In second year, we did a project based on Le Corbusier's five points and it was helpful to see examples of how he worked.	Allowed me to be more confident in my design.

(continued)

TABLE 9.1 *(continued)*

Instructor habit or character trait	Detailed example	How this made the learner feel
Showing examples of real-life applications when explaining a new concept	I thought it was helpful to get a definition of something (a type of construction in construction documents class) then see the drawing of it, and the only way it stuck was to see an actual photo. Also, going to the construction site probably helped me learn more than anything.	This made me feel like I have a better understanding of the material.
Managing content		
Using section reviews within long projects	We had a difficult project once and we had a review in every segment of the project. It was a good time to ask general questions.	It made me feel the instructor cared and was concerned about if we understood it or not.
Posting lecture notes or pictures online/Blackboard	When teachers post notes or slides on the internet it is very helpful to students who have to miss class, especially for studying purposes. Also, things missed in class can be reiterated.	I feel like the teacher really cared about us and wanted us to succeed.
Going over the material we learned from the day at the end of class and emphasizing the key points of the day	After an hour lecture of material the professor would then go back and review the key points of the lecture, making sure we got them written down in our notes.	It made me feel grateful that they took the time to make sure we understood so we could be successful in the class.
Reviewing material from last class at the beginning of each class period	The professor reviewed the material from the week before at the beginning of every class to make sure we didn't forget it over the week.	This helped a lot and highlighted the most important information of the previous class.
Making a semester schedule that is too difficult to understand	This teacher made a due date flow chart and class semester schedule that was too complicated and difficult to read. It made an easy class complicated and made it easy to miss due dates.	I felt stressed and continuously lost in the class.
Communication and availability		
Teachers that you can get to know on a different level than just the person that lectures	I have a number of teachers that share what they do outside of class including their jobs, projects, where they came from, and if they are married or have kids.	I feel a mutual respect and the ability to go in and ask questions. I feel I know them rather than they just lecture and that's it.

(continued)

TABLE 9.1 *(continued)*

Instructor habit or character trait	Detailed example	How this made the learner feel
Speedy email responses!	Since all projects are digitally created, our progress is always documented as a jpg file. Whenever I need help with my progress, I always send a file via email to my professor. What was *very* helpful was how quickly I got a response back. Frequent email checking ensures getting back to the student faster.	Email communication is easier . . . *much* easier, which automatically makes any student feel better about both the relationship she has with the teacher and satisfaction with feedback given from your professor.
Individual meetings and critiques	Some instructors I've had like to do one-on-one desk critiques during the design process to see progress and help with transformation.	I felt like the teacher cared about my work and that I was given extra help because of this one-on-one situation.
Visiting desks daily to meet with students	Every day in studio, I felt that I was given equal attention for questions, concerns, etc.	I felt very good because it was obvious the teacher cared.
Being available for students outside of class	Our professors frequently stop in studio during "non-studio" times to see if we need any help or guidance	Felt like they really cared, wanted me to do well and push myself. It showed they care about you enough to come to school when they don't have to be there.
Guiding learners		
Helping develop the student's idea—not just giving them a new one	I had a professor who basically just told the students what to build and didn't help them develop the ideas they had come up with.	It made me feel like my design or idea wasn't worth developing.
Correcting students' artwork while they are out of the room during class break	Rather than helping me realize what I was doing wrong, the teacher erased my charcoal and redrew my picture while we were on break.	I felt as if he couldn't teach, he decided to "fix" my drawing and I was not even in the room to learn from it. It angered me that he would erase my drawing.
Pushing us to improve and work hard	I had a studio teacher who was hard on us and really pushed us to do better and improve. A lot was expected and we always had stuff to do.	I felt that the teacher really cared and just wanted us to do our best and that's why we were being pushed.
Showing examples related to what we were doing to give us ideas and help	One instructor I had would bring examples to class of other projects that related to the project we were currently working on. They would also bring examples of their own work to motivate us.	It motivated me to work on improving my designs and also gave me an insight into how my instructor designs.

(continued)

TABLE 9.1 *(continued)*

Instructor habit or character trait	Detailed example	How this made the learner feel
Sharing software shortcuts and tricks with the entire class	I love it when a professor shows someone a quicker way to do something in studio. Then he/she shares it with everyone.	Good. Like they want us to be efficient. Also, this helps eliminate thoughts of favoritism.
"I'll show you once, you show me twice"	This tip was very effective in a Cad class I took. The teacher got real tired of showing us the same thing over and over, so the rule by the end was he'd do it once, and we had to start over and show him twice so we were less likely to forget.	Confident that I would remember the process.
Getting on my computer and looking at my things when I'm away from my desk	I returned to studio to find a professor editing a paper of mine on my computer without my permission.	I felt violated and disrespected. I'm sure he had good intentions, but I found it completely inappropriate.
Being conscious of due dates in multiple classes	This is a demanding field. Sometimes the act of learning can get lost in the rush to get things done. I have had several teachers that will check in with the students to make sure they don't have many things due on the same day.	It makes you feel respect for the teacher because you know they are respecting you and trusting you when you tell them that you have too much to do. It also adds time for the student to feel they have time to learn the material, not just fly through it.
Classroom interaction and management		
Calling on specific people to answer questions in class	When no one would volunteer an answer, this professor would pick a name from the roster to answer the question.	It made me pay attention to the questions in case she called on me, but it made me anxious about being forced to answer in front of the class.
Reviewing previous lecture at the beginning of each class with practice test review questions	I had a class that began everyday with a five-question quiz that had potential test questions based on the previous lecture.	Good because I knew what types of questions would be on the test while refreshing my memory of the subject.
Not being present during labs	I had a teacher one time who never visited any of our labs. I thought it would have been beneficial to at least stop in once in a while to meet the students and see how things were going.	I felt like the teacher didn't really care to know who we were or if we were obtaining the right information.
Retreating from class discussion	One of my professors started discussions and mostly let it go wherever the students wanted to take it.	We often got off topic (quite a bit) and seldom ended up talking about the literature we were supposed to be discussing.

(continued)

TABLE 9.1 *(continued)*

Instructor habit or character trait	Detailed example	How this made the learner feel
Learning every student's name!	I had a teacher once that either refused or didn't even try to remember my name. Even after answering several questions in class, the teacher had to ask me my name when I went to talk to them after class!	It made me feel like the teacher didn't care if I was in the class or not, and that I wasn't worth their effort.
Talking to us the entire time we were trying to concentrate on drawing	I remember I felt I always lost concentration on my drawing I was trying to concentrate on at the moment because I felt like I needed to listen to what he was trying to teach us.	I just felt frustrated because I didn't know what to concentrate on more at the time.
Not having time for class	I had an instructor who stated that he was busy when things were requested of him. He said he couldn't get things done by class time, but he would try.	It was very frustrating because if he didn't have time, I felt like he shouldn't be teaching the class. It made me feel like the class was his last priority.
Having lectures or showing PowerPoint presentations that are disconnected from the current project	Time is precious and when an hour is used to talk about work not related to the current project, it's almost a waste of time. If a teacher shows their work or someone else's work, I feel it would be better to show how it can relate or inspire us with the current project.	I feel frustrated when I don't see a connection between me as a student and the work shown from the teacher.
Bringing food to class	One of my professors would bring snacks to class sometimes. Since it was a discussion-based class, it really helped break the ice and make everyone more awake and ready to participate.	It made me feel good and I looked forward to the class.
Tests and grading		
Giving extra credit in unfair ways	I had a teacher who would give us a 1/3 letter grade increase (extra credit) for sitting in the front row during a lecture—or for asking one of the first three questions during/after the lecture.	I felt like my tuition money was a waste—I couldn't sit in a chair for three hours to ensure that I got a seat in the front. I felt cheated out of a chance.
Including and implementing student suggestions in the class structure	My teacher listened to our comments and would let us vote which day of the test week we wanted the exam on to try to avoid having a lot of students having multiple tests in one day.	I felt like I made a difference and that I was valuable.

(continued)

TABLE 9.1 *(continued)*

Instructor habit or character trait	Detailed example	How this made the learner feel
Online instruction		
I am in an online course because I need to work during the class time.	All of the sudden the professor will post on Discussion Board that we need to be in class the next day. No excuses!	I was very frustrated because I cannot call in the day before and take work off. I felt like the professor could care less about anything else we were doing.

THE INDIVIDUAL VOICE OF THE INTERIOR DESIGN EDUCATION EXPERIENCE

These essays illustrate the human experience tapestry from which learning springs and reveal the diversity of perspectives that characterize interior design education. As a snapshot in time, they further embody the state of the interior design profession, itself growing and evolving toward increased effectiveness, visibility, and service to its public. It is tempting to speculate about the issues, challenges, and successes interior design educators will see fit to write about five, ten, or fifty years hence, for it is we, the current seekers of knowledge, who will help lay the foundation for what is to come. In this way, our responsibility is not only to those who are our contemporaries but to the generations of interior design educators, practitioners, and students who will later take the stage.

ENDNOTES

1. Ralph, E. (1998). *Motivation Teaching in Higher Education: A Manual for Faculty Development.* Stillwater, OK: New Forums Press; Weimer, J. (1993). *Improving your classroom teaching*, vol. 1. London: Sage.

CHAPTER 10

The Teaching and Learning Physical Environment

The Studio II class was beginning a project to design a small conference/work space for a non-profit environmental group. The project would require the student teams to fully understand the client's business model and mission, develop a concept, then apply principles of proxemics, anthropometrics, and space planning to their solutions.

The new multimodal classroom facility offered the students a one-stop shopping approach for its design process activities. To kick off the project, the instructor grouped the twenty students into the lecture-presentation area to explore the non-profit organization's website. Moving in the room's breakout lounge table areas, the learners then split into their teams and began to coordinate their programming approach. Later the learners would use the room's digital docking port/drafting stations to sketch preliminary solutions, applying Internet-based research materials simultaneously to influence their emerging decisions. Several team members would also take advantage of the room's rapid prototyping area to mock up quick 3D study models in cardboard to test their ideas. As teams moved through the project's phases, the team practiced their digital presentation in the nearby presentation rehearsal area during time between classes in the department's Learning Center. The project presentations culminated where the project began—in the classroom's lecture-presentation area. Teams showed their printed large boards on the pinup walls and their digital animation presentation on the smart board screen. Their 3D physical models on the area's rotating presentation table were projected to a wall screen behind using the room's opaque projector. Audio and video of the teams' presentations were linked via live feed to monitors in the nearby Learning Center, giving underclassmen a glimpse of their next course's expectations.

In his article *Imperatives for Change in Higher Education*, Prakash Nair describes current higher education facilities as "physical relics of a bygone era" that show our "continued preference for a mass-production model of education in a world that demands a highly customized education for each child."[1] Nair's comment belies the winds of change that have buffeted American school facilities throughout United States history. At various eras in time, educational facilities' appearances have been directly reflective of influences including the assembly line, the business model, and more lately, the expectations of members of the Baby Boom Echo generation (those born between 1980 and 1995) that have entered higher education's doors within the last ten years. Indeed, quickly changing attitudes concerning education as well as technology are exerting pressures on campus facilities to embrace new paradigms of learning and teaching that are at once exciting and jarring.

There are several reasons why an understanding of teaching and learning facilities principles and influences are helpful for interior design educators on the front lines of teaching:

- Interior design program administrators and educators are the primary, long-term users of educational facilities with their constantly changing cadre of learners and are consequently the recipients of its benefits or liabilities to mental and physical well-being.
- Studies suggest facilities impact the success of learners' educational experiences.
- Cultural impacts of technology, economic concerns, and evolving attitudes about learning from both research and the public are acting to quickly evolve facilities into new forms.
- The appearance and functionality of learning environments have much to say about the perception of credibility, capability, and currency of academic programs of study, both for learners and the institution's accrediting bodies. Consequently, the appropriateness of facilities can affect learner enrollments and the ultimate thriving of the department and institution for better or worse.

This chapter will explore some of the influences on facilities decision making campuses experience today. It will then provide an overview of current research about the needs of those that inhabit higher education facilities. Last, it will explore the appearance of new teaching and learning spaces that seek to respond to both new influences on its physical form and amenities.

EDUCATIONAL FACILITIES' INFLUENCES AND PRESSURES THROUGH HISTORY

Before exploring current influences on interior design teaching and learning facilities, it may first be revealing to review the pressures that shape higher education facilities in general, both historic and present. As influences on the campus as a whole go, so go influences on departments of design.

In his article *Big Change on Campus*, facilities manager David Pearce Snyder provides a whirlwind historic tour of the academic campus form and the current pressures it is now facing:

> The concept of higher education is far from new, and the existence of the first university was purportedly 4,500 years ago. Professional graduate schools followed in Egypt 200 years later and the first public universities appeared in Rome in about 75 CE. Successive universities in the ancient, gothic, renaissance, pre-industrial, and post-industrial ages were all by and large demonstrative of the teacher-controlled instructional environment still with us in the current age.[2]

Given the university model's long existence and seeming immovability from this paradigm, current advances in technology and exponential explosion of available information are exerting powerful changes on physical classrooms and related spaces.

CURRENT AND FUTURE CHALLENGES AND INSTITUTIONS' RESPONSES

The nature of higher education is labor-intensive, a cost that is difficult to reduce through enhanced efficiency or other cutbacks. Consequently, tuition costs have risen 300% over the last twenty-five years, twice the rate of inflation. This fact, plus the growing economic gap between the haves and the have-nots, has opened up an opportunity for nimble, for-profit postsecondary schools. By using lower-cost part-time faculty and cost-efficient existing buildings, these organizations are capturing a growing segment of the education-buying market.[3] Public universities find themselves in a crunch: they cannot significantly reduce their labor costs, and yet the buying consumer perceives less and less value for their dollar as tuition costs continue to rise. Some institutions are finding relief in rethinking their physical facilities. A number of strategies may be on the horizon:

- In response to the growing popularity of the business model, institutions are considering outsourcing many of their services, including custodial, groundskeeping, and even administration services to cut costs. This change will have ramifications on the facilities these groups use and maintain.
- Because facilities (especially aging buildings) can be especially costly to institutions, some may decide to sell off their campus and its buildings to a private property management firm or real estate investment trust and then lease back the properties. This will have implications for the expansion, retrofitting, and maintenance of these buildings, as their care would then be the responsibility of a profit-driven third party.[4]
- Due to economic pressures and demands of non-traditional learners, institutions will continue to convert proportions of their traditionally instructed curricula to electronic-mediated forms, becoming centers of e-learning. This decision is supported by research that suggests online learners have small increases in their cognitive, affective, and behavioral outcomes over learners experiencing traditional instruction.[5] However, instructors typically find that online courses require more preparation than they anticipated and take more time to administer than traditional courses.[6] Conversion of curricula to off-campus access will presumably compel the reallocation of facilities to accommodate the reduced number of on-site learners.
- University institutions are becoming increasingly conscious of those academic programs that possess profit potential. While pressures on academics to bring in grant projects has existed for some time, the increasing competition perceived from private, for-profit schools may compel some public universities to spin off their professional schools, including architecture and interior design, to become independent institutions that are marketplace-viable. These new independent entities may still physically reside on campus but would have separate business plans.[7] The facilities implications for these organizational changes can vary by institution. Another possibility is the inclusion of allied disciplines within technology parks adjacent to the college campus, reports Mark Johnson with HGA Minneapolis. "This trend has been talked about a lot, but now it is actually happening. The bricks and mortar are being put in place."[8]
- In an embrace of the business model, educational institutions are looking with new eyes on the value of private business

collaborations of various scope with academic departments. These "incubator" initiatives offer outside funding, real-world exposure to processes, and networking opportunities to learners.
- Institutions are recognizing that today's learner pool is far more diversified than in the past. Eventually, youth enrollments will decline with the cessation of the Echo Boom generation. In an effort to extend influence and maintain economic health, some institutions are reaching out to retirees with lifelong learning opportunities.[9] This has the effect of enhancing the use of facilities during off-hours and adding a self-supporting profit center. With the addition of nearby retiree housing, the university thereby strengthens relationships to the local residential population and enjoys the stability of a less volatile pool of learners.
- Economic pressures on public institutions imply that these organizations must be in a constant state of fundraising. To avoid deferring maintenance on facilities, a 40%-level endowment should be established and preserved. With the current average for alumni endowed giving of 17%, it is likely that many facilities are not being maintained adequately.[10]

CULTURAL AND TECHNOLOGICAL FACTORS INFLUENCING HIGHER EDUCATION FACILITIES DESIGN

Among the many factors influencing the new construction and renovation of academic buildings, two particularly stand out in current literature. The expectations and attitudes toward higher education as exhibited by the Echo Boom generation and quickly changing technologies both rest front and center amongst decision influences.[11]

A review of current literature in college facilities planning and management suggests the following intangible influences on physical academic learning spaces.[12]

- *Adoption of the learner-centered model:* Research in multiple intelligences and brain-based learning are significantly altering previous preconceptions in how people learn. Academic discussion is now exploring the impact of 24/7 learning, the impact of direct experience on individual learning, and the establishment of patterns, relationships, and connections as a means to build cognitive frameworks. The primacy of these discoveries is having deep impacts on the design of learning facilities and runs starkly counter to the instructor-centered model that has dictated higher education procedures for generations.
- *My Space versus our space:* Echo Boom learners expect increased personal residential space, and the floor plans of new dormitories reflect this trend. Amenities such as retail, fitness, and parking garages are new dormitory inclusions. At the same time, the concept of "learning" is leaking beyond the walls of dedicated classrooms into shared "in-between spaces" that foster collaboration and community. Previous barriers erected between "off time" and "time on task" are breaking down, coupled with expectations of instant information access.
- *The end of the 9-to-5 work mentality:* Echo Boomers both work and socialize at all times of the day. Just as the concept of "classroom" and "lounge" are being rethought, so is the concept of the traditional eight-hour workday. Institutions are responding by accommodating behaviors in places previously thought inap-

propriate. For example, Goucher College now recognizes that the library is a place where students, work, eat, socialize, and even nap.[13]

- *Thinking beyond the traditional isolated degree:* Educational institutions are beginning to respond to society's needs that transcend a specific discipline. New, merged content areas such as nano-ecology and environmental sociology are in turn influencing the placement of departments and campus buildings. This movement is promoting cross-discipline collaborations while still maintaining a sense of community and cohesiveness. Clustered buildings can create "neighborhoods" and strategic placement of buildings can prompt learners to pass through an allied area to reach their main destination.

  Universities are also rethinking the traditional four- to six-year degree and considering a certification model that recognizes that learning is a lifelong endeavor. The Department of Engineering Professional Development at the University of Wisconsin offers both onsite and remote electronic learning and its continuing academic structure enhances the institution's financial return. This new structure has important ramifications for facilities that accommodate its activities.[14]
- *Learner motivation:* Learners are expecting more natural, stimulating environments that increase their comfort and thereby maintain positive motivation. Natural light and wireless connectivity can assist in achieving this goal. Giving learners a measure of control over factors such as air and light levels can increase satisfaction. One institution installed a link to a local radio station in its learner café to inject a positive mood into the space.[15]
- *Collaboration:* Dialogue and information sharing lead to problem solving. Open spaces that are less structured than classrooms are offering the venue for impromptu, productive multi-person meetings. Technology interfaces and food and refreshments are bolstering an atmosphere of contribution and sharing.
- *Personalization and inclusion:* The computer is now fifty years old, and the maturing of the computer user permits more user-regulàted access to technology. That is, it is now more feasible to place computers in underutilized areas and offer laptop programs that foster a sense of inclusion and connectivity. Reliable virus programs permit users to have control over the downloading of software without administrator consent. Physical facility cues can help reinforce a sense of openness and uncritical acceptance, for example, wider doorways and flexible furniture that allow learners to customize their education experience by the moment. Intentional audio cues detectable upon entering a space can be used to clue learners into a space's quiet/calm or noisy/animated function.
- *Flexibility:* Two continuous decades of rapid technological change has made staying flexible crucial in academic facilities. As it is difficult to tell the exact nature of the next must-have technology, facilities managers are opting to keep their physical renovation options as open as possible. Mobile and wireless networks can make repurposing spaces simpler and less physically intrusive. In today's facility designs, technology is often an afterthought imposed after the fact on existing infrastructure. Open plan designs and subfloor systems that permit a wide variety of reconfigurations offer the opportunity to implement flexibility into a design from its inception. The utterly open-plan, mixed-use room has challenges of acoustics, temperature, and student activity. For this reason, a mix of open and closed

environments often work well to suit various activities.

Ideally, the academic physical learning facility should be a positive reflection of the goals of administration, faculty of all categories, and its learners. It is the physical representation of the intangible quest for knowledge and thus reflects the institution's vision and strategy for successful learning.

OTHER INTERIOR ENVIRONMENT CONSIDERATIONS

By their nature, the design and construction of public spaces is a complex undertaking that must respond to the influences from multiple stakeholders. Some of these factors are only coming to light through recent research.

Sustainability and Indoor Air Quality

In December 2002, the United Nations passed Resolution 57/254, which established the United Nations Decade of Education for Sustainable Development (2005–2014). Urged on by Echo Boom generation grassroots efforts, sustainability is going the way of the Americans with Disabilities Act concepts in the 1990s: toward an accepted and universally assumed ethical mindset that directs an accountable course of action. It is difficult to find an educational or building organization that is not engaged in this issue at some level in its activities.[16]

Some states are creating green design standards for K-12 institutions such as California's Collaborative for High Performance Schools, which seeks to unify local, unconnected efforts. Higher education across the country has similarly embraced the movement toward campus sustainability. Many universities and colleges are in various stages of organizing events and codifying procedures to integrate sustainability into their existing practices.[17]

Green campus task forces and initiatives offer design educators a unique way to contribute to the campus improvement dialogue. Interior design graduate students are also drawn to the timeliness and urgency of this mission, and the compelling nature of the topic can result in thesis-supporting grants, as the example in Figure 10.1 describes. This also offers a natural path for academic research with a readily available experimental test case of one's own department facilities and user participants.

Indoor air quality is one of many issues underneath the sustainability umbrella. Despite the critical impact on breathable air for young people who often spend the majority of their days in school, awareness of this issue in academic construction context is only recently coming to light. "In my humble opinion, the two areas [where] we ought to be most concerned about the quality of air are the two areas that we have probably done the least—healthcare institutions and schools," notes Carl Smith, chief executive officer of the non-profit sustainability organization GreenGuard.[18]

Research suggests that a classroom's indoor environmental quality can in fact impact student health, performance, and attendance. In a recent study, 45% of surveyed classrooms had elevated levels of carbon dioxide, a compound linked to increased frequency of health symptoms and absenteeism.[19] The solution is adequate ventilation to manage the spread of disease in these high-use areas, as well as vigilant ongoing maintenance.

Acoustics

Learning often involves intense concentration, especially in the case of complex top-

GREENER THAN LANDIS

An FSU Sustainable Campus and Community Initiative grant project funded by Florida Campus Compact and the Florida State University Center for Civic Education and Service

Rachelle McClure
Master of Fine Arts Candidate

Eric Wiedegreen
Major Professor and Chairperson of the Florida State University Department of Interior Design

Jill Pable
Committee Member and Assistant Professor of Interior Design, Florida State University

GOALS AND OBJECTIVES OF PROPOSED PROJECT

Goal 1: Increase awareness of the benefits of sustainable building practices among Florida State University administration, planning staff and students. This serves the larger goal of sustaining an active dialogue that may ultimately result in future campus construction choices that are positively influenced by sustainability principles.

Objective 1: Research the environmental costs associated with conventional campus building practices and externalities.
Objective 2: Using objective data, the team will create a detailed comparison study of both hard and soft costs associated with selected sustainable buildings and conventional buildings. Hard costs are those that can be definitively quantified such as reduced energy expenses. Soft costs include such items as a decrease in employee sick days and worker productivity. This factual analysis seeks to objectively identify the financial and wellness benefits of sustainable buildings.
Objective 3: Develop select case studies of other universities that have been successful in adopting and implementing sustainable building plans. This background research will provide data regarding the positive effects sustainable buildings have on the community, the campus and the financial bottom-line.
Objective 4: Evaluate select building products used on college campuses, including Florida State University, to explore cost-benefit opportunities that may exist in their use or exclusion.
Objective 5: Present the study's findings to Florida State University's facilities planners, managers and administration.

Goal 2: To help FSU make their sustainable buildings an active interdisciplinary learning practice.

Objective 1. To research how other universities have integrated interdisciplinary approaches to their sustainable buildings.
Objective 2. To disseminate this research to Florida State University.

Figure 10.1 A 2007 grant awarded to a graduate student of the Florida State University Department of Design provided funds for travel to multiple campuses to gather facts on sustainability. This information in turn supports the analysis of current campus conditions at FSU and the development of a set of recommendations. The grant also provides a venue for interior design students to build public awareness for sustainable building practices through their construction of an information kiosk. By R. McClure, E. Wiedegreen, & J. Pable (2007), *More Green than Landis*. A grant funded by The FSU Sustainable Campus and Community Initiative by the Florida State University Center for Civic Education and Service.

ics that engage learners in high levels of cognition. Distracting occurrences can serve to interrupt activities and lessen the ability of learners to internalize content well. A recent acoustic study of K-12 classroom environments may also have lessons for designers of higher education classrooms:

- Noise can cause irritation, discomfort, distress, and frustration.
- Whispering, speech, corridor sounds, and scraping chairs were found to be the most disturbing.
- Poor ventilation leads to opening windows which can exacerbate noise intrusion.[20]

Reverberation can also be a problem in learning environments, especially in discussion and lecture environments. Interior finish materials are often to blame in that hard, impervious surfaces such as vinyl composition tile and painted drywall are attractive to facilities designers in their ease of maintenance and cost-efficiency and thus are often specified. Solutions include sound baffles and thoughtful sequestration of sound-critical tasks from more active areas in the space plan.

Furnishings

Effective specification for furniture for learning is influenced in part by several emerging problems among current college learners. These issues are collectively detrimental to musculoskeletal health:

1. Despite heady declarations of the move toward "paperless workplaces," today's college learners often tote around alarmingly heavy backpacks. Not surprisingly, one recent research study suggests this can contribute to musculoskeletal problems even before learners reach college age.[21] Care should be taken in the design of lockers and other related items to minimize bending and cantilevering that can exacerbate spinal injuries. Hooks and shelves for hanging backpacks in restroom stalls should be extra heavy duty.
2. The increasing use of technology can affect sitting duration, posture, and overall spinal health. As learners spend increasing amounts of uninterrupted time in front of computers, the advice to move frequently from sitting to standing positions often gets lost in intense concentration. Spinal compression can result.
3. The increasingly frequent specific use of laptops can be especially problematic. While laptops excel in their connectivity and portability, there is often little agreement between keyboard height and tabletop height, increasing the proclivity for carpal tunnel syndrome and poor posture in general. Tabletop stands for laptops that elevate the keyboard to a more appropriate height can simultaneously raise screen level, lessening learners' need to look down at uncomfortable angles.

Besides ergonomic considerations, the overall diversity of learner body sizes can make furniture comfort for all difficult to achieve. The growing awareness of bariatric furniture (furnishings for the obese) in the healthcare industry has not yet fully been addressed in educational furnishings, and the results of this negligence can be unfortunate.[22]

Given the current emphasis on flexibility in learning activities, furnishings must increasingly respond to multiple functions. "Instead of cramming in little tablet arm chairs that are not conducive to moving around, almost every new table and chair is [now] on casters," says Lynnette Bush Clouse, the di-

Figure 10.2 Inflatable igloos create temporary enclosures for group meetings in the Saltire Centre of Glasgow Caledonian University. Joint Information Systems Committee e-Learning and Innovation Team (2006), *Designing Spaces for Effective Learning: A guide to 21st century learning space design.* Retrieved 6/30/07 from www.jisc.ac.uk/uploaded_documents/JISClearningspaces.pdf. Bristol, UK: Higher Education Funding Council for England (HEFCE).

rector of interiors and project manager for Ohio University.[23] Furnishings must also respond to increasingly collaborative activities with workstations sufficiently large to accommodate several students at once. Stackable chairs can help with reconfiguration needs, according to DesignGroup, Inc., designers of Ohio University's library learning center.[24]

It is interesting to note that learners are likely to adapt to a given furnishings layout rather than alter it to suit their individual needs.[25] Therefore, cues should be present that signal that reconfiguration is easy and acceptable. Figure 10.2 shows one unique solution that celebrates flexibility through its inflatable, seemingly temporary nature.

Wayfinding

The blurring of learning and lounging spaces is leading to the trend of mixed-use facilities on campuses. Thus, a classroom may be located alongside a lounge, a refreshment area, faculty offices, and gallery exhibition areas. Similarly, modern architectural building types sometimes obscure visual cues such as main entrances and locations of amenities like water fountains and restrooms. In such situations, intuitive user navigation may be elusive. Thus, effective wayfinding methods become quite important in the functioning of the space.

In the article *Forecasting Higher Education's Future*, Ann Day recounts designer A. Kenneth Roos' ideation to reestablish needed visual wayfinding cues for visitors:

> Just as iconic buildings become readily recognized campus landmarks, sculpted forms within buildings can mark unique activity. A distinctly colored wall can identify the entrance to a financial service center; descriptive floor patterns, like breadcrumbs on a forest path, can be a guide to an instructor's office. A stair clad in free flowing, overscaled guardrails can symbolize the way to a second floor coffee house. Special features such as backlit, translucent wall panels can become a beacon for a message center and make a distinctive design statement.
>
> Representative design features, rhythmic floor patterns and lighting all clarify wayfinding, create familiarity and enrich the student experience. A confusing conglomerate of activities and services within a building can be architecturally transformed into a place of familiarity and comfort by creative interior design.[26]

DESIGN TEACHING AND LEARNING FACILITIES

There is surprisingly little past and current specific literature on the design of higher education facilities dedicated to the design fields such as interior design and architecture. This represents a gap in the knowledge base that interior design researchers are uniquely positioned to remedy, both from their content knowledge and their day to day practical experience of inhabiting teaching facilities.

What Makes a Quality Design Department Facility?

The book *Designing for Designers: Lessons Learned from Schools of Architecture* by Jack Nasar et al. (Fairchild Books) promises to offer practical insights stemming from extensive post-occupancy evaluation case studies of architecture, landscape architecture, and interior design higher education facilities nationwide.[27] The post-occupancy instrument is discussed next, along with points noted as most meaningful to users within design teaching and learning facilities.

A Post-Occupancy Evaluation Tool and its Findings

As a means to better understand users' reactions to architectural teaching and learning spaces and thus design better ones in the future, architectural researcher-educators Jack Nasar, Henry Sanoff, and Nate Perkins developed a post-occupancy evaluation survey to gauge user satisfaction with architectural teaching facilities.

The survey was structured in six main parts:

- Context of the building
- Massing
- Interface of the building, such as its treatment of public and private spaces and its relationship to the site
- Wayfinding
- Socio-spatial considerations
- Comfort

Figure 10.3 provides an excerpt of this survey, which was administered at six different

7. FOR YOUR *LEAST SATISFYING* SPACE YOU LISTED ABOVE, HOW WOULD YOU RATE EACH OF THE FOLLOWING?

	Very poor	Poor	Fairly poor	Neutral	Fairly good	Good	Very good	Not applicable
Adequacy of space								
Lighting								
Acoustics								
Temperature								
Odor								
Esthetic Appeal								
Security								
Flexibility of Use								
Accessibility for persons with disabilities								
Other (specify)								

8. FOR YOUR *MOST SATISFYING* SPACE LISTED ABOVE, HOW WOULD YOU RATE EACH OF THE FOLLOWING?

	Very poor	Poor	Fairly poor	Neutral	Fairly good	Good	Very good	Not applicable
Adequacy of space								
Lighting								
Acoustics								
Temperature								
Odor								
Esthetic Appeal								
Security								
Flexibility of Use								
Accessibility for persons with disabilities								
Other (specify)								

Figure 10.3 The Nasof/Sanoff/Perkins Post-Occupancy Evaluation survey includes specific questions about various characteristics of users' most favorite and least favorite spaces within the campus design building in an effort to understand its socio-spatial qualities. J. Nasar, H. Sanoff, & N. Perkins, et al. (2007, May 31), The Architecture of Architecture Schools. A presentation at the 2007 National Conference of the Environmental Design and Research Association, Sacramento, California.

architectural academic institutions across the United States and Canada.[28]

As a part of the study, co-author Nate Perkins assessed the learner and instructor responses of the landscape architecture facility at Guelph University. The responses yielded interesting information that often echoes the general observations just explained and sometimes highlight overlooked qualities that might similarly be applied to interior design teaching and learning facilities.

- *Visibility and location:* Learners observed that seeing lights on and activity from outside of the building was a motivating influence.
- *Proximity:* Space plan distances for communication and collaboration in

learner-to-learner interactions as well as learner-to-instructor engagements were key. In order for learners to seek out instructor feedback, Perkins recommends that learners can reach instructors for meaningful discussions in less than thirty seconds.

- *Quality of materials:* Furnishings, fixtures, and equipment were specified to endure the extensive abuse that will occur. Objects and surfaces that last and still work and look appropriate if worn were highly regarded.
- *Tradition and personalization:* Often overlooked, this quality spoke to the potential for evocative features of facilities to embed themselves in learners' memories long after their educational experience there had concluded. The ability for learners to leave behind evidence of their time there was seen as particularly meaningful as a means of claiming ownership, particularly since learners are not permitted to "imprint" on their transitory dormitory spaces. Actions such as carving one's name on a windowsill, or leaving lasting evidence of one's existence at a cold desk for the next occupant gave learners the ability to mark their space.
- *Flexibility:* Movable furniture and interior partitions were highly regarded by users. Portable technology that could activate and repurpose spaces was conducive to learning. Access 24/7 was similarly noted as important for feeling kinship and the privilege of being accepted into the academic program.
- *Networking and connection:* Student-maintained lounge areas for impromptu meetings and brainstorming were considered the nexus of ideation.
- *Control:* Instructors remarked on the importance of office location. Avoidance of key intersections for the offices relieved faculty of unnecessary disruption and endless provision of directions to first-time visitors. Learners remarked positively on the ability to control ventilation, temperature, and light to suit their individual needs.[29]

DESIGN TEACHING AND LEARNING SPACE ARCHETYPES

The diverse nature of interior design education activities calls for facilities that meet these challenges. Box 10.1 describes a basic laundry list of spaces typically required by an interior design department in a higher education institution. Each institution, of course, has specific needs that would drive additions and edits to this generic list when planning for a new or updated facility.

Current literature and thinking on higher education facilities points to a future of teaching and learning spaces that respond flexibly to different learning styles and instructional techniques. When compared to the common fixed seat and table classrooms of today, the contrast is clearly evident.

Is Learning Really Resulting from these New Ideas?

It is worthwhile to ask if this new, almost amorphous style of facility is in fact an enhancement to real, long-term knowledge for interior design learners. Researcher Muhbub Rashid attempted to answer this question in a 2007 study comparing interior design learners in a human factors class that first used a traditional classroom with fixed furnishings and ordinary technology. At the semester halfway point, the same room was then converted to an "innovative design" with flexible furnishings, moveable whiteboards, and lounge chairs in addition to table-based seating that

BOX 10-1 CHARACTERISTICS AND EQUIPMENT FOR ACADEMIC SPACES

Interior design program facilities requirements vary greatly. This basic list can be used to brainstorm specific needs.

1. Lecture and other non-studio learner spaces

- Stadium seating (or alternately, flat floor with moveable tables/chairs)
- Amply deep table surfaces
- Exit placed so as not to disrupt presentations
- Pinup space for class exercises
- Technology-smart equipment
  - Opaque projector and LCD projector
  - Software that permits instructor control of learners' laptops
  - Smart board
  - Digital controls for showing multiple images simultaneously
  - DVD player

2. Studio learning spaces

- Multimodal to support digital and traditional presentations, computer-based work, team collaboration, 3D model building, printing, and project assembly

3. Critique and exhibition spaces

- Lighting gallery for product/light/shadow demonstrations
- Loose seating that stacks
- Can be secured and surveilled
- Public access
- No conflict with proximity to or circulation for scheduled classes
- Large lockable cases for 2D and 3D work
- Access to kitchenette for catered events
- Technology support for variety of digital exhibits and presentations
- Daylight control

4. Learner support spaces: Learning centre

- Presentation rehearsal space
- Screens for close-captioned presentations beamed from classrooms
- Team collaboration space
- Lounge space
- Food/refreshments
- Ample digital ports in different seating modes
- Wired headphones for multimedia learning
- Print center
- Table access for quiet study
- Smart board
- Dedicated lockers and private space

(*continued*)

BOX 10-1 (continued)

5. Learner support spaces: Other
- CAD laboratory with 2D and 3D printing
- Spray booth
- Modelmaking lab
- Woodworking lab
- Materials library with computer access
- Color copier with swipe/payment access
- Design periodical/book library with copier access
- Mat cutter

6. Learner cold desks, either as supplementary or in-class work areas

7. Seminar room for small conference-room based classes and faculty meetings

8. Storage
- Student work retained for accreditation purposes
- Teaching materials
- Gallery display pedestals and easels
- Paper and administration files and archives
- Software and hardware equipment

9. Instructor spaces
- Offices for full-time and part-time faculty
- Graduate teaching assistant offices
- Guest speaker or visiting scholar office
- Lounge with kitchenette
- Support spaces
  - Copy/collate area
  - Mailboxes
  - Research space
- Staging space (lockable) for grading large projects
- Restroom for faculty

10. Graduate-specific facilities
- Research desks
- Reserved technology such as printers and computers

instructors and learners used for the remainder of the semester. The researcher compared learner behavior, learner perceptions of the environment, and learner academic performance in both settings.

Using observation techniques, the study results suggested several learner behavior advantages to the new room design, including increased interaction with class colleagues, increased interaction with the instructor, and enhanced independent learner behavior when working in breakout teams. Learners also reported a significant preference for the new space, noting its seating options and reconfigurability among the advantages. The researcher hypothesized that the enhanced project scores that emanated from the learners' increased information sharing was made possible in part by the "innovative" room's flexible setup.[30] Additional research will help lend support to these preliminary findings.

Exemplars from Other Design Fields

Other fields are similarly rethinking the nature of their curricula and the facilities design that supports these new approaches to learning. Faculty at the Massachusetts Institute of Technology Engineering Department, for example, observed that engineering education and real-world demands on engineers were drifting apart during the 1990s. The department's industry partners began to find that graduating students, while technically adept, lacked social and entrepreneurial skills required in real-world engineering situations. In response, faculty overhauled curriculum and created the CDIO initiative. This Conceiving–Designing–Implementing–Operating process embodied an approach of experiencing the concrete and then applying the experience to the abstract. This implied new inclusion of design/build projects early in the curricula, team approaches to learning, and interdisciplinary partnerships in problem solving. The facilities response to this new strategy involved a multi-million dollar overhaul to the existing Aeronautical Laboratory into a series of four large rooms each dedicated to one step of the CDIO process. Fifteen other engineering institutions are now implementing the CDIO model.[31]

What Might a Twenty-first-Century Design Learning Facility Look Like?

The many influences acting on the design of the twenty-first century classroom may cause it to look distinctly different than the standard issue classroom of today. Design programs are incorporating enhanced architectural features into their spaces, such as collaborative group areas and flexible classrooms that reflect the extended hours design students often spend working on projects. For example, the new classroom building of the Department of Interior Architecture at University of North Carolina Greensboro accommodates student furniture projects in the wide corridors and features natural light in many areas that reduces heating and cooling costs. See Figures 10.4 through 10.6 for examples of these and other details.

The Joint Information Systems Committee, a division of Great Britain's Higher Education Funding Council for England (HEFCE), gathered case studies of new teaching and learning facilities that respond to many of the new demands this chapter describes. Three facility types are discussed here.

- *The multimodal classroom:* Research is leading to increasing respect for learner-led and active learning techniques as suitable augmentation to traditional instructor-led activities. The physical classroom that can best handle these different strategies is one with flexible and changeable components. In Figures 10.7 and 10.8, AMA Alexi Marmot Associates show a prototypical higher education learning room that seeks to address the dynamics of these challenges.[32] Key among them is the ability for segments of the class population to be involved in different things simultaneously. This new concept places the instructor on the sidelines as a director of learning and the learners as the primary guides in their own discovery. However, the flexibility of the room also permits the instructor to gather all together for a singular activity when appropriate.
- *The classroom that emphasizes process:* The University of Strathclyde's Department

Figure 10.4 Student cold desks at the Department of Interior Architecture promote collaboration in a light-filled environment at the University of North Carolina, Greensboro. Photo courtesy of Anna Marshall-Baker.

of Design, Manufacture, and Engineering Management employs a strong ethos of product realization from design to manufacture and supports the hands-on use of the design process to model real-world processes for its learners. Classroom activities feature problem solving and scenario-based learning strategies undertaken in linked zones within a single unifying, collaborative room. There may be advantages to this approach in that learning is kept fresh by changing the modes of knowledge negotiation between lecture-presentation, technology-assisted self-discovery, 2D and 3D manipulation, and collaborative teamwork. The room partitions could be sufficiently distinct to manage the acoustics of the various activities. As technology changes, space allocations can be readjusted to accommodate new needs.[33] Figure 10.9 depicts this classroom arrangement.

- *Classroom-supplemental learning centers:* To accommodate today's reality of

Figure 10.5 A group critique space provides a flexible room configuration and high, open ceilings, offering true color rendition for presented projects. Department of Interior Architecture, University of North Carolina, Greensboro. Photo courtesy of Anna Marshall-Baker.

24/7 learning, impromptu interchange, and collaboration, design departments may need to rethink learner spaces that are supplemental to dedicated teaching classrooms. The Learning Center concept creates a learning and social hub that facilitates blended activities, as shown in Figures 10.10 and 10.11. This type of space permits learners to make productive use of their between-hours for studying, relaxing, and socializing, team meetings, and background research. The design of these spaces should carefully manage the various modes of sound level and passageway intrusion to minimize conflict.[34]

- *Classroom-supplemental materials centers:* Many interior design programs have long recognized that learners require access to the materials of the trade during their educations. However, the future may dictate that the role of these materials libraries evolve to embrace testing, manipulation, and collaborative research. The University Co-op Materials Resource

Figure 10.6 The Natuzzi Lounge offers students a relaxed environment to access reference materials. Department of Interior Architecture, University of North Carolina, Greensboro. Photo courtesy of Anna Marshall-Baker.

General teaching spaces

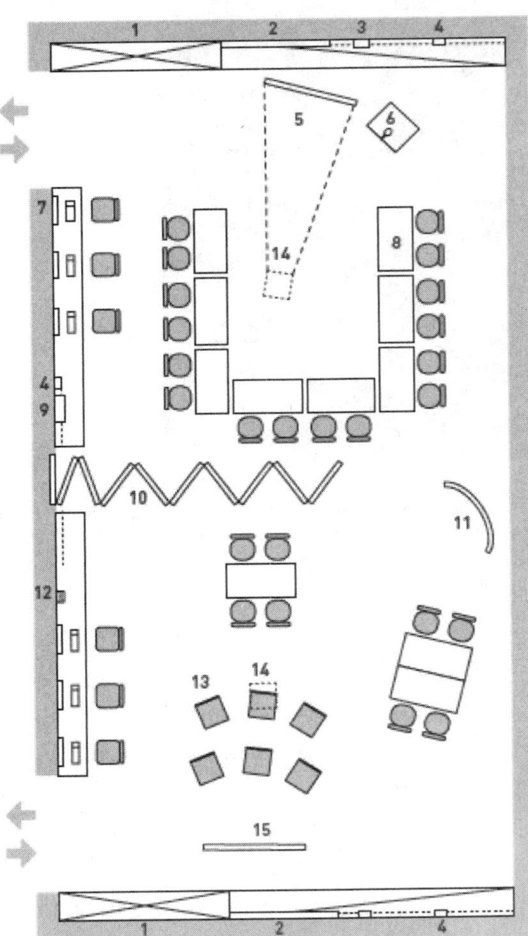

1 Lockable storage and recharging facility for wireless tablet PCs

2 Whiteboard

3 Receiver for voting devices

4 Power sockets

5 Mobile interactive whiteboard

6 Lectern with control panel for lighting and power/network points

7 Wired computers

8 Foldaway tables

9 Charger for voting devices

10 Folding/sliding acoustic wall

11 Free-standing magnetic surface/partition

12 Wireless hub

13 Stackable chairs

14 Ceiling-mounted projection

15 Video conferencing facility

This floor plan gives prototype designs for two teaching spaces. It does not represent designs in any particular institution.
Source: AMA Alexi Marmot Associates

Figure 10.7 Interactive whiteboards and reconfigurable partitions and furnishings characterize this dynamic space capable of accommodating multiple learning techniques at the same time. By AMA Alexi Marmot Associates. In Joint Information Systems Committee e-Learning and Innovation Team (2006), *Designing Spaces for Effective Learning: A guide to 21st century learning space design*. Retrieved 6/30/07 from www.jisc.ac.uk/uploaded_documents/JISC learningspaces.pdf. Bristol, UK: Higher Education Funding Council for England (HEFCE).

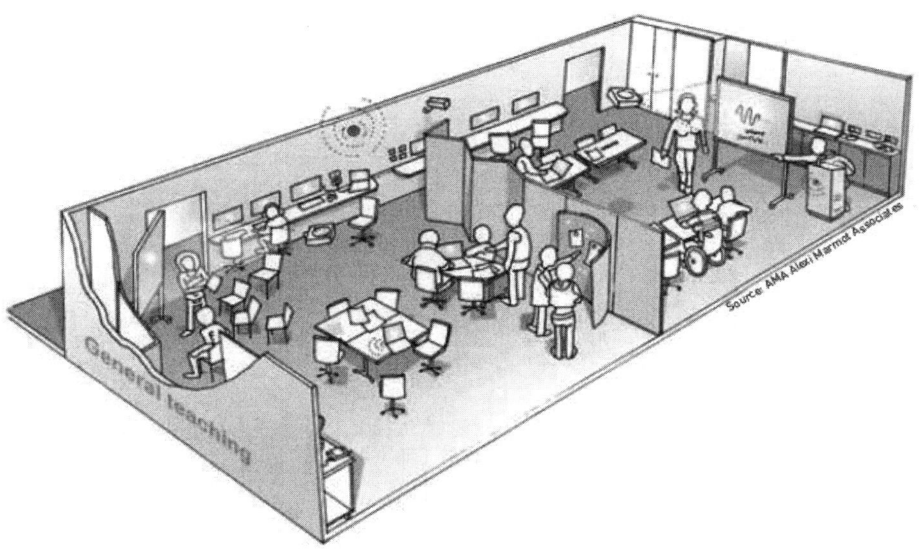

Figure 10.8 **A perspective of the multimodal classroom. By AMA Alexi Marmot Associates. In Joint Information Systems Committee e-Learning and Innovation Team (2006). *Designing Spaces for Effective Learning: A guide to 21st century learning space design.* Retrieved 6/30/07 from www.jisc.ac.uk/uploaded_documents/JISClearningspaces.pdf. Bristol, UK: Higher Education Funding Council for England (HEFCE).**

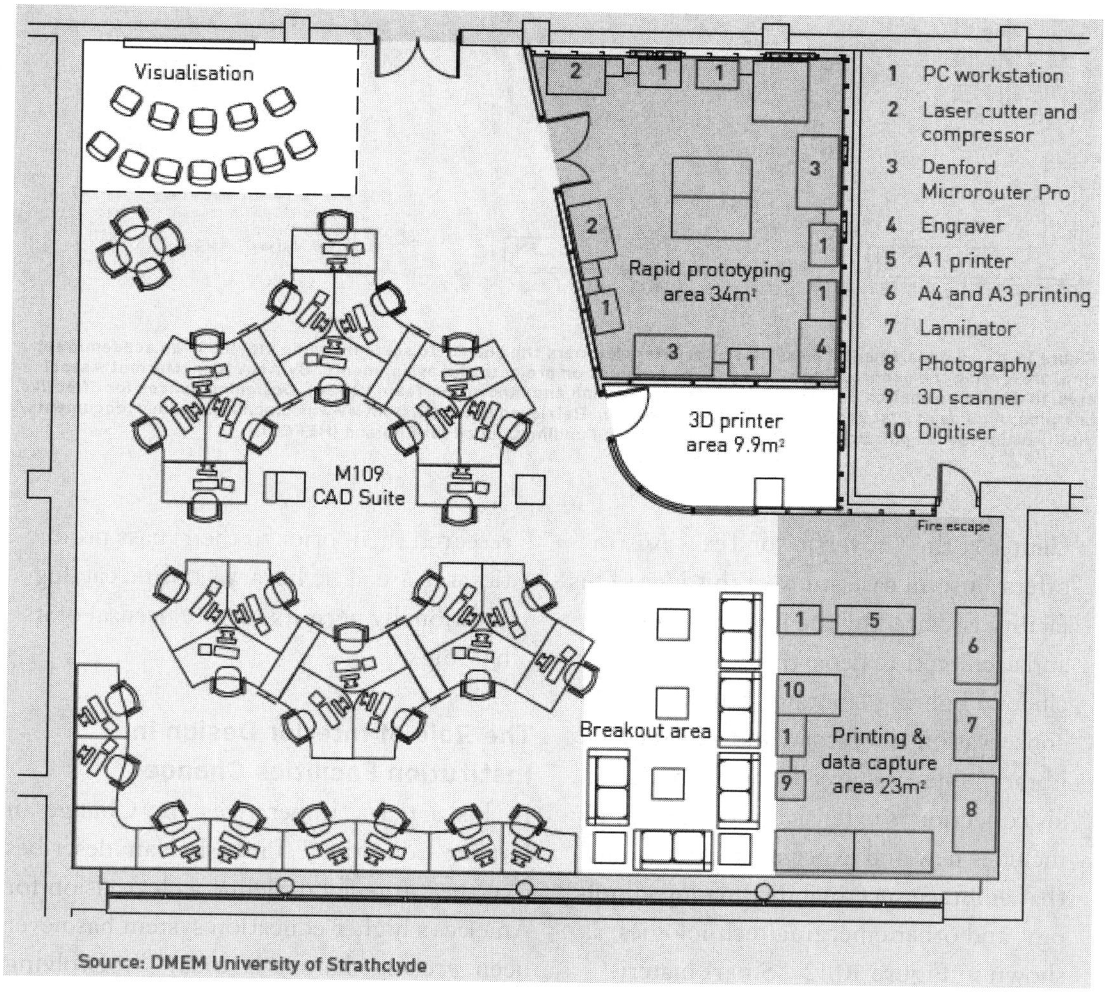

Figure 10.9 **The University of Strathclyde's multimodal rapid prototyping classroom offers ideas for interior design studio classroom design. The rapid prototyping area could be translated as a 3D model building facility for interior design purposes. By AMA Alexi Marmot Associates. In Joint Information Systems Committee e-Learning and Innovation Team (2006), *Designing Spaces for Effective Learning: A guide to 21st century learning space design.* Retrieved 6/30/07 from www.jisc.ac.uk/uploaded_documents/JISClearningspaces.pdf. Bristol, UK: Higher Education Funding Council for England (HEFCE).**

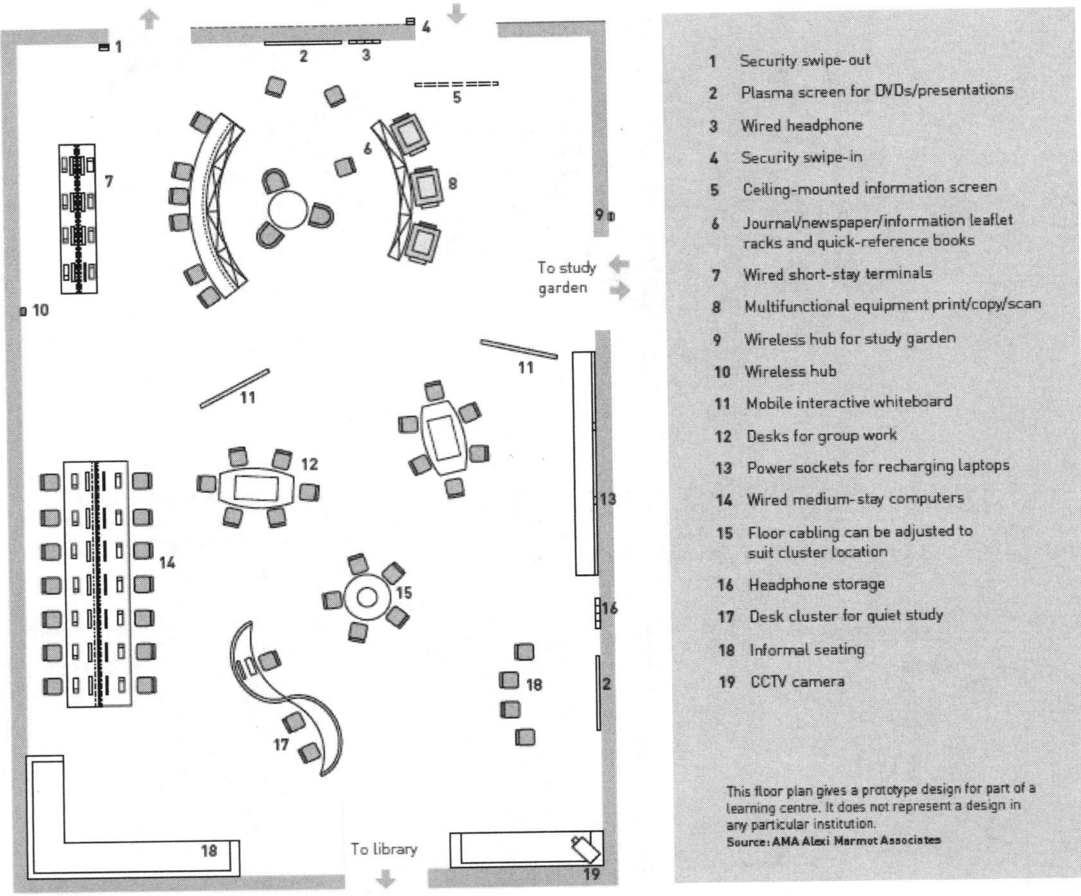

Figure 10.10 A departmental learning center offers learners the chance to socialize while staying in an academic setting, presenting the opportunity for productive progress on projects and assignments. By AMA Alexi Marmot Associates. In Joint Information Systems Committee e-Learning and Innovation Team (2006), *Designing Spaces for Effective Learning: A guide to 21st century learning space design*. Retrieved 6/30/07 from www.jisc.ac.uk/uploaded_documents/JISClearningspaces.pdf. Bristol, UK: Higher Education Funding Council for England (HEFCE).

Center at the University of Texas Austin offers a useful case study of this idea. This facility is shared by the interior design and architecture departments and includes a lighting laboratory, architectural conservation laboratory, and a materials library. The Resource Center's materials collection is extensive and increasingly includes new and experimental materials that embrace sustainability, nanotechnology, and other emerging technologies, as shown in Figure 10.12. "Smart materials" such as phase-change polymers and environmentally reactive metal alloys are included in the library's quickly changing holdings so that graduate students can research them prior to their mass production release. The library's online catalog additionally permits off-site perusal of its holdings.[35]

The Role of Interior Design in Institution Facilities Change

In his article "Imperatives for Change in Higher Education," Prakash Nair describes that the "urgency to define a clear vision for America's higher education system has never been greater than it is today"[36]. Evolving thinking in how learners internalize content, new expectations of the Echo Boom population, and increased competition are but three of many issues that are exerting dramatic

Figure 10.11 Concept sketch of a learning center prototype. By AMA Alexi Marmot Associates. In Joint Information Systems Committee e-Learning and Innovation Team (2006), *Designing Spaces for Effective Learning: A guide to 21st century learning space design.* Retrieved 6/30/07 from www.jisc.ac.uk/uploaded_documents/JISClearningspaces.pdf. Bristol, UK: Higher Education Funding Council for England (HEFCE).

Figure 10.12 The Materials Lab in the University Co-op Materials Resource Center at the University of Texas, Austin, features new and experimental materials that learners can study first-hand. Photo courtesy of Samuel Duncan.

influence on the very nature of higher education. Despite the many financial pressures that are often decried as the main drivers of college and university decision making, great need can lead to great innovation, both in curricular design and the creation of facilities that support its goals. In this time of significant change, interior design instructors and researchers are well positioned through their knowledge and professional occupation to make a significant and positive contribution to this critical dialogue.

ENDNOTES

1. Nair, Prakash. (January 2003). Imperatives for Change in Higher Education. *DesignShare: The International Forum for Innovative Schools.* Retrieved 7/1/07 from http://www.designshare.com/Research/Nair/HigherEd/imperatives. p. 1.
2. Snyder, D. (January/February 2006). Big Change on Campus. *Facilities Manager.* Retrieved 6/30/07 from http://www.appa.org/FacilitiesManager/article.cfm?ItemNumber=2550&patentid=2540.
3. Snyder reports that the number of four-year, for-profit schools in America increased from 79 to 194 during the 1990s, which represents a 266% increase in a ten-year period. Conversely, the number of public and nonprofit four-year institutions rose from 595 to 613 institutions during the same period, representing an increase of only 3%.
4. Snyder explains that many corporations have been doing this for years, but "for a college or university, it's a stunning thought."
5. Blomeyer, R. & Guerrero, R. (Spring/Summer 2004). Further Research Suggests Classroom Technology Use Has Positive Impact on Student Performance. *Educational Technology News 4*(1): 2–4.
6. See Tallent-Runnels, Mary K., et al. (Spring 2006). Teaching Courses Online: A Review of the Research. *Review of Educational Research 76*(1): 93–135; Dahl, J. (2003). How Much Are Distance Education Faculty Worth? *Distance Education Report* 7(14): 5–7; and Zhang, P. (1998). A Case Study on Technology Use in Distance Learning. *Journal of Research on Computing in Education, 30:* 398.
7. Snyder, D. (January/February 2006). Design department administrators and faculty should consider both the opportunities and liabilities of this situation carefully. For example, industry partnerships that this model might afford can bring significant facilities upgrades in the form of furnishings, finishes, and equipment, including costly technology. However, the temptation to endorse certain products (because they happen to be used in the department) suggests a cautious approach so as to maintain a neutral academic standing.
8. Babcock, R. (August 2005). Schoolhouse Rocks: Exploring the Future of Learning Environments. *Buildings.* Retrieved 6/30/07 from www.buildings.com/Articles/detail Buildings.asp?ArticleID=2650.
9. Kressley, K. & Huebschmann, M. (November 1, 2002). The 21st Century Campus: Gerontological Perspectives. *Educational Gerontology 28*(10): 835–851.
10. Fisher and Miller advise that "at all times, a capital campaign should either be underway or in the planning stages. In addition to the annual fund, heavy emphasis should be placed on prospect research, major gifts, and planned giving." Fisher, J. & Miller, S. (January 2000). From Here to 2010. *College Planning and Management 3*(1). Retrieved 7/30/07 from http://www.peterli.com/archive/cpm/35.shtm, pp. 24–25, 28–29, 32–35. This point is worth considering when a classroom educator aspires to certain positions in higher administration. While the allure of increased responsibility and social standing can be great, reality suggests that fundraising campaigns, letter-writing, and consistent event attendance to encourage giving can take the glow off the position for some.
11. It is notable to observe that the first of these influences itself reflects a vast change in the forces driving many areas of decision making of academic institutions—it is not administration or faculty who are driving change, but instead the consumers of education and their bill-paying families or employer sponsors. The Echo Boom learner population is expected to peak in 2013 at approximately 18 million students.
12. For further detail on these influences, see Dordai & Rizzo. (November 1, 2006). Echo Boom Impact (College Admissions for Baby

Boomers). *American School and University* 79(3). Retrieved 6/30/07 from *Expanded Academic ASAP* database. Thomson Gale; Fisher & Miller. (2000); Joint Information Systems Committee. (2006). Joint Information Systems Committee e-Learning and Innovation Team. *Designing Spaces for Effective Learning: A Guide to 21st Century Learning Space Design*. Retrieved 6/30/07 from http://www.jisc.as.uk/uploaded_documents/JISClearningspaces.pdf; Snyder. (January/February 2006);Nair (2003); and Trends in Education. (January 2006). *College Planning & Management*. Retrieved 6/30/2007 from http://www.peterli.com/archive/cpm/1041.htm.

13. Says Goucher College's Sanford Unger, "The library should be a place where you feel comfortable enough to fall asleep, wake up, get a cup of coffee or tea and resume studying at any time." In Dordai & Rizzo. (2006), p. 2. Unger's interview does not include a description of where students are allowed to sleep or if special sleeping accommodations or furnishings are provided for this activity.
14. Nair, P. (January 2003). p. 5.
15. Joint Information Systems Committee e-Learning and Innovation Team. (2006). Funded by Higher Education Funding Council for England (HEFCE): Bristol, UK.
16. In Education: Campus Compact, green schools.net, the Sustainable Campus Information Center at http://www.sustainable campus.org/universities.html. In the building industry: ASHRAE (American Society of Heating, Refrigerating and Air-Conditioning Engineers), IDEC (Interior Design Educators Council), ASID (American Society of Interior Designers), IIDA (International Interior Design Association), USGBC (United States Green Building Coalition), NCIDQ (National Council for Interior Design Qualification), CIDA (Council for Interior Design Accreditation), and AIA (American Institute of Architects).
17. The Sustainable Campus Information Center (http:www.sustainablecampus.org/universities.html) lists the following institutions (that are known to have programs of interior design) as participating in sustainability events and developing policies that embrace sustainability at the campus level: Arizona State University, Cornell University, Florida State University, Michigan State, University of Florida, University of Kentucky, University of Michigan, University of North Carolina, and Washington State University.
18. As quoted in Babcock. (August 2005).
19. Shendell, D., Prill, R., & Fisk, M., et al. (2004). Associations between Classroom CO_2 Concentrations and Student Attendance in Washington and Idaho. *Indoor Air 14*(5): 333–341.
20. Bowman, E. & Enmarker, I. (2004). Noise Annoyance Affects Learning. *Environment and Behavior (36)2*: 207–228.
21. Milanese, S. & Grimmer, K. (2004). School Furniture and the User Population: An Anthropometric Perspective. *Ergonomics 47*(4): 416–426.
22. As instructors, we have watched as significantly obese learners have attempted to use provided tablet-armed lecture desks. This is not only clearly uncomfortable, but serves to point out the comparisons of their body girth to others which must be similarly disquieting. Some institutions mandate "accessible" desks with a traditional chair and 2' × 6' table surface which can be helpful, though less so if a wheelchair-assisted learner is using it.
23. As quoted in Babcock. (August 2005).
24. Ibid.
25. Joint Information Systems Committee e-Learning and Innovation Team. (2006).
26. A. Kenneth Roos is a principal of Einhorn Yaffee Prescott, Architecture & Engineering, P.C. Day, A., ed. Forecasting Higher Education's Future. *College Planning and Management* 7(1): 10–12, 14–16. Retrieved 6/30/07 from http://www.peterli.com/archive/cpm/580.shtm.
27. Nasar, J., Preiser, W. & Fisher, T. (2007). *Designing for Designers: Lessons Learned from Schools of Architecture*. New York: Fairchild.
28. Nasar, J., Sanoff, H. & Perkins, N. (2007). The Architecture of Architecture Schools. A presentation at the 2007 National Conference of the Environmental Design and Research Association, Sacramento, California.
29. Nasar, Jack, Sanoff, Henry, & Perkins, Nate, et al. (2007). The Architecture of Architecture Schools. A presentation at the 2007 National Conference of the Environmental De-

sign and Research Association, Sacramento, California.
30. Rashid, M. (2007). Physical Design of University Classrooms & Learning Outcomes: A Quasi-Experiment. A presentation at the 2007 National Conference of the Environmental Design and Research Association, Sacramento, California.
31. For more information see "Reforming Engineering Education: The CDIO™ Initiative." *Aero|Astro MIT Department of Aeronautics and Astronautics.* Retrieved 7/3/07 from http://web.mit.edu/aeroastro/academics/cdio.html.
32. Joint Information Systems Committee e-Learning and Innovation Team. (2006).
33. Ibid.
34. Ibid.
35. Duncan, S. (2007). UT Collections. A press release for The University Co-op Materials Resource Center at the University of Texas Austin.
36. Nair, P. (January 2003), p. 1.

GLOSSARY

Not wishing to appear foolish, Simone immediately went to her office following the faculty meeting to look up the definition of the word pedagogy. *She had never come across this term, and faculty at the meeting were speaking as though it had some important (and common-knowledge) meaning to the courses being discussed.*

As with most fields, terms considered common language to those deeply immersed in a specialized field may be perplexing to others. Interior design education is no exception. While purely design-oriented terms are universal among educators and practitioners, a distinct language sometimes appears within the educational realm. Often this is due to the foundational concepts shared with other academic fields and the need to communicate effectively across disciplinary boundaries.

Here we present and define many of the common terms used by design educators and introduced throughout the book.

Absolute grading Holds learner performance up to an unchanging objective "yardstick" of achievement level. This often means awarding points for performance on course requirements. Relative grading is another, different approach to grading.

Adjunct faculty Faculty hired on a temporary basis—typically to teach courses, sometimes to engage in specific scholarship or creative work and service assignments. Adjunct faculty are sometimes appointed for one course and at other times for an entire academic term.

Andragogy A theory developed by Malcolm Knowles that describes how adults learn. Often the term is used to describe learning in general for college and other adult students. When teaching using a paradigm of andragogy, the instructor's role is to facilitate learning. This is based on learner-centered approach and often uses an approach of scaffolding to provide more support in the early stages of a course, gradually removing that support as students become increasingly more self-reliant.

Associates Degree Typically a two-year degree, an Associates Degree prepares graduates with training to directly enter an occupational field or, if designed as a transfer course of studies, to replace the first two years of a four-year degree. Associates Degrees are usually conferred by community colleges or junior colleges, which may be private or public institutions.

Asynchronous This form of course delivery is found most often with distance education; it accomodates differing time zones and learner schedules and recognizes that learners may process information at differing rates. Learning activities are designed to be completed when learners are not necessarily online at the same time. Threaded discussion boards are one example of an asynchronous learning activity.

Baby Boomer Persons who were born between 1943 and 1960. This age group includes the parents of the Millenial generation.

Baccalaureate Degree An academic degree conferred by a college or university upon those successfully completing a program of undergraduate studies. Sometimes referred to as a Bachelors Degree. In most colleges and universities, this traditional degree occurs over a period of four years.

Bachelors Degree An academic degree conferred by a college or university upon those successfully completing a program of undergraduate studies. Sometimes referred to as a Baccalaureate Degree. In most colleges and universities, this traditional degree occurs over a period of four years.

Bell curve This form of relative grading assumes an average for the class based on the location of the mean score. The bell curve is a symmetrical curve representing the normal distribution. Using a bell curve (this is often simply referred to as "curving" a grade) forces the evaluation of students into a bell-shaped distribution where the bulk of students receive a "C". Other grades are distributed based on a standard deviation from the mean score.

Blackboard An online learning software. The software serves as a communication interface between instructors and learners and also between learners. The software possesses features including email, realtime chat, group communication, grading, and anonymous survey administration. Learners can upload digital assignments to instructors, and instructors can make digital resources available to learners. Blackboard and WebCT merged in 2005; the product is now called WebCT (http://www.WebCT.com).

Bloom's taxonomy Bloom suggested (in 1956) a hierarchical system of ordering thinking skills from lower to higher, with the higher levels including all of the cognitive skills from the lower levels. The taxonomy contains six levels: knowledge, comprehension, application, analysis, synthesis, and evaluation. This framework provides a common structure for learning and the measurement of that learning (i.e., examinations).

CIDA An acronym for Council for Interior Design Accreditation, the official change of name for the Foundation for Interior Design Education and Rearch (FIDER) effective January 2006. This organization facilitates reviews of undergraduate and first professional graduate degree programs that lead to an accredited status. More than 150 programs are currently accredited.

Cognitive (learning) Cognitive learning style refers to the manner in which learners receive, store, retrieve, transform, and transmit information. It reflects the ways people think about and process information—for example, as right-brained, global thinkers or left-brained, analytical thinkers.

Cold desk A learner workspace within an institution's facility that is dedicated to and used by a single learner for a described period of time. For example, an institution may provide cold desks for all interior design juniors for an academic year. Conversely, hot desks are used by learners only during the time of a class meeting and are then surrendered to another learner when the next class begins.[1]

College Depending on the context, college may refer to an institution of higher learning that grants the bachelor's degree; an undergraduate division or school of a university offering courses and granting degrees in a particular field; a school (sometimes, but not always, a university) offering special instruction in professional or technical subjects; or the students, faculty, and administration of such a school or institution.[2]

Copyright and fair use laws The "ownership" of intellectual property contained in an original work, regardless of whether the work is published on paper, on the Internet, or on a video or movie format. Instructors who access such materials must be familiar with and abide by laws that govern how they can be made available to learners. The full text of the TEACH Act can be viewed at www.copyright.gov/legislation/pl107-273.html#13301. A helpful summary of the TEACH Act is available at learningforlife.fsu.edu/ctl/explore/bestPractices/docs/TEACHAct.pdf.

Course materials Books, online content, and other sources for information that supplement and support class goals and objectives.

Curricular map An effective tool to develop, examine, alter, and communicate the building of knowledge and experiences throughout a program of study leading to the successful completion of a degree; sometimes referred to as a "flow chart." Curricular maps are utilized among faculty and administrators to develop a course of study, to trace construction of learning in a particular track of knowledge, and to communicate to learners the path of learning they are on.

Curriculum A group of courses intentionally selected to relate to each other in pursuit of identified goals. Higher education institutions often have a dedicated curriculum, or collection of courses, that define their undergraduate and/or graduate degree programs.

Curriculum vitae (CV) or Vita A document that describes one's educational background, teaching experience, and other skills. A vita (singular) is also called a "CV" or vitae. It is usually longer than a resume and is often required as a part of a university teaching or research position application package and when applying for tenure or promotion.[3]

Desk copy A free copy of a course text provided to instructors at no charge. Desk copies are usually provided by publishers if the instructor verifies they have adopted the text for their learners' use and that the learners must purchase the resource.

Desk critique or desk crit Desktop critiques most often occur during studio classes, where the instructor is moving from desk to desk to discuss with each student some aspect of their progress or project. Desktop critiques are less threatening to the student than pinup critiques. Participants in desktop critiques are often only the instructor and affected student; however, some "official" critiques may also occur in this manner. At the end of a design development phase of a design project, for example, students may be instructed to arrange all of the appropriate descriptive drawings, materials, and manufacturers' literature on their desktop for a crit involving the instructor, other students, and invited guest critics.

Evaluation copy A free copy of a course text provided to instructors at no charge. An evaluation copy is provided to an instructor so they can review its contents for possible adoption for a course. Sometimes publishers will bill an instructor for the cost of an evaluation copy unless the text is actually adopted.

Experiential learning A learning strategy that engages students in hands-on "learning by doing" activities. Design-build courses, for example, can involve learners in constructing a house. Experiential learning can also engage students in specialized activities, such as serving as crew on a boat voyage as a means to learning yacht design.

FIDER An acronym for the Foundation for Interior Design Education Research, a non-profit organization that develops standards for interior design education for colleges and universities in the United States and Canada.[4] Programs of interior design that submit to the accreditation review process undertake self-assessment and submit to peer review. The organization's name was changed in 2006 to the Council for Interior Design Accreditation. Nearly 150 programs are accredited as of August 2007.

Formative assessment Formative assessment is designed to provide feedback and information for the purpose of learning, developing, and improving. The feedback from a formative assessment is not so much a formal grade as a monitoring of learning progress, and it refers to the process of generating and providing information to students about their performance with the specific purpose of helping them to improve. Feedback is an important element in formative assessment. Strictly speaking, formative assessment is designed to facilitate academic learning and growth while opportunity still exists for development to occur.

Full-time equivalent (FTE) A system to measure student enrollment. Colleges and universities vary in the number assigned to a full-time student. FTEs can also be used to measure the activities of an educator such as teaching and research.

Full-time faculty Faculty engaged in the full-time (often defined as more than 32 hours per week) pursuit of delivering education and associated activities at an institution of higher learning. Full-time status is not correlated with a particular "rank"; the positions of instructor, lecturer, assistant professor, associate professor, and full professor may each be filled by full-time faculty members.

Full-time student A student taking the standard amount of courses in a quarter or semester. Most curricula compute the total number of semesters to complete a degree assuming that a student will maintain a full-time pace of course completion.

Generation X The cohort of individuals born between 1961 and 1981.

Grading rubric A matrix often used for assessment or feedback. In most rubrics, the text on the left vertical of the matrix are descriptions of attributes or tasks, the top horizontal contains a descriptor of performance, and each resulting rectangle in the matrix contains a detailed description of the qualities that lead to a particular letter or numerical grade. Grading rubrics are helpful in maintaining a standard when multiple sections of a particular course are taught by more than one instructor.

Hot desk Learner workspace provided by an institution for use only during the time of a class meeting; the workspace is then surrendered to another learner when the next class begins. Conversely, a cold desk may be assigned to a learner for their exclusive use for an entire year.

IDCEC The Interior Design Continuing Education Council (IDCEC) promotes lifelong learning and professional development for the interior design profession by serving as central entity for the sharing of CE information, approval, and registration; it also provides strategic planning for CE programming and activity.[5]

IDEC An acronym for Interior Design Educators Council, founded in 1963 and "dedicated to the advancement of education and research in interior design. IDEC fosters exchange of information, improvement of educational standards, and development of the body of knowledge relative to the quality of life and human performance in the interior environment." IDEC members are interior design educators, practitioners, researchers, scholars, graduate students, and administrators in institutions of higher education. Membership is also offered to individuals who are interested in interior design education and the activities of IDEC.[6]

Instructional strategy An approach to providing learning activities that result in successful knowledge building in learners. Instructional strategies may include (among others) lectures, specific assignments, examinations, and critique methods.

Instructor Term used to describe a person whose occupation is teaching or who imparts knowledge to a learner or facilitates learning activities. The term additionally refers to a specific employment rank at some institutions: a rank below assistant professor that does not lead to tenure.

Interdisciplinary Communication and/or collaboration amongst several disciplines. Interdisciplinary projects are an increasingly popular strategy in interior design education, pairing interior design students with students from other career areas such as architecture, communication, English, nursing, and many other fields.

Journal of Interior Design (JID) A refereed scholarly publication dedicated to issues concerning the design of the interior environment.

Learning objectives Learning objectives describe a desired outcome of learning and are described in terms of knowledge, skill, or attitude. Effective learning objectives are specific and measurable. Learning objectives are an important component of the course objective section of a syllabus.

Learning strategies An instructor tactic for successfully imparting knowledge to learners. There are numerous learning strategies. Seven of the most common strategies are lecture, discussion, team learning, seminar, case study, role playing/simulation, and narrative/drama.

Learning styles Each person learns slightly differently, and several theories exist to define specific styles of learning. Learning styles identify the way learners ingest and process information and then apply it to situations.

Measurable outcomes Outcomes illustrating that learning objectives have been met; they are described in terms of specific, observable, and measurable behaviors or products.

Millennial generation Cohort of individuals born between 1982 and 2002.

Multiple intelligences A theory developed by Howard Gardner in 1983 recognizing that people have aptitudes for learning in areas not measured by standard IQ tests. The original seven intelligences (body/kinesthetic, interpersonal, intra-personal, logical/mathematical, musical/rhythmic, verbal/linguistic, and visual/spatial) have been subsequently expanded to at least eight (to include naturalistic).

Non-traditional student A student who diverges from the typical track of entering a higher education institution directly after completing high school. Non-traditional students are chronologically older than traditional students.

Part-time faculty Faculty member who teaches a reduced load of courses. Typically, a part-time faculty member is not tenured, though other employment protections may exist. Also sometimes called an adjunct faculty member or adjunct instructor.

Part-time student A student taking less than the traditional 12-hour course load in a semester. Standards for a "traditional course load" vary by institution.

Pedagogy The art and science of teaching others. The term is often used in the academic world to describe teaching approaches in courses. The paradigm of pedagogy is typically teacher-centered and concentrates on techniques of imparting knowledge to students.

Performance objectives Definition of a specific outcome that must be achieved in order to successfully accomplish a task or course. Performance objectives are statements of particular elements of knowledge or of a particular skill or attitude that a learner should display as a result of the learning activity. A set of performance objectives is typically included in the course objectives portion of a syllabus to describe desired outcomes of a course. Particular performance objectives may be included on assignments or project descriptions to assist students in focusing their learning.

Pinup critique or crit A learning activity in which each student displays their work on a project or assignment on a vertical surface (often a pinnable surface) and proceeds to describe their work verbally. Attendees (often this will be the professor, other students, and any invited critics) typically make comments to the presenting student or ask questions that either lead the presenting student to critical observations of their own work or aid in the critics' understanding of what is shown. Often the pinup critique may be referred to as a "jury," but sometimes it is handled much as a poster session at a conference.

Prep time "Preparation time" is the time required for preparing to teach a session of a course. This time requirement varies by course, instructor experience, and familiarity with the course content. On average, three hours of preparation time are necessary for one hour of instruction the first time a new class is taught.

Relative grading A system and philosophy of grading that adjusts individual grades to reflect the group's performance. Relative grading is often called "grading on a curve" and is contrasted with the alternative approach of absolute grading.

Research I institution A university category created by the Carnegie Foundation for the Advancement of Teaching to designate those institutions that award at least twenty doctoral degrees per year (excluding doctoral-level degrees that qualify recipients for entry into professional practice). In 2006, the designations of Research I & II, Doctoral I & II, and Doctoral/Research—Extensive/Intensive were changed to RU/VH: Research Universities (very high research activity), RU/H: Research Universities (high research activity) and DRU: Doctoral/Research Universities.[7]

Research and creative scholarship Although requirements vary at each institution, examples of research and creative scholarship include general traditional research studies, grants and the dissemination of results, writing published in scholarly (refereed or peer-reviewed) journals, and creative projects gaining recognition through awards.

Reserve reading A technique for making content available to learners. Often used for resources that are difficult to replicate for large quantities of learners. Institution libraries often have reserve reading procedures that permit learners to access real or digital copies of works in a controlled fashion.

Rubric A helpful reference tool providing a comparative performance benchmark for learners that equates test and project performance to a letter grade and grade point average. The four-point grading scale (4 points for an A to 1 point for a D) is widely accepted in higher education. Some instructors like to provide a description of "what an A looks like" that goes beyond stated university standards for such a grade (*see* Grading rubric).

Schedule or course schedule A document given to learners that describes the course dates for activities, critiques, exams and/or project due dates. Schedules often list the topics to be addressed in lecture or lab or the general daily activity (field trip, guest speaker, presentations, etc.). Some educators provide an expanded outline indicating sources to be read and assignments to be completed on particular days.

Schema-based learning system A strategy where knowledge is chunked together and scaffolded to achieve higher levels of learning.

Summative assessment Summative assessments certify level of achievement and are what instructors typically think of as "grading." In a summative assessment, the instructor is assessing the extent and quality of student performance based on expectations for knowledge and skills. The overall assessment is often subdivided to provide evaluation of particular criteria deemed important to achieve the goals and objectives established for the assignment, exam, project, or overall course.

Syllabus An orienting document made available to learners at the beginning of the semester that represents an understanding of course intent and methods between the instructor and the learners. Typically, it contains instructor contact information, an overview of the course goals and objectives, and a description of how learners will be assessed for a course grade. Syllabi can also explain project details and department policies.

Synchronous Interaction between instructor and learner at the same time, whether in an online or face-to-face setting.

Teaching evaluation An instrument often used by an institution to document teaching performance and effectiveness for merit, tenure, or promotion purposes. Many institutions require that learners perform a teaching evaluation by answering a series of questions at or near semester's end to assess instructor success.

Teaching load The total number of courses an instructor teaches or facilitates during a single quarter or semester. Standards vary by institution. A "3/2" load means that the instructor teaches three courses in the fall semester and 2 courses in the spring semester.

Teaching philosophy A statement written by an instructor that identifies his or her personal values and priorities for teaching. Some institutions require a teaching philosophy statement as a component of an application for a teaching position.

Teaching portfolio This showcase document contains examples of materials used in particular classes and developed by the instructor to teach a course; it also contains a philosophy of teaching, critical writing regarding the effectiveness of the materials, and examples of student product in the course. A teaching portfolio may be used during the promotion or tenure process to determine an individual's growth in effective teaching, but it is just as important as a self-reflective tool for improvement.

Tenure-seeking or tenure-track Refers to a job position at a tenure-granting university or college. Typically, a person in a tenure-seeking or tenure-track position is at the rank of assistant professor, although rank and tenure are not directly related.

Terminal degree A post-secondary degree considered by the academic community to be sufficient for an academic teaching and/or research position. A Master of Fine Arts (MFA) degree is considered by most institutions to be a terminal degree. Other institutions may require a Ed.D. or Ph.D. as a minimum qualification.

Traditional student A student who enters a higher education institution directly after completing high school.

Transformational (or transformative) learning Learning strategies that provide students the opportunity to become aware of their assumptions and how those assumptions may limit their conclusions and actions. A transformed learner is emancipated from previous assumptions; he or she is empowered to embrace a more inclusive and integrated perspective and to engage in actions that put this new understanding into play.[8]

WebCT WebCT is a registered proprietary e-learning product that many universities use. WebCT and Blackboard are the most widely used web tools that provide learning opportunities through the Internet. Information for classes is maintained by instructors, and collaboration and communication are possible through digital means. Blackboard and WebCT merged in 2005; the product is now called WebCT (http://www.WebCT.com).

ENDNOTES

1. Adapted from Merriam, S. B. & Caffarella, R. S. (1991). *Learning in Adulthood.* San Francisco: Jossey-Bass, p. 159.
2. Adapted from *The American Heritage Dictionary of the English Language*, 4th ed. (2003). Boston: Houghton Mifflin.
3. McKay, D. Curriculum Vitae. Retrieved 7/28/07 from About.com: Career Planning at http://careerplanning.about.com/od/resumewriting/g/def_vitae.htm.
4. Council for Interior Design Accreditation. Retrieved 7/25/07 from http://www.accredit-id.org/history.html accessed 8/28/07.
5. Interior Design Continuing Education Council. Retrieved 8/28/07 from http://idcec.org.
6. Interior Design Educators Council. Retrieved 8/28/07 from http://www.idec.org.
7. The Carnegie Foundation for the Advancement of Teaching. (2006). Basic Classification Description. Retrieved 7/28/07 from http://www.carnegiefoundation.org/classifications/index.asp?key=791.
8. Cranton, P. (1994). *Understanding and Promoting Transformative Learning: A Guide for Educators of Adults.* San Francisco: Jossey-Bass, p. 92.

REFERENCES

Chapter 1: The Importance of Interior Design Teaching and Learning

Buchanan, R. (December 2000). *Design and the Organization of Learning.* Keynote address at the Re-Inventing Design Education in the University Conference. Perth, Western Australia.

Design Intelligence. (December 13, 2006). America's Best Architecture & Design Schools. Available at http://www.di.net/article.php.

Dinot, C. (December 2000). Looking for Design in the Twenty-First Century University. Keynote address at the Re-Inventing Design Education in the University Conference. Perth, Western Australia.

Jackson, B. (December 2000). Supra-Design: Transforming Design Education for the Age of Lifelong Learning. Presentation at the Re-Inventing Design Education in the University Conference. Perth, Western Australia.

Chapter 2: The Nature of Interior Design Education

Note: Information regarding characteristics of the "Silent Generation" retrieved 5/17/07 from http://library.thinkquest.org/23440/silent.html.

Anderson, D., Honey, P. & Dudek, M. (2007). Interior Design's Social Compact: The Missing Aspect of Our Quest for Professional Legitimacy. In proceedings of the International Interior Design Educator's Council Conference*: Design and Social Justice.* Austin, TX, 91–98.

Anderson, James (March 2000). Tailoring Assessment to Student Learning Styles. In *Assessment to Promote Deep Learning. AAHE Bulletin.* Available at http://aahebulletin.com/public/archive/styles.asp.

Benjamin, E. (1998). Declining Faculty Availability to Students Is the Problem—But Tenure Is Not the Explanation. *American Behavioral Scientist 14*: 716–735.

Blackburn, R. & Lawrence, J. (1997). Faculty Research. In Philip Altbach, ed., *Contemporary Higher Education: International Issues for the Twenty-First Century.* New York: Garland.

Bloom, B. S., et al. (1956). *Taxonomy of Educational Objectives Handbook 1: Cognitive Domain*, London: Longman Group Ltd.

Board of Regents of the University of Wisconsin System. (2006). Academic Programs and Resources. University of Wisconsin-Madison. Retrieved 8/28/07 from http://www.wisc.edu/about/facts/acprograms.php.

Bowles, M. (2007). *Design:* The Next Generation. *IIDA Perspective* (Winter): 26–31.

Brooks, D. (2007). Integrated Learning Theory: Applications in Teaching. Available at dwb4.unl.edu/dwb/Research/TheoryPaper/CompTh.html.

Brunner, L. (2006). Are There Lasting Effects of a Schema-based Learning System in the Interior Design Studio? *Proceedings of the 2006 International Interior Design Educators Council.* Scottsdale, AZ.

Carnegie Foundation for the Advancement of Teaching. (1989). *The Condition of the Professoriate: Attitudes and Trends, 1989.* Princeton, NJ: Carnegie Foundation for the Advancement of Teaching.

Carnevale, A. P. & Fry, R. A. (2000). *Crossing the Great Divide: Can We Achieve Equity When Generation Y Goes to College?* Princeton, NJ: Educational Testing Services.

Carroll, S. (January 18, 2007). Teaching Excellence Series: Enhancing Interaction. Seminar at Florida State University, Tallahassee, FL.

Chickering, A. W. & Gamson, Z. F. (1987). Seven Principles for Good Practice in Undergraduate Education. *AAHE Bulletin 39*(7): 3–7.

Coleman, C. & Sosnowchik, K. (September 2006). *Interior Design Trends and Implications.* Grand Rapids, MI: Council for Interior Design Accreditation.

DeBard, R. (2004). Millennials Coming to College. *New Directions for Student Services* (106): 33–45.

Donovan, J. (2003). Changing Demographics and Generational Shifts: Understanding and Working with the Families of Today's College Students. Retrieved 6/23/07 from http://www.colostate.edu/Depts/SAHE/JOURNAL2/2003/Donovan.htm.

Fisher, J. & Miller, S. (January 2000). From Here to 2010. *College Planning and Management, 3*(1). Retrieved 7/1/07 from http://www.peterli.com/archive/cpm/35.shtm.

Gardner, H. (1993). *Frames of Mind: The Theory of Multiple Intelligences,* New York: Basic Books.

Gibney, F. & Luscombe, B. (March 20, 2000). The Redesigning of America. *Time.* Retrieved 7/1/07 from http://www.time.com/time/magazine/article/0,9171,996372,00.html.

Gohn, L. A. & Albin, G. R., eds. (2006). *Understanding College Student Subpopulations.* National Association of Student Personnel Administrators. (NASPA).

Hall, D. (2002). *The Academic Self: An Owner's Manual.* Columbus, OH: The Ohio State University Press, pp. xii–xiii.

Hansen, E. J. (November 1998). Essential Demographics of Today's College Students. *AAHE-Bulletin.* Teaching Ideas #8. Retrieved 4/3/07 from www.Emporia.edu/tec/tchid08.html.

Hodgins, W. & Conner, M. (Fall 2000). "Everything You Ever Wanted to Know about Learning Standards but Were Afraid to Ask." *Learning in the New Economy e-Magazine (LiNE Zine).* Retrieved 06/09/07 from www.linezine.com/2.1/features/wheyewtkls.htm.

Howe, N., & Strauss, W. (2000). *Millennials Rising: The Next Great Generation.* New York: Vintage Books, pp. 43–44.

Interior Design Educators Council. (2006). *Defining Graduate Education in Interior Design.* White paper produced by the IDEC Graduate Education Committee. Available at www.idec.org.

Johnson, H. E. & Schelhas-Miller, C. (2000). Don't Tell Me What to Do, Just Send

Money: The Essential Parenting Guide to the College Years. New York: St Martin's Griffin.

Kalwarski, T., et al. (April 25, 2006). 50 Best Jobs in America. *Money Magazine*. Retrieved 6/30/07 from http://money.cnn.com/magazines/moneymag/moneymag_archive/2006/05/01/8375749/index.htm.

Kellogg, C. (January 2006). Learning from Studio. *DesignIntelligence 4*. 15–16. Mann, T. (2004). *Time Management for Architects and Designers*. New York: Norton.

Kolb, D. A., Boyatzis, R. E. & Mainemelis, C. (2000). Experiential Learning Theory: Previous Research and New Directions. In R. J. Sternberg & L. F. Zhang, eds., *Perspectives on Cognitive, Learning, and Thinking Styles*. Hillsdale, NJ: Lawrence Erlbaum.

Kucko, J. & Gabb, B. (2000). Students Today and Professionals Tomorrow: A Sometimes Challenging Position. *Interiors and Sources* (May): 188–191.

Levine, A. & Cureton, J. S. (1998). What We Know about Today's College Students. *About Campus*, *3*(1): 4–9

McCoy, J., Guerin, D. & Portillo, M. (2006). Who Are We? Beginning Markers of Accredited Interior Design Programs. In the proceedings of the *2006 International Interior Design Educators Conference*. Scottsdale, AZ.

Nair, Prakash. (January 2003). Imperatives for Change in Higher Education. *DesignShare: The International Forum for Innovative Schools*. Retrieved 7/1/07 from http://www.designshare.com/Research/Nair/HigherEd/imperatives.

Niederhelman, M. (Summer 2001). Education Through Design. *Design Issues 17*(3): 83–87.

Oluwasanmi, N. A. (2000). Tuition: Impossible. *Smart Money* (September): 146–154.

Pable, J. (2000). *Sketching Interiors at the Speed of Thought*. NY: Fairchild.

Perlstein, R. (n.d.). What's the Matter with College? *New York Times Online*. Retrieved 7/20/07 from http://nytimes.com/marketing/collegeessay/essay.html.

Richardson, J. (Winter 1999). Tenure in the New Millennium: Still a Valuable Concept. *National Forum, The Phi Kappa Phi Journal 79*(1): 19–24.

Rittel, H. & Webber, M. (1973). Dilemmas in a General Theory of Planning. *Policy Sciences*, *4*(2): 155–169.

Scott, B. R. & Daniel, B. V. (2001). Why Parents of Undergraduates Matter to Higher Education. In B. V. Daniel & B. R. Scott, Eds., Consumers, Adversaries and Partners: Working with the Families of Undergraduates. *New Directions for Student Services*, no. 94. San Francisco: Jossey-Bass, 83–89.

Shell, Duane F. & Brooks, David W. (2007). The Unified Learning Model: Implications for Learning and Teaching. A working paper.

Snyder, D. (January/February 2006). Big Change on Campus. *Facilities Manager*. Retrieved 6/30/07 from http://www.appa.org/FacilitiesManager/article.cfm?ItemNumber=2550&parentid=2540.

University of Wisconsin: Academic Programs and Resources. Retrieved 6/24/07 from www.wisc.edu/about/facts/acprograms.php. Van der Ryn, S. (2005). *Design for Life*. Layton, UT: Gibbs Smith.

Wallis, C. & Steptoe, S. (December 18, 2006). How to Bring our Schools Out of the 20th Century. *Time*. Retrieved 8/28/07 from http://www.time.com/time/magazine/article/0,9171,1568480,00.html.

Waxman, L. & Clemons, S. (2007). Student Perceptions: Debunking Television's Portrayal of Interior Design. *Journal of Interior Design 32*(2): v–ix.

Zemke, Ron, Raines, Claire & Filipczak, Bob. (2000). *Generations at Work : Managing the Clash of Veterans, Boomers, Xers, and Nexters in Your Workplace.* New York: AMACOM.

Chapter 3: Course Preparation

Alvermann, D. (1986). Graphic Organizers: Cueing Devices for Comprehending and Remembering Main Ideas. In J. F. Baumann, ed., *Teaching Main Idea Comprehension.* Newark, DE: International Reading Association, 210–255.

Anderson, T. & Armbruster, B. (1984). Content Area Textbooks. In R. C. Anderson, J. Osborn, Y. & R. J. Tierney, eds., *Learning to Read in American Schools: Basal Readers and Content Texts.* Hillsdale, NJ: Erlbaum, 193–226.

Bloom, B. S., et al. (1956). *Taxonomy of Educational Objectives Handbook 1: Cognitive Domain.* London: Longman Group.

Designing a Learner-Centered Syllabus. (n.d.). University of Delaware. Retrieved 3/2/07 from http://cte.udel.edu/syllabus.htm.

Drawbaugh, C. (1984). *Time and Its Use: A Self-Management Guide for Teachers.* New York: Teachers College Press.

Filene, P. (2005). *The Joy of Teaching.* Chapel Hill, NC: University of North Carolina Press.

Goldhaber, M. (April 7, 1997). The Attention Economy and the Net. *First Monday: Peer Reviewed Journal on the Internet* 2(4). Retrieved 7/30/07 from http://www.firstmonday.dk/issues/issue2_4/goldhaber/.

Grunert, Judith. (1997). *The Course Syllabus: A Learning-Centered Approach.* Bolton, MA: Anker Publishing Company.

Heinich, R., Molenda, M., Russell, J., Smaldino, S. (2002). *Instructional Media and Technologies for Learning,* 7th ed. Englewood Cliffs, NJ: Prentice Hall.

Hinrichsen, B., et al. (April 1–5, 2002). *A Study of Faculty Workload as a Means of Improving the Student Learning Environment.* Paper presented at the Annual Meeting of the American Educational Research Association, New Orleans, LA.

How to Write Objectives and Outcomes. Retrieved 4/12/07 from www.assessment.uconn.edu/docs/HowToWriteObjectivesOutcomes.pdf.

Indiana State University's *Instructional Design and Teaching Styles* Reference Guide.

Information and Library Services. (2007). Copyright and Fair Use in the Classroom, on the Internet, and the World Wide Web. University of Maryland University College. Retrieved 7/19/07 from http://www.umuc.edu/library/copy.shtml#teacher.

Lorch, R. (1989). Text-signaling Devices and Their Effects on Reading and Memory Processes. *Educational Psychology Review* 1: 209–234.

Mann, T. (2004). *Time Management for Architects and Designers.* NY: Norton.

Mayer, R. (1985). Structural Analysis of Science Prose: Can We Increase Problem-solving Performance? In B. Britton & J. Black (eds.), *Understanding Expository Prose.* Hillsdale, NJ: Erlbaum, 65–87.

McKeatchie, W. (1986). *Teaching Tips: A Guidebook for the Beginning College Teacher.* Lexington, MA: Heath.

Ramsden, P. (1984). The Context of Learning. In F. Marton, D. Hounsell & N. Entwistle, eds, *The Experience of Learning.* Edinburgh: Scottish Academic Press.

Robinson, D. (1994). Textbook Selection: Watch Out for "Inconsiderate" Texts. In K. Pritchard & R. Sawyer, eds. *Handbook of College Teaching.* Westport, CN: Greenwood Press, 415–422.

Wachter, J. & Carhart, C. (2003). *Timesaving Tips for Teachers,* 2nd ed.. Thousand Oaks, CA: Corwin Press.

Webb, J. (2000). Virtual Textbooks: Creating a Specialized Text for Interior Design Courses. *Proceedings of the 2000 International Interior Design Educators Conference.* Calgary, Alberta, Canada.

Woolcock, M. (2007). *Constructing a Syllabus.* The Harriet W. Sheraton Center for Teaching and Learning, Brown University. Retrieved 3/2/2007 from http://www.brown.edu/Administration/Sheridan_Center/publications/syllabus.html.

Chapter 4: Managing and Guiding Learning

Amor, C. & Wilson, J. (March 2004). Collaboration Studio: Correlation between Design Outcome and Personality Types. In the proceedings of the 2004 International Interior Design Educator's Conference: *IDEC Taking the Lead.* Pittsburgh, PA.

Anderson, B., et al. (March 2004). Strategies for Implementing Group Work and Teaming in Interior Design Education. In the proceedings of the *2004 International Interior Design Educators Conference.* Pittsburgh, PA.

American Psychological Association. (n.d.). Using the New Bloom's Taxonomy to Design Meaningful Learning Assessments. In *APA Online Applying Assessment Strategies in Psychology.* Retrieved 7/9/07 from http://www.apa.org/ed/new_blooms.html

Bosworth, K., et al. (n.d.) What Is Your Classroom Management Profile? From *Teacher Talk.* Retrieved 7/9/07 from http://education.indiana.edu/cas/tt/v1i2/what.html.

Bowman, D., et al. (1999). The Educational Value of an Information-Rich Virtual Environment. *Presence 8*(3): 317–331.

Bruner, J. (1985). Narrative and Paradigmatic Modes of Thought. In Eisner, E., ed. *Learning and Teaching the Ways of Knowing.* Chicago: Chicago: University of Chicago Press.

Carroll, S. (January 18, 2007). Teaching Excellence Series: Enhancing Interaction. Seminar at Florida State University, Tallahassee, FL.

Chickering, A., ed. *The Modern American College.* San Francisco: Jossey-Bass.

Christensen, C. (1987). *Teaching and the Case Method.* Boston: Harvard Business School.

Cooke, S. (2007). The Care of Making—Towards a Theory of Design Benevolence. *Proceedings of the 2007 Hawaii International Conference on the Arts & Humanities.* Honolulu, HI, 44.

Council for Interior Design Accreditation. (2006). *Professional Standards.* Grand Rapids, MI: Council for Interior Design Accreditation.

Creed, T. (1993). The Seven Principles . . . Not! *American Association for Higher Education Bulletin 45*(7): 78–80.

Danko, S., Meneely, J. & Portillo, M. (2006). Humanizing Design through Narrative Inquiry. *Journal of Interior Design 31*(2). Retrieved 3/28/07 from http://www.idec.org/publication/JID31.2.pdf.

Davidson, C. & Ambrose, S. (1995). Leading Discussions Effectively. *The Teaching Professor*, *9*(6): 8.

Davis, J. (1993). *Better Teaching, More Learning.* Phoenix, AZ: Oryx.

Denton, H. (1997). Multidisciplinary Team-based Project Work: Planning Factors. *Design Studies*, *18*(2): 158.

Dunkin, M. & Barnes, J. (1986). Research on Teaching in Higher Education. In M. Wittrock, ed., *Handbook on Research on Teaching*, 3rd ed. New York: Macmillan, 754–777.

Ekeler, W. (1994). The Lecture Method. In K. Pritchard & R. Sawyer, eds. *Handbook of College Teaching: Theory and Applications.* Westport, CT: Greenwood Press.

Fiechtner, S. & Davis, E. (1985). Why Groups Fail: A Survey of Student Experiences with Learning Groups. *The Organizational Behavior Teaching Review 9*(4): 58–73.

Filene, P. (2005). *The Joy of Teaching.* Chapel Hill, NC: University of North Carolina Press.

Frederick, P. (1994). Classroom Discussions. In K. Pritchard & R. Sawyer, eds. *Handbook of College Teaching: Theory and Applications.* Westport, CT: Greenwood Press.

Gale, R. (2006). The "Magic" of Learning from Each Other. The Carnegie Foundation for the Advancement of Teaching. Retrieved 7/22/07 from http://www.carnegiefoundation.org/perspectives/.

Gardner, H. (1993). *Frames of Mind: The Theory of Multiple Intelligences,* 10th anniversary ed. New York: Basic Books.

Groat, L. & Wang, D. (2002). *Architectural Research Methods.* New York: Wiley.

Hackman, J. (1983). A Normative Model of Work Team Effectiveness. Technical Report no. 2. Research Project on Group Effectiveness. Office of Naval Research Code 442, Yale School of Organizational Management.

King, A. (1993). From Sage on the Stage to Guide on the Side. *College Teaching 41*(1): 30–35.

Kleiner, C. & Lord, M. (November 2, 1999). The Cheating Game: "Everyone's Doing It," from Grade School to Graduate School. *U.S. News & World Report,* 55–66.

Lawson, B. (1997). *How Designers Think.* New York: Architectural Press.

Linton, H. (2003). *Portfolio Design,* 3rd ed. New York: Norton.

Lupton, R., Chapman, K. & Weiss, J. A Cross-National Exploration of Business Students' Attitudes, Perceptions, and Tendencies Toward Academic Dishonesty. *Journal of Education for Business* 75(4): 231–235.

Lyons, R, Kysilka, M. & Pawlas, G. (1999). *The Adjunct Professor's Guide to Success.* Boston: Allyn & Bacon.

Magnan, R., ed. (1990). *147 Practical Tips for Teaching Professors.* Madison, WI: Atwood Publishing.

Mann, T. (2004). *Time Management for Architects and Designers.* New York: Norton.

Martin, N. & Shoho, A. (January 2000). Teacher Experience, Training and Age: The Influence of Teacher Characteristics on Classroom Management Style. Paper presented at the Annual Meeting of the Southwest Educational Research Association, Dallas, TX.

Martin, N. & Yin, Z. (January 1997). Attitudes and Beliefs Regarding Classroom Management Style: Differences between Male and Female Teachers. Paper presented at the Annual Meeting of the Southwest Educational Research Association, Austin, TX. McCown, R., et al. (1996). *Educational Psychology: A Learning-centered Approach to Classroom Practice,* Canadian ed. Scarborough, ON: Allyn & Bacon.

Master Teacher. (n.d.). You Can Handle Them All: A Reference for Handling over 117 Misbehaviors at School and Work. Retrieved 7/9/07 from http://www.disciplinehelp.com/teacher/list.cfm?cause=All.

McKeatchie, W. (1986). *Teaching Tips: A Guidebook for the Beginning College Teacher.* Lexington, MA: Heath.

McMurtry, K. (November 2001). E-cheating: Combating a 21st Century Challenge. *THE Journal.* Retrieved 3/3/2007 from http://thejournal.com/articles/15675_5.

Michaelsen, L. (1994). Team Learning. In K. Pritchard & R. Sawyer, eds. *Handbook of College Teaching: Theory and Applications.* Westport, CT: Greenwood Press, 150–152.

Miller, N. & Webb, J. (March 2004). Firewalking: Threading Your Way through Team Assessment. *Proceedings of the 2004 International Interior Design Educators Conference.* Pittsburgh, PA.

Miyahara, A. (March 2003). Theory and Practice: The Need for a Discourse in Design Education. *Proceedings of the 2003 International Interior Design Educators Council Conference.* San Diego, CA, 44.

Moore, M. (Winter 1988). Narrative Teaching: An Organic Methodology. *Process Studies, 17*(4): 248–261. Retrieved 4/15/07 from http://www.religion-online.org/showarticle.asp?title=2765.

Pable, J. (April 2002). Giving Back: Student-Generated Product Research for Practitioner Benefit. In the proceedings of the 2002 International Interior Design Educator's Conference: *The Mesas and the Mysteries: On the Edge of Imagination/Green Design.* Santa Fe, NM, 99–100.

Pable, J. (March 2007). 3D Graphics in Design: A Comparison of Educator and Practitioner Attitude, Use and Perceptions of Student Preparedness. In the proceedings of the International Interior Design Educators Council Conference: *Design and Social Justice*, Austin, TX, 273–283.

Park-Gates, S., Marshall-Baker, A., Bowker, J., Cross, L., Germona, J., & Sawyers, J. (April 2002). Effects of Group Interactive Brainstorming on Creativity. In the proceedings of the 2002 International Interior Design Educators Council Conference: *The Mesas and the Mysteries: On the Edge of Imagination/Green Design.* Santa Fe, NM, 46–47.

Ralph, E. (1997). The Power of Using Drama in the Teaching of Second Languages: Some Recollections. *The McGill Journal of Education 32*(3): 273–288.

Ralph, E. (1998). *Motivation Teaching in Higher Education: A Manual for Faculty Development.* Stillwater, OK: New Forums Press.

Rossiter, M. (2003). Narrative and Stories in Adult Teaching and Learning. Ericdigests.org. Retrieved 4/15/07 from http://www.ericdigests.org/2003-4/adult-teaching.html.

Santrock, J. (2005). *Adolescence.* New York: McGraw-Hill.

Tuckman, B. (1965). Developmental Sequence in Small Groups. *Psychological Bulletin 63*(8), 384–399.

University of Washington (n.d.). Faculty Resource on Grading. Retrieved 3/3/07 from http://depts.washington.edu/grading/practices/guidelines.html.

Waxman, L. (2007). Getting Them to Talk. A presentation of the Teaching Tidbits: Successful Teaching Strategies Workshop facilitated by Denise Guerin at the International Interior Design Educators Council Conference, Austin, TX.

Weaver, R., Kowalski, T. & Pfaller, J. (1994). Case-Method Teaching. In K. Pritchard & R. Sawyer, eds. *Handbook of College Teaching: Theory and Applications.* Westport, CT: Greenwood Press.

Woolcock, M. (2007). Constructing a Syllabus. The Harriet W. Sheraton Center for Teaching and Learning. Brown University. Retrieved 3/2/07 from http://www.brown.edu/Administration/Sheridan_Center/publications/syllabus.html.

Yin, R. (2003). Case Study Research. New York: Sage.

Chapter 5: Studio Learning

Awwad-Rafferty, R. (2006). Designing in Two Worlds: Shoshone Bannock Tribes Inspire an Alternative Worldview for Interior Design Studio. *Proceedings of the 2006 International Interior Design Educators Council.* Scottsdale, AZ.

Beecher, Mary Anne. (Spring, 2006). Designing Criticism: Integrating Written Criticism in Interior Design Education. *Journal of Interior Design 33*(3): 54–61.

Bender, D. & Vredevoogd, J. (2006). Using Online Education Technologies to Support Studio Instruction. *Educational Technology & Society 9*(4): 115

Clemons, S., et al. (2007). Infusing Third Place Theory into a Studio Environment: A Qualitative Inquiry. *Proceedings of the 2007 International Interior Design Educators Council.* Austin, Texas.

Ernest L. Boyer, E. & Mitgang, L. (1966). *Building Community: A New Future for Architecture Education and Practice.* Princeton, NJ: Carnegie Foundation.

Kellogg, C. (January 2006). Learning from Studio. *DesignIntelligence 4:* 15–16.

Miller, N., Sattar, H. & Gentry, M. (2006). A Shifting Paradigm: Integrating Critical Thinking with the New Learning Styles of the Millennium Generation. *Proceedings of the 2006 International Interior Design Educators Council.* Scottsdale, AZ.

Ochsner, J. (2000). Behind the Mask: A Psychoanalytic Perspective on Interaction in the Design Studio. *Journal of Architectural Education* (May): 195.

Watson Zollinger, S. & Salmi, P. Re-Thinking Studio Critique: Three New Strategies. *Proceedings of the 2006 International Interior Design Educators Council.* Scottsdale, AZ, March 28–April 2.

Chapter 6: Teaching and Learning at a Distance

Academic Media Services. Washington State University. Retrieved 5/24/07 from whets.wsu.edu.

Bacon, P. & Bagwell, D., Jr. (2005). *Creating Online Courses and Orientations: A Survival Guide.* Bridgeport, CT: Libraries Unlimited.

Bender, D. M. & Vredevoogd, J. D. (2006). Using Online Education Technologies to Support Studio Instruction. *Educational Technology & Society 9*(4): 114–122.

Brooks, D. (2007). Integrated Learning Theory: Applications in Teaching. Available at dwb4.unl.edu/dwb/Research/TheoryPaper/CompTh.html.

Chickering, A. & Ehrmann, S. C. (October 1996). Implementing the Seven Principles: Technology as a Lever. *AAHE Bulletin 49*(2): 3–6.

Conrad, R., & Donaldson, J. A. (2004). *Engaging the Online Learner: Activities and Resources for Creative Instruction.* San Francisco: Jossey-Bass.

Fisher, M. (2003). *Designing Courses and Teaching on the Web.* Latham, MD: Rowman & Littlefield Education.

Gordon, D. (2003). *Better Teaching and Learning in the Digital Classroom.* Cambridge, MA: Harvard Education Press.

Iverson, K. (2005). *E-Learning Games: Interactive Learning Strategies for Digital Delivery.* Upper Saddle River, NJ: Pearson Education.

Jones, S., (2002). *The Internet Goes to College.* Washington, D.C.: Pew Internet & American Life Project.

Ko, S. & Rossen, S. (2004). *Teaching Online: A Practical Guide.* 2nd ed. Boston, MA: Houghton Mifflin.

Levine, S. L. & Wake, W. K. (2000). *Education of Artists. Hybrid Teaching: Design Studios in Virtual Space.* Presented to the National Conference on Liberal Arts and the Education of Artists. SVA, New York.

National Forum on Information Literacy, http://www.infolit.org.

Media Literacy, http://www.medialiteracy.net/research/definition.shtml.

Porter, L. R. (2002). *Virtual Classroom Distance Learning with the Internet.* Canada: Wiley.

Salmon, G. (2004). *eModerating: The Key to Teaching & Learning Online*, 2nd ed. London: Taylor & Francis Books.

Shank, P., ed. (2007). *The Online Learning Idea Book.* New York: Wiley.

Shank, P. & Sitze, A. (2004). *Making Sense of Online Learning: A Guide for Beginners and the Truly Skeptical.* New York: Wiley/Pfeiffer.

Wenger, E. (June 1998). *Communities of Practice: Learning as a Social System, Systems Thinker.* Cambridge, MA: Cambridge University Press.

Wenger, E. (1999). *Communities of Practice: Learning, Meaning, and Identity.* Cambridge, MA: Cambridge University Press, 1999.

Chapter 7: Trends in Interior Design Teaching and Learning

Note: References on technology courtesy of Katherine Ankerson; references on sustainability courtesy of Lisa Tucker; references on social justice courtesy of Jill Pable; references on K-12 interior design education courtesy of Stephanie Clemons.

Bentivenga, V. et al. (2002). A Vision and Methodology for Integrated Sustainable Urban Development. *Building Research & Information 30*(2): 83–94.

Benyus, J. (1997). *Biomimicry.* New York: William Morrow.

Berke, P. (2000). Are We Planning for Sustainable Development? *Journal of the American Planning Association 66*(1): 21–33.

Bontje, M. (2004). From Suburbia to Post-suburbia in the Netherlands: Potentials and Threats for Sustainable Regional Development. *Journal of Housing and the Built Environment 19*(1): 25–47.

Clemons, S. (1994). "Pat's Place": A Child's Animated Storybook. *IDEC Southwest Regional Meeting Proceedings.* El Paso, TX, 17–19.

Clemons, S. (1998). Computer Animation: A Tool for Teaching Design Fundamentals to Elementary School Students. *Journal of Interior Design 24*(1): 40–47.

Clemons, S. (1999). Development of Interior Design Career Information for Dissemination to Students in Grades Six through Eight. *Journal of Interior Design 25*(2): 45–51.

Coleman, C. & Sosnowchik, K. (September 2006). *Interior Design Trends and Implications.* Grand Rapids, MI: Council for Interior Design Accreditation.

Davis, S. (2004). *Designing for the Homeless: Architecture that Works.* Berkeley: University of California Press.

Dohr, J. (October 1992). Six Predictions: The Future of Interior Design. *Interior Design 63*(14): 131.

Duany, R., Wheeler, J. & Schubert, R. (2006). No Compromise: The Integration of Technology and Aesthetics. *Journal of Architectural Education 60*(2): 8–17.

Edwards, A. (2005). *The Sustainability Revolution.* Gabriola Island, BC: New Society Publishers.

Eyler, J. & Giles, D., et.al, (2001). *At a Glance: What We Know about the Effects of Service-Learning on College Students, Faculty, Institutions and Communities: 1993–2000*, 3rd ed. Retrieved 9/19/05 from http://www.servicelearning.org/lib_svcs/pubs/index.php from the National Service Learning Clearinghouse.

Frequently Asked Questions About Hate Crimes and Hate on the Internet. (n.d.). Retrieved 5/1/06 from Partners Against Hate, http://www.partnersagainsthate.org/about_pah/index.html.DOE. (2005). Annual Review. Retrieved 3/23/07 from http://www.eia.doe.gov/basics/energybasics101.html.

Gateway, T. N. S. (January 2007). The Natural Step/U.S. Retrieved 3/26/07, from http://www.naturalstep.org/com/nyStart/.

Gibney, F. & Luscombe, B. (March 2000). The Rebirth of Design. *Time Magazine*, http://www.time.com/time/archive/preview/0,10987,996372,00.html.

Guy, S. & Farmer, G. (2001). Reinterpreting Sustainable Architecture: The Place of Technology. *Journal of Architectural Education 54*(3): 140–148.

Hanna, K. (2005). Planning for Sustainability: Experiences in Two Contrasting Communities. *Journal of the American Planning Association 71*(1): 27–40.

Hunger and Homelessness Survey: A Status Report on Hunger and Homelessness in America's Cities. (December 2005) Retrieved 12/5/05 from United States Conference of Mayors at http://www.usmayors.org/uscm/hunger survey/2005/HH2005FINAL.pdf.

Hyllegard, K., Ogle, J. & Dunbar, D. (2003). Sustainability and Historic Preservation in Retail Design: Integrating Design into a Model of the REI Denver Decision-making Process. *Journal of Interior Design 29*(1, 2): 32–49.

Kaufman, W. (December 12, 2006). *Mileage Ratings Drop as EPA Changes Car Tests.* Retrieved 10/14/07 from National Public Radio at http://www.npr.org/templates/story/story.php?storyId=6612913.

Matthews, D. (2000). Making Connections Between Virtual Reality and the Design Process: A Media and Language for Presenting Interiors in Four Dimensions. *Interior Design Educators Council International Conference Proceedings*, p. 54.

McDonough, W. (1992). *The Hannover Principles: Design for Sustainability.* Retrieved 3/26/07 from http://www.mcdonough.com/principles.pdf.

McDonough, W. & Braungart, M. (2002). *Cradle to Cradle: Remaking the Way We Make Things.* New York: North Point Press.

McLennan, J. (2004). *The Philosophy of Sustainable Design.* Kansas City, MO: Ecotone Publishing.

Pable, J. (July 2006). Homelessness and the Design Response. *Implications: A Newsletter by InformeDesign 4*(7): 1–6. Available at http://www.informedesign.umn.edu/.Minneapolis: University of Minnesota.

Papanek, V. (1982). *Design for the Real World: Human Ecology and Social Change*, 2nd ed. Chicago: Academy Chicago Publishers.

Portillo, M. & Rey-Barreau, J. (1995). The Place of Interior Design in K-12 Education and the Built Environment Education Movement. *Journal of Interior Design 21*(1): 39–43.

Price, C., Zavotka, S. & Teaford, M. (2004). Implementing a University-Community-Retail Partnership Model to Facilitate Community Education on Universal Design. *The Gerentologist 44*(5): 697–702.

Schmidt-Bleek, F. B. (2000). Factor 10 Manifesto. Retrieved 3/26/07 from http://www.factor10-institute.org/pdf/F10Manif.pdf.

State of Minnesota Sustainable Design Guidelines (MSBG). (2006). Center for Sustainable Building Research, College of Design, University of Minnesota. Retrieved 3/26/07 from http://www.msbg.umn.edu/downloads_v2_0/guidelines.pdf.

Tucker, L. M. (2002). The Void between Sustainability and Historic Preservation. Paper presented at the Interior Design Educators International Conference. Santa Fe, NM.

Van der Ryn, S. (2005). *Design for Life.* Salt Lake City, UT: Gibbs Smith.

Van der Ryn, S. & Cowan, S. (1996). *Ecological Design.* Washington, D.C.: Island Press.

Worldwatch Institute. (2006). State of the World 2005. Retrieved 9/15/06 from http://www.worldwatch.org/node/3942

Why We Take Action. (n.d.). Retrieved 4/25/06 from Responsible Wealth.org, http://www.responsiblewealth.org/aboutrw/whywe act.html.

Chapter 8: Improving Teaching and Learning

Adams, John V. (1997). *Student Evaluations: The Ratings Game.* Inquiry *1*(2): 10–16. Retrieved 8/23/07 from Virginia Community College System, www.vccaedu.org/inquiry/inquiry-fall97/i12-adam.html.

Arreola, R. A. (1995). *Developing a Comprehensive Faculty Evaluation System.* Bolton, MA: Anker Publishing.

Center for Teaching and Learning. (2005). Effective University Teaching: Reflecting on and Responding to Your Course Evaluations. Retrieved 8/23/07 from http://ctl.stanford.edu/effect_univ_teach.pdf.

Course Evaluation and Revision: Chapter 14—Improving Your Teaching with Feedback. Retrieved 8/13/07 from learningforlife.fsu.edu/ctl/explore/onlineresources/docs/Chptr14.pdf.

Enhancing Education @ Carnegie Mellon. Retrieved 8/23/07 from www.cmu.edu/teaching/assessment/15sturatings.html

Hazari, S. & Schno, D. *Leveraging Student Feedback to Improve Teaching in Web-based Courses.* Retrieved 8/23/07 from www.thejournal.com/the/printarticle/?id=14146.

McGill Centre for University Teaching and Learning. How Professors Can Use Student Course Ratings to Improve Teaching and to Prepare for Tenure/Promotion/Merit Decisions: Research-based Suggestions. Retrieved 8/13/07 from www.mcgill.ca/files/tls/ratinfo1.pdf.

Chapter 9: Essays and Inspirations

Ralph, E. (1998). *Motivating Teaching in Higher Education: A Manual for Faculty Development.* Stillwater, OK: New Forums Press.

Weimer, J. (1993). *Improving Your Classroom Teaching*, vol. 1. London: Sage.

Chapter 10: The Teaching and Learning Physical Environment

Aero|Astro MIT Department of Aeronautics and Astronautics. (n.d.). Reforming Engineering Education: The CDIO™ Initiative. Retrieved 7/3/07 from http://web.mit.edu/aeroastro/academics/cdio.html.

Babcock, R. (n.d.). Schoolhouse Rocks: Exploring the Future of Learning Environments. *Buildings.* Retrieved 6/30/07 from http://www.buildings.com/Articles/detailBuildings.asp?ArticleID=2650.

Blomeyer, R. & Guerrero, R. (Spring/Summer 2004). Further Research Suggests Classroom Technology Use Has Positive Impact on Student Performance. *Educational Technology News 4*(1): 2–4.

Bowman, E. & Enmarker, I. (2004). Noise Annoyance Affects Learning. *Environment and Behavior 36*(2): 207–228.

Dahl, J. (2003). How Much Are Distance Education Faculty Worth? *Distance Education Report* 7(14): 5–7.

Day, A., ed. (January 2004). Forecasting the Future of Higher Education. *College Planning and Management, (7)*1. Retrieved 6/30/07 from http://www.peterli.com/archive/cpm/580.shtm, 10–12, 14–16.

Dordai, P. & Rizzo, J. (November 2006). Echo Boom Impact (College Admission for Baby Boomers). *American School and University 79*(3). Retrieved 10/14/07 from http://asumag.com/DesignPlanning/university_echo_boom_impact/index.html.

Fisher, J. & Miller, S. (January 2000). From Here to 2010. *College Planning and Management 3*(1). Retrieved 7/1/07 from http://www.peterli.com/archive/cpm/35.shtm.

Joint Information Systems Committee e-Learning and Innovation Team. (2006). Designing Spaces for Effective Learning: A Guide to 21st Century Learning Space Design. Bristol, UK: Higher Education Funding Council for England (HEFCE). Retrieved 6/30/07 from http://www.jisc.ac.uk/uploaded_documents/JISClearningspaces.pdf.

Kressley, K. & Huebschmann M. (November 2002). The 21st Century Campus: Gerontological Perspectives. *Educational Gerontology 28*(10): 835–851.

Milanese, S. & Grimmer, K. (2004). School Furniture and the User Population: An Anthropometric Perspective. *Ergonomics 47*(4): 416–426.

Nair, P. (January 2003). Imperatives for Change in Higher Education. *DesignShare: The International Forum for Innovative Schools.* Retrieved 7/1/07 from http://www.designshare.com/Research/Nair/HigherEd/imperatives.

Nasar, J., Preiser, W., & Fisher, T. (2007). *Designing for Designers.* NY: Fairchild Books.

Nasar, J., et al. (May 2007). The Architecture of Architecture Schools. A presentation at the 2007 National Conference of the Environmental Design and Research Association, Sacramento, CA.

Niederhelman, M. (Summer 2001). Education Through Design. *Design Issues 17*(3): 83–87.

Rashid, M. (May 2007). Physical Design of University Classrooms & Learning Outcomes: A Quasi-Experiment. A presentation at the 2007 National Conference of the Environmental Design and Research Association, Sacramento, CA.

Shendell, D.G., Prill, R., & Fisk, M., et al. (2004). Associations between Classroom CO_2 Concentrations and Student Attendance in Washington and Idaho. *Indoor Air 14*(5): 333–341.

Snyder, D. (January/February 2006). Big Change on Campus. *Facilities Manager.* Retrieved 6/30/07 from http://www.appa.org/FacilitiesManager/article.cfm?ItemNumber=2550&parentid=2540.

Tallent-Runnels, M., et al. (Spring 2006) Teaching Courses Online: A Review of the Research. *Review of Educational Research* 76(1): 93–135.

Zhang, P. (1998). A Case Study on Technology Use in Distance Learning. *Journal of Research on Computing in Education, 30*: 398.

Definitions

Carnegie Foundation for the Advancement of Teaching. (2006). Basic Classification Description. Retrieved 7/28/07 from http://www.carnegiefoundation.org/classifications/index.asp?key=791.

Council for Interior Design Accreditation. Retrieved 7/25/07 from http://www.accredit-id.org/history.html.

Cranton, P. (1994). *Understanding and Promoting Transformative Learning: A Guide for Educators of Adults.* San Francisco: Jossey-Bass.

Interior Design Continuing Education Council. Retrieved 8/28/07 from http://idcec.org.

Interior Design Educators Council. Retrieved 8/28/07 from http://www.idec.org.

McKay, D. Curriculum Vitae. *About.com: Career Planning.* Retrieved 7/28/07 from http://careerplanning.about.com/od/resumewriting/g/def_vitae.htm.

Merriam, S. B. & Caffarella, R. S. Learning in Adulthood. San Francisco: Jossey-Bass, 1991.

The American Heritage Dictionary of the English Language. 4th ed. (2003). Boston, MA: Houghton Mifflin.

INDEX

Note: Italic page numbers indicate material in tables or figures.

D

E

M